Targeting: The Challenges of Modern Warfare

Paul A.L. Ducheine · Michael N. Schmitt
Frans P.B. Osinga
Editors

Targeting: The Challenges of Modern Warfare

ASSER PRESS

Springer

Editors
Paul A.L. Ducheine
Faculty of Military Sciences
Netherlands Defence Academy
Breda
The Netherlands

Frans P.B. Osinga
Faculty of Military Sciences
Netherlands Defence Academy
Breda
The Netherlands

Michael N. Schmitt
Stockton Center for the Study of International Law
United States Naval War College
Newport, RI
USA

ISBN 978-94-6265-071-8 ISBN 978-94-6265-072-5 (eBook)
DOI 10.1007/978-94-6265-072-5

Library of Congress Control Number: 2015946061

Published by T.M.C. ASSER PRESS, The Hague, The Netherlands www.asserpress.nl
Produced and distributed for T.M.C. ASSER PRESS by Springer-Verlag Berlin Heidelberg

Printed on acid-free paper

Springer Science+Business Media B.V. Dordrecht is part of Springer Science+Business Media (www.springer.com)

Foreword

Targeting is not only the most vital, but also one of the most challenging processes during military operations. When targeting, our efforts should be focused on successfully engaging identified and prioritized targets on both the operational "joint" level and the tactical level. The targeting process has evolved from having a primarily kinetic/lethal emphasis, with hardly any consideration for collateral damage, to our current operational domain, characterized by operations among the people and heavily influenced by modern (social) media. In addition, targeting is no longer a process primarily focusing on air assets, but over the past two decades has come to incorporate a host of military engagement capabilities.

As Commander of Regional Command South in the ISAF-operation in Afghanistan, I experienced this change of the environment in which the targeting process had to be used. For example, rules of engagement became more restrictive and the availability of resources increased. In addition, armed unmanned assets entered into the inventory. Throughout, the watchful eyes of the social and regular media were constantly upon us, impacting on our military operations. As a primary reaction, our targeting process tended to shift from one that attached scarce resources to identified and prioritized targets to a process that primarily avoided collateral damage. This was not the solution. We found that the information domain had to be included as well.

These developments have implications. Incorporating the information domain into the targeting process broadens the definition of a "target". The availability of unmanned resources expands the inventory of assets. And what about the near future when capacity for cyber operations and perhaps even autonomous systems become available?

The changes create political, legal, and ethical issues. Some of these concerns are based on a misunderstanding of the targeting process, but others require more in-depth discussion, as well as guidance and decisions from politicians and military leaders. *Targeting: The Challenges of Modern Warfare* contributes to this dialogue and, in doing so, creates more clarity for our men and women on operations.

Mart de Kruif
Lieutenant General
Commander of the Royal Netherlands Army
(Former Commander RC-South ISAF, 2008–2009)

Preface

Issues about targeting have always been central to warfighting, but in the twenty-first century a variety of factors have conspired to make this basic task an extraordinarily complex endeavour. Of course, there has been the emergence of ever-more lethal technology that can create a much greater potential for unintended consequences, particularly with respect to the incidental death or injury of civilians and damage or destruction of their property. At the same time however, technology has permitted the emergence of weaponry capable of being used in an extraordinarily precise manner. Still, targeting issues continue to bedevil commanders, policymakers, and their lawyers.

The reason for this is in great part due to technological and organizational developments in the international media community which very often permit the almost instantaneous broadcast of battlefield events—to include the graphic results of targeting—around the globe. In addition, we are increasingly seeing soldiers and others equipped with either official or unofficial video recording devices that likewise allow the capture of combat in real time. These too have a propensity to find their way into the global information marketplace, often without official approval.

In short, publics around the world have a much greater opportunity to view the consequences of targeting in ongoing conflicts, and do so before governmental authorities have an opportunity to evaluate what is appearing on television screens and computer monitors around the world. It is not uncommon for such visual depictions to be accompanied by informed or—often—*uninformed* commentary as to the legitimacy of the attack. At the same time, there is a greater cognizance of international law, to some extent because of its utility in facilitating transnational business activities occasioned by the rise of globalized commerce. Collectively, these factors result in a world where strict adherence to the rule of law in armed conflict is expected and required.

It is this unique and, in many ways, unprecedented, environment that makes this volume so exceptionally valuable. Targeting is the *sine qua non* of the international law of armed conflict (or international humanitarian law, as some call it) because intrinsic to it are the central tenets of civilized combat: distinction, proportionality, military necessity, and humanity.

There was a time, perhaps, that adhering to these principles was a relatively simple thing. Belligerents wore uniforms and military objects were so unique that there was typically little dispute as to the propriety of their designation as lawful targets.

Today, however, much of that has changed. Contemporary conflicts frequently involve nonstate actors who wear civilian clothing and embed themselves in civilian areas. What is more is that many of the technologies essential to modern warfighting are "dual use," that is, as valuable and indispensable to civilians as they are to belligerent militaries. Paralleling this development is the fielding, as already noted, of weaponry capable of extraordinary precision.

As a result, force very often can be applied with an accuracy that could be only dreamed about in earlier eras. Yet, despite the seeming progress of the ability to scrupulously honor the demands of legal and moral targeting, controversy about targeting has, if anything, actually increased. In part, this may be the result of modern militaries being a victim of their own success, for widely advertised surveillance and precision strike capabilities have raised public expectations well beyond what the law requires, and perhaps even beyond what the chaos and friction of war would ever be able to satisfy.

What this volume does is to gather together in one place the very best of the current thinking about targeting. It is intellectually holistic and comprehensive in that it not only lays out the history and context of targeting, it details its application in specific circumstances.

Beyond the law itself, it grapples with the thorny ethical, technical, and political issues associated with targeting decisions, especially in a coalition environment where differing perspectives about particular operations can result in constraining policies, to include guidelines not necessarily mandated by the law of armed conflict. Furthermore, the book deals with not just the law, but with the procedures applicable to the law's actual operations in various armed conflict situations.

The end product is a volume that is not only a phenomenal work of legal and military scholarship, it is written and organized in a way that is readily accessible not just to lawyers, but also to nonlawyers, including commanders, policymakers, and others involved in the art of war. What is more is that it will be extremely useful to members of the media and other opinion makers because it clarifies the often misunderstood legal aspects of the law of targeting. Wherever one stands on the use of force in a particular circumstance, the value and legitimacy of whatever position is taken must be built on a clear understanding of the law as it is.

What differentiates this book from other efforts to address (the law of) targeting is that it is informed by authors who have real-world experience dealing with the complexity of targeting in actual combat situations. While there are certainly many distinguished scholars around the world whose erudition as to the law, *per se*, cannot be questioned, their assessments may be insufficiently grounded in a keen understanding of the technical capabilities of the weaponry and the methodologies of their use in armed conflict.

Importantly, this book is not just a retrospective as to the law of targeting, but one that looks ahead to grapple with what will surely be the next generation of targeting issues. These include questions arising from the development and fielding of autonomous weapons systems. While there is a movement afoot to develop an international consensus on barring the introduction of the weapons, it is this writer's view that not only will such efforts ultimately fail, their failure is actually desirable. Indeed, autonomous weapon systems have the potential, if properly used consonant with the law of armed conflict, to significantly increase the likelihood that force will be used in a way that minimizes not only the risk to civilians but also to combatants by decisively unhinging its warfighting capability without necessarily destroying every element of the same.

Of course, it is quite unlikely that every reader will agree with every position taken by every author in this book. Indeed, one should not expect that even within the book the authors will consistently agree with each other in every instance. That is the nature of a volume that aims to collect the very best thinking from the widest selection of experts. Yet, the book's organization makes it a ready reference for anyone confronted with these issues.

The killing of another human being even when permitted by international law can never be taken lightly. Of course, everyone—and particularly those in the armed forces—wishes that human nature might someday evolve to the point where conflicts can be resolved peaceably in a way that preserves human dignity and freedom. Regrettably, there is little to suggest that such a day is coming in time soon.

Until it does, we must live by the truism often attributed to Cicero that "only the dead have seen the end of war." That being the case, it is all the more important that at those times when force must be used in a just cause, it be applied in a way that comports to the law, serves the best interests of humanity, and honors the consciences of the men and women called upon to use it. To serve that noble end is the real purpose of this book.

Charles J. Dunlap Jr.
Major General, USAF (Ret.)
Duke University School of Law
Durham, North Carolina

Contents

Editors and Contributors

About the Editors

Brigadier-General Professor Paul A.L. Ducheine is a Professor for Cyber Operations and Cyber Security at the Netherlands Defence Academy and a Professor of the Law of Military Cyber Operations at the University of Amsterdam. Trained at the Netherlands Royal Military Academy, he joined the Engineer Corps in 1988 and changed to the Army Legal Service in 1998. He holds a Master of Science degree in Public Administration as well as a Master degree and a Ph.D. in Law.

Professor Michael N. Schmitt is the Charles H. Stockton Professor and Director at the Stockton Center for the Study of International Law at the United States Naval War College. He is also Professor of International Law at Exeter University in the United Kingdom, Senior Fellow at the NATO Cyber Defence Center of Excellence in Tallinn Estonia, and Fellow at the Harvard Law School Program on International Law and Armed Conflict. Professor Schmitt served in the United States Air Force for 20 years as a Targeting Officer and Judge Advocate specializing in operational law.

Air-Commodore Professor Frans P.B. Osinga is Professor of Military Operational Art and Sciences, Chair of the War Studies Department at the Netherlands Defence Academy (Faculty of Military Sciences), and member of the Faculty's Managing Board. Trained at the Royal Military Academy, he joined the Royal (NLD) Airforce in 1987 as a F-16 pilot. He defended his Ph.D. in 2005 on the relation between war, science and strategic thinking (of John Boyd).

Contributors

Hans Boddens Hosang is the Deputy Director of Legal Affairs for the Netherlands Minister of Defence, and Head of the International and Operational Law Department, Legal Affairs Division, NLD MoD. He is a Ph.D. Researcher at University of Amsterdam (topic: Rules of Engagement).

Professor Christopher Coker is Professor of International Relations at the London School of Economics. He is a serving member of the Washington Strategy Seminar; the Institute for Foreign Policy Analysis (Cambridge, Mass); the Black Sea University Foundation; the Moscow School of Politics; and the IDEAS Advisory Board. He is a member of the Executive Council for the Belgrade University International Summer School for Democracy and also President of the Centre for Media and Communications of a Democratic Romania.

Professor Coker is a regular lecturer at the Royal College of Defence Studies (London); the NATO Defence College (Rome), the Centre for International Security (Geneva) and the National Institute for Defence Studies (Tokyo).

Professor Martin L. Cook is Admiral James B. Stockdale Professor of Professional Military Ethics at the College of Operational and Strategic Leadership at the US Naval War College. He is also co-editor of The Journal of Military Ethics and a board member of Parameters. Professor Cook was previously a professor of philosophy and deputy department head at the Philosophy Department at the US Air Force Academy from 2004 to 2009. He was also a professor of ethics at the US Army War College from 1998 to 2003 and the Elihu Root Chair of Military Studies in 2000.

Lieutenant-Colonel Chris De Cock (Royal Belgian Airforce) is a legal advisor and Head of the Operational Law Section, Armed Forces Legal Service of the Belgian Ministry of Defence. He is a member of the visiting teaching staff at the International Institute of Humanitarian Law in San Remo and senior lecturer at the Royal Military School in Brussels. He holds Master degrees in the fields of Aeronautical and Military Sciences, Law, Political Sciences, Public Management, Security, and Defense. Since 2004, Lieutenant-Colonel De Cock (GS) has participated in operations in Afghanistan, counter-piracy and counter-narcotics operations, and Operation Unified Protector.

Professor Terry D. Gill is Professor of Military Law at the University of Amsterdam and the Netherlands Defence Academy and was first Assistant and later Associate Professor of Public International Law at Utrecht University from 1985 until 2013. He is Director of the Research Program on the Law of Armed Conflict and Peace Operations at the Amsterdam Centre for International Law and of the Netherlands Research Forum on the Law of Armed Conflict and Peace Operations (LACPO). He is Editor in Chief of the Yearbook of International Humanitarian Law and is on the editorial board of the Journal of Conflict and Security Law and the Journal of International Peacekeeping. He was Fulbright Visiting Scholar at Columbia University and Visiting Fellow at Cambridge University, the International Institute of Humanitarian Law (San Remo), University of Coimbra and University of Granada. Professor Gill is the co-editor/author of The Handbook of the International Law of Military Operations (Oxford University Press 2010) and of numerous publications in the areas of the use of force, international humanitarian law, and related topics.

Phillip R. Pratzner Jr. retired as a Colonel in the United States Air Force in 2013. He spent 17 years in targeting duties, serving in four Air and Space Operations Centers, and in Europe, the Pacific, the Republic of Korea and the Middle East/ Central Asia. Pratzner was the first Commander of the Air Force Targeting Center from 2009 to 2011. His last duty was the Director of Intelligence for United States Air Forces Central Command. He wishes to thank the Air Force Targeting Center at Langley Air Force Base, under the command of Colonel Mike Flaherty, for its generous devotion of time, ideas and willingness to listen and critique his ideas for this chapter.

Lieutenant-Colonel Dr. Bryan Price (US Army) is the Director of the Combating Terrorism Center and an Assistant Professor in the Department of Social Sciences at the United States Military Academy at West Point. He is a former aviator and current FA59 strategist who has served in a variety of command and staff positions in operational assignments, including deployments to both Iraq and Afghanistan. He holds a Bachelor of Science degree in History from the United States Military Academy, a Master of Arts in International Relations from St. Mary's University, and a Master of Arts and Ph.D. in Political Science from Stanford University.

Captain Mark P. Roorda (Royal Netherlands Marine Corps) is a Ph.D. researcher, War Studies Department, Netherlands Defence Academy and Amsterdam Centre of International Law, University of Amsterdam. He holds a Bachelor's degree in War Studies (Netherlands Defence Academy) and a Master's degree in Law (University of Utrecht). He was trained and deployed as a JTAC in Afghanistan (ISAF, 2013).

Lieutenant-Colonel Jeffrey S. Thurnher joined the United States Army in March 1997. A Judge Advocate, Lieutenant Colonel Thurnher has deployed to Kosovo and Afghanistan as part of multi-national forces. He currently serves as a Legal Advisor for the NATO Rapid Deployable Corps in Münster, Germany. His previous assignment was as a Military Professor in the International Law Department at the US Naval War College. Lieutenant Colonel Thurnher holds degrees from the University of Virginia, the College of William and Mary, the US Army Judge Advocate General's Legal Center and School, and the US Naval War College. He has published numerous articles, including ones that earned the 2009 American Society of International Law's Lieber Society Military Prize, the US Naval War College's Vice Admiral James H. Doyle, Jr., Military Operations and International Law Prize in 2012, and the Lieber Society's Richard R. Baxter Military Prize Certificate of Merit for 2013.

Lieutenant-Colonel Eric Widmar (US Army) is a Judge Advocate in the United States Army. Lieutenant Colonel Widmar served four tours in Afghanistan as the senior legal advisor to a Joint Special Operations Task Force and one tour in Iraq as the legal advisor to a US Army Airborne Infantry Brigade. He currently serves as the Chief of Administrative and Military Law, US Army Pacific (Pacific Command). His previous assignment was as Military Professor of International Law and Associate Director for Law of Land Warfare, Stockton Center for the Study of

International Law, US Naval War College. Lieutenant Colonel Widmar holds degrees from the United States Military Academy at West Point, Brigham Young University, the US Army Judge Advocate General's School, and the US Naval War College, where he received the William S. Sims Award as the Distinguished Graduate and the US Naval War College's Vice Admiral James H. Doyle, Jr., Military Operations and International Law Prize in 2013.

Chapter 1
Introduction

Paul A.L. Ducheine, Michael N. Schmitt and Frans P.B. Osinga

Abstract This book offers a multidisciplinary treatment of targeting. Historically, destruction of enemy forces and equipment has been the primary, albeit not exclusive, means of securing ultimate victory. Today, after a long evolutionary process and enabled by technological developments, the contemporary effects-based approach in targeting aims to achieve specified effects on and beyond the battlefield. It involves 'affecting' a variety of intended audiences through a combination of military and other means and methods of warfare which vary from classic military kinetic lethal actions, such as employing bombs, guns or torpedoes, to 'unorthodox' non-military, non-kinetic and non-lethal activities like financial actions, lawfare and information operations. This volume comprises three parts. Part I explores the context of targeting, covers the evolution of targeting and explains the current targeting process and characteristics. Part II offers an overview of the legal and ethical constraints on targeting as an operational process. Part III surveys contemporary issues in targeting such as the potential advent of autonomous weapon systems, 'non-kinetic' targeting, targeting in multinational military operations and leadership decapitation in counter-terrorism operations. It is intended for use in military training and educational programmes, as well as in Bachelor and Master degree-level courses on topics such as War Studies and Strategic Studies.

Keywords Targeting · Warfare · Military operations · Use of force · War

---

P.A.L. Ducheine (✉)
Cyber Operations and Cyber Security, Netherlands Defence Academy, Breda, The Netherlands
e-mail: pal.ducheine.01@mindef.nl

M.N. Schmitt
Stockton Center for the Study of International Law, United States Naval War College, Newport, Rhode Island
e-mail: Schmitt@aya.yale.edu

F.P.B. Osinga
War Studies Department, Netherlands Defence Academy, Breda, The Netherlands
e-mail: fpb.osinga@mindef.nl

P.A.L. Ducheine et al. (eds.), *Targeting: The Challenges of Modern Warfare*,
DOI 10.1007/978-94-6265-072-5_1

Contents

1.1 Targeting

To date, robust assessments of contemporary targeting practice and theory have been hobbled by the propensity of the various disciplines involved to speak only to members of their own community. This book responds to that impediment by offering a multidisciplinary treatment of the subject. It accordingly brings together experts from a variety of fields to consider targeting in a manner that is accessible to colleagues outside their respective disciplines.

Targeting can briefly be defined as the deliberate application of capabilities against targets to generate effects in order to achieve specific objectives. It is about the application of means (weapons) of warfare to affect addressees (people or objects) using a variety of methods (tactics) that create effects contributing to designated goals. Targeting, accordingly, represents the bridge between the ends and means of warfare.

The targeting process is not a nascent one, although it has evolved dramatically over time. Historically, destruction of enemy forces and equipment has been the primary, albeit not exclusive, means of securing ultimate victory. Attrition of enemy forces through their defeat on the battlefield was calculated to lead to the enemy's capitulation, either by rendering the enemy State unable to field and use its armed forces effectively or by inducing it to refrain from sending those forces into battle.

In this traditional approach, the relationship between targeting and its effects was linear and somewhat unsophisticated. While targeting made possible the achievement of effects at the tactical, operational and strategic levels of war when combined with manoeuvre and other components of warfare, such effects were typically achieved only when enemy forces faced each other on the battlefield.

The advent of aerial warfare in the twentieth century dramatically altered this dynamic. It allowed a belligerent's forces to leap beyond the front line and thereby extend the conflict into the enemy's heartland. This capability made possible targeting strategies that were non-linear, direct and sophisticated in design. Such strategies shortened the link between targeting and the enemy's decision-making processes.

Achieving effects that did not directly relate to an enemy's military wherewithal was not an entirely new phenomenon. The classic examples of doing so were blockade at sea and siege on land. However, with the advent of long-range aircraft, only the laws of neutrality limited the geographical scope of the battlefield.

The first full employment of this new approach was the strategic bombing campaigns in World War II. Of course, the shift in approach did not signal the end of targeting at the tactical level. But conceptually, military thinkers began to view targeting less as simply a way to denude the enemy forces of their battlefield capability and more as one of achieving particular effects, whether those effects were framed in terms of immediate destruction of enemy forces or achieving second- or third-order results that optimized operational and strategic-level objectives. Today, targeting as a means of realizing specified effects characterizes military operations in all military domains—land, sea, air, space, and cyber—and on all levels of command—strategic, operational and tactical.

In recent decades, military operations have moved beyond the realm of warfare proper to include, for instance, the generation of effects during peace support and stabilization operations. Such operations necessitate the application of the same effects-based approach that has been fully embraced in traditional combat during an armed conflict. Consequently, targeting is now employed to produce a wide array of effects serving a variety of purposes. These ends can be of a military nature, but may also include political, economic, social, or psychological ones; all are intended to somehow contribute to overarching express or implied goals of the State conducting a targeting operation. To paraphrase Clausewitz, effects-based targeting is the epitome of the continuation of politics by other means.

The effects-based approach involves 'affecting' intended addressees of an effect through a combination of military and other means and methods of warfare. These vary from classic military kinetic lethal actions, such as employing bombs, guns, or torpedoes, to 'unorthodox' non-military, non-kinetic, and non-lethal activities like financial actions, lawfare or information operations. In the twenty-first century, targeting can best be described as a comprehensive process for the coordinated use of all instruments available to a State that have the potential of generating desired effects.

A further important shift in operational targeting concepts involves the 'addressees' of targeting. By the effects-based approach, desired effects can operate on other than enemy combatants, civilians directly participating in hostilities, or military objects. Increasingly, addressees include civilians (who are protected against direct kinetic attack), stakeholders, neutral actors, and enemy supporters. This represents a paradigm shift in the sense that the development of non-kinetic methods and means of warfare such as cyber operations opens the legal door in some instances to the targeting of civilians and civilian objects, including those of non-belligerent States, despite their protection from kinetic attacks under international humanitarian law.

Considered in its entirety, targeting serves as a coordination and decision-support mechanism that synchronizes the application of military and non-military means to produce both physical and non-physical effects. It enables targeteers to plan and execute operations and activities comprehensively, efficiently, and effectively. At the same time, it enables commanders to use force (or assets and resources) more economically by providing them additional options with which to accomplish their mission. In many instances, the effects-based approach lends itself to greater clarity by increasing the availability of transparent mission accomplishment options, thereby facilitating (ex post and ex ante) assessments of the legitimacy of activities and operations, as well as enhancing legal and operational accountability. The focus on effects, and the availability of more options, also simplifies the delineation of command and control (who does what) responsibilities and the distinction between supporting and supported tasks (who supports who). Finally, the effects-based approach allows the political, moral, and legal sensibilities of all States involved in a multi-national operation, to be better reflected in targeting operations.

As suggested above, the targeting process adapts to, and reflects, technological and social developments. Perhaps most illustrative in the technical context is the use of the digital domain and digital instruments alongside, or in lieu of, conventional weaponry. Responsiveness to social change has been illustrated in the Herculean efforts to mitigate and prevent collateral damage during armed conflict.

1.2 Purpose and Audience

This book takes a distinctly multidisciplinary perspective on targeting practice and theory. Therefore, it surveys contemporary conceptual and doctrinal approaches, current technological and organizational developments, and the strategic, military-operational, moral, and legal issues that targeting in the face of the evolving battlefield presents.

The project is a joint effort between the Netherlands Defence Academy (Faculty of Military Sciences) and the United States Naval War College (Stockton Center for the Study of International Law). The book is intended for use in military training and educational programmes, whether practical or academic in character, including those at Command and Staff and War Colleges. It is also meant for use in Bachelor and Master degree-level courses on such topics as War Studies and Strategic Studies. In addition to its use in the classroom, the book should prove useful for journalists, NGOs, international organizations, judicial bodies, and other individuals and entities that deal with the legal and practical ramifications of warfare in general, and targeting in particular. Sadly, much of today's public targeting debate evidences a distinct lack of understanding as to the goals, context, practice, and technological and operational underpinnings of targeting. For example, the abuse of the notion of collateral damage in public and governmental discussion is often the unintentional result of confusion about, and conflation of, the fields of international law, military operations, and policy implementation. This book aims to help alleviate such obstacles, thereby allowing the debates to occur at a more mature and sophisticated level.

1.3 Structure

This volume comprises three parts. Part I explores the targeting environment by addressing the context in which it occurs (Chap. 2), presenting the history and development of (aerial) targeting doctrine (Chap. 3), and explaining the current targeting process and characteristics (Chap. 4).

Part II offers an overview of the various constraints on targeting as an operational process. It examines the legal framework that applies to the resort to force by States—*ius ad bellum*—through military operations (Chap. 5). It first sets forth the legal framework applicable to the conduct of hostilities that is found in the law of armed conflict, also referred to as *ius in bello* or*Ius in bello* international humanitarian law (Chap. 6). However, law is not the only normative framework constraining (and enabling) targeting. Therefore, ethical constraints have also been considered (Chap. 7). Rules of Engagement (Chap. 8) bring together all of the factors shaping a targeting operation These rules are the operationalization of military, legal, diplomatic, political, moral, and other factors.

The book concludes with Part III, which surveys contemporary issues in targeting. Sparking hot debate with respect to methods and means of targeting is the possible advent of autonomous weapon systems in military operations (Chap. 9). The controversy is ongoing and shows no sign of being settled soon. The phenomenon of so-called 'non-kinetic' targeting is likewise a topic of current interest, particularly as a means of complementing or replacing traditional kinetic strikes (Chap. 10). Recent conflicts, particularly that in Afghanistan, have highlighted the complexity of organizing and executing targeting in multinational military operations and, thus, such targeting in that environment merits consideration in this book (Chap. 11). Finally, the very purpose of targeting—to generate designated effects by affecting selected addressees—is assessed using the case study of leadership decapitation in counter-terrorism operations, a topic that has generated controversy in virtually all of the disciplines associated with the practice and theory of targeting (Chap. 12).

Acknowledgments The authors would like to thank the contributors to this volume, all of whom came to the project armed with extensive academic or practical background in targeting … or both. It was our professional and personal pleasure to work with each of them. We would also like to thank Philip van Tongeren and Marjolijn Bastiaans at Asser Press for their valued support of this effort and Sasha Radin at the United States Naval War College for her tireless efforts throughout the editing process.

Finally, we hope this work contributes to the realization of the goal to which every member of every nation's armed forces must commit him or herself—the effective and efficient achievement of legitimate military objectives in a manner that minimizes the inevitable destruction and suffering that attends warfare.

Part I
Context

Chapter 2
Targeting in Context

Christopher Coker

Abstract This essay discusses three aspects of the targeting challenge from the time of the ancient Greeks: the 'who', 'what', and 'how'. With respect to the first, we would appear to have broken with past convention and adopted a policy of targeted killings of enemy commanders or political leaders. We have done so in response to a demand of the hour made possible by technology—the need to manage risks. Targeting has become a risk management exercise in all but name. With regard to the second, we are trying to be more precise when aiming at the centre of gravity and to reduce collateral damage to a minimum. We are trying, in a word, to be more 'humane'. And with respect to the last, technology now allows us to target from a distance without endangering military personnel, at the risk, however, of producing a problem never before encountered in war: dissociation.

Keywords Drone · Risk · Targeted killing · Surveillance · Centre of gravity · Humane · Dissociation

Contents

C. Coker (✉)
International Relations at the London School of Economics, London, UK
e-mail: c.coker@lse.ac.uk

P.A.L. Ducheine et al. (eds.), *Targeting: The Challenges of Modern Warfare*,
DOI 10.1007/978-94-6265-072-5_2

2.1 Introduction

In a passage from Thucydides' *History of the Peloponnesian War*, we find a brief exchange between a Spartan prisoner of war and an Athenian soldier who asks his captive whether his fellow Spartans, who have chosen so bravely to die rather than surrender the day before, had been men of honour. The Spartan replies that a weapon would be worth a great deal if it could distinguish a gallant man from a coward.[1] Of course, no weapon can.

It was Thucydides who called war 'the human thing', the only definition he was prepared to provide. It is human because it derives its impetus from the social context of the time. It is the context that is all-important for the 'who', the 'what', and the 'how' one targets. In the fifth century BC, men targeted other men; armies targeted each other. Even today, however, where people are usually targeted from the third dimension of war—the air—a drone pilot operating an Unmanned Aerial Vehicle (UAV) over the skies of Afghanistan does not know whether he is killing men who are brave or cowards. The drone pilot, it is true, may share an intimacy with his targets that is unique in history; he can follow his targets to weddings and funerals, and if he is curious watch them having sex thanks to infrared cameras.[2] Pilots can profile behaviour, and take out people they consider to be terrorists. But while a drone pilot may be able to see more than any pilot has seen before, his breadth of vision does not allow him to see the man within. He might have greater oversight of the battlefield than ever, but this affords him no greater *insight* into the moral status of the man he has in his sights.

The 'who' is only part of another context—the 'what'. We have been targeting for centuries what Clausewitz called 'the centre of gravity'. It is a concept derived from Newtonian mechanics, and one that has perhaps decreasing purchase in a digital age. But every century has a recognised centre of gravity and every army has tried to target it, though not always with success. Instead of engaging the Persians in close combat, the Scythians retreated into the vastness of the Steppes. As nomads they had no capital city to capture and no trade routes to cut off. Instead, they vanished over the horizon, harrying the invaders in skirmishes and ambushes by mounted archers. In exasperation, the Persian King Darius issued a challenge to 'stand and fight like men'. The reply from one of the Scythian kings was made famous by Herodotus: 'Know this of me, Persians. I have never fled for fear of any man.'[3] But because they had no cultivated land to waste and no towns to capture, they also had no reason to engage the Persians in battle. They had nothing to defend but the graves of their fathers. Find them and the Persians would get their battle. In the end, they never did, and so were forced to retreat'.

---

[1]Lendon 2005, pp. 2, 47.

[2]Catherina 2011.

[3]Asprey 1994, p. 3.

In the course of history, war changed. It began to involve the will of a society and its people to fight on. Europe, claimed the philosopher Hegel in the early nineteenth century, had reached the stage when its citizens no longer fought for the security of life or the property of the individual, but were willing to hazard both for a greater end. In the modern age, societies were ready to fight wars for freedom or for a cause. It was the readiness of the citizen to sacrifice his life in the service of the State that, for Hegel, constituted the last phase of history. Inevitably, the centre of gravity was located in the sprawling urban cities of the industrial world, and in the workers and citizens who were conscripted to fight either at the front or in the factories. Today we target terrorist networks, non-State actors, and jihad tourists, the 'linchpin' of collective violence.

As for the 'how' of targeting, this has been almost entirely the outcome of technology in the modern era. In the late nineteenth century weapons became area-killing devices; individual soldiers were encouraged to fire not at a specific enemy but at the area in which several enemies might be found. It just so happens that in recent years we have been offered targeting choices we have never had before, and some of these I will discuss. None of this, however, takes away from what Thucydides told us long ago, that without strategic wisdom, targeting is useless.

2.2 Who

Targeted killings have never been popular. The Duke of Wellington was aghast when one of his artillery officers wanted to fire on Napoleon during the battle of Waterloo. Aristocrats did not target each other except in duels. This was an era of so-called 'cabinet wars', when armies preferred to out-manoeuvre, rather than out-fight each other. Today, argued an essayist of the period, 'war is waged so humanely, so deftly and with so little profit, that it could be compared without paradox to civil trials'.[4] Of course, fashions change in war as in every other aspect of life. It is impossible to extrapolate from any period of history into the future and assume that things will be the same. As the most unpredictable of all activities, war is particularly unsuitable for the sort of trend analysis in which so many experts put their faith. A graph of eighteenth century combat deaths would have given no hint of the slaughter that was to come in the French Revolutionary and later Napoleonic wars. Nevertheless, the targeting of commanders who are also political leaders (Napoleon being one) has been generally avoided throughout history for a very obvious reason. Political decapitation may help you win a battle, but not necessarily a war. Someone has to surrender.

[4]Bell 2007, p. 49.

Even in World War II (as close to total war as any conflict has come), the Allies preferred not to target German commanders and the Americans targeted only one Japanese commander, Admiral Yamomoto, in 1943. On the eve of D-Day, the MI6 chief, Sir Stewart Menzies, wrote to the Foreign Office to explain why he was calling off a campaign of assassinations:

> We prepared a list of names which represent the most important German personalities and paramilitary formations believed to be in France. We do not believe, however, their removal will have much, or indeed any, effect on the efficient functioning of so widespread and highly organised a machine.

The Chairman of the Joint Intelligence Committee concurred:

> I agree with C in disliking the scheme, not out of squeamishness, as there are several people in this world whom I could kill with my own hands with a feeling of pleasure, and without that action in any way spoiling my appetite, but I think that it is the type of bright idea that in the end produces a good deal of trouble and does little good … Also, the Germans may take reprisals on our prisoners, and at that game they always win.[5]

As noted by Shashank Joshi, in his review of two recent books, Jeremy Scahill's *Dirty Wars* and Mark Mazzetti's *The Way of the Knife*, these arguments have been progressively abandoned. Both books document the rapid emergence of a new and probably enduring epoch in American security policy. Drone strikes in particular (so-called 'signature strikes') have now become almost the norm.

There are a number of explanations for this. The first is that information is becoming an increasingly important military instrument, as well as a major determinant of tactical and operational effectiveness. It is considered to be a force multiplier; it is also part of winning the 'narrative' by minimising collateral damage. While in the past information was seen mostly as an enabler of more efficient and accurate targeting, information these days is seen as an end in itself.

Second, drone strikes are really a form of policing rather than pacifying—not producing security, but reducing insecurity to manageable levels, as we do crime at home. This is why it makes sense for the CIA, as well as the regular military, to carry out many of these strikes. George Tenet, the Director of the Central Intelligence Agency at the time of 9/11, was originally appalled that he should be asked to go into the assassination business. By 2013, Scahill tells us, President Obama's appointee to the same post—John Brennan—was known as the 'Assassination Tsar'.

Targeted assassinations are not new; they were pioneered by the Israelis back in the 1990s. It was in this period that the Israeli Defence Force (IDF) seems to have adopted the maxim that successful armies need to instil 'terror in the hearts of their enemies'. This maxim can be seen in a number of policies that became fundamental during the second intifada. The most well known of these is what have been called 'targeted killings', or 'extra-judicial executions'. These practices have taken many forms, ranging from the detonation of terrorist leaders' mobile phones

---

[5]Joshi 2013, p. 44.

to helicopter strikes in densely populated areas. Crucially, the IDF opted not only to strike at purely military ringleaders, but also to take out a number of individuals whose function was partly or wholly political. The assassinations in 2004 of Sheikh Ahmed Yassim, the spiritual leader of Hamas, and his successor, Abdel-Aziz al-Rantisse, are cases in point. While these operations drew widespread criticism in the outside world, Israel maintained that its actions had significantly weakened the infrastructure of the movement.

None of this should be surprising, however, because it is reflective of the way we have been policing our societies at home. War, Clausewitz reminds us, is part of the pattern of social life. It is a microcosm of society and its norms. Signature strikes are based on behavioural profiling that is as old as the way we have been policing our societies since the 1980s. In terms of surveillance, successful policing has depended increasingly on the information that provides the algorithmic methods of modern risk assessment. Crime control and policy are particularly connected with a 'culture of control', a term which was coined to describe a society in which the perennial desire for security, risk management and the taming of chance have been so magnified and reinforced with regulations that surveillance has become a norm in practically every area of life. In the UK, the Home Office spends a significant portion of its crime prevention budget on CCTV cameras and face-recognition 'smart' technology. Corporations actively monitor consumer choice every time a credit card is swiped or an internet site visited. We have NETFLIX suggestions for what we should watch next based on what we have viewed before. On Amazon and Google we are profiled by what we read as well as watch. The global positioning system can track mobile phone users, and the same, of course, goes for GPS systems in cars.

In Britain, the Ministry of Defence is investing in neural network technology for pattern-matching to enable the security services to scan faces in a crowd and cross-reference them to known troublemakers.[6] Very soon we will be able to programme computers to recognise patterns and relationships that we cannot recognise in each other—body language if you will—that betray anxiety, even perhaps an intention to plant a bomb.[7] The Department of Homeland Security has Future Attribute Screening Technology (FAST) to identify potential terrorists using 'virtual' signs such as body language with a 70 % success rate (however this is measured). The point is that law enforcement agencies take pre-emption seriously in stopping crime before it is committed.

Data processing systems are also improving all the time. CCTV cameras can now be patched into information retrieval systems to facilitate a 'knowledge brokering' function which goes far beyond pinpointing people as they move about.

---

[6] Norris 1999, p. 217.

[7] This is explained in a presentation by Moglen (2012) at Re:Publica (Berlin), around 16 min, he recalls a statement from a Senior White House Official: 'The Governments wants a social graph of the US.'

Police forces go in for concentrated surveillance at high-risk locations and times;[8] hence, for example, the rise of drink-drive blitzes and random alcohol checks on weekends and public holidays. Both constitute a new *risk-focused* pattern of policing, which is intended through reconnaissance to establish the extent of the risk that either criminals or people involved in criminally negligent activity (drink driving) pose to the rest of us. Law enforcement agencies have begun replacing human police officers with efficient, all-seeing algorithms and the intelligence of the algorithms is continually growing. Speed cameras can now pick out newcomers to an area. Increasingly, these cameras are capable of making sense of human behaviour on CCTV. Algorithms are being tested that can identify—in real time—faces in a crowd or people with a particular gait. 'Predictive policing' systems built by IBM sift through vast records of past offences, weather patterns, social media use, and other contributing factors to display maps showing where offences are likely to occur, prompting police to boost patrols at specific times. Surveillance identifies a risk before it goes critical. To prevent it from going critical, we are encouraged to go for target devaluation.

In other words, our societies seek total knowledge of people. Surveillance enables the State to make biographical profiles of the population in order to determine their probable behaviour at some undetermined date. Thus, not only is it possible to follow an individual as he moves through space, but it is also possible to assess his moral worth at the same time, using information contained on a database.[9] This is called 'social sorting', an inclusive and exclusive process that is central to what the management of risk is fast becoming.

The same is increasingly true of targeting in war. It remains to be seen how successful drone strikes have been. The 'who' involves the 'what'—the enemy's centre of gravity. In Pakistan, the Americans have taken out training camps, and targeted the leadership of Al-Qaeda. The US campaign, however, seems to be less aimed at high value targets (only about 2 % of all drone deaths are aimed at targets such as Al-Qaeda Central members or militant leaders in Afghanistan or Pakistan); the main targets are usually low-level insurgents.[10]

Even now, it is impossible to estimate the real effects of drone strikes—whether tactical brilliance yields any real strategic reward. 'Is it creating a new generation of terrorists' is a question often asked. In the tribal areas of Pakistan, parents report taking their children out of school out of fears for their safety, and students speak of their diminished ability to concentrate.[11] Accounts such as these serve as

---

[8]Bauman and Lyon 2012, p. 47.

[9]Lyon 2007, p. 107.

[10]International Human Rights and Conflict Resolution Clinic at Stanford Law School and the Global Justice Clinic of New York University School of Law (2012) Living under drones: death, injury and the trauma to civilians from US drone practices in Pakistan. www.livingunderdrones.org/wp-content/uploads/2013/10/Stanford-NYU-Living-Under-Drones.pdf. Accessed 19 December 2013.

[11]See Amnesty International (2013) and Human Rights Watch (2013).

a reminder that the harm of the US drone campaign goes beyond the significant toll of civilian lives lost (a matter also much disputed).

2.3 What

The 'what' of targeting is part of the social discourse of war, and discourses are always changing. For good or ill, the Western discourse is a liberal one. And technology is the single most important factor in delivering the means by which liberal societies can fight in a liberal manner. Technology makes it possible, as we shall see, to keep faith with traditional ethical practices much more than in the past. It also poses new ethical problems, for all technologies have side effects. Liberal societies still find the world stubbornly resistant to their ideas of how war should be waged.

Consider the reaction in 1911 to the first aerial bombing. An Italian airman threw grenades out of his monoplane onto Turkish troops in Libya. The world's press was outraged at the 'unsporting' nature of the venture on a very specific ground. The soldiers below were unable to retaliate. In fact, Turkish troops shot down an Italian airplane with rifle fire the following week. Less than 40 years later, Allied bombers were pummelling German cities (in retaliation, of course, for German raids).

It is striking that the Great Powers largely abided by the Geneva Protocol banning Chemical Weapons,[12] even though a few years earlier they had employed such weapons in the field. A strong military case was made for the use of gas before the American attack on Iwo Jima, but Roosevelt rejected the idea. More surprisingly, Hitler too prohibited their use even though they were central to the Final Solution ('Endlösung'). In part, this may have been out of fear of reprisals, or in part, quite possibly, because he had been gassed himself. In their book *A Higher Form of Killing*, the authors note that Raubkammer, where the Germans tested chemical weapons, was the only major military proving ground that Hitler never visited, perhaps with devastating consequences.[13] At least one American commander, Omar Bradley, later claimed that a sustained chemical counter-attack would have made all the difference between success and failure on the Normandy beaches.[14]

Now, in an attempt to be even more 'humane', we not only have banned certain technologies, but also have invented non-kinetic means of dealing with the enemy. We have non-lethal weapons in their third generation that, though still not widely used in combat zones, allow us to neutralise our enemies without taking

[12]Protocol for the Prohibition of the Use in War of Asphyxiating, Poisonous or other Gases, and of Bacteriological Methods of Warfare, 17 June 1925, 94 LNTS No 2138 (1929).

[13]Harris and Paxman 2002.

[14]The Economist (2013) The history of chemical weapons: the shadow of Ypres.

them out: sonic bullets that give you the mother of all headaches; super-glue guns that glue you to your weapon; and corrosive chemicals that dissolve the wings on a plane before it has had a chance to take off. All of these weapons, according to the commander of the US Marine Corps unit in Somalia in February 1995, showed "a reverence for human life and … commitment to the use of minimum force."[15] This is what humane warfare promises, the chance for the first time to eliminate the incivility of modern warfare. As Alvin and Heidi Toffler wrote some years ago:

> Non-lethality emerges not as a simple replacement for war, or an extension of peace, but as something different. It is something radically different in global affairs, an intermediate phenomenon, a pausing place, an arena for contests where more outcomes are decided bloodlessly.[16]

What we are targeting, however, is a centre of gravity which increasingly is public opinion. Winning the narrative is the name of the game and to win it we have to be humane. This derives from three imperatives, all of which require us to *humanise* war. The first is old-fashioned Western humanism. Governments used to measure the cost of war in terms of money, lost production, or the number of soldiers killed or wounded. Rarely did they attempt to measure its cost in terms of individual human suffering. Enemies were stripped of their humanity. Little thought was given to individuated death. Democracies had no more compunction than their enemies in raining down death and destruction on the heads of citizens, even children. 'Two years ago, we would all have been aghast at the idea of killing civilians', complained George Orwell in 1942.[17] 'I remember saying to someone during the Blitz… "in a year's time you will see headlines in the *Daily Express*: *Successful raid on Berlin orphanage. Babies set on fire*"'.[18]

Today, by contrast, we are inclined to individualise both death and human suffering more than ever before, especially when targeting. The US, claimed Madeline Albright at the time of the Kosovo War, spent as much time trying to limit deaths on the other side as it did its own. Even the ethics of war is no longer determined by abstract concepts as in the past. Ethics is a human endeavour and present-day humanism is reflected in the wish of civil society to reduce the incivility of warfare, both for the soldiers who serve in society's name and the enemies with which our societies find themselves at war.

We are doing so because we can technologically. We tried to accomplish this, of course, much earlier, back in the 1890s, but advances in modern weaponry, such as automatic weapon fire, massed artillery bombardment, and aerial bombing, resulted in greater inhumanity still—wars of bloody attrition. Today, we see little value in 'area killing' or the targeting of civilians. In the future, we will continue

---

[15]Cited in Freedman 1998, p. 16.

[16]Toffler and Toffler 1994.

[17]Orwell 1968, p. 496.

[18]Ibid.

to become more discriminating. In the first Gulf War (1991) precision-guided weapons accounted for only 8 % of ordinance drops. During the second Gulf War, the invasion of Iraq twelve years later, they counted for nearly 100 %. 'The calibration of destruction' was the title of an article which appeared in *The Economist* in January 2010. 'Smaller, cleverer and more accurate munitions are changing warfare'.[19] The article was about *Perseus*, a 2000 lb bomb that incinerates almost everything in an area the size of two dozen football fields. Just outside that area, it sucks oxygen from the air, crushing anyone to be found there by a pressure wave. The weapon is not that different from napalm. What is surprising is that it is endorsed by the Human Rights Watch,[20] a humanitarian non-governmental organisation based in New York, largely because the weapon can be employed selectively and humanely; it spares the lives of people while destroying a bunker housing biological or chemical weapons. It can sterilise germ warfare laboratories. It can be put to use humanely.

The corollary of this is that we are also increasingly interested in reducing the material and human destructiveness of the battlefield, in limiting damage to the environment and human habitat. A 1954 Convention on Cultural Property permits countries to nominate 100 buildings that cannot be targeted by an enemy (in Britain, St Paul's Cathedral, but interestingly not Westminster Abbey, is on the list).[21]

We also fight humanitarian wars—Kosovo was supposed to be the first, though it may well have been the last. There was little humanity in the twentieth century. Marxists and non-Marxists alike were usually dismissive of the claims of small people to nationhood, not to mention 'unhistorical peoples' who got in the way of progress. In mediating humanity through the nation in arms or the revolutionary State, locked in a historic struggle against ancient adversaries, even democracies put principles first and individual human suffering second. In making the world 'safe for democracy', few Americans asked themselves whether democracy could be made safe for the world. Today, we fight for others as well as ourselves. We have extended our concept of humanity from the local community to the imagined community of the nation-State, and further afield still to the global village. "We are all internationalists now", claimed Britain's Prime Minister 22 days into the Kosovo War.[22] And you cannot fight humanitarian wars inhumanely. Even if we accept that selective targeting cannot work—that air power and cruise missiles do not always allow ethical choices and that we cannot target the evils of the world with the blunt instruments in our possession—we will insist on being more humane in targeting than we have in the past.

---

[19]The Economist (2010) The calibration of destruction.

[20]Ibid.

[21]Convention for the Protection of Cultural Property in the Event of Armed Conflict. The Hague. 14 May 1954. 249 UNTS 240.

[22]Blair 1999.

Something more profound, however, is behind this new attitude towards targeting—risk management. Humanity, in fact, is not something that has only recently been 'discovered'. Up until now it has been difficult to conduct war humanely. Back in 1916 when the German military was arguing for an unrestricted submarine campaign against Britain, it tended to dismiss civilian objections as *Humanitatsdusehei*, or mere 'humanitarian babbling'.[23] In fact, the debate over whether or not to press ahead with unrestricted submarine attacks on allied shipping went far beyond humanitarianism; it involved a discussion about the political consequences of being *seen* to be more inhumane than the enemy when fighting. To invoke today's fashionable phrase, it was all about who owned the narrative.

The German Chancellor initially resisted the generals' demands for unrestricted submarine warfare for fear it would bring the US into the war. Clausewitz would have cautioned restraint. The principal object of the military art, he tells us, 'is to prevent the trembling balance from suddenly turning to our disadvantage and the half-war from changing into a complete one'.[24] Ultimately, both the decision to go to war and the decision to adopt submarine warfare three years later represented a failure of political leadership for which the Chancellor himself must be held partly responsible. He simply did not fight his corner hard enough. The consequences of the campaign were indeed devastating. Apart from the humanitarian concerns about drowning innocent passengers on ships like the *Lusitania*, which had been torpedoed two years earlier, it also meant breaking international law (no small matter when the President of the US was a moralist like Woodrow Wilson).

Today, we are always enjoined to anticipate the negative effects of our decisions; we are urged continually to bring the future into a calculative relation to the present. And this was also the dynamic of the U-Boat debate in 1916–1917, with a critical difference. The Germans externalised the risks, such as the response of neutral countries to putting their own shipping in danger by continuing to trade with the UK and the risk that the US would be bounced into war by public opinion. We now tend to *internalise* risks in the form of consequence management. The distinction does not lie in the fact that the risks the German High Command chose to incur were measurable in a way that many risks we run today are not. The real difference is that the costs of incurring them have become unacceptably high. We have become consumers, not producers, of risk, and have greater difficulty than ever in legitimising the risks we ask others to take (including our own citizens, or members of coalitions to which we belong, by virtue of the fact that they are implicated in every decision we take).

Consequence management (as the internalisation of risk) was clearly in evidence in Kosovo in 1999. Precision air strikes enabled NATO to coerce the Serbian government without inflicting much direct damage on the population,

---

[23] Stone 2007, p. 99.

[24] von Clausewitz 1982, p. 401.

although collateral damage could not be eliminated altogether. When it failed to make progress, the Alliance was forced to bomb a large number of industrial plants. The most important target of all was the Serbian power grid. Some of the bombs contained carbon fibre spools, which instead of destroying the generators, merely short-circuited the transformer yards, putting out the lights in the major cities for anywhere between 8 and 24 hours. As soon as the Serbs managed to get the power working again, more air strikes could be carried out using non-lethal carbon fibre bombs.[25] As a medium-sized economy, Serbia was also small enough to allow precision targeting to achieve its objectives without major damage, although the long-term consequences of the bombing campaign were greater than NATO was willing to acknowledge at the time. In Pančevo and Novi Sad, two towns that vied for the title of 'the most bombed town in Serbia', the once thriving car factories that provided jobs were devastated.

Kosovo was the first example of consequence management evolving into a doctrine—an effects-based approach to war. An effects-based operation is a methodology in which the desired effect of an action, regardless of its scope, has to be identified first. In the air attack with which the invasion of Iraq (2003) began, the first concern of the Americans was to negate the effectiveness of the enemy's air defences without necessarily destroying Iraqi aircraft on the ground. The country's air defence system was rendered useless by a series of tailored actions that included selective hard strikes against key command and control nodes (if pilots have no instructions, no radar to guide them, and no communications, they are unlikely to be effective), as well as a series of 'soft strikes' (feeding false data into Iraqi information systems and infecting them with computer viruses).[26]

In this regard, writes Alan Stephens, the term 'effects based operation' has come to define a *philosophy* of war more than a doctrine. The object is to achieve a specific effect and to avoid both predicted and unpredicted consequences at the lowest affordable cost. But as a philosophy of risk management it also has drawbacks, for the impact of an air strike, as an example, is not always obvious at the time.[27] Even more significantly, it is not necessarily apparent even at the point of impact. The political fallout is often latent, or in other words invisible to everyday perception. Hazards may externalise symptoms only later in the day and they often reach a critical mass before they are appreciated. It is the interval between action and impact (as a *latent* symbol) that is frequently critically important in determining whether public support for war can be retained.

The modern battle-space, in other words, is a fiendishly complex environment. At staff colleges these days, students are taught that the more risks go unacknowledged at the time, the more likely they are to multiply later. And when the risks are latent, the cost is liable to be all the greater when the time bomb finally explodes. This is especially problematic given the speed of modern war. Targeting decisions

[25] Ignatieff 2001, p. 107.

[26] Stephens 2007, p. 134.

[27] Adam 2003, p. 219.

have to be taken quickly. Whatever is effective in the medium term is usually preferred, irrespective of the attendant consequences. Immediate successes tend to result in complacency. Success, however temporary, is often taken to be its own reward.

2.4 How

Until the twentieth century targeting was the responsibility of the army and navy. Once war took to the third dimension it became not only a major concern, but also the chief function of the air force. Only six years after the *Wright Flyer* had taken to the air, Parliamentarians in Britain expressed apprehension about the *immoral* bombing, thus identifying—years before major aerial bombardment became a possibility—the real strategic centre of gravity: morale. The MPs recognised that the application of air power in this way could have consequences beyond potential physical damage to infrastructure and buildings. 'We do not know', contended one, '[w]hat destructiveness [aircraft] will cause in our laws, customs and convenience, but these matters will no doubt be adjusted'.[28] These matters, adds Peter Lee, would be adjusted far more quickly than MPs could have imagined at the time.[29]

In war, changes have always been made to customs and laws (it is part of war's Darwinian ability to adapt to every environment). But the *internal* adjustments to the psyche and our emotional register are perhaps the most important of all. Throughout history it has not been morality that has been especially effective. Technology has made the critical difference in warfare—take the sword and shield, the arquebus, rapid fire small arms, aircraft, and missiles. Technology offers choices. It opens doors and closes others. It happens that today technology offers a more diverse set of targeting options than ever before. Once targeting is combined with changing moral codes and ethical precepts, as well as new technologies, the 'who' of targeting transforms very quickly.

The real game changer, however, is the elimination of risk—a first in warfare. This may have resulted in the unforeseen progressive dissociation of pilots from the activity in which they are engaged. To be dissociated from one's actions is not the same as to be distanced or divorced; it is to be disembodied (it is to lack feeling, sensitivity). We learn only by seeing and we see 'feelingly'. To see feelingly is to allow reason to move us within the constraints of the suffering body, which is why Wittgenstein concluded that the body in pain is the most graphic reflection of the human soul. The challenge of all military technology in the past hundred years is that it creates death while destroying the experience of it. It is much easier to

---

[28]House of Commons Debate, Naval and Military Aeronautics, 2 August 1909, vol 8, cc1564–617. http://hansard.millbanksystems.com/commons/1909/aug/02/naval-and-military-aeronautics. Accessed 19 December 2013. Idem: Lee 2013, p. 73.

[29]Lee 2013, p. 134.

become desensitised, distanced from the consequences of our actions. It is quite another thing to become altogether disconnected from what our actions mean for others. By acting without meaning we are in danger of being stripped of our moral core.

For the Allied bombers of World War II the issue was distance and the fear that war was becoming a mere routine. Some crew members called themselves 'freight-engineers', others 'aerial taxi drivers'. They returned from their missions, wrote one, 'bored in a way no-one had ever been bored before'.[30] But the point is that however distanced they were from their targets, they remained at risk all the time. By August 1943, the Germans were shooting down as many American B-24 and B-17s as replacement crews and planes arrived in England. A plane could be shot down by anti-aircraft fire or intercepted in the air by fighters. The crews were exposed to other hazards as well, including respiratory infections from which they continued to suffer well into the peace. A man's courage is his capital, wrote Lord Moran—the call on the bank may be the daily drain of the front line, or it may be a sudden draft which threatens to close the account. And he found this to be as true for the pilots of Bomber Command as it was for the infantrymen or tank crews on the ground. 'The pilot enters upon the summer of his career, a period of confidence, success and achievement… But the summer months must pass, and when autumn comes the picture of the pilot's distress is not so different from that of a soldier or sailor, only the colouring varies'.[31] The extent of that 'colouring' was caught vividly many years later in one of the most powerful war novels to emerge from the experience of World War II, Joseph Heller's *Catch-22*.

All this is history. 'Our major role is to sanitise the battlefield', a service airman is quoted as saying in Peter Singer's book, *Wired for War*.[32] Today, even bomber pilots no longer face the risks they did. Unlike B-52 pilots in Vietnam, pilots in the present day are rarely in danger of being shot down. Embedded with the B-1 Bomber Squadron in the early days of Operation Enduring Freedom, the journalist Mark Bowden concluded that for the pilots war had become almost entirely cerebral, not visceral; it required them to invest little emotional energy into the task at hand.[33] Almost immune from danger, they clocked up the hours in the sky like business executives, and, like the latter, could go home to their families in 48 hours from a mission over Afghanistan, in time to see the latest episode of *Friends*.

And one of the most important questions is what the experience of selective targeting, or targeted killing, is doing to the pilots concerned. For if distance was a twentieth century problem, dissociation or disconnection is a twenty-first one. Paul Kahn, Professor at Yale Law School, claims that both distance and disconnection 'propel us beyond the ethics of warfare', but the two are actually quite different.[34]

---

[30]Piette 1995, pp. 76–77.

[31]Holmes 2004, p. 214.

[32]Singer 2009, p. 34.

[33]Bowden 2002.

[34]Singer 2009, p. 432.

One US Air Force Colonel in command of a Predator Squadron told Singer that the young pilots under his command did not know what was really going on; they were semi-detached from the action.[35] We talk of pilots being distanced when they cannot see the effects of their bombing; we talk of drone pilots being disconnected or dissociated when they have an impaired understanding of war itself. And dissociation is becoming a theme of many Hollywood films, including Ridley Scott's *Body of Lies*, in which the CIA boss, played by Russell Crowe, orders a drone strike against terrorists from the comfort of his own office, while the agent in the field, played by Leonardo Di Caprio, living an offline life, gets tortured, blown up, and at one point beaten to a pulp. Dissociation is likely to arise when we live a largely online life.

One interesting question—a first in targeting—is what the technologies used by the pilots and gunners are doing to their brains. It is not so much a failure to understand the experience or decode the meaning of an activity. Something much more may be involved. Our brains are engaged less directly and more shallowly in information processing. We may become more efficient in our undertakings but less aware of what it is that we are doing. One of the problems is that we process information out of context and therefore find it difficult to be reflective about what we process. After all, what we are doing in multi-tasking is shifting our attention from one job to the next, learning to be more skilful at a superficial level. The area in which we are becoming more skilled is that of visual attentional processing—the speed at which we can shift our visual attention without at the same time gaining an insight into what lies behind the picture. Nicholas Carr quotes Patricia Greenfield, a developmental psychologist at UCLA, whose research found that new strengths in visual-spatial intelligence tend to go hand in hand with the weakening of 'de-processing' that underpins inductive analysis, critical thinking and the full use of our imagination. And this can actually be measured in changes of neural circuitry. Our brains, in fact, are becoming more computational; they are beginning to function like computers. We can increase 'the pace of the stream'. We can process the flow of information even faster than before, but we may be doing so at the risk of becoming emotionally shallow.[36]

Or is this the proper way of looking at the question? Quite another method is involved if we invoke Actor Network Theory (ANT), an approach to social theory and research originating in the field of science studies and developed by scholars such as Bruno Latour and John Law.[37] Broadly speaking, ANT is a constructivist approach that avoids essentialist accounts of events or innovations (explaining a successful theory by saying it is true and others are false). It is different from other sociological network theories for its distinct material DOS semiotic approach.

The point is that non-animate machines, like drones, do not lie outside social relationships. There is no difference in the ability of technology and humans to act.

---

[35]Singer 2009, p. 367.

[36]Carr 2011, p. 133.

[37]Law 1992.

Take a car. It is a system with many electronic and mechanical components hidden from the view of the driver, which is why the latter tend to see a car as a single object, not a system of which he or she is a part. And it is generated by the principle of generalised symmetry (i.e., differences between humans and machines are created in the network of relations). John Law offers another example. When he writes a text he is communicating with a reader, though the two will probably never meet in person. The communication is made possible by the computer on which he has typed the article, the paper on which it is written, and the printing press that is used to publish it. The argument is that these 'technologies' participate in the social world. They help shape it and are necessary to the social relationship between author and reader. In some measure, it might even be said that they overcome the reader's reluctance to read the text.[38] If machines are part of the social world we take for granted, they are likely to play an even larger role in the future. The theory rejects the claim that either the machine or human being is determinate in the final instance (that one drives the other). Both are inextricably interlinked. It is a radical theory, of course, because it also rejects the idea that we are necessarily special.

This raises an even more radical question: what do we mean by 'people'. What counts as a person is generated by a network of relationships with other people and other things. And a machine, too, is not an inanimate object after all; it relies on human designers and users. It is contended that the process, as it deepens, will give rise to a new category of people–machine, or the 'inhuman'.[39] The term is unfortunate, but it is one that is intended to blur the distinction between the two and, in the case of machine ethics, suggests that one day, perhaps quite soon, we will not know whether the ethical arises from man or machine. It would also be fair to say that whenever we have wanted to be ethical in the modern era, we have been entirely reliant on technology anyway, from precision guided munitions to non-lethal weapons.

All this is vitally important in respect to drones, as the technology will continue to become more autonomous. The US Air Force Research Laboratory at Wright-Patterson Air Force Base (Dayton, Ohio) is expecting to have operational by 2015 a suite of on-board sensors that will allow drones to independently detect another aircraft and manoeuvre to avoid it. Quite soon, drones will be able to start processing information that they are looking for, rather than sending back an endless video stream that requires hours of intense analytic analysis and interpretation, and is heavily human-intensive. And one day in the not too distant future, drones will be able to independently dock with Air Force tankers in mid-air.[40]

At some point in the future they may even be able to take ethical decisions on our behalf. When drones can be programmed with moral algorithms equivalent to

[38] Law 1992 pp. 381–382.

[39] Thrift 1994, p. 197.

[40] Coker 2013.

the moral heuristics programmed into us by natural selection, there will be little need of pilots. At best they will be on the loop, not in the loop, acting as managers, not operators, checking to see that the programmes work and the heuristics are being adhered to. This will represent a major threshold in the future of war; man and machine will be taking targeting decisions together, in a partnership that blurs the ultimate distinction between the two.

References

Adam B (2003) The risk society and beyond: critical issues for social theory. Sage, London

Amnesty International (2013) Will I be next? US drone strikes in Pakistan. http://www.amnestyusa.org/sites/default/files/asa330132013en.pdf. Accessed 13 May 2014

Asprey R (1994) War in the shadows: the classic history of guerrilla warfare from ancient Persia to the present. Little and Brown, New York

Bauman Z, Lyon D (2012) Liquid surveillance: a conversation. Polity, Cambridge

Bell D (2007) The first total war: Napoleon's Europe and the birth of modern warfare. Bloomsbury, London

Blair T (1999) Doctrine of the international community (22 April 1999). PBS NewsHour . www.pbs.org/newshour/bb/international/jan-june99/blair_doctrine4-23.html. Accessed 19 Dec 2013

Bowden M (2002) The Kabul dance (1 November 2002). The Atlantic. www.theatlantic.com.magazine/archive/2002/11/the-kabul-ki-dance/302610/. Accessed 19 Dec 2013

Carr N (2011) The shallows; how the internet is changing the way we think, read and remember. Atlantic, London

Catherina F (2011) Ethical conflicts of killing without risk (19 November 2011). The Times. http://www.thetimes.co.uk/tto/news/world/article3231479.ece. Accessed 9 May 2014

von Clausewitz C (1982) On war. Penguin, London

Coker C (2013) Warrior geeks: how 21st century technology is changing the way we fight and think about war. Oxford University Press, New York

The Economist (2010) The calibration of destruction (28 January 2010). http://www.economist.com/node/15391218. Accessed 9 May 2014

The Economist (2013) The history of chemical weapons: the shadow of Ypres (31 August 2013). The Economist. http://www.economist.com/news/briefing/21584397-how-whole-class-weaponry-came-be-seen-indecent-shadow-ypres. Accessed 9 May 2014

Freedman L (1998) The revolution in strategic affairs, Adelphi Paper, No 318. International Institute for Strategic Studies, London

Harris R, Paxman J (2002) A higher form of killing: the secret history of chemical and biological warfare. Random House, New York

Holmes R (2004) Acts of war: the behaviour of men in battle. Cassell, London

Human Rights Watch (2013) Between a drone and Al-Qaeda: the civilian cost of US targeted killings in Yemen. http://www.hrw.org/sites/default/files/reports/yemen1013_ForUpload_1.pdf. Accessed 13 May 2014

Ignatieff M (2001) Virtual war: Kosovo and beyond. Chatto and Windus, London

Joshi S (2013) America's killing spree. The World Today 69:7. http://www.chathamhouse.org/sites/default/files/public/The%20World%20Today/2013/AugSep/WT0413Joshi.pdf. Accessed 12 May 2014

Law J (1992) Notes on the theory of the Actor Network; ordering, strategy and heterogeneity. Systems Practice 5:4

Lee P (2013) Return from the wilderness; an assessment of Arthur Harris' moral responsibility for the German city bombings. Air Power Rev 16:1 (Spring)

Lendon JE (2005) Soldiers and ghosts: a history of battle in classical antiquity. Yale University Press, New Haven
Lyon D (2007) Surveillance studies: an overview. Polity, Cambridge
Moglen E (2012) Why freedom of thought requires free media and why free media require free technology, Re:Publica 2012 (Berlin) http://www.youtube.com/watch?feature=player_embedded&v=sKOk4Y4inVY. Accessed 12 May 2014
Norris C (1999) The maximum surveillance society: the rise of CCTV. Berg, London
Orwell G (1968) Penguin essays of George Orwell. Penguin, London
Piette A (1995) Imagination at war: British fiction 1939–1945. Papermac, London
Scahill J (2013) Dirty wars: the world is a battlefield. Serpent's Tail, London
Singer P (2009) Wired for war: the robotics revolution and conflict in the 21st century. Penguin, London
Stephens A (2007) Effects-based operations and the fighting power of a defence force. In: Olson J (ed) New wars. Files on defence and security 4/2007, Oslo, pp 131–149
Stone N (2007) World War 1: a short history. Allen Lane, London
Thrift N (1994) Inhuman geographies: landscapes of speed, light and power. In: Cloke P, Doel M, Matless D, Phillips M, Thrift N (eds) Writing the rural: five cultural geographies. Paul Chapman, London
Toffler A, Toffler H (1994) War and anti-war: survival at the dawn of the 21st century. Warner Books, London

Chapter 3
From Douhet to Drones, Air Warfare, and the Evolution of Targeting

Frans P.B. Osinga and Mark P. Roorda

Abstract Through the prism of the experience of air warfare, this chapter identifies key factors that have shaped targeting. These include technological developments, organizational structures, and processes and inter-service competition for scarce resources. Moreover, targeting is informed by perspectives on the nature of the political mandate and objectives, by the type of war, by intelligence on the nature of the opponent, and by assumptions that are derived from experience, doctrine, or strategic theory. It is, of course, shaped by societal norms. Targeting's evolutionary process is one of solving technical and informational obstacles to finding and hitting targets. It is characterized by a trend in increased munitions accuracy and pinpoint attack capability against objects of an ever-decreasing physical signature in ever-shortening response times, and, if necessary, from ever-increasing distances from the target. The evolution is also a story of constant organizational learning, rediscovery, and theorizing about and experimenting with new targeting planning tools and processes. Moreover, there is a constantly swinging pendulum between the poles of centralized and decentralized control, with a strong tendency toward stringent political oversight. Finally, norms play an increasing role. As this chapter will argue, contemporary targeting challenges emanate from a paradox—as targeting accuracy has reached an unprecedented level, so too has the societal demand for risk-mitigation, precisely because of demonstrated targeting capabilities.

Keywords War · Targeting · Innovation · Strategic bombing · Collateral damage · Legitimacy

---

F.P.B. Osinga (✉) · M.P. Roorda
War Studies Department, Netherlands Defence Academy, Breda, The Netherlands
e-mail: fpb.osinga@mindef.nl

M.P. Roorda
e-mail: mp.roorda@mindef.nl

P.A.L. Ducheine et al. (eds.), *Targeting: The Challenges of Modern Warfare*,
DOI 10.1007/978-94-6265-072-5_3

Contents

3.1 Introduction: Air Warfare and Targeting

The current state of the art of targeting in Western militaries derives from a long evolutionary process that is intertwined with the history of air warfare.[1] An analysis of this evolution discloses persistent challenges and dominant trends, which are key to understanding the complexity of targeting, current targeting practices, and contemporary targeting dilemmas. This chapter is chronologically structured into four periods: air warfare through World War II (WW II); the Cold War; the post-Cold War period; and events since 9/11. Each section will discuss key campaigns that illustrate the most important developments in targeting practices.[2]

Through this prism of the development of air warfare, the chapter aims to identify key factors that, over time, have shaped how targeting is understood and organized into contemporary warfare. Technological development is obviously a dominant factor, but not necessarily the most important one. Organizational structures and processes also shape targeting, as does inter-service competition for scarce resources. Moreover, it is informed by perspectives on the nature of the political mandate and objectives, by the type of war or conflict, and by intelligence on the nature of the opponent. It is also inspired, knowingly or otherwise, by assumptions, derived from experience, doctrine, or strategic theory, about the causal logic that explains why force (lethal or otherwise) will produce a specific

[1]For a full definition, see Allied Joint Doctrine For Joint Targeting AJP-3.9, 2008, p. 1.

[2]As targeting doctrine in the West is heavily shaped by American experiences and capabilities, and as these are thoroughly documented, this chapter leans heavily on American case studies.

effect. Finally, in the articulation of mandates, directives, targeting limitations, and Rules of Engagement (ROE), targeting is shaped by societal, political, and professional norms that include, but often also transcend, rules of a strictly legal nature. Indeed, as this chapter will argue, contemporary targeting challenges emanate from a paradox—targeting accuracy has reached an unprecedented level, but so too has the societal demand for risk-mitigation, precisely because of such capabilities.

3.2 Targeting Until 1945

3.2.1 The Emergence of Targeting

3.2.1.1 From Frontline to Fire Support to Rear-Area Bombardment

Arguably, targeting (in the contemporary meaning of the concept) did not evolve until World War I (WW I). Up to and including WW I, ground combat tactics and equipment were primarily designed to engage the enemy's front-line troops directly; attack its fortifications and logistical facilities; disrupt routes of approach to the enemy's position so as to hamper reinforcement; or deceive and distract the enemy by firing at positions away from the location of a planned offensive.

The introduction of air power changed this reality. It added a third dimension, one that gave militaries the capability to target elements beyond the frontline engagement zones. Commanders could now choose to use their aerial resources in direct support of fighting troops, for destroying nearby logistical nodes in an effort to cut resupply of the enemy's forces, or for attacking even distant targets of greater strategic value. When, in the opening weeks, Germany used Zeppelins to bomb civilians in Liege, Antwerp, and Warsaw, the United Kingdom planned a strategic raid on Zeppelin production facilities in Cologne and Düsseldorf, to be conducted by the Royal Naval Air Service.[3] On both sides, specialized aircraft and bomber squadrons rapidly came into service and, while not yet understood in its present form, the concept of rear-area strategic bombing was born. However, with the rise of air power technology, the issue of target selection arose as a problem requiring high-level consideration. The option of strategic bombing generated debates concerning the rationale and legitimacy for selecting specific targets, in particular when those targets concerned civilian infrastructure. Prioritization of targets became a contentious issue between army and air force officers, one colored by organizational interests as much as by operational arguments.

[3] Tucker et al. 1999, p. 13; Benbow 2011, p. 29. For a general history of the role and evolution of air power in the Great War, see Kenneth 1991.

3.2.2 The Interbellum

3.2.2.1 Strategic Bombing Theory

The nascent strategic bombing capability, together with a desire to avoid the terrible attrition-style warfare that marked WW I, inspired air power theorists of the interbellum period like Julio Douhet, Billy Mitchell, and Hugh Trenchard. All argued that air power offered a method of waging war beyond the traditional ground-centric paradigm. Indeed, they argued that in the era of total war it would be necessary to attack the opponent's capacity and will to continue war. Such attributes, they contended, reside in government, industry, and the population at large. Consequently, the immunity of civilians from the effects of war had become strategically untenable.

Douhet argued that strategic bombing would have to target vital societal centers such as industry, transport infrastructure, communications centers, the government, and the will of the people. The effect of such a campaign on public morale would be so great that it would force the population to overthrow its government. To accomplish the destruction of the will of the people, Douhet contemplated the sequential use of several types of munitions to render the greatest effect. Mitchell also saw great utility in the strategic bombing of vital centers, as well as attacks on high-value military targets such as battleships. His followers at the Air Corps Tactical School (ACTS) further emphasized the merits of attacking key economic nodes. The father of the Royal Air Force (RAF), Trenchard, meanwhile argued for targeting railways, airfields, communication and transportation networks, and industrial centers.[4] The common thread among these theorists was the conviction that strategic attacks would either change the behavior of the enemy's government through the threat of civil uprising, social collapse, fear, or economic paralysis, or that they would bring about military defeat by causing enemy operational paralysis.

3.2.2.2 Metaphors and Assumptions

Their assumptions concerning this causal logic, however, were not based on experience or proven technology, but rather informed by a deterministic Newtonian mindset, coupled with a sophisticated yet underdeveloped analysis of the workings of modern industrialized societies (alongside a separate desire to justify the establishment and maintenance of an independent air force).[5] The arguments were characterized by the liberal use of metaphor to bolster them. Societies were considered fragile, with social cohesion prone to collapse like a 'house of cards' from fear and

---

[4]This very brief description does not do justice to the work of these theorists. For outstanding discussions of air power theory development during the interbellum see, for instance, McIsaac 1986; Meilinger 1997, in particular Chaps. 1–6; Biddle 2003b; Overy's excellent 2013 tome The Bombing War, Europe 1939–1945 (Overy 2013), in particular Chap. 1; and Faber 2015.

[5]Faber 2015; Watts 1984, Chap. 7 in particular.

terror of attack. Modern industrial societies were likened to spider webs, dependent on effective links between critical nodes that make up the network of society. The underlying assumption was that identifying the critical industrial and infrastructural nodes in the system would allow one to calculate precisely how much explosive would suffice to destroy sufficient targets to paralyze the enemy's entire social and economic system.

These ideas also echoed political and societal fears prevalent among European nations. The German attacks on London in 1917 with Gotha bombers, which created massive panic among Londoners, had convinced many of the potential of this new weapon in the future. But while effective rhetorically, the arguments proved less convincing in practice. Most importantly, the capabilities did not yet exist to meet the aspirations of the air power advocates. Before 1939, the technology and economic resources to develop and produce large, complex bomber aircraft simply were not available, even for industrially developed powers such as the United States and Germany. In countries like the USSR, Germany, and France, strategy and doctrine still focused on land warfare, thereby precluding the development of strategic aerial bombing capabilities. And only in the United States and United Kingdom was the political climate sufficiently receptive to allow the development of a strategic preference for long-range bombing. British leaders overcame the moral objections by characterizing strategic bombers as a new form of deterrent. In an era when air defense was still woefully ineffective, bombers could bring the war to the enemy, thus avoiding another war of attrition.[6]

3.2.2.3 Norms: Security Concerns Before Morality

At this stage in the development of air warfare, norms played little role in strategic bombing theory. In 1899, European powers had agreed to prohibit the discharge of explosives from balloons. However, when several countries managed to use dirigibles to some military effect, strategic considerations trumped humanitarian concerns.[7] Customary law and the Hague Conventions of 1899 and 1907 were the only existing legal frameworks governing targeting at the beginning of WW I. Bombing strategy was constrained primarily by the basic rules prohibiting indiscriminate attacks and limiting targets to military objectives, which, at the time, included more than just military forces and objects. The concept of total war encompassed the targeting of virtually anything supporting the war effort, including infrastructure, industry, labor, and the population's will. Targeting civilians was an acceptable strategy insofar as it was directed at the morale of the enemy population as a military objective.[8]

---

[6]See Overy 1998, pp. 11–17, 72–73.

[7]For an excellent concise overview of the development of norm in air warfare until 1945, see Biddle 1994, pp. 140–159.

[8]Reynolds 2005, p. 10.

After WW I, the creation of a normative consensus against the bombing of civilians was almost impossible. First, the embryonic bombing raids had suggested what terrifying destructive power might await and the great political effect to which it could be put. Second, such destruction appeared to promise a quick end to war. Geopolitical turbulence during the interbellum period, and the evident rise of German power after 1933, precluded a ban on strategic bombing. There was consensus that terror bombing of civilians was immoral and unlawful, but this did not necessarily preclude the deterrent role that countries such as the United Kingdom envisioned for their bomber forces. Consequently, prior to the outbreak of WW II, the norm against bombing civilians was weak. It certainly was not internalized by the organizations responsible for the planning and prosecution of the air war.[9]

3.2.3 *World War II (WW II)*

3.2.3.1 Targeting Morale

Morale, rather than specific industries, became the prime target of nighttime strategic bombing by RAF's Bomber Command in WW II. For Prime Minister Winston Churchill, it served, until 1942, the political purposes of striking at the heart of Germany at a time when other options for fighting back were unavailable and of temporarily satisfying Stalin's demands for opening a second front in the West. During the second half of the war, British and American forces coordinated their strategic bombing activities in the Combined Bomber Offensive (CBO), the objective of which had been laid down in the Casablanca Directive of January 1943: "the progressive destruction and dislocation of the German military, industrial and economic system, and the undermining of the morale of the German people to a point where their capacity for armed resistance is fatally weakened." This directive placed strategic bombing in the context of the wider strategy of the liberation of Europe.[10]

Post-war analysis of the CBO indicated that while it played a vital role in the overall Allied victory, German society, like that of the United Kingdom in 1940, proved very resilient despite the large-scale destruction of cities and industry. Morale broke at the local level, but not beyond. Victims of bombing raids were preoccupied with mere survival and the German government was easily able to suppress any potential unrest or uprising. Moreover, technology had not achieved pre-war aspirations. Navigation and target identification proved very difficult, in particular in European weather conditions, and bomb-aiming devices were not

[9]Thomas 2001, p. 125. This section merely touches upon the question whether norms influenced targeting. The debate on the morality of the bombing campaigns at the time, and the previous decades, merits greater attention than is possible in this chapter.

[10]For the development of the CBO, see Overy 2013, in particular Chap. 6.

particularly precise, despite rapid development of navigational aids. In addition, the intensity of the bombing campaign was less than intended. Weather frequently forced air raids to be aborted and German air defenses caused attrition rates that were often unsustainable, thereby necessitating temporary cessation of operations. Key German manufacturers also dispersed their production facilities, enabling them to continue production of military equipment, albeit with long-term negative consequences in terms of efficiency and innovation. Finally, Allied target selection was erratic, with debates about the type of targets that were most valuable (oil, synthetic rubber, transport, cities, military industry, ball bearing factories, or the Luftwaffe) continuing throughout the war between senior air commanders, between air commanders and their colleagues from other services, and between commanders and political leaders.[11] As a result, the air campaign was incoherent in direction and intensity before 1944.

3.2.3.2 Intelligence and Organization

While the unrealistic pre-war assumptions may be criticized in hindsight, the theorists did break new ground. At least in the case of ACTS, they consciously attempted to develop a model of modern society, regarding it as a complex system of interdependent subsystems, together with a plausible theory as to how to create strategic effects through aerial bombing. But while the financial and economic crisis of the interbellum period had suggested that industrial economies were fragile, this was uncharted territory, doctrinally as well as academically. As Overy stated, the bombing campaigns had muddled strategies because so little was known about the effect large-scale bombing was having on an enemy's economy or war-willingness.[12] Meaningful measures of success, beyond those that crudely assessed the devastation of built-up areas, were lacking.[13]

Recognizing those problems, the CBO inspired the creation of targeting organizations. The United Kingdom established the Enemy Branch of the Ministry of Economic Warfare, which conducted detailed target analysis for RAF Bomber Command. Having initially relied on the aforementioned organization, in 1942 the United States created the Enemy Objectives Unit, with the task of providing targeting information to the Eighth Air Force. Another organization that played an important role in supporting US targeting policies in the European theater was the Committee of Operations Analysts (COA), which eventually evolved into the first Joint Target Group. The COA consisted of prominent lawyers, academicians, businessmen, and regular officers tasked with providing a comprehensive analysis of the German war economy in sufficient time to guide the proposed combined

[11] For a detailed analysis of the effectiveness of CBO, see Overy 1980; and Overy 2013, Chaps. 6 and 10 in particular.

[12] Overy 2013, p. 611.

[13] Overy 2013, p. 337; Glock 2012, p. 156.

bomber offensive. They specifically looked for bottlenecks in the war-making capability of the Axis and Axis-controlled countries, and developed criteria to measure first-order (whether the bombs created the damage require) and second-order success (whether the damage had the expected impact on the targeted industrial sector and the anticipated ripple effect beyond it). Within the bomber commands and numbered air forces, operations-analysis sections were established to assess different tactical and technical aspects of aerial bombardment, such as bombing accuracy, the use of bomb fuses, and radio and radar countermeasures. In the European, North African, and Pacific theaters, target analysis, selection, and prioritization became institutionalized in the form of target committees (such as the Combined Strategic Targets Committee) that produced advice for the Allies' senior commanders and political leaders.[14]

3.2.3.3 Disagreements

The implementation of the CBO, and the functioning of these various targeting committees and boards, also demonstrated that target selection was a highly sensitive and contentious topic. National differences, service interests, and operational responsibilities resulted in differing perspectives on targeting priorities. The 1942 Casablanca Directive masked a fierce disagreement between US senior commanders and their British counterparts. The American commanders bemoaned the absence of a well-developed plan underlying RAF operations. The United States, in contrast, had developed Air War Plans Directive-42, which recalled the British commitment to wear-down Germany prior to a land invasion, and included a prioritized set of seven target categories: (1) the German air force, (2) submarine buildings, (3) communications, (4) electric power, (5) oil, (6) aluminum production, and (7) synthetic rubber. It encompassed 177 targets and would, the plan suggested, require 132,090 tons of bombs and 66,045 sorties (the precision with which the numbers were presented betrayed a rather deterministic mindset). The Casablanca Directive did not resolve the matter, despite the direct involvement of Winston Churchill and Franklin D. Roosevelt, and instead simply tolerated both national preferences. While in practice the two approaches were indistinguishable in terms of destructive impact, the compromise resulted in the establishment of separate bombing organizations without a unified commander with sufficient command authority to establish targeting priorities for both forces.[15]

At the operational level, disagreement further marked targeting discussions. There were debates in the Mediterranean and Pacific theaters, with army commanders emphasizing interdiction and close air support (CAS), navies demanding

---

[14]This draws from the excellent detailed Chaps. 2 and 3 on British and U.S. air offensives in Hall 1998; and Overy 2013, in particular Chap. 6. The following studies offer concise and focused overviews: Meilinger 1999; Schmidt 1993; Moeller 1994; and Ballew 2011.

[15]Overy 2013, pp. 305–308.

support for maritime blockades, and air forces stressing the need for air defense and strategic bombing. In the European theater, differences in priorities came to the fore during the run-up to Operation Overlord, the Allied invasion of Normandy. The British and American commanders of the strategic bomber forces argued for unrelenting bombing of German cities and industries—thus maintaining their autonomy—while those immediately responsible for Operation Overlord favored shifting scarce strategic bomber resources to the interdiction of the transport network and the achievement of air superiority.

3.2.3.4 Targeting Lessons Disregarded

WW II had demonstrated that the proper selection of vital targets, through rational planning based on the systematic study of available intelligence, is critical to the successful application of air power. Performing such a function requires an organization with a high degree of analytical competence. As the post-war analysis of the United States Strategic Bombing Survey (USSBS) stated:

> The importance of careful selection of targets for air attack is emphasized by [our] experience. Our strategic intelligence ... at the outset of the war was highly inadequate .... [I]f a comparable lack of intelligence should exist at the start of a future national emergency, it might prove disastrous.... The present shortage of trained and competent intelligence personnel give[s] cause for alarm and require[s] correction.[16]

Yet, at the end of the war, most targeting organizations were disestablished and expertise in joint targeting was generally lost. Despite the existence of relevant doctrine, major Western military operations following WW II have generally been marked by the lack of a standing inter-service targeting organization with the necessary proficiency, procedures, ready access to intelligence and command authority.

3.2.3.5 Norms

WW II demonstrated the weakness of the norm against bombing civilians. It restrained bombing in the first year of the war, but broke down rapidly once German bombers struck UK cities after similar catastrophic attacks against Warsaw and Rotterdam. Once the norm crumbled, incentives for restraint disappeared, resulting in a spiral of retaliation. US commanders objected to morale bombing, considering it to be barbaric and contrary to national values. However, political imperatives (to strike back at Nazi Germany), operational and strategic considerations, and technical limitations combined to overshadow any ethical objections. This remained the case even once those limitations had been resolved,

[16] The United States Strategic Bombing Surveys (European War) (Pacific War) 1987, pp. 39 and 117.

victory looked assured, and intelligence had demonstrated the cruel futility of morale bombing.[17] In the Pacific, with the dropping of two atomic bombs, moral considerations proved even less relevant.

3.3 Targeting During the Cold War

Following WW II, aerial targeting both improved and regressed. The introduction of nuclear weapons eventually resulted in an enormous targeting organization within the US military, with the nuclear strategies of both superpowers promising destruction on an unprecedented scale. In contrast, during the conventional, but limited, Korean and Vietnam wars, the United States applied stringent constraints on bombing campaigns. However, in spite of its earlier experiences, the same problems re-emerged with respect to target selection, bombing technologies, coordination, and differences in doctrine. Hard-won lessons of WW II were disregarded or made subservient to service interests, with unity of command, in particular, proving persistently difficult to achieve.

3.3.1 The Korean War

When the United States entered the war in Korea it lacked the organization, intelligence personnel, databases, or target materials needed to support the application of joint air power on the Korean peninsula. No organization in the US Air Force maintained and analyzed data on North Korean targets and no inter-service target selection organization existed. Nor was there any target analysis unit, akin to the Economic Effectiveness Unit, to assess the Korean society and military in detail and develop realistic and meaningful measures of effectiveness. These omissions were felt immediately once a ground offensive was considered.

3.3.1.1 Targeting Organization

Differences over targeting priorities centered on two issues. First, the Navy and the Air Force disagreed over how to integrate land- and sea-based air assets into a coherent air striking force. Second, the Army and the Air Force disagreed doctrinally about the level of air effort appropriate for CAS.[18] Army commanders felt

---

[17] See Thomas 2001, pp. 136–146.

[18] For debates concerning the air war in Korea, see, e.g., Mark 1994, Chap. 8; Winnefeld and Johnson 1993, Chap. 5; Crane 2000; Schmidt 1993; and Moeller 1994. For comprehensive and very detailed studies of air operations in the Korean War, see Hone 1998, pp. 469–527; and Futrell 1997.

that the Air Force did not provide enough air support, while Air Force leaders felt the Army did not appreciate or understand the ability of airpower to influence the battlefield in ways other than through support of the close-in battle.

To solve the differences over airpower priorities and target selection, in July 1950 General Douglas MacArthur, then Commander-in-Chief United Nations Command and Commander of US Armed Forces in the Far East (USAFFE), formed a Joint Operations Center (JOC) and General Headquarters Target Group (GHQTG). The GHQTG board consisted of four senior staff officers, two from the Army and one each from the Air Force and the Navy. This board had four tasks: (1) advise on offensive airpower in conformance with the daily situation; (2) recommend selection and prioritization of targets; (3) recommend measures to assure coordinated use of airpower; and (4) maintain an analysis of target systems and assigned priorities. The JOC initially suffered from poor communication and the absence of doctrine dealing with joint targeting and the control of air operations of the different services. It eventually became a tactical air mission tasking organization that brokered requirements and resources. However, targeting decisions often had to be referred to the GHQTG. As the members of this entity were not experts in air-target selection, it was replaced by the Far Eastern Command (FEC) Target Selection Committee, made up of expert senior officers from each service, with respect to its targeting responsibilities.[19]

3.3.1.2 Targets

This committee developed viable interdiction campaigns designed to cut off the flow of supplies to communist forces operating in South Korea. The first major US strategic bombing campaign against North Korea began in late July 1950. Although strategic targets in China and the USSR were off-limits because the Korean War was considered a 'limited' one, the campaign was approached much along the same lines as the major offensives of WW II. Following the Chinese intervention in November 1950, MacArthur ordered an enhanced bombing campaign in North Korea, including incendiary attacks against arsenals and communications centers. The campaign targeted, in particular, the Korean side of bridges across the Yalu River. Targets also included hydroelectric stations and dams (indispensible for rice farming), usually to destroy downstream roads, bridges, and railroads, rather than starve the North Korean civilian population. Pyongyang and other towns were annihilated. As with the aerial bombing campaigns in WW II, the objective was not only to destroy North Korea's war infrastructure and isolate frontline units, but also specifically to shatter enemy morale.[20]

---

[19]On command problems, see in particular Winnefeld and Johnson 1993: The Renewed Clash of Service Air Command and Control Doctrines.

[20]See Pape 1996, pp. 160–61; and Hone 1998, p. 488.

The extensive bombing raids on North Korea continued until the armistice agreement was signed between communist and United Nations forces on July 27, 1953.[21] While initial interdiction operations in 1950 greatly affected North Korean ground advances, the overall results were disappointing. Destruction inflicted, tonnage dropped, and sorties flown—then understood to be the measures of success—did not necessarily translate into a degradation of the enemy's will and capacity to fight; the industrial capacity required to sustain the fight and meet the logistical demands of the North Korean land forces was low, in particular once the front became static. Flawed analogizing to the campaign against Germany, mirror imaging, and the absence of meaningful measures of effectiveness for the specific theater were all apparent during the conflict.

3.3.1.3 Inter-service Disagreements

Inter-service tension reared its head when the Navy stopped taking part in the FEC Target Selection Committee, citing poor target selection and multiple tasking. This prevented the truly integrated and effective use of airpower. The Navy argued that ensuring sea control and protection of the sea lines of communication outside the Korean air campaign context required it to retain control of its aircraft. Unified command of air assets was further hindered by the limited communications equipment on Navy vessels, which could not handle the large volume of encrypted messages required for the planning and coordination of joint air operations. By the end of the conflict, the Navy had simply carved out an Area of Responsibility in the northwestern part of Korea. Indeed, the penchant for staking out subregions for aircraft of one service, or one organization within a service, characterized most of the Korean War air operations.[22] This could have had serious operational and strategic consequences, but for an abundance of air assets that compensated for the lack of unity in targeting. Eventually, the Korean War saw the employment of several more-or-less separate air forces: a strategic bomber command, US Navy air assets, the US Marine Corps Air Wing, and the US Fifth Air Force, each of which generally conducted its own bombing campaign independent of the ebb and flow of ground operations.[23]

3.3.1.4 Norms

Norms had limited impact initially. Political imperatives, rather than humanitarian ones, drove US President Harry S. Truman's administration to prohibit the Air

[21]Meilinger 2007, p. 161. A total of 320,000 interdiction sorties were flown by the services combined, destroying or damaging a total of 5,087 bridges, 2,345 locomotives, 41,882 rail cars and 111,623 vehicles.

[22]Winnefeld and Johnson 1993, p. 53.

[23]Winnefeld and Johnson 1993, p. 53.

Force from bombing near the borders of China and the USSR. But, internationally, the bombing of civilian targets under the guise of military necessity started to attract criticisme and condemnation, including from other Western countries. This was especially the case once the war became a stalemate in 1952. For the US State Department, unfavorable public and legislative opinion became a factor to take into account, which in turn resulted in restrictions on targeting plans. An international sensibility was emerging that bombing attacks resulting in many civilian deaths (as had happened in Pyongyang), even if they were not aimed at the civilian population *per se*, were an illegitimate means of warfare. While this norm was not yet internalized in MacArthur's targeting organization, and produced differences of opinion between the military and political authorities, it at least forced States to consider the political costs they might incur by offending international opinion.[24]

3.3.2 *The Vietnam War*

The war in Vietnam would see a continuation of inter-service disagreements. Problems again included quarrels between the Navy and Air Force about command and control (C2) of air strikes in North Vietnam, and arguments between ground commanders and the Air Force concerning the weight of effort needed to support US ground operations in South Vietnam, including by means of CAS. The Air Force now also needed to take into account the significant air-defense capabilities of North Vietnam. This required large numbers of offensive bombing sorties against airfields and surface-to-air missile (SAM) systems, as well as the employment of scarce electronic warfare (EW) and suppression of enemy air defenses (SEAD) capabilities. Offensive technology had matured, with enhanced precision, but so too had air-defense technology.[25]

3.3.2.1 Political Influence

Aggravating these problems were the facts that the US Presidents were keen to limit the scope of the war to avoid active Chinese and Soviet intervention and to employ air power as a strategic coercive instrument for applying pressure on North Vietnam. Both desires resulted in direct political influence on—and control of—the targeting process. There were thus two air wars—one of an operational and tactical nature that focused on the ground war within Vietnam, the other of a

---

[24]Thomas 2001, pp. 150–151.

[25]In 1972, each offensive sortie during the Linebacker campaign required four EW sorties in protective support. Allocation and prioritization became acute issues.

strategic nature that aimed to influence Hanoi's will to continue the fight. Targeting decisions were subsequently made at different headquarters at different levels, a complex process.[26]

Political influence manifested itself early on when President Lyndon B. Johnson rejected a strategic attack plan developed by Air Force Chief of Staff General Curtis LeMay against ninety-four targets designed to destroy North Vietnam's capability and will to resist. Instead of this aggressive plan, Johnson preferred a gradual escalation strategy, which evolved into the 1965–68 Rolling Thunder interdiction campaign, and later, until 1972, into Linebacker I and II. The first phase of Rolling Thunder was calculated to destroy the emerging industrial base of North Vietnam, while the second sought to degrade North Vietnam's ability to infiltrate troops and supplies into South Vietnam. The third phase of the campaign attacked industrial and transportation infrastructure in and around Hanoi, Haiphong, and buffer zones near the Chinese border, while the fourth was a de-escalation of the bombing to promote negotiations. The psychological operation that accompanied this campaign included dropping an estimated one billion leaflets and other pieces of printed material, together with radio broadcasts warning civilians to stay away from military objects subject to attack.[27]

Operations Linebacker I and II were conducted to encourage the North Vietnamese to bring the conflict to a close. The eleven-day bombing campaign of approximately 1,369 sorties targeted military installations, rail yards, petroleum stocks, bridges, roads, electric power production facilities, and steel works believed to support the North's war effort. The dual-use infrastructure supported the civilian economic base as well as North Vietnam's ability to conduct military operations. Both campaigns aimed not only to degrade North Vietnam's ability to continue the war, but also to signal the seriousness of the US commitment and to induce North Vietnam to seek peace.[28]

3.3.2.2 Process and Organization

Target development, selection, and approval involved not only the President, but also the theater commander and the Joint Chiefs of Staff (JCS) at the Pentagon. The process began in the Pacific, with the Rolling Thunder Coordinating Committee (RTCC). This joint targeting team, which originally comprised Air Force and Navy components, focused on coordinating and resolving conflicts relating to operations in the Southeast Asia area. Key responsibilities included coordinating the production of compatible target lists and target materials for each

[26]For detailed discussions, see Hone 1998, pp. 491–516; and Winnefeld and Johnson 1993, Chap. 6: Vietnam, 1965–1968: Regression and Progress.

[27]The literature on the Vietnam bombing campaigns is extensive. For brief but detailed discussion, see, e.g., Hone 1998. For a detailed analysis, see Clodfelter 1989.

[28]Thomas 2001, p. 152.

area of responsibility. It also published a monthly proposed target list that provided input directly to the Chairman of the Joint Chiefs of Staff.

In parallel, the Rolling Thunder Targeting Team (RTTT) in Washington DC was responsible for preparing targeting recommendations for bombing North Vietnam. These recommendations often included advice to escalate in light of North Vietnamese rejection of US proposals. The Chairman would present them to the Secretary of Defense and the President during the so-called 'Tuesday Luncheon'. Once the President approved the target list, rarely entirely in line with the JCS recommendation, it went back to the RTCC, which then divided the list into two parts (for Air Force and Navy), eliminated any de-confliction issues, and distributed it for implementation. However, Strategic Air Command (SAC), located in Omaha, retained control of the B-52 targeting in the theater, thereby magnifying the coordination difficulties. Overall, this fragmented process, and direct Presidential scrutiny of individual targets, degraded the effectiveness of the campaign and resulted in animosity between the military and political authorities.[29]

3.3.2.3 Inter-service Disagreements

Tactical air operations in Vietnam, as in Korea, were characterized by inter-service disagreements concerning targeting priorities. First, naval commanders refused to give up their aircraft to an Air Force commander during Rolling Thunder. As a solution, both the Air Force and the Navy were allowed relative autonomy in conducting air strikes. To that end North Vietnam was divided into seven 'Route Packages', with primary responsibility for attacking targets in each zone assigned to either the Air Force or the Navy.

This de-confliction mechanism, however, introduced coordination problems for interdiction and CAS missions, the second area of disagreement. Despite a dramatic increase in sorties dedicated to CAS in support of the growing ground war, problems remained due to the many simultaneous, independent air operations being conducted under different commanders. This situation produced an uneven flow of support. Often, too many aircraft answered requests for ground support, while at other times, there were either critical no-shows or slow response times (twenty to thirty minutes).

The later assignment of a single manager for in-theater air operations created a more centralized process, which made a major difference in the effectiveness and timeliness of CAS. Still, the most important factor for keeping the ground commanders satisfied was simply the large number of aircraft—and therefore sorties—available to handle their requests. Prioritization is not an issue when there is no shortage of assets.

[29] See Hone 1998, pp. 500–501.

3.3.2.4 Norms

Norms played an ever-increasing role for strategic, political, and humanitarian reasons. The common perception that US bombing in Vietnam was indiscriminate and disproportionally harmful to civilians seems incorrect. Far more than in previous wars, sensitivity to civilian casualties constrained bombing. For instance, areas within thirty miles of Hanoi and ten miles of Haiphong were restricted areas requiring White House approval for targeting. Areas within ten miles of Hanoi and four miles of Haiphong were prohibited. Targets in populated areas were to be avoided and SAM sites within those areas could only be hit if they were actually firing at US aircraft. The valuable dam and dike system was placed off-limits to bombing, while certain other objects that could have been lawfully struck were also placed also off-limits at times.

The White House occasionally promulgated instructions specifically designed to limit the risk of civilian casualties: striking only under optimal weather conditions to allow visual identification of targets; using an attack axis that minimizes the risk for collateral damage in case the bombs fell long or short; and using precision munitions. ROE even forced aircrew to accept risk to a level beyond what international law demanded. Indeed, targeting guidelines and restrictions were for the most part considerably more stringent than required by international law.

Political priority was placed on the avoidance of civilian casualties, in particular to avoid the perception that civilians were being targeted. Public opinion, including in the United States, had condemned early air attacks and, by 1966, the administration was keenly aware that domestic and world opinion would not accept destruction of Vietnamese infrastructure to the level that a successful coercive campaign would probably require. The norm against bombing civilians had become more important than the international law governing the issue.[30]

3.4 The First Post-Cold War Decade

3.4.1 Operation Desert Storm

Desert Storm stands as a pivotal campaign in the evolution of targeting. On the one hand, it displayed many of the familiar inter-service debates and involved the employment of weapon platforms developed during the 1960s and 1970s. On the other, it saw novel command arrangements, new surveillance and offensive technologies, and fresh targeting philosophies. It was in this first post-Cold War campaign that the influence of modern 24/7 media, and a resulting sensitivity to images of slaughter and collateral damage, made itself felt. This was manifested

[30] Thomas 2001, pp. 155–158.

in a new sensibility among Western politicians and publics, a development that would increasingly affect military interventions in the following two decades.

In terms of targeting, the opening phase of the liberation of Kuwait in January 1991 seemed familiar. Following NATO doctrine, it was characterized by offensive counter-air operations intended to degrade the extensive Soviet-style Iraqi air defense system in order to gain air superiority. Moreover, it saw traditional air interdiction operations against Iraqi armor, logistics, and infrastructure as well as CAS against dug-in Iraqi troops. This was in line with the Blitzkrieg-inspired US 'AirLand Battle' concept that had been developed from the mid-1970s onward.[31] Yet, the 39 days of massive precision air strikes, including conventional strategic attacks against targets in downtown Baghdad, that preceded the four-day ground campaign broke with expected pattern of operations.

The United States had developed a non-traditional four-phased offensive plan to make the most of its technological superiority. Phase I would consist primarily of a strategic air campaign. In phase II, the geographical focus of efforts would shift to the Kuwait Air Campaign. Phase III would be dedicated to the attrition of Iraqi ground power and isolation of the Kuwait battlefield. Only phase IV was recognizable as following the AirLand Battle doctrine, in that it was during this final phase that the actual ground invasion would commence.

3.4.1.1 Technology for Targeting

In addition to cruise missiles, an abundance of modern offensive aircraft, superior C2 infrastructure and training and an array of Electronic Warfare (EW) assets, two technologies were pivotal for enabling this new approach.[32] Advances in the precision of detection, identification, and attack capabilities constituted the first. Instead of delivering a typical load of four unguided bombs on a single target, Precision-Guided Munitions (PGM)-equipped fighter bombers could now attack multiple targets in one sortie. The use of PGMs thus led to a dramatic 13:1 differential between precision and non-precision attacks.[33] Intense day and night air attacks with PGMs offered the possibility of relatively quick success against old-fashioned armed forces relying on massed mechanized ground combat. In February 1991 almost two entire Iraqi divisions were destroyed from the air during their advance to Al Kafji, after being detected by a Joint Surveillance Target Attack Radar System (JSTARS) air-ground surveillance aircraft. Iraqi brigades lost more in half an hour of air attacks than during eight years of war against Iran.[34] In the

[31]See, e.g., Citino 2004, Chaps. 7 and 8.

[32]The following short overview of the 'lessons' of Desert Storm is based on several sources. Besides Cohen and Keaney 1995 and Hallion 1992, see Gordon and Trainor 1995, For a well researched counterpoint on the alleged decisive impact on Iraqi ground units, see Press 2001, pp. 5–44.

[33]Hallion 1992, p. 205.

[34]Titus 1996, p. 19.

Kuwaiti theater, coalition air attacks managed to destroy in excess of 50 percent of Iraqi armor and artillery equipment. Iraqi ground troops surrendered in the thousands after being pounded by B-52 strikes or following leaflet drops threatening such attacks. It appeared that 'everything that moves can be seen and everything than can be seen can in principle be hit.'[35]

This was a significant break with past experience. Interdiction and CAS had always been considered risky missions that required vast numbers of aircraft with only limited chances of achieving significant effects. Now one fighter could attack several targets in one mission. The result was a drastic shortening of the time required and the risk involved for ground units to complete the coalition victory. It rendered archaic the traditional notion of massing a large ground force to confront an opponent, particularly on a 'field of battle.'[36]

In addition, relentless PGM attacks on trucks and bridges were used to effectively halt the movement of units within the Kuwaiti theater and the flow of supplies to the Iraqi frontline. Thus, Iraqi resistance was effectively neutralized before it could make contact with Western troops, while substantial movement by Iraqi forces was made virtually impossible, either through physical destruction or through the demoralizing effect of attacks.[37] Desert Storm also suggested that military operations need not necessarily entail massive civilian casualties and that collateral damage to civilian infrastructure can be controlled. In addition, the risk for coalition troops was lower than expected. The age of mass warfare that had existed since WW I was drawing to a close.

Stealth was the second icon. Air Force F-117s could operate deep into enemy territory from the first moment of the war, sometimes attacking two targets per mission in the Baghdad area, which sported the highest density of air defense systems in the world. Not only did stealth accord immense operational value, it also provided an indispensable improvement in efficiency. Whereas a typical non-stealth attack package required thirty-eight aircraft to enable eight to deliver bombs on three targets, only twenty F-117s were required to simultaneously attack thirty-seven targets in the face of strong air defenses. The result was a dramatic rise of intensity of attack. To illustrate, during 1943 Allied bombers attacked 123 target complexes in Germany. In contrast, during the first twenty-four hours of Desert Storm, 148 target complexes were attacked.

3.4.1.2 Targeting Philosophy

While such new capabilities could have been employed in accordance with the AirLand Battle doctrine, a new targeting philosophy, inspired by the potential of

[35]Cohen 1996, p. 44.

[36]Hallion 1992, pp. 121–123.

[37]For a good discussion of this distinction, see Hosmer 1996, Chap. 10.

stealth, EW, and precision weapons, was incorporated in the overall joint campaign plan. Colonel John A. Warden III, a visionary campaign planner working in the Checkmate Division at the Pentagon, devised the targeting concept of parallel warfare, which implied a rediscovery of conventional strategic attack. Updating the interbellum ideas of the ACTS, Warden had recognized that precision, standoff, and stealth capabilities offered new possibilities for strategic attacks against multiple target-categories—centers of gravity—of a nation state. His so-called 'five-ring' model distinguished five subsystems that, combined, comprised the 'enemy system': military units, population, organic essentials (energy, water, food supply, etc.), critical infrastructure and, most important, leadership. Even if targets were in the vicinity of civilian objects, the development of precision weapons meant that it was now possible to attack them near simultaneously in order to rapidly degrade the functioning of the entire enemy system.[38]

Indeed, instead of the traditional model, by which a country's defeat first required decisive victory over its armed forces, Desert Storm heralded the 'inside-out' model. Overwhelming air power capabilities offered the potential to strike at the heart of a country (the regime) from the first moment of a campaign, crippling the enemy's strategic command capabilities before attacking fielded forces, and thus potentially paralyzing its entire system.[39] Instead of focusing exclusively on the armed forces, new options were now available, such as regime targeting and precise infrastructural disruption, which could have direct strategically significant effects. The new approach held out the promise that several smaller-scale physical and non-physical attacks—with less destructive power—conducted simultaneously on vital and interdependent targets could achieve disproportionate strategic outcomes. With each bomb likely to strike within yards of a target, targeteers could now think in terms of the specific first- and second-order effects that needed to be achieved, instead of merely hoping targets would be destroyed. Effects-Based Operations (EBO) as a targeting philosophy emerged.

3.4.1.3 The Targets

The joint air campaign plan largely refined and developed Warden's initial plan, Instant Thunder (so named to explicitly contrast it with Rolling Thunder).[40] It rested on four principles: target the regime, not the Iraqi people; minimize civilian casualties and collateral damage; minimize US and allied losses; and pit US strengths against Iraqi weaknesses.

---

[38]See, e.g., Warden 1995, pp. 40–55. For an elaborate discussion of Warden's ideas, see Olson 2007.

[39]For a balanced account of the strategic air offensive against Iraq, see Davis 1998.

[40]Instant Thunder was designed to offer a strategic offensive retaliation option for the Joint Force Commander, General Norman Schwarzkopf, in the event Iraq decided to strike into Saudi Arabia while US troops were still in the build-up phase.

Applying his five-ring model on Iraqi political, military, and economic systems, Warden and his planning team recognized seven core strategic target sets. The first, national leadership, and second, military and civil C2, should be attacked in order to put physical and psychological pressure on the regime, demonstrate its vulnerability to the Iraqi people, and reduce its capacity to command Iraqi forces, i.e., to isolate, incapacitate, and paralyze it. In traditional fashion, electric power generation, oil refineries, distribution, and storage were also listed ('organic essentials' in Warden's five-ring model), as well as transport infrastructure to isolate the Kuwaiti battle area (railroads and bridges). The final three target sets pertained to military capabilities: nuclear, biological, and chemical (NBC) weapons together with associated research and development (R&D) and production facilities; military support capabilities; and Scud ballistic missiles. The destruction of Iraqi air defenses was added to the list as a prerequisite for any offensive air operation.

The Joint Force Commander, General Norman Schwarzkopf, included Warden's plan as an integral part of the joint air-ground campaign plan designed to achieve the political objectives: liberating Kuwait and ensuring the security and stability of Saudi Arabia and the Persian Gulf. Achieving these objectives also required direct attacks on Iraqi ground troops, in particular the backbone of the Iraqi regime's offensive power and domestic power base, the Republican Guard Divisions.[41] Central Command (CENTCOM) Operations Order (OPORD) 91-001 listed seven key military objectives to achieve the political aims: (1) attack Iraqi political-military leadership and C2; (2) gain and maintain air superiority; (3) sever Iraqi supply lines: (4) destroy known NBC production, storage and delivery capabilities; (5) destroy known NBC capabilities; (6) destroy Republican Guard forces in the Kuwait Theater of Operations (KTO) and (7) liberate Kuwait City with Arab forces. Due to the unanticipated rapid achievement of objective (2), the campaign quickly focused on the subsequent phases and related target sets. Figure 3.1 shows the apportionment of sorties per target category.[42]

3.4.1.4 Command Arrangement

The organization of the targeting process also saw a marked improvement compared to the Korean and Vietnam wars.[43] For the first time, a single commander for air operations—a Joint Force Air Component Commander (JFACC)—controlled all the theater aircraft, including those of the Navy. Schwarzkopf designated US Air Force General Charles Horner as the JFACC, responsible for all air operations in support of Desert Storm. Horner's instrument for orchestrating air operations, after developing the joint air campaign plan, was the Air Tasking Order

[41]See Hallion 1992, pp. 150–155; Davis 1998, pp. 540–554.

[42]Source: Desert Storm Target Sets (030226-D-9085 M-006), at http://www.defense.gov/news/briefingslide.aspx?briefingslideid=110.

[43]For a concise focused discussion of the command arrangements, see in particular Winnefeld and Johnson 1993, Chap. 8.

Target Categories	Strikes
Iraqi Ground Forces	23430
Airfields	2990
Scuds	1460
SAMs	1370
LOCs	1170
Military Industry	970
NUC/Bio/Chem	970
IADS (KARI)	630
Telecomms/C3	580
Oil	540
Naval Targets	370
Electric Power	345
Leadership	260

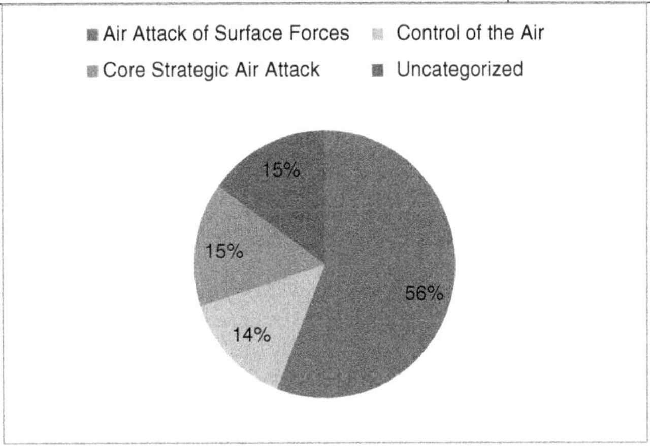

Source: http://www.defense.gov/DODCMSShare/briefingslide/110/030226-D-9085M-006.jpg	

Fig. 3.1 Coalition air-to-surface strikes by functional area

(ATO), which was much more directive and comprehensive than 'coordination control' or 'mission direction' as exercised in the Korean War and Vietnam War respectively.[44] The strategic component of targeting was developed in detail by the Special Planning Group, nicknamed the 'Black Hole,' while tactical strikes against Iraqi ground troops in and around Kuwait were planned by the so-called KTO Cell. Another important doctrinal innovation was the Joint Targeting Coordination Board, which Schwarzkopf installed just prior to the ground war, and to which he assigned the Deputy Commander-in-Chief, US Army Lieutenant General Calvin Waller, as head. Waller became responsible for reviewing the targets nominated by the ground commanders and apportioning aircraft in support of the battlefield preparation plan, so as to ensure all services saw their interests appropriately cared for in the air sortie apportionment.

3.4.1.5 Disagreements

This did not prevent the familiar inter-service debates. Naval planners, for instance, believed that the JFACC had erected a C2 system that was too rigid to take advantage of the flexibility of naval aviation. Carrier planners had become accustomed to independent, autonomous operations and chafed under the restrictions of General Horner's centralized control and the taskings he issued in order to separate missions and prevent fratricide. The Navy subsequently decided to limit representation in the planning and targeting process, thereby creating friction and distrust between Navy in-theater staff and the JFACC throughout the campaign.

Air Force-Army disagreements also flared up, particularly as the launch of the ground war approached. The US Army and Marine Corps ground commanders objected to what they perceived as a very low level of support by the Air Force for the preparation and shaping of the battlefield. Approaching G-Day, the planned start of the ground offensive, they argued that too much effort, occupying too many assets, was being spent on attacking strategic targets and that not enough air support was being allocated to support ground operations. In reality, however, only 7 percent of all sorties were dedicated to strategic attack; the KTO Cell was responsible for the planning of more than 80 percent of the total coalition air effort.[45] Doctrinal differences also emerged with Army, Marine, and Navy officers challenging Air Force officers as to the relevance and priority of targets. They also questioned whether some targets labeled as strategic were in fact military in nature.[46]

Several reasons explain why the JFACC targeted only approximately one-third of ground-nominated targets. Schwarzkopf's primary concern was to diminish the strength of the Republican Guard and he therefore prohibited the JFACC from

[44]Winnefeld and Johnson 1993, p. 107.

[45]Davis 1998, p. 554.

[46]Winnefeld and Johnson 1993, p. 136.

attacking other enemy units determined as being below 50 percent of their combat strength. Transparency to corps commanders was not enhanced by the fact that Schwarzkopf also acted as both the Land Component Commander (LCC) and Joint Force Commander (JFC). As such, he interacted directly with Horner. The lack of a separate LCC meant the corps commanders did not have a component commander equivalent to General Horner to whom they could go with their target requests. Instead, last-minute orders to strike higher priority targets by Schwarzkopf redirected aircraft away from the corps-nominated targets.

3.4.1.6 Intelligence Problems

Both strategic attacks and tactical air operations were hampered by the fact that the US Air Forces Central Command (CENTAF) and CENTCOM intelligence organizations lacked sufficient information about the Iraqi infrastructure and economy. Moreover, they could not keep up with the high volume of data produced by the large number of daily offensive air strikes (Desert Storm deployed 2,780 US fixed-wing aircraft, which flew more than 112,000 individual sorties). To circumvent these problems, strategic strike planners in the Black Hole approached other intelligence organizations and outside consultants, a practice resembling that of WW II. Air combat wings meanwhile developed an informal battle-damage assessment (BDA) network to share squadron-level assessments of videotape recordings from strike aircraft.

Intelligence support at the corps level lagged behind the actual Iraqi order of battle. This time-lag meant that the corps targeteers, who had no idea of the debilitating effects of the intense air offensive on Iraqi warfighting capabilities, used outdated and inaccurate reports for target nominations, often submitting targets that had already been attacked.[47]

3.4.1.7 A New Standard

The end result of Desert Storm was that through this novel campaign design, informed and enabled by a combination of advances in targeting organization, targeting concept, and air-power technologies, the coalition effectively neutralized Iraq with decisive air attacks. Using stealth technology alongside large packages of EW aircraft, decoy drones, and attack aircraft armed with both PGMs and free-fall weapons, the coalition defeated Iraq's sophisticated air-defense system, thereby enabling attacks on key nodes in its electrical infrastructure, C2 structure, and intelligence apparatus. As a result, Iraq was unable to coordinate an effective response to the coalition's other military operations. While this did not obviate the need for ground operations—ground forces still had to eject Saddam Hussein's

[47]Davis 1998, pp. 556–557.

forces from the KTO and secure the liberation of Kuwait—the new precision targeting capabilities set the stage for a ground offensive in which the coalition could exploit a weakened enemy. Another remarkable feature was that, despite massive air strikes on dual-use facilities and on government and military complexes in urban areas, the level of collateral damage and the number of civilian casualties were, while still substantial, unprecedentedly low.[48] Most analysts agree that Desert Storm nearly amounted to a 'revolution in warfare,' or at least inspired developments that have given rise to a markedly different mode of warfare. These developments, related closely to increased political and public expectations as to the precision of attacks and avoidance of collateral damage, have had long-term consequences for targeting doctrine.[49]

3.4.2 NATO over the Balkans: Post-modern Warfare Emerges

3.4.2.1 Coercing While Peacekeeping

In the new, complex and poorly understood Balkans peacekeeping and peace-enforcement missions of the early 1990s, with ground forces tied to strict non-aggressive ROE, NATO commanders and politicians alike turned to the aforementioned targeting options to deter or coerce leaders of the various ethnic factions.[50] This approach generated debate among Western academics and military planners as to the optimal coercive strategy.[51] Echoing the strategic bombing theories of the interbellum period and Cold War deterrence theories, proposed 'coercive mechanisms' included: 'decapitation' and 'incapacitation' (paralyzing the country or its military apparatus by eliminating command nodes or by disrupting command processes); 'punishment' and 'risk' (increasing the cost to the enemy of achieving a strategic aim); and 'denial' (eliminating the enemy's means to carry out its strategy, thus reducing the chance of success). The intensity of attacks was also a topic of debate, with one doctrinal school advocating the application of massive and continuous 'decisive force' in order to achieve maximum political and military shock, while others favored gradually increasing intensity so as to provide room for political maneuver.

By the mid-1990s, these targeting approaches and the enhanced ability to strike accurately combined to serve as the basis for the concept of effects-based operations (EBO).[52] EBO recognized that forces must be able to produce a variety of

---

[48]Thomas 2001, p. 159.

[49]See Hallion 1992, p. 252; and Cohen and Keaney 1995.

[50]Cohen 1994, pp. 109–124. See also Farrell 2002, p. 286.

[51]See, e.g., Mueller 1998, pp. 182–228.

[52]The EBO concept was developed by David Deptula, an assistant to John Warden, and key planner of the strategic component of the Desert Storm air campaign. See Deptula 1996. For the historical pedigree of EBO, see Meilinger 2007.

desired military and political effects, not merely massive destruction. Tailored to the type of conflict and specific political objectives, it does so through the application of movement, supply, attack, defense, and maneuver tailored to achieve functional, systemic, and psychological effects beyond the immediate physical results. Understanding how to achieve such effects requires detailed and up-to-date knowledge of how the various subsystems of the opponent behave.[53] Few of these emerging insights informed either strategic thinking in headquarters or targeting by operations centers during the Balkans peace operations.

3.4.2.2 Deny Flight

Targeting during NATO's Deny Flight operation highlighted the extent to which the advantages high technology can offer are conditional on an appropriate strategy and suitable context. European aircraft were not widely equipped with PGMs and their operations were hindered by the weather. Lacking a well-established and proven peacekeeping doctrine, coalition forces operated in a politically constrained environment, under a limited UN mandate and with very strict ROE. Their pin-pick air strikes on targets of limited strategic value were, unsurprisingly, ineffective. Instead of escalating to achieve dominance, ground and air commanders were required to de-escalate tense situations. Avoidance of risk for peacekeepers on the ground and for politicians in their capitals trumped military necessity and strategic impact. Indeed, political restrictions often mandated that targeteers and aircrew avoid hitting significant military targets unless they were firing on NATO assets. Any targeting error, no matter the precautions taken, could result in civilian casualties that would produce dramatic media footage and, so it was feared, undermine the credibility and legitimacy of the NATO mission. This sensitivity was not lost on the warring factions. Skillful manipulation of the media, the hiding of military assets among civilians and civilian infrastructure, and hostage-taking of UN observers by various ethnic factions served as effective counter-coercion tactics.[54]

Only after the 1995 Srebrenica massacre did NATO take steps to create the proper conditions for the effective use of force. When operation Deliberate Force commenced in August of that year against Bosnian Serb forces, the effect of modern Western air power, in fortuitous simultaneity with a Croat ground offensive, was visible (albeit only employed in a limited coercive campaign). The Serb leadership stood powerless against an air offensive that destroyed the military capabilities it needed to defend against the Croats. As a result of this relatively low-risk endeavor, all military and political objectives were attained. Safe areas were no

[53]For an exchange which neatly summarized this debate, which has been ongoing since 1991, see Pape 1997. pp. 93–114; Watts 1997, pp. 115–71; Mueller 1997, pp. 182–228. For a description of the emergence of EBO as a doctrinal concept, see, e.g., Mann et al. 2002.

[54]See, e.g., Byman and Waxman 2002, Chap. 5; Jakobsen 1998, pp. 70–109; Jakobsen 2000, pp. 1–22; Byman and Waxman 1999, pp. 107–120.

longer threatened, heavy weapons were removed from designated areas and Sarajevo's airport and roads to the city reopened. More importantly, the path to a peace agreement had been secured.[55]

3.4.2.3 Allied Force: Politics, No Strategy

Strategy was once again lacking over Kosovo between March 24 and June 27, 1999. Following a year of fruitless diplomatic efforts, NATO, led by the United States, conducted a limited air campaign to halt the continuing human-rights abuses that were being committed against the citizens of the Kosovo province by the forces of Serbian President Slobodan Milošević. The limited intensity of the first air strikes (only forty-eight sorties a day, versus 1,300 daily during Desert Storm) conveyed neither power, nor a sense of commitment, thus violating guidance that literature on deterrence and coercive diplomacy offered. Force escalation only became an accepted option once NATO credibility was at stake.

When that occurred, however, many were surprised at the success of the campaign. A combination of factors forced Milosevic's hand. These included a shift in Russia's diplomatic support for the Serb leadership; increasing intensity of Kosovo Liberation Army activities; NATO perseverance in the face of setbacks; and exhaustion of possible Serb countermoves. All came into play after and because of the continued limited air campaign, which lasted 78 days and involved thirty-eight thousand combat sorties of 829 strike aircraft.[56] Global Positioning System (GPS)-guided PGMs offered all-weather and night precision navigation and attack capabilities. With PGMs accounting for 40 percent of the ordnance delivered, the trend of using precision weapons was continued. By flying at high altitudes and by launching weapons from stand-off ranges, NATO casualties were avoided; only two aircraft were downed.[57] In the end, NATO achieved its goals at low losses and costs, especially considering estimates of the number of ground forces that would have been required for a forced entry into Kosovo (in excess of one hundred thousand).

3.4.2.4 Disagreement over Strategy and Targets

Success masked the immense problems those responsible for the execution of the campaign experienced, such as deficiencies in strategy, planning, operational

---

[55] See Owen 2010. A total of 293 aircraft flew 3,515 sorties in two weeks to deter Serb aggression. Compared to Desert Storm, the percentage of PGMs used was much greater, totaling 98 percent of US and 28 percent of non-US ordnance delivered.

[56] For balanced analysis of the Kosovo operation, see Posen 2000, pp. 39–84; Byman and Waxman 2002; Daalder and O'Hanlon 2000; and in particular Lambeth's very detailed operational analysis, NATO's Air War for Kosovo, A Strategic and Operational Assessment, Lambeth 2001.

[57] McInnes 2002, p. 92. To appreciate this accomplishment, two decades earlier, the United States lost sixteen B-52 bombers in just 11 days during the Linebacker II campaign against North Vietnam.

concept, and day-to-day command of the operation.[58] The campaign began under the guidance that it would last only 2–3 days and involve only fifty targets. Attuned to internal NATO sensitivities, the Supreme Allied Commander Europe (SACEUR), US General Wesley Clark, had five goals: (1) minimizing loss of friendly aircraft; (2) impacting Serb military and security forces in Kosovo; (3) minimizing collateral damage; (4) achieving the first three in order to hold NATO together; and (5) protecting allied ground forces in neighboring Bosnia, especially, from Serb raids.[59] The plan set forth a gradual approach, one that assumed Milošević would be sufficiently impressed given the strategic impact of Deliberate Force a few years earlier.

Instead of a gradual approach, the US JFACC, Lieutenant General Mike Short, had wanted to use Desert Storm-style overwhelming parallel strikes against centers of gravity, including targets in Belgrade. By way of a comparison with Desert Storm, he stated that this campaign was more 'constant drizzle' than Instant Thunder.[60] It seemed not to be aimed at achieving clear-cut strategy goals, but rather more akin to random bombing of military targets. There was no effects-based target analysis, just attacks on targets that key NATO governments happened to approve. Such approvals could change on short notice. Political consensus, rather than military and strategic value, often dominated decision-making. Disunity was a major concern for SACEUR with France, Germany, Italy, and Greece harboring major misgivings about the war. Responsibility for managing the war, and approving targets and target categories, was therefore delegated to five States: the United States, UK, France, Germany, and Italy.

3.4.2.5 Targets

The air war started slowly in terms of the numbers of missions flown and targets struck. It was a phased operation with air defenses as first-priority targets. The second phase consisted of attacks against Serb army, police, and paramilitary units operating below the 44th parallel (including Kosovo). The third phase, if and when approved, would involve strategic infrastructure targets like power stations, communication facilities, and government buildings in and around Belgrade. Once the initial assumptions proved invalid, however, NATO planners rapidly had to identify a large number of valid targets, which proved a problem.

Serb military capabilities comprised the default target category. However, while targets such as Serb forces, tanks, and artillery in Kosovo were obviously legitimate and politically uncontroversial, their destruction was of little value from the perspective of a coercive strategy. Moreover, in light of the requirement for visual

---

[58]For an enlightening detailed assessment, see Lambeth 2001, Chap. 7. See also Kometer 2007, pp. 96–99.

[59]See Clark 2002, pp. 183–84 and 346; and Byman and Waxman 2000, p. 85.

[60]Lambeth 2001, p. 195.

identification of targets by pilots, these often small, fleeting targets in mountainous terrain were hard to detect, track, and engage from high altitude. Low altitude operations, however, were prohibited due to the risk posed by the mobile Serb air defenses.[61] Strict ROE, high political sensitivity, and tactical failures combined to undermine the campaign's coercive effect.

Gradually, other target categories were approved, with the implicit aim of affecting the civilian population's morale so as to isolate Milosevic and generate public pressure to end the war. The targets attacked included 11 railroad bridges, 34 highway bridges, 29 percent of Serbia's ammunition storage facilities, 57 percent of its petroleum reserves, all its oil refineries, 14 command posts, over one hundred aircraft, and 10 military airfields. Targets also included electrical and broadcast services, news media, and two of Milošević's homes, which were reportedly used as C2 facilities.[62]

3.4.2.6 Command: Allied Force Problems in the Targeting Organization

The sustained nature of Operation Allied Force highlighted the deficiencies of NATO C2 capabilities more than had the low-intensity air strikes of Deny Flight and Deliberate Force. The Combined Air Operations Center (CAOC) in Vicenza was neither staffed nor trained for a sustained campaign. It lacked both state-of-the art air C2 software tools to plan and communicate complex offensive ATOs and the necessary targeting specialists. Command relationships were a muddle. US national command lines were mixed with NATO command lines and instead of adhering to established arrangements, in which the JFACC reported to his direct chief, Commander Allied Air Forces, Southern Europe (COMAIRSOUTH), SACEUR decided to command the air operation himself, using ad hoc informal communication formats such as email and, in light of the geographical spread of key players, video teleconferences (VTCs). This did little to foster trust among subordinates or provide the formal guidance required in a proper planning process.

BDA processes, once again, proved slow, requiring two independent sources to confirm a target kill. As a result, it sometimes took days to receive confirmation of air strike success from intelligence sources that might be located in the United States or United Kingdom. The security classification of sources also prevented the free-flow of data among NATO nations.[63] Thirty-seven days were required to develop a smooth-running target development process and it was only on day forty-seven that the first Joint Integrated Prioritized Target List (JIPTL) was

[61]Lambeth 2001, pp. 133–134.

[62]U.S. Department of Defense 2000.

[63]Kometer 2007, pp. 160–164.

published.[64] Finally, political debates within NATO as to the legitimacy of escalating the war, and of the targeting of Serb infrastructure and facilities, further hindered operations.

3.4.2.7 Shortening the Sensor-to-Shooter Time

The BDA problem was not new. During Desert Storm, Iraq's Scud missile launchers could not be engaged due to the long sensor-to-shooter time.[65] Deny Flight and Deliberate Force demonstrated that Serb troops were adaptive opponents who quickly learned to exploit caves, underground facilities, dispersal of equipment and troops, use of decoys, and, if necessary, concealment within refugee convoys. These tactics negated the asymmetric edge that air power conferred upon Western forces. Neither NATO nor US air operations centers had fully incorporated lessons learned from this experience when Allied Force commenced, which resulted in problems when the Serbs moved their SA-3 SAM systems every few hours. The Serbs also were helped by leaks from within the CAOC that provided them advance warning of ATO targets.[66] As a result, they were able to fire 815 SAMs. The SAM threat prevented NATO from employing potent but vulnerable AC-130 gunships and Apache attack helicopters, which could have been very effective against the small Serb infantry groups. It also forced NATO planners to dedicate 30 percent of every attack wave to the SEAD mission.

There was initially no process or team in the CAOC to deal with targets that emerged during the execution of an ATO, although an ad hoc "flex-targeting" team was finally assembled near the end of the campaign's first month. This team coordinated coalition efforts to detect, identify, and engage emerging Serbian targets that could not wait for inclusion in a subsequent ATO. It developed three different approaches. The first was to apportion ATO sorties to "alert flex." They were expressly assigned to engage emerging targets identified during the ATO cycle. The second was to re-role missions, either on the ground or once airborne, that had been tasked to hit a preplanned target. This approach tended to have a negative effect on ATO execution as it diverted resources from a previously prioritized military objective. The third approach was to dedicate aircraft to orbits in and around the Kosovo Engagement Zone. These missions typically employed fighters as forward air controllers, using non-traditional intelligence, surveillance, and reconnaissance (ISR) methods (unaided and aided sight, as well as on-board reconnaissance or infrared targeting pods) to search defined areas in order to identify targets, assess collateral damage potential, and engage or report them to other fighters and C2 agencies.

---

[64] Lambeth 2001, p. 212.

[65] Around 2,500 sorties were tasked with Scud hunting, with 1,500 strikes against Scud-related sites or production facilities. There was not one confirmed Scud destroyed.The time between target detection and that information reaching a pilot was up to fourteen hours.

[66] Lambeth 2001, p. 206.

Sensor-to-shooter timeliness improved. Instrumental in this were two E-8 JSTARS aircraft that directed airborne controllers and strike aircraft against potential targets of opportunity. Improvised processes were developed to disseminate information from sensors to shooters. They included processing data received from live Predator Unmanned Aerial Vehicle (UAV) imagery, developing targets and passing them to orbiting strikers for prosecution, and using U-2s to transmit possible SA-6 locations to F-15Es for engagement. Still, the results were disappointing. Over thirty thousand total combat sorties were flown; although thousands were tasked to find and kill Serbian military forces in and around the KEZ, success was marginal at best.

The paucity of time-sensitive targeting (TST) capabilities necessitated centralized control. The lack of doctrine and process at the operational level, inherent in the novel character of TST, translated into inadequate (almost non-existent) JFC and JFACC guidance on what should be classified as a flex-target and how it should be prioritized against the ATO targets. Finally, casualty avoidance and collateral damage weighed heavily in these TST decisions, contributing further to the requirement for centralized control of flex-targeting engagements. These concerns and restrictions increased after the widely publicized mistaken bombing of the Chinese embassy, and the unintended destruction of a civilian passenger train crossing a legitimate bridge target.[67]

3.4.2.8 Norms

Concern for collateral damage, civilian casualties, and the safety of its own troops dominated NATO political decision-making to an unprecedented degree during the campaign. This was not lost on Milošević's regime, which made deliberate attempts to exploit Western political and societal sensitivities. It increased civilian casualties, for instance, by commingling military personnel with civilian refugees and by generating enormous refugee flows in order to create humanitarian crises, including in neighboring countries. In addition, Serb troops and equipment were dispersed and hidden throughout the countryside in civilian homes, barns, schools, factories, and monasteries. Serb forces also located themselves within civilian traffic and used human shields to protect military equipment.[68] Indeed, Milošević made collateral damage the centerpiece of his wartime political campaign. Serb state media regularly brought Western journalists to sites of alleged collateral damage incidents, successfully leading European politicians to demand fewer civilian casualties. General Clark later admitted that NATO lost the propaganda war.

[67]For an enlightening study of accidents in recent wars, see Larson and Savych 2006. See Chap. 3 for the key 'misfortunes' during Allied Force.

[68]See Posen 2000, pp. 39–84.

Allied Force raised the bar for Western militaries even higher than it had been set during Desert Storm.[69] The operation redefined the acceptable in terms of civilian casualties and collateral damage. 'Clean' war had by 1999 become the public and political expectation and, as a result, the norms regarding protection of civilians now took center stage. Low likelihood of collateral damage became the "litmus test to pick a target," General Short observed. Similarly, General Klaus Naumann, Chairman of the NATO Military Committee at the beginning of the war, explained that NATO had three guiding principles: "We had first of all to avoid if possible any of our own casualties and fatalities; secondly we were told to avoid collateral damage to the extent possible; and thirdly, bring it to a quick end."[70] The new norms reflected a shift in the *mentalité collective* concerning acceptable post-Cold War methods in warfare in which vital interests were not threatened.[71]

3.4.2.9 Media

One key factor in this shift in norms was the mediatization of war. Allied Force was presented as a virtual event, less a representation of real war than a spectacle. Michael Ignatieff described NATO's war in Kosovo as a virtual war, and the way that such 'humanitarian' wars have been experienced by Western publics as spectator-sport warfare.[72] Media could now transmit real-time footage of military action, sometimes creating highly suggestive and evocative, but unbalanced, images. Allied Force demonstrated how tactical events can have immediate and disproportionate strategic implications of which targeteers need to be conscious.

Paradoxically, political and societal concern for the safety of Western troops has meant that the use of stand-off air power is increasingly considered essential to maintain public support. However, at the same time, this has been severely criticized on the grounds that it seems to transfer the risk of going to war onto the target society.[73] Likewise, the new opportunities that PGMs offer in the targeting of

---

[69]See Larson and Savych 2006, pp. 43–57 for the Al Firdos incident during Desert Storm. The Al Firdos accident that killed two to three hundred civilians highlighted the increasing aversion for civilian casualties and the dramatically strengthened bombing norm. The target was a functioning C2 bunker in Baghdad, and thus a legitimate military target; however, unbeknownst to US planners, it was also used during nighttime as a bomb shelter for Ba'ath party family members. Precisely because it was located in an urban area, the planners had decided to attack it at night when the risk of civilians nearby was low. Exploited by Saddam Hussain in the media, it was a moral, political and strategic crisis because it threatened the stability of the coalition and international support. The result was that Chairman of the JCS, General Colin Powell, put Baghdad off limits for further strategic attacks.

[70]Thomas 2001, p. 164.

[71]See, e.g., Latham 2002; McInnes 2002; Maoz and Gat (eds) 2001, in particular Luttwak 2001 and Gat 2001.

[72]Ignatieff 2002.

[73]See Shaw 2005, in particular Chap. 4. For a broader discussion on the Risk Society, see, e.g., Rasmussen 2006; and Coker 2009.

governmental, economic, and infrastructural objects, while avoiding WW II levels of destruction to cities, has also received criticism from ethicists. Campaigns against infrastructure are said to be of limited strategic value because they, so the argument goes, are of unproven military utility, harken back to WW II morale bombing, put civilians unnecessarily in danger, and violate civilian immunity. At the same time, they are justified using the euphemistic and apologetic term 'collateral damage' to suggest unintentionality, inevitability, adherence to humanitarian law and thus legitimacy. Instead of utilizing the new capabilities to strike previously prohibited objects, the West has an enhanced responsibility to avoid collateral damage and civilian casualties.[74] The employment of precision weapons to avoid casualties has become an ethical norm, a social imperative and a reality that no government in of an advanced society can ignore.[75]

3.5 Into the Twenty-First Century

The first decade of the twenty-first century witnessed a number of important developments in targeting capabilities and processes, all driven by operational needs, technical advances, and societal expectations. They included the refinement and widespread application of dynamic and time-sensitive targeting and the gradual introduction of UAVs—drones—first as a surveillance, and later a strike, platform. It also saw the application of high-tech targeting capabilities in an irregular warfare context against small groups of insurgents. The new Western capabilities drew praise for improved accuracy, but also led to growing media and political scrutiny and criticism. This, in turn, inspired the rise of 'lawfare,' the attempt by opponents to create images that suggest Western militaries cause disproportionate collateral damage and civilian casualties, thereby undermining the perception of legitimacy. In response, Western militaries focused increasingly on collateral damage mitigation procedures in the targeting process.

3.5.1 Operation Enduring Freedom: Targeting Non-State Actors

3.5.1.1 Improving Targeting Capabilities

In the wake of Allied Force, the US Air Force's leadership recognized the need to improve CAOC performance; command, control, communications, computers, intelligence, surveillance, and reconnaissance (C4ISR) capabilities and

[74]See, e.g., Shue 2010, pp. 2–8; Smith 2002; Thomas 2006; and Crawford 2013.

[75]Gat 2001, p. 86.

architecture; and system-wide data-link capabilities, with the CAOC serving as the hub thereof. Moreover, the concept of TST was pushed to the forefront and formalized in doctrine.[76] These initiatives dovetailed with a Pentagon-wide program designed to stimulate Network Centric Warfare, which entails using data-links to create a network of sensors, 'shooter platforms' and command nodes. The network facilitates the rapid dissemination of information to anyone who may need it, from the highest to the lowest levels. This reduces response times and increases operational tempo.[77] In particular, it condenses the 'sensor-to-shooter' interval, which significantly enhances air–land cooperation.[78]

When Operation Enduring Freedom began, these new processes, procedures, and doctrines were not firmly established in the joint community; they subsequently proved indispensable. The United States was confronted with an enemy trained in dispersed guerilla fighting in mountainous terrain, with an impressive track record against Soviet forces and domestic rivals. The enemy had no significant infrastructure that would lend itself to strategic coercive leverage or application of Warden's five-ring model in an intense paralyzing campaign. With the battle situated in a non-supportive Muslim region in which ground invasion was precluded, it was neither obvious nor predetermined that the United States would emerge victorious. If it did, it was likewise unclear whether victory would be achieved at a relatively low cost in terms of destruction and losses.

3.5.1.2 The Operation

Phase I of the operation consisted of a series of limited air strikes against air-defense sites, training camps, and government facilities. On the first night, 31 targets using 50 cruise missiles, 15 bombers, and 25 attack aircraft were prosecuted. Once these targets were destroyed, progress stalled until the insertion of Special Operations Forces (SOF), which marked commencement of phase II. With only three to five hundred SOF troops actually within Afghan territory, the United States managed, by uniting and empowering local opposition factions (the Northern Alliance, totaling no more than 15,000 men), to evict a force of 60,000 Taliban fighters and topple the regime. This was, in essence, an air campaign

[76]Eventually, these became a category of so called time-critical targets. The 2001 US Joint Pub 3–60 Joint Doctrine for Targeting defined time-sensitive targets as "air-, land- or sea-based targets of such high priority to the friendly force that the JFC designates them as requiring immediate response because they pose (or will pose) a danger to friendly forces or because they are highly lucrative, fleeting targets of opportunity."

[77]Rumsfeld 2002, pp. 20–32. For a comprehensive overview of these developments, see, e.g., Kagan 2006.

[78]For a concise description of the tenets of Transformation, see Farrell et al. 2010, Chap. 2. For a thorough overview of the evolution of air command and control, see Kometer 2007. The concept of NCW is discussed in detail in Alberts 1999. Another influential volume is Arquilla and Ronfeldt 1997.

conducted in conjunction with, and supported by, SOF and friendly indigenous fighters. It required a relatively limited operation of one hundred combat sorties a day, amounting to a total of 38,000 sorties, of which 6,500 were strike sorties that dropped a total of approximately 17,500 munitions with an accuracy rate of 75 percent (as compared to 45 percent in Desert Storm). A new type of GPS-guided munition, the Joint Direct Attack Munition (JDAM), proved very effective. The operation was enabled by an unprecedented array of ISR platforms, which flew 1,300 sorties. Novel elements included the employment of armed UAVs and the use of JDAM-equipped B-1, B-2 and B-52 bombers in close coordination with SOF ground controllers. The usage of PGMs again increased, this time up to 60 percent, with an average of 1.66 PGMs delivered per sortie (versus 0.32 in Desert Storm). The use of PGMs had become the norm.[79]

3.5.1.3 Joint SOF and Air Operations

Because of the widely dispersed nature of the Taliban and elements of al-Qaida, the air component and SOF elements operated in concert to detect and identify emerging enemy targets. Ground units used GPS target-locating and laser-target designating equipment to guide strike aircraft and PGMs to targets. Because of the lack of "traditional" preplanned ATO targets (e.g., infrastructure, integrated air defenses, C2), the preponderance of air tasking in Enduring Freedom involved interdicting enemy forces or logistics discovered real-time by ISR or SOF (which called in ten to thirty targets per day).[80] By the midway point of the operation, 'flex-targeting' dominated, with 80 percent of sorties taking off without a specific assigned target.[81] Instead, JSTARS, UAVs, signals intelligence (SIGINT) platforms and SOF acted as eyes. They spotted pop-up targets and relayed time-sensitive, up-to-date target information to shooter platforms that were either inbound or already circling in the vicinity, and subsequently handed over the aircraft to forward air controllers. This approach not only applied to TSTs, but also regular air support, in particular because many SOF teams found themselves in close contact with Taliban fighters who had learned to conceal themselves from airborne detection.[82] The networking of US forces offered an impressive reaction capability, with response times averaging only twenty minutes (and sometimes within minutes). This combination of air power and small SOF units working in cooperation with proxy forces has been described as the 'Afghan model.' It belied any argument that high-tech weapon systems are useless against insurgents.

[79]Lambeth 2005, pp. 247–252. This book is the most detailed open source study of the campaign.

[80]Lambeth 2005, p. 260.

[81]Fyfe 2005, p. 11.

[82]For this argument, see in particular Biddle 2003a, pp. 31–46.

3.5.1.4 Command Arrangement: Centralized Tasking

Although the fact that most of these tactical arrangements were devised during ongoing operations might suggest highly decentralized planning, this was not the case. CENTCOM's state-of-the-art CAOC at Prince Sultan Air Base in Saudi Arabia conducted the air portion of the operations. Detailed target planning and tasking was initially centralized at CENTCOM and CENTAF in Tampa, Florida, and not at the CAOC. Several factors explain this division of labor. The CAOC was neither fully manned nor had training with the novel air C2 facilities and procedures been conducted. Inter-service doctrinal disagreements over the target prioritization, as well as political sensitivity about collateral damage, supported the tendency to centralize. Moreover, SOF units were unfamiliar with the standard air–land coordinating procedures, were not equipped to receive ATOs, and could only function as forward air controllers. The involvement of the Central Intelligence Agency (CIA) also made coordination at the CENTCOM level necessary. Finally, the large number of sensors, bandwidth capacity, and live high quality video stream allowed CENTCOM to conduct the operation from afar.[83] ISR platforms were data-linked with both headquarters and strike aircraft, and could distribute target information across the command network, almost in real time (often within five–ten seconds).[84]

Lack of doctrine concerning authority for TST decisions complicated matters. Centralized TST control was inefficient. Both CENTCOM and its air component, CENTAF, had their own TST procedures, resulting in a lack of integration and synchronization. The two organizations used different methodologies with respect to Desired Mean Point of Impact (DMPI) selection, Collateral Damage Estimation (CDE), weapon-target pairing, and use of the Common Operating Picture (COP). In the first three areas, CENTCOM tended to use more conservative methods and estimates than CENTAF. The differing solutions generated by the two organizations initially created trust issues between them, which resulted in double-checking each other's work, thereby increasing the execution timeline. Collateral damage considerations and coalition sensitivities dominated as the primary emphasis. Final approval for most TST nominations was also centralized at the senior levels of CENTAF and/or CENTCOM; indeed, some leadership targets were reserved for the Secretary of Defense. The notion of remote control by politicians and generals through a 'seven-thousand-mile screwdriver' was born. The result of all of these factors was classic friction.

---

[83]Kometer 2007, pp. 129–137.

[84]Lambeth 2005, p. 254. See 254–258 for a detailed description of the linking of various platforms.

3.5.2 *Operation Iraqi Freedom*

3.5.2.1 Targeting Technology

As far as targeting is concerned, Operation Iraqi Freedom merged many aspects of Desert Storm and Enduring Freedom. It benefited from continuing investments in information and communications technology and ISR systems, as well as the fact that all strike aircraft in the inventory were now equipped with day and night sensors and PGMs. Munitions also had increased accuracy. Miss distance was often less than 3 feet, which allowed smaller yield bombs to be used, in turn reducing the risk of collateral damage. The demand for risk limitation by early 2003 resulted in extensive collateral damage mitigation methods, doctrinal publications, new procedures and new software tools to aid planning.

These efforts benefitted from data accumulated during a decade of bombing campaigns.[85] The United States introduced a computer program, nicknamed "Bug-Splat", to calculate the risk that bomb blast and fragments might affect civilian objects near a pre-planned target. Each potential target could be examined for proximity to civilians or civilian property. Officially named the Fast Assessment Strike Tool—Collateral Damage (FAST-CD), it generated blob-like images resembling squashed insects that precisely modeled the potential damage produced by a particular type and size of bomb, dropped by a particular aircraft flying at a particular altitude. FAST-CD took account of the characteristics of terrain and the objects being struck in order to forecast an often irregular pattern of damage. If the predicted risk of collateral damage was deemed too high, targeting specialists could attempt substituting either a smaller weapon or one with a delayed fuse—which lets a bomb penetrate first and then detonate—or try changing the type of aircraft or its angle of attack.

3.5.2.2 Air-Land Integration

Iraqi Freedom joint planning also reaped the benefits of the experience of Enduring Freedom.[86] In March 2002, Operation Anaconda, which resulted in US fatalities, had reaffirmed the importance of close planning and execution cooperation between air and land units. It resulted in organizational improvements in that regard and focused attention on the need for training and equipping tactical air control teams. Air-land integration at ever-lower tactical levels was facilitated through the assignment of air liaison officers and joint tactical air controllers to companies and, as required, even platoons. In addition, several high-level joint experiments and training exercises were conducted, focused on Scud hunting,

[85]See Crawford 2013, pp. 351–356; Graham 2003; US Department of Defense 2000.

[86]For detailed analysis see Mahnken and Keaney 2007; Murray and Scales 2003; Woodward 2004; and Cordesman 2003.

dynamic targeting, solving C2 problems, smoothing joint targeting processes, and testing various planning software tools.[87] As a result of the Afghanistan lessons-learned, there were also significant improvements in joint and service doctrine vis-a-vis TST processes and training. One of the key TST lessons from previous conflicts was the importance of defining and prioritizing the different target categories. This and other lessons were reflected in the *Commander's Handbook for Joint Time-Sensitive Targeting*, which was published as a resource for the joint community.[88]

3.5.2.3 Time-Sensitive-Targeting

For the campaign, a time-sensitive target—a target identified within the ATO cycle and requiring immediate response—included Iraqi military leadership and non-military regime C2; weapons of mass destruction (WMD) delivery systems and equipment; terrorists and their facilities; and mobile WMD labs. A Dynamic Target (DT)—a target identified within the ATO cycle as being of significant importance to all components such that it should be struck during the ATO period given available assets—encompassed long-range radars; air-defense components; anti-aircraft artillery (AAA) pieces; and SAM systems. A Joint Critical Target—a target identified within the ATO cycle that does not meet TST or DT criteria, but is important enough for strike during the cycle—included elements of C2 and communications. Finally, Emerging Targets—targets that meet sufficient criteria to be considered and developed as a target, but where the criticality and time sensitivity is initially undetermined— embraced mobile tactical SAMs; mobile artillery; and massed enemy ground forces. For each category, the relevant command and target approval authority were clearly delineated,[89] with leadership targets requiring the highest level of approval.

3.5.2.4 Planning

The final campaign plan aimed at seizing key objectives as rapidly as possible. It also sought to prevent Iraq from using WMDs against coalition troops and Scud-type missiles against Israel or destroying oil fields. Iraq was divided into the Western, Northern, and Southern sectors, each with a different focus. Applying the Afghan model, large numbers of SOF troops operated in the West and North of Iraq as part of a closely integrated team of airborne sensors, command nodes, and offensive aircraft to detect and neutralize potential launches of Scud-type

[87]Kometer 2007, p. 203.

[88]US Joint Forces Command, Joint Warfighting Center, Commander's Handbook for Joint Time-Sensitive Targeting, 22 March 2002.

[89]Fyfe 2005, pp. 18–19.

missiles, and to restrict Iraqi freedom of movement on the ground. The South would see the rapid ground advance toward Baghdad, preceded and accompanied by massive air support. In contrast to Desert Storm, the plan sought to leave as much Iraqi infrastructure intact as possible. The goal was to effect regime change while causing the Iraqi population as little suffering as possible. Therefore, the strategic attack portion of the plan included targeting only C2 networks, regime security forces, select palaces, government ministries, command bunkers, and WMD facilities.[90]

Planning for these targets benefited from the long preparation time, which spanned more than a year. Applying a systems approach and effects-based philosophy, the impact point for each target for the first seventy-two hours of the campaign was developed and eventually reviewed in a conference involving intelligence agencies, CENTCOM planners, and weapons experts of the relevant services. As these strategic target sets were developed, planning continued for gaining air superiority and supporting the ground campaign. This involved planning for on-call CAS, interdiction, destruction of Iraqi ground forces, and support for the SOF component commander.[91] To further enhance flexibility, about 15,000 sorties were allocated for combined "kill-box" interdiction and CAS missions that would attack JIPTL targets, but could also respond to CAS requests.[92]

3.5.2.5 Results

The 'spear' of the attack consisted of 125,000 coalition ground forces. Iraqi forces numbered 400,000, including some 100,000 well-trained and equipped Republican Guard troops. In the South, US Secretary of Defense Donald Rumsfeld placed his trust in the concept of Network Centric Warfare, which involved precision bombing, a small, fast-moving ground-attack force and heavy reliance on SOF and air power. Air–ground surveillance systems, unmanned aircraft and SOF located conventional Iraqi forces as a stream of strike aircraft delivered ordnance. Once again, a critical component of the targeting process was the ability of US and coalition ISR assets to find and fix time-sensitive Iraqi targets. Eighty US and coalition ISR platforms, flying approximately a thousand sorties, supported the effort, while space-based assets provided operational- and tactical-level support, including Iraqi missile-launch detection.[93]

A TST mission opened the campaign with a 20 March attack using cruise missiles and an F-117 against Iraqi leadership. The efficiency of the TST process was

[90]Lambeth 2013, p. 33. This is the most detailed study as far as targeting and command and control is concerned.

[91]Lambeth 2013, p. 35. See the entire Chap. 1 for a detailed overview of the joint planning process.

[92]Kometer 2007, p. 204.

[93]Fyfe 2005, p. 21.

such that, in some cases, it took as little as twelve minutes to destroy a confirmed target; at times, this was only five minutes after detection. A key factor in this capability, apart from training and technical connectivity, was the fact that, in contrast to and because of experiences in Enduring Freedom, the US Commander, General Tommy Franks, delegated full authority to the JFACC and CAOC to develop target lists and to conduct collateral damage estimates.[94] As a result, top-down tactical control was largely avoided. Overall, targeting had improved dramatically in accuracy and responsiveness since Desert Storm.[95]

As a result, the coalition destroyed a thousand tanks and reduced the Republican Guard by 50 percent in a single week. Most Iraqi armor and artillery was neutralized before it could deploy against coalition ground forces and many Iraqi troops fled their armor once the first bombs started hitting them, allowing for a very rapid advance toward Baghdad. Even urban operations saw enhanced air strike effectiveness. Intense intelligence preparations had produced detailed maps featuring codes for individual buildings in specific areas of Baghdad, thereby facilitating CAS coordination with ground troops. In the North, the combination of SOF, ISR, CAS, and cooperation with Peshmerga irregular forces managed to fix and attrite thirteen Iraqi divisions.[96] In the West, no Scud or similar missile was launched.

3.5.3 Fighting Terrorists, Insurgents, and Public Opinion

These new air capabilities also enabled NATO's operations in Afghanistan from 2003 onward, including Counter-Insurgency (COIN) operations as part of the International Security Assistance Force (ISAF). Intense air–land integration proved challenging because of the vast distances involved, caveats imposed by nations on the use of their units, and limited NATO Air C2 capabilities. Yet without rapid and precise offensive air support for troops in contact (which occurred daily), as well as air reconnaissance for convoy protection and the detection and tracking of enemy movement, ground operations in such vast, barren, and underdeveloped terrain were vulnerable, less effective, and sometimes barely feasible.[97] Enhanced precision created trust among ground troops in calling in CAS at distances well within the traditional thousand-meter safe distance. Moreover, new Rover equipment allowed forward air controllers and pilots to share the same air-to-ground image of the target, which helped avoid fratricide. Such capabilities also facilitated urban engagements.

---

[94]Lambeth 2013, p. 203.

[95]See Lambeth 2013, Chap. 4 for key accomplishments.

[96]See Andres 2007a, pp. 52–64; and Andres 2007, pp. 69–88.

[97]Mueller 2010, pp. 47–65. See for an up to date discussion of air power in COIN, Hayward (ed) 2009.

3.5.3.1 Drones, SOF Teams, and Leadership Targeting

These air–ground engagement capabilities were also used for counter-terrorist operations in Afghanistan, the Afghanistan-Pakistan border area and Iraq. Indeed, from the perspective of targeting, what stands out as novel in operations since Iraqi Freedom is the proliferation of the use of UAVs for surveillance, and, increasingly, also in the combat and leadership-targeting role. In fact, the first sortie of Enduring Freedom was conducted by an armed Predator UAV operated from an airbase near Las Vegas some 7,000 miles away.

Literally thousands of small, medium, and large UAVs have since been deployed in Iraq and Afghanistan as part of COIN operations. The advantages are obvious. Small UAVs can be launched, operated, and recovered by deployed surface forces, affording them organic reconnaissance capability. This offsets their usually slow transit speeds (typically between one and two hundred knots). For adversaries, this makes exposure outside buildings or forests a risky activity. Armed UAVs, or the combination of manned fighter aircraft alongside a UAV equipped with a targeting pod, have proved able to strike key leaders and small groups of Taliban insurgents. They are especially suited for politically delicate missions, such as the targeting of al-Qaeda militants in Pakistan and Yemen by the CIA.

The practice of leadership targeting has grown rapidly since 2009.[98] Drone strikes have fast become the icon of the Western post-modern style of warfare. Equipped with small Hellfire missiles, drones engaging in leadership-targeting missions are the final link in a long, intricate targeting chain involving numerous military and civilian intelligence agencies, foreign intelligence sources, legal advisors, and sometimes even senior political leadership. The key features that drones offer for these leadership attacks are real-time streaming video and very accurate sensors, which enables individuals to be found, tracked and, if their identity is confirmed, killed. This demonstrates how the technology and organization of targeting, developed for conflict between States, has also proved effective in engaging violent non-State actors. With missions now targeting small groups or even individuals with single PGMs from remote distances, such developments illustrate the dramatic target granularity in modern warfare.

3.5.3.2 Media and Adaptive Opponents: Lawfare

Experiences in Afghanistan also demonstrate the conditional nature of technological superiority during campaigns against adaptive opponents that occur in full view of the media. The Internet and corresponding prevalence of social media have given rise to so-called “War 2.0”, which offers non-State actors in particular

[98] The literature on so called drone warfare is extensive. For a representative overview, see Osinga 2013.

a powerful asymmetric edge—a new virtual front where norms are employed as weapons. Digital media are cheap and allow simple production and rapid global distribution of material, as well as the easy manipulation—i.e., spin—of events as they occur. This means that the connection between the popular perception of the war and the physical battlefield is more immediate, and therefore more volatile, than ever before. Web 2.0 media penetration compresses the operational level of war. It gives each tactical action immediate strategic impact.[99] Indeed, most challenges with targeting no longer revolve around technological, doctrinal, or organizational factors. Instead, problems emanate from the mediatization of war, Western norms, and public perceptions of legitimacy. Each of these factors produces pressure for increased transparency, accuracy, and accountability. Then, there is 'lawfare,' and its exploitation of such sensitivities by adaptive opponents through media spin.[100]

3.5.3.3 The Israeli Experience

The Israeli experience during the past decade has featured such dynamics.[101] In particular, the Israeli Air Force (IAF) has honed its skills in the targeted killing of key leaders of Hamas and the Hezbollah through the use of data-linked surveillance UAVs, combat helicopters, and fighter aircraft. This, combined with persistent unrest and casualty aversion, contributed to a belief on the part of many civilian and military leaders that air power offers a low-cost (primarily in terms of casualties) means of retaliating against, and defeating, adversaries. In essence, Israel has leveraged new precision weapons and the fusion of intelligence sources to craft a counter-terrorism strategy. The effect has been periods of 'quiet' in which demonstration of the ability to acquire accurate intelligence and capability to employ deadly force against key individuals served as a deterrent; although violence was not eliminated, it was limited to a level with which Israeli society could cope.[102]

In the summer of 2006, Israel applied this model to stop Hezbollah from firing Katyusha rockets into Israeli communities and to secure the return of two abducted soldiers (Operation Change of Direction). In part, this low-risk strategy was effective. The IDF eliminated approximately 500 of Hezbollah's most effective fighters and forced many of the others to evacuate the areas south of the Litani River. The IAF destroyed roughly half of the unused longer-range rockets,

---

[99]See in particular Rid and Hecker 2009, for a detailed account of the use of social media by insurgents groups.

[100]See Dunlap 2009, pp. 34–39.

[101]This section draws in particular from Krebs 2009, pp. 141–156; and from Brun 2010, pp. 297–324. For a detailed analysis see also Arkin 2007.

[102]This section on Israeli counter terrorism practices involving leadership targeting draws from Wilner 2011a, pp. 740–772; Stahl 2010, pp. 111–133; Wilner 2011b, pp. 3–37; Inbar and Shamir 2013, pp. 1–23; Byman 2006; Rid 2012, pp. 124–147; and Henriksen 2012.

along with much of the Lebanese infrastructure used to resupply Hezbollah. As it demonstrated again in December 2008 during Operation Cast Lead, as well as in subsequent operations against Hamas in the Gaza Strip, its established network of multiple UAVs, fighter aircraft, and artillery allows it to strike targets precisely within minutes, and sometimes seconds, of a launch being detected.

3.5.3.4 Coping with Asymmetric Media Operations

On the other hand, air power was unlikely to be able to produce the desired outcome against a hybrid opponent like Hezbollah that lacks high-value targets, such as industrial facilities and robust C2 nodes. Instead, the main targets were Hezbollah leadership and its fielded forces and weapons. Hidden amongst civilians and frequently moved, they were extremely difficult to target. From standoff positions, there was no way to distinguish between non-uniformed Hezbollah fighters and Lebanese civilians. As a result, IDF attacks inevitably contributed to the tally of 1,100 Lebanese civilian casualties. Mingling with civilians and hiding in mosques or day-care centers were tactics of dubious moral standing, but the collateral damage it elicited had the effect of rallying and recruiting sympathizers to Hezbollah's cause. Turning to its sophisticated media organization to showcase the damage in Lebanon, and portraying (sometimes through manipulation of video material) the Israeli attacks against civilians as indiscriminate, disproportionate, and inhumane, Hezbollah was able to generate sympathy among the domestic Lebanese audience and produce international condemnation of the IDF's actions. It is therefore clear that Hezbollah understood the increasing importance of winning the media-battle.[103] In response, the IDF implemented several measures to ensure the validity of targets (more detailed intelligence, involving lawyers to review targets) and to reduce the risk of collateral damage (through increased employment of low collateral damage munitions). In addition, it issued warnings to civilians by distributing hundreds of thousands of leaflets, and even phone calls to some families in high-risk areas.[104]

3.5.3.5 Norms and the Drone-Warfare Debate

Counterproductive media coverage at both the local and global level was also the main reason why, in Afghanistan, ISAF Commander General Stanley McChrystal took pains in July 2009 to limit the risk of civilian casualties by drastically curtailing the use of force. As he stated, "Air power contains the seeds of its own destruction if we do not use it responsibly. The tactical gains do not outweigh the

[103] Hamas likewise has exploited the protected status of mosques, schools and civilians homes to hide weapons caches. See Erlanger 2009.

[104] Cordesman 2009. See for a extensive analysis Lambeth 2011.

costs."[105] Drone strikes, in particular, have incurred international moral outcry and condemnation. The criticism is sometimes based on biased information, policy advocacy, unverifiable casualty data, outdated research, or ignorance of the facts of real-world targeted killing procedures. Drone strikes, it is claimed, kill too many innocent civilians. Thus, the entire practice of targeted killing with drones is condemned as dangerously immoral and as a cause of an erosion of Western prestige.[106]

According to the critics, 'remote killing' has made 'killing too easy' and is 'unethical' because only one side to a conflict is at risk of attack, while the other side can remain several thousand miles from the front. Drone operators are also said to be at risk of failing properly to assess the consequences of their actions; they operate in a virtual reality as merely a cog in a machine, with targets represented by symbols rather than experienced as real humans. As a result, moral disengagement seems likely to occur. The physical anonymity of both target and operator is said to lead to the de-individuation and de-humanization of war, and thus to lowering the threshold for deciding to attack. The risk of a 'playstation' mentality lurks not far in the background.[107]

In addition, according to some analysts, drones may create risk-free warfare as an option for politicians. Risk-free war promotes endless war, as there is no incentive to end it. It also leads to limitless expansion of the battlefield. Not only do drones make it easier to go to war, but they also may make it easier to keep them going. And when the target is global terrorism, fighting it may encompass the globe.[108] Concern for the ease with which international norms regarding sovereignty can be violated has resulted in condemnation in a UN report.[109] There is also a blowback effect for drone strikes, in that, according to some analysts, they have driven scores of young men to join al-Qaeda and affiliated groups. Another strand of criticism claims there is little evidence that simply targeting leaderships can defeat terrorist organizations. Finally, it is argued that there is a lack of transparency and legal accountability with respect to targeting procedures.[110]

Most of these arguments have been countered in detailed analysis.[111] Indeed, a UN Rapporteur in 2013 stated, "If used in strict compliance with the principles of international humanitarian law, remotely piloted aircraft are capable of reducing the risk of civilian casualties in armed conflict by significantly improving the

---

[105]As quoted in Crawford 2013, p. 19.

[106]The three main databases are: The New America Foundation 2013; Roggio and Mayer 2013; The Bureau of Investigative Journalism 2011. See further Cole et al. 2010; New America Foundation 2012; The Bureau of Investigative Journalism 2012; Heller 2013, pp. 94–103.

[107]Bandura 1999, p. 193; Alston and Shamsi 2010.

[108]Miller 2011.

[109]U.N. Human Rights Council 2013a.

[110]Becker and Shane 2012. See also Boyle 2013, pp. 6–9; U.N. Human Rights Council 2010, p. 3; U.N. Human Rights Council 2013b.

[111]See for instance Byman 2013; Frank 2013; Savage 2012; Johnston 2012, pp. 47–79; and book length nuanced analysis such as Williams 2013; and Strawser (ed) 2013.

situational awareness of military commanders."[112] The President of the International Committee of the Red Cross likewise stated that drones "allow belligerents to carry out their attacks more precisely against military objectives and thus reduce civilian casualties and damage to civilian objects, in other words, to exercise greater precaution in attack."[113] Nevertheless, public criticism has resulted in a deliberate decrease in the number of drone-strikes and an increase in the transparency of the procedures surrounding drone strikes.[114]

3.6 The Story-Arc of Targeting

The story-arc of targeting stretches from the strategic bombing theory of Douhet to the contemporary experience of drone warfare. This chapter sought to illustrate how the experience of air warfare has shaped targeting, and, in doing so, highlight those key factors that influence targeting practices in general. As illustrated, targeting's story-arc is one of solving technical and informational obstacles concerning (1) the location and identification of targets, (2) navigating to the target, and (3) accurately delivering munitions. It also reflects an upward trend in the accuracy of munitions and in the capability to conduct pin-point attacks against objects of an ever-decreasing physical signature, in ever-shortening response times, and, if necessary, from ever-increasing distances from the target. Targeting is the story of continuous organizational learning, forgetting, and rediscovery; of theorizing about and experimenting with new targeting planning tools and processes; and of the development of new, more precise, munitions and ever-improving data communications and ISR capabilities. Increasing versatility, flexibility, and integration between the armed services mark targeting practices, but they are equally characterized by the constant swing of the pendulum between the poles of centralized and decentralized control. This reflects a strong tendency towards stringent political oversight, sometimes down to the level of tactical detail, and at times exercised from capitals thousands of miles away.

A final central theme in the story arc is the interplay with societal and political norms. Risk-avoidance has become a paramount concern for military commanders and their political superiors. Western militaries have increasingly been forced carefully to consider every potential consequence of their attacks, and to take all possible precautions to avoid them. Indeed, opponents of Western militaries have proven very agile in exploiting this sensitivity. They are enabled by the proliferation of tools such as camera-equipped cell phones, YouTube, and Twitter—the cyberspace targeting means and methods of warfare for the information age. As a result, the involvement of legal advisors is now more common than

[112] U.N. Human Rights Council 2013c, p. 23.

[113] Statement in Kellenberger 2011.

[114] Baker 2013.

ever in the targeting processes. Even so, norms and perceptions, rather than law, matters most in the current media saturated era. The call for instant accountability is incessant.

The debate over drone warfare merely accentuates the paradox that the ability to attack with unprecedented precision has raised the bar for future operations. On the one hand, the increase in accuracy of weaponry has broadened the realm of targetable objects and inspired new strategic approaches that promise military success that can be achieved with fewer casualties on all sides. On the other, since Desert Storm's images of cruise missiles flying through the streets of Baghdad, the 'CNN effect' is such that extraordinary precision has become expected. It is now a public and political ethical norm, and thus a military one.[115] Targeting errors gain instant attention and condemnation. In contrast with the World Wars, where the certainty of massive civilian casualties did not inhibit the wholesale bombing of cities, today the risk of collateral damage has become highly problematic, even when legitimate targets are struck and civilian casualties result from the deliberate tactics of defenders who seek to exploit Western sensitivities.

Now that individuals can be targeted, it has been observed that the morality and legitimacy of the practices of war are undergoing fundamental transformation. Whereas traditional practices and the laws of war defined 'the enemy' in terms of categorical group-based judgments that turned on status (a person was an enemy because he was a member of the opposing army), we are entering a world that implicitly or explicitly requires the individuation of the responsibility of specific persons before the use of military force can be justified, at least as a moral and political matter.[116] This harkens back to the observations Christopher Coker made in the aftermath of Allied Force, when he noted that avoiding casualties and destruction is a humanizing trend that is the only way to maintain legitimacy for conducting combat operations: "To be just, wars have to be humane. Western societies can now only fight wars which minimize human suffering, that of their enemies as well as their own. They are trying to humanize war. It is the great project for the twenty-first century."[117] And, as he predicted correctly in 2002, there is no way back—we can only go forward.[118]

References

Alberts D et al (1999) Network centric warfare. CCRP Press, Washington DC

Alston P and Shamsi H (2010) A killer above the law? The Guardian, 2 Aug 2010

Andres R (2007a) Deep attack against Iraq. In: Keaney T, Mahnken T (eds) War in Iraq, planning and execution. Routledge, London

[115]Thomas 2001, pp. 162–164.

[116]Isscharoff and Pildest 2013, pp. 1522–1523.

[117]Coker 2002, pp. 2–5.

[118]Coker 2002, p. 13.

Andres R (2007b) The Afghan model in Northern Iraq. In: Keaney T, Mahnken T (eds) War in Iraq, planning and execution. Routledge, London

Arquilla J, Ronfeldt D (1997) In Athena's Camp, preparing for conflict in the information age. RAND, Santa Monica

Arkin W (2007) Divining vsictory, airpower in the 2006 Israel-Hezbollah War. Air University Press, Maxwell AFB, Alabama

Baker P (2013) Pivoting from a war footing, Obama Acts to Curtail Drones. The New York Times, 23 May 2013

Ballew B (2011) The enemy objectives unit in World War II. Master thesis, School of Advanced Military Studies, Fort Leavenworth, Kansas

Bandura A (1999) Moral disengagement in the perpetration of inhumanities. Pers Soc Psychol Rev 3(3):193–209

Becker J, Shane S (2012) Secret kill list proves a test of Obama's principles and will. The New York Times, 29 May 2012

Benbow T (ed) (2011) British naval aviation: the first 100 years. Ashgate Publishing, Ltd

Biddle S (2003a) Afghanistan and the future of warfare. Foreign Affairs 82(2):31–46

Biddle T (1994) Air Power. In: Howard M et al (eds) The laws of war. Yale University Press, New Haven

Biddle T (2003b) Rhetoric and reality in air warfare: the evolution of British and American ideas about strategic bombing, 1914–1945. Princeton University Press, Princeton

Boyle M (2013) The costs and consequences of drone warfare. International Affairs 8(1):1–29

Brun I (2010) The second Lebanon War, 2006. In: Olson (ed) A history of air warfare. Potomac Books, Washington DC

Byman D (2006) Do targeted killings work? Foreign Affairs 85(2):95–111

Byman D (2013) Why drones work, the case for Washington's weapon of choice. Foreign Affairs 92(4):32–43

Byman D, Waxman M (1999) Defeating US Coercion. Survival 41(2):107–120

Byman D, Waxman M (2000) Bosnia Kosovo and the great air power debate. Int Secur 24(4):5–38

Byman D, Waxman M (2002) The dynamics of coercion. CUP, Cambridge

Citino R (2004) Blitzkrieg to Desert Storm. University Press of Kansas, Lawrence, Kansas

Clark WK (2002) Waging modern war, Kosovo and the future of Combat. Public Affairs, New York, Bosnia

Clodfelter M (1989) The Limits of Air Power. The Free Press, New York

Cohen E (1996) A revolution in warfare. Foreign Affairs 75(2):37–54

Cohen E, Keaney T (1995) A Revolution in Warfare? Air Power in the Persian Gulf. Naval Institute Press, Annapolis

Cohen E (1994) The mystique of US airpower. Foreign Affairs 73(1):109–124

Coker C (2002) Humane warfare. Routledge, London

Coker C (2009) War in the age of risk. Polity, Cambridge

Cole C, Dobbing M, Hailwood A (2010) Convenient killing: armed drones and the 'Playstation' mentality. http://dronewars.net/2010/09/20/convenient-killing-armed-drones-and-the-play-station-mentality-2/. Accessed 21 May 2015

Cordesman A (2003) The Iraq War, strategy, tactics, and military lessons. CSIS, Praeger, Westport

Cordesman A (2009) The "Gaza War": a strategic analysis. Center for Strategic and International Studies, Washington DC http://csis.org/files/media/csis/pubs/090202_gaza_war.pdf. Accessed 21 May 2015

Crane C (2000) American Airpower Strategy in Korea, 1950–1953, University Press of Kansas

Crawford N (2013) Accountability for killing, moral responsibility for collateral damage in America's Post-9/11 wars. OUP, Oxford

Daalder I, O'Hanlon M (2000) Winning ugly, NATO's War to save Kosovo. Brookings Institution Press, Washington DC

Davis R (1998) Strategic bombardment in the Gulf War. In: Hall R (ed) Case studies in strategic bombardment. US Government Printing Office, Washington DC
Deptula D (1996) Effects based operations, change in the nature of warfare. Aerospace Education Foundation, Arlington
Desert Storm Target Sets (030226-D-9085 M-006). http://www.defense.gov/news/briefingslide.aspx?briefingslideid=110. Accessed 21 May 2015
Dunlap C Jr (2009) Lawfare: a decisive element of 21st century warfare? Joint Forces Quarterly 54:34–39
Erlanger S (2009) A Gaza War full of traps and trickery. The New York Times, 11 Jan 2009
Faber P (2015) Paradigm lost, airpower theory and its historical struggles. In: Olson J (ed) Airpower reborn, the strategic concepts of John Warden and John Boyd. Naval Institute Press
Farrell T (2002) Humanitarian intervention and peace operations. In: Baylis J, Wirtz J, Gray C (eds) Strategy in the contemporary World. OUP, Oxford
Farrell T, Terriff T, Osinga F (eds) (2010) A transformation gap? American innovations and European military change. Stanford University Press, Stanford
Frank U (2013) The five most common media misrepresentations of UAVs. In: Aaronson M, Johnson A (eds) Hitting the target? How new capabilities are shaping international intervention. Whitehall Reports 2–13, RUSI, London. https://www.rusi.org/downloads/assets/Hitting_the_Target.pdf. Accessed 21 May 2015
Futrell R (1997) The United States air force in Korea, 1950–1953, US Government Printing Office, Washington DC
Fyfe J (2005) The evolution of time sensitive targeting, CADRE Research Paper 2005-2. Air University, Maxwell AFB, Alabama
Gat A (2001) Isolationism, appeasement, containment, and limited war: Western Strategic Policy from the Modern to the "Postmodern" Era. In: Maoz Z, Gat A (eds) War in a changing world. The University of Michigan Press, Ann Arbor
Glock J (2012) The evolution of air force targeting. Air & Space Power J 26(6):146–174
Gordon M, Trainor B (1995) The General's War: the inside story of the conflict in the Gulf. Little, Brown and Company, Boston
Graham B (2003) Bugsplat computer program aims to limit civilian deaths at targets, The Washington Post, 22 Feb 2003
Hall R (ed) (1998) Case studies in strategic bombardment, air force history and museums program, Washington DC
Hallion R (1992) Storm over Iraq, air power and the Gulf War. Smithsonian Institution Press, Washington DC
Hayward J (ed) (2009) Air power, insurgency and the "War on Terror". RAF Centre for Air Power Studies, Cranwell
Heller K (2013) 'One Hell of a Killing Machine': signature strikes and international law. J Int Crim Justice 11(1):94–103
Henriksen D (2012) Deterrence by default? Israel's Military Strategy in the 2006 War against Hizballah. J Strateg Stud 35(1):95–120
Hone T (1998) Strategic bombing constrained. In: Hall R (ed) Case studies in strategic bombardment. Air force History and Museums Program, Washington DC
Hosmer S (1996) Psychological effects of US air operations in four wars, 1941–1991. RAND, Santa Monica
Ignatieff M (2002) Virtual war: Kosovo and beyond. Colin McInnes, Boulder, London
Inbar E, Shamir E (2014) Mowing the grass: Israel's strategy for protracted intractable conflict. J Strateg Stud 37(1):65–90
Issacharoff S, Pildes R (2013) Targeted warfare: individuating enemy responsibility. New York Univ Law Rev 88(5):1521–1599
Jakobsen P (1998) The Yugoslav wars. In: Jakobsen P (ed) Western use of coercive diplomacy after the Cold War. MacMillan, London

Jakobsen P (2000) Reinterpreting western use of coercion in Bosnia-Herzegowina: assurances and carrots were crucial. J Strateg Stud 23(2):1–22
Johnston P (2012) Does decapitation work? Assessing the effectiveness of leadership targeting in counterinsurgency Campaign's. Int Secur 36(4):47–79
Kagan F (2006) Finding the target, the transformation of American military policy. Encounter Books, New York
Kellenberger P (2011) Key note address to the 34th roundtable on Current Issues of International Humanitarian Law, San Remo, 8 Sept 2011. https://www.icrc.org/eng/resources/documents/statement/new-weapon-technologies-statement-2011-09-08.htm. Accessed 24 May 2015
Kenneth L (1991) The first air war, 1914–1918. The Free Press, New York
Kometer M (2007) Command in air war. Air University Press, Maxwell AFB, Alabama
Krebs S (2009) Air Power's role in Asymmetric Operations: the Case of the Second Lebanon War. In: Hayward J (ed) Air power, insurgency and the war on terror. Centre for Air Power Studies, Cranwell
Lambeth B (2001) NATO's air war for Kosovo, a strategic and operational assessment. RAND, Santa Monica
Lambeth B (2005) Air power against terror, America's conduct of Operation Enduring Freedom. RAND, Santa Monica
Lambeth B (2011) Air operations in Israel's war against Hezbollah: learning from Lebanon and getting it right in Gaza. RAND, Santa Monica
Lambeth B (2013) The unseen war, allied air power and the takedown of Saddam Hussein. Naval Institute Press, Annapolis
Larson E, Savych B (2006) Misfortunes of war: press and public reactions to civilian deaths in wartime. RAND, Santa Monica
Latham A (2002) Warfare transformed: a Braudelian perspective on the 'Revolution in Military Affairs'. Eur J Int Relat 8(2):231–266
Luttwak E (2001) Blood and computers: the crisis of classic military power in advanced postindustrialist societies and the scope of technological remedies. In: Maoz Z, Gat A (eds) War in a changing world. The University of Michigan Press, Ann Arbor
Mahnken T, Keaney T (eds) (2007) War in Iraq. Planning and execution, Routledge, Abingdon
Mann E III, Endersby G, Searle T (2002) Thinking effects, effects-based methodology for joint operation. Air University Press, Maxwell AFB, Alabama
Maoz Z, Gat A (eds) (2001) War in a changing world. The University of Michigan Press, Ann Arbor
Mark E (1994) Aerial interdiction in three wars, Center For Air Force history. US Government Printing Office, Washington
McInnes C (2002) Spectator- sport warfare, the West and contemporary conflict. Westview Press, Boulder
McIsaac D (1986) Voices from the central blue: the air power theorists. In: Paret P (ed) Makers of modern strategy. Princeton University Press, Princeton
Meilinger P (1997) The paths of Heaven, the evolution of airpower theory. Air University Press, Maxwell AFB, Alabama
Meilinger P (1999) Air warfare, an historical perspective. In: Finn C (ed) Effects based warfare. Joint Doctrine and Concepts Centre, Shrivenham
Meilinger P (2007) A history of effects based air operations. J Mil Hist 71(1):139–167
Miller P (2011) When will the U.S. drone war end? The Washington Post, 17 Nov 2011
Moeller M (1994) The sum of their fears: the relationship between the Joint Targeting Coordination Board and the Joint Force Commander. Master thesis, School of Advanced Airpower Studies, Air University, Maxwell AFB, Alabama
Murray W, Scales R (2003) The Iraqi war. A military history. Harvard University Press, Cambridge
Mueller K (1998) Strategies of coercion: Denial, punishment and the future of air power. Secur Stud 7(3):182–228

Mueller K (2010) Air Power. In: Denemark R (ed) The international studies encyclopaedia, vol I. Wiley-Blackwell, Oxford
Olson J (2007) John Warden and the renaissance of American air power. Potomac Books, Washington
Osinga F (2013) Drone warfare, bounding the debate. In: Amersfoort H et al (eds) Moral responsibility and military effectiveness. Asser Press, The Hague
Overy R (1980) The air war, 1939–1945. Stein and Day Publishers, New York
Overy R (1998) Strategic bombardment before 1939. In: Hall R (ed) Case studies in strategic bombardment. Air Force History and Museums Program, Washington DC
Overy R (2013) The bombing war, Europe 1939–1945. Allen Lane, London
Owen R (2010) Operation Deliberate Force. In: Olson J (ed) A history of air warfare. Potomac Books, Washington DC
Pape R (1996) Bombing to win. Cornell University Press
Pape R (1997) The limits of precision guided air power. Secur Stud 7(2):93–114
Posen B (2000) The war for Kosovo: Serbia's political-military strategy. Int Secur 24(4):39–84
Press D (2001) The myth of air power in the Persian Gulf War and the future of war. Int Secur 26(2):5–44
Rasmussen M (2009) The risk society at war. Cambridge
Reynolds J (2005) Collateral damage on the 21st century battlefield: enemy exploitation of the law of armed conflict, and the struggle for a moral high ground. Air Force Law Rev 56:1–109
Rid T (2012) Deterrence beyond the State: The Israeli experience. Contemp Secur Policy 33(1):124–147
Rid T, Hecker M (2009) War 2.0: irregular warfare in the information age. Praeger, Westport
Roggio B, Mayer A (2013) Charting the data for U.S. airstrikes in Pakistan, 2004–2013. Long War J. 8 February 2013. http://www.longwarjournal.org/pakistan-strikes. Accessed 24 May 2015
Rumsfeld D (2002) Transforming the military. Foreign Aff 81(3):20–32
Savage C (2012) Top U.S. security official says 'Rigorous Standards' are used for drone strikes, The New York Times, 30 April 2012
Schmidt E (1993) Targeting organizations. Master Thesis, School of Advanced Airpower Studies, Air University, Maxwell AFB, Alabama
Shaw M (2005) The new Western way of war. Polity Press, Cambridge
Shue H (2010) Targeting civilian infrastructure with smart bombs, the new permissiveness. Philos Public Policy Q 30(3/4):2–8
Smith T (2002) The new law of war: legitimizing H-Tech and infrastructural violence. Int Stud Q 46:355–374
Stahl A (2010) The evolution of Israeli targeted operations: consequences of the Thabet operation'. Stud Conflict Terrorism 33(2):111–133
Strawser B (ed) (2013) Killing by remote control: the ethics of an unmanned military. Oxford University Press, Oxford
The Bureau of Investigative Journalism (2011) Covert US strikes in Pakistan, Yemen and Somalia: our methodology, 10 August 2011. http://www.thebureauinvestigates.com/2011/08/10/pakistan-drone-strikes-the-methodology2/. Accessed 24 May 2015
The Bureau of Investigative Journalism (2012) Covert Drone War, 12 November 2012. http://www.thebureauinvestigates.com/category/projects/drones/. Accessed 24 May 2015
The New America Foundation (2012) Counterterrorism strategy initiative, the year of the drone. http://webcache.googleusercontent.com/search?q=cache:MVKRnajpmIgJ:counterterrorism.newamerica.net/drones+&cd=1&hl=en&ct=clnk&gl=us
The New American Foundation (2013) The year of the drone: methodology, 15 Jan 2013. http://counterterrorism.newamerica.net/drones/methodology
The United States strategic bombing surveys (European War) (Pacific War) (1987) Air University Press. Maxwell AFB, Alabama

Thomas W (2001) The ethics of destruction: norms and force in international relations. Cornell University Press, Ithaca, Norms and Force in International Relations
Thomas W (2006) Victory by Duress: civilian infrastructure as a target in air campaigns. Secur Stud 15(1):1–33
Titus J (1996) The Battle of Khafji: an overview and preliminary analysis. CADRE, Maxwell Air Force Base, Alabama
Tucker S, Wood L, Murphy J (eds) (1999) The European powers in the first World War: an encyclopedia. Taylor & Francis
U.N. Human Rights Council (2010) Report of the Special Rapporteur on extrajudicial, summary or arbitrary executions, 28 May 2010. http://www2.ohchr.org/english/bodies/hrcouncil/docs/14session/A.HRC.14.24.Add6.pdf. Accessed 24 May 2015
U.N. Human Rights Council (2013a) Pakistan: Statement by the UN Special Rapporteur on human rights and counter-terrorism, 15 March 2013. http://www.ohchr.org/en/NewsEvents/Pages/DisplayNews.aspx?NewsID=13148&LangID=E. Accessed 24 May 2015
U.N. Human Rights Council (2013b) Report of the Special Rapporteur on extrajudicial, summary or arbitrary executions, 9 April 2013. http://www.ohchr.org/Documents/HRBodies/HRCouncil/RegularSession/Session23/A-HRC-23-47_en.pdf. Accessed 24 May 2015
U.N. Human Rights Council (2013c) Report of the Special Rapporteur on the promotion and protection of human rights and fundamental freedoms while countering terrorism, New York, 1 March 2013. http://daccess-dds-ny.un.org/doc/UNDOC/GEN/N13/478/77/PDF/N1347877.pdf?OpenElement
U.S. Department of Defense (2000) Report to Congress: Kosovo/Operation Allied Force After Action Report, 31 January 2000. http://www.dod.mil/pubs/kaar02072000.pdf. Accessed 24 May 2015
Warden J (1995) The enemy as a system. Airpower J 9(1):40–55
Watts B (1997) Ignoring reality, problems of theory and evidence in security studies. Secur Stud 7(2):115–171
Watts B (1984) The foundations of US air doctrine. Air University Press, Maxwell AFB, Alabama
Williams B (2013) Predators: the CIA's Drone War on al Qaeda. Potomac Books, Washington DC
Wilner A (2011a) Deterring the undeterrable: coercion, denial, and delegitimization in counterterrorism. J Strateg Stud 34(1):3–37
Wilner A (2011b) Fencing in Warfare: threats, punishment, and intra-war deterrence in counterterrorism. Secur Stud 22(4):740–772
Winnefeld J, Johnson D (1993) Joint air operations: pursuit of unity in command and control, 1942–1991. Naval Institute Press, Annapolis
Woodward B (2003) Plan of Attack. Simon and Schuster, New York

Chapter 4
The Current Targeting Process

Phillip R. Pratzner

Abstract This chapter examines the current targeting process. It begins by defining targeting as the process of selecting and prioritizing targets and matching the appropriate response to them, considering operational requirements and capabilities. The essential elements of targeting are highlighted: a process orientation, awareness of one's own capabilities, and, perhaps most significantly, a linkage to a specific requirement. It then defines what the targeting process is not: arbitrary, fixated on the impossible or random. Next, this chapter lays out the targeting process by examining the US and NATO deliberate processes, along with their identical F2T2EA (Find, Fix, Track, Target, Engage, Assess) dynamic process. The author describes a targeting process that encompasses four steps: (1) objectives and guidance; (2) planning; (3) execution; and (4) assessment. This chapter identifies six dynamics that inform and influence the current targeting process: (1) tension between the art and science of targeting; (2) equal demands to both speed up and slow down the targeting cycle; (3) high demand for precision; (4) avoidance or at least mitigation of collateral damage; (5) non-lethal capabilities, increasingly relevant in today's targeting; and (6) cognitive approach as the bedrock targeting principle. The author concludes by examining the future of the targeting process through the lens of robotics. As Artificial Intelligence increases, precision becomes more exact, the need for human beings in the loop lessen and greater isolation occurs from actual combat on the ground. These are unnerving possibilities that could impact targeting dynamics. For now, targeting remains focused on influence and coercion, leading one to the inescapable conclusion that targeting is a human activity. And this human activity, undertaken by humans and focused on other humans, drives the current targeting process.

P.R. Pratzner (✉)
Asymmetric Operations Sector, Johns Hopkins University Applied Physics Laboratory, 11100 Johns Hopkins Road, Laurel, MD 20723-6099, USA
e-mail: phillip.pratzner@jhuapl.edu

P.A.L. Ducheine et al. (eds.), *Targeting: The Challenges of Modern Warfare*,
DOI 10.1007/978-94-6265-072-5_4

Keywords Targeting · Process · Precision · Collateral · Non-lethal · Cognitive · Robotics

Contents

4.1 Introduction

In April 2011, three events occurred simultaneously in different areas of the world with seemingly no connection. In Afghanistan, a US soldier called for immediate close air support through an established protocol, waiting only minutes for the International Security Assistance Force (ISAF) aircraft to arrive to assist in this counterinsurgency operation. In Germany, operational planners at the Air and Space Operations Center at Ramstein Air Base, Germany, planned and adjusted potential operations in Libya as part of the operation that would soon be known as Odyssey Dawn (2011). The execution of this operation was only days away; it would not be a counterinsurgency, but rather a major combat operation (MCO). In the Republic of Korea (ROK), representatives from all four US services and their ROK counterparts contemplated the best way to synchronize a combined operation should hostilities break out on the Korean peninsula. The time horizon for this operation was not days away, but rather months or even years, and the operation might include elements of a counterinsurgency, an MCO, or even humanitarian operations. Despite the substantial differences in the geographical location, temporal planning dimension, and type of military operation, there was a common thread in all these events: the targeting process was at work.

The goal of this chapter is to examine the current targeting process. First, the author will lay out what it is, and what it is not. Second, the four parts of the process, which can be applied to understanding any targeting process, will be explored. Third, the author will discuss six dynamics that inform, and in many cases dominate the current targeting process. Finally, the future of the targeting process will be examined through the lens of robotics.

4.2 The Targeting Process Defined

Targeting is the process of selecting and prioritizing targets and matching the appropriate response to them, considering operational requirements and capabilities.[1] We see in this definition several key elements: a process orientation, awareness of one's own capabilities, and, perhaps most significantly, linkage to a specific requirement. Targeting must logically begin with an objective, which drives the subsequent steps of this process. Based on what targeting is, three conclusions can be made as to what targeting is not. First, targeting is not arbitrary, since it follows an identifiable process. Second, it cannot be fixated on the impossible, since it must be based, on capabilities actually possessed. These capabilities can include air-based, land-based and sea-based assets; comprise a mix of kinetic and non-kinetic weapons; and operate in multiple domains, to include cyberspace. Third, targeting is not random because it is focused on a requirement, and by inference an objective. In sum, targeting has three elements: process, capabilities, and requirements. With this established, we now take a closer look at the process.

4.3 The Steps of the Targeting Process

At first glance, one could conclude that there are at least two targeting processes to consider, one focused on deliberate targeting (future, scheduled plans)[2] and the other centered on dynamic targeting (targets identified too late for deliberate targeting).[3] The deliberate process contains six steps in the methodologies of the US Military and North Atlantic Treaty Organization (NATO). Both emphasize that these cycles are iterative. There is substantially similarity between the two processes, as Fig. 4.1 illustrates.

[1] JCS, Joint Pub 3-60 2013, p. I-1. NATO, AJP-3.9 2008, p. 1–1.

[2] JCS, Joint Pub 3-60 2013, p. II-1 and NATO, AJP-3.9 2008, pp. 1–2.

[3] JCS, Joint Pub 1-02 2013, p. 84 and NATO, AJP-3.9 2008, pp. 1–2.

Steps of Process	United States Military	NATO
1	End State and Commander's Objectives	Commander's Objectives, Guidance and Intent
2	Target Development and Prioritization	Target Development, Validation, Nomination and Prioritisation
3	Capabilities Analysis	Capabilities Analysis (including Weaponeering)
4	Commander's Decision and Force Assignment	Force Planning and Assignment
5	Mission Planning and Force Execution	Mission Planning and Execution
6	Assessment	Combat Assessment/ Measurements of the Effectiveness of the Attack

Fig. 4.1 Comparison of US Military's (JP 3-60 2013, p. II-3) and NATO's (NATO, AJP-3.9 2008, p. 2–1) Deliberate Joint Targeting Cycle

The similarities do not end with the deliberate cycle, but extend into the dynamic targeting cycle as well.[4] The US Military and NATO subscribe to a dynamic targeting cycle best known by its acronym, F2T2EA—Find, Fix, Track, Target, Execute and Assess.[5] This process emphasizes speed and equips the war fighter with an intellectual framework to constrain, by necessity, the available options. The sole purpose is to remain focused on a target, track it wherever it goes, and then execute a military option as expeditiously as possible. This requires a singularity of purpose that the deliberate cycle does not necessarily embrace. But like the deliberate cycle, it is iterative.

Additionally, four distinct steps characterize both the deliberate and dynamic cycles: (1) objectives and guidance; (2) planning; (3) execution; and (4) assessment. To be certain, there are variables that differentiate how a specific operation's targeting process is carried out—namely, the goal itself, the time allotted for planning, the means or capabilities, and the tools available to assess. Every targeting event, however, whether by a nation-State or non-State actor, can be viewed through the prism of these four steps. This is valid on all levels, from the strategic and operational to the tactical. It also applies to all weapon types, whether they be air-based, sea-based or land-based. A discussion of each step follows.

[4]AJP-3.9 2008 describes this process as the "Time Sensitive Targeting" Process; for the sake of brevity, the author will refer to this as dynamic targeting. Within the US military and NATO, professionals often use the terms "Time Sensitive Targeting" and "Dynamic Targeting" interchangeably.

[5]JCS, Joint Pub 3-60 2013, pp. II-21–22, NATO, AJP-3.9 2008, p. A-5.

4.3.1 Objectives and Guidance

A clear and achievable objective, with guidance that follows, is perhaps the most critical step to ensure targeting success. Practitioners have long understood this, and applaud the good examples as much as they loathe the bad. For many, Operation Desert Storm (1991) provides an excellent example, in that a monumental task (extracting Iraq from Kuwait) occured in a mere 42 days.[6] Conversely, many operational planners were frustrated by the arguably bad example provided by Operation Allied Force (1999), which lasted 78 days. Its objectives not only changed, but guidance was often confusing and disjointed. German General Klaus Naumann, then Chairman of NATO's military committee, stated, '[w]e need to find a way to reconcile the conditions of a coalition war with the principles of military operations such as surprise and overwhelming force. We did not apply either in Operation Allied Force … and this cost time, effort, and potentially additional casualties'.[7] There is little doubt that Desert Storm provides examples of multiple poor tactical decisions and Allied Force furnishes many good ones, but in evaluating the objectives and guidance step of the targeting process, practitioners are nearly united in the conclusion that these operations exemplify the right and left boundaries.

We find that in order to start 'right', the writings of Von Clausewitz and Sun Tzu are as pertinent today as they were in their own day. Clear and achievable objectives and guidance are driven by policy aims, an understanding of the nature of the conflict, the quality of the intelligence, and the capabilities possessed by the actor or actors involved. Where the objective is insufficient because it is vague, impractical, or based on faulty intelligence, the burden of success falls on the other parts of the cycle (planning, execution, and assessment). Often, the activities associated with these efforts will shape new, refined objectives and guidance to reflect the operational reality. Whether good, bad or somewhere in between, these are deliberate activities; hence, objectives and guidance are clearly linked to the deliberate targeting process.

The evidence is not as clear with dynamic targeting, given that its first step is to 'find' a target. Do objectives and guidance apply to dynamic targeting? The answer is an emphatic yes. Practitioners have long understood that dynamic targeting success requires clear and achievable objectives and guidance. It rarely

---

[6]Mann 1985, p. 87. Also, the author uses the dates of 17 January 1991–28 February 1991, specifically the time period of the Desert Strom operation to arrive at 42 days. Many consider the start date as 2 August 1990, the day Iraq invaded Kuwait, and the start of Operation Desert Shield. But targeting execution did not start in earnest until Desert Storm, so 17 January 1991, in the author's estimation, is the most accurate way to measure the time dimension of this operation.

[7]Priest 2003, p. 54 and DoD 2000, p. 127. Although the Department of Defense presented a very favourable picture of the operation in this report, there are several areas where it identifies problems and challenges at the political-military strategic level.

occurs in a vacuum, devoid of anything other than a single target or purpose. A parent headquarters, such as a combatant command, Joint Task Force (JTF), or a Combined Air and Space Operations Center (CAOC), will ordinarily establish guidelines for execution, priority of tasks, and specific Rules of Engagement (ROE). In the US and NATO targeting systems, dynamic targeting has been focused in the past decade on individual actors; in many instances, the target has been designated a High Value Individual (HVI). Yet even in these cases, considerable thought, clear rules on execution, and specific guidance on priorities (since many dynamic targeting scenarios occur simultaneously) are the rule and not the exception. As planners consider dynamic targeting in an MCO, units and even pieces of equipment, such as a SCUD Transportable Erector Launcher, may rise to the highest priority. Guidance is required to deal with these targets as well.

The evidence is therefore indisputable: objectives and guidance start the targeting process. They may be clear and achievable, and drive the other steps effectively while remaining flexible enough to be iteratively modified. They may also be vague and uninformed, presenting challenges throughout the targeting process. This can not only limit the effectiveness of the operation, but also cause catastrophic failure if not remedied. The first impact, whether good or bad, is felt in the next step.

4.3.2 Planning

Like objectives and guidance, planning is applied to both deliberate and dynamic targeting. The quality of planning is a direct result of four factors: (1) time; (2) intelligence related to the planning; (3) competency in the targeting tradecraft; and (4) the mental agility to change the plan as the environment evolves. The importance of time cannot be overstated. Although information and communications technology (ICT) has enabled many lower end functions to be automated, there are necessary steps—command direction and course checks, legal reviews, proper vetting of individual targets, etc.—that demand time to properly complete. More time often enables better and increased quantities of intelligence as well, given the availability of intelligence planners and the intelligence, surveillance, and reconnaissance (ISR) assets at their disposal.

More time has not always equated to greater success, but nearly any US or NATO targeting planner would see it as a significant plus.[8] Two operations illus-

[8]This comment is based on the author's 17 years of targeting experience, including involvement in nine major contingency or deliberate targeting planning efforts and dozens of smaller efforts in seven different combatant commands. In every single effort, more time to plan was viewed by the author and other targeting professionals as highly desirable.

trate this advantage. First, when Israel began hostilities during the Six Day War in 1967, they were executing a plan which had taken years to develop. Egypt, the most formidable foe aligned against them, saw their Air Force decimated within the first hours of the conflict. The Israeli Air Force knew how and when to hit it. Mordechai Hod, the Israeli Air Force Chief of Staff, described the plan in this way: 'Sixteen years planning had gone into those initial 80 min'.[9] The second example is the US plan for Operation Desert Storm. Born of the efforts of the Air Force's Checkmate Planning Cell in the Pentagon augmented by planners from 9th Air Force, a targeting plan that evolved over a six-month period neutralized Iraqi defenses and enabled a very short 100-hour ground campaign to extract Iraq from Kuwait.

As important as time is the intelligence that supports it. The right intelligence can overcome the inherent disadvantage of limited time. Quantity—the number of ISR sensors, the extent of the human intelligence network, the size of the analytical team evaluating the raw intelligence—is vital. Targeting campaign success is replete with examples in which the greater quantity of intelligence was the decisive advantage. However, more ISR sensors at one's disposal cannot overcome a complex adaptive enemy aiming to win at the strategic level. The Vietnam War (1960s–1970s) was instructive in this way for the US, as was the 2006 Israel-Hezbollah War (Operation Change of Direction) for Israel. In both cases, significant quantities of intelligence did not equate to strategic success. These examples illustrate that something else is at work. In simple terms, the quality of intelligence—a deep understanding of the enemy through intense study, modelling of potential reactions to friendly actions, a thorough knowledge of the enemy's ability to take blows and adapt—matters at least as much as the quantity.

Related to this is the third factor, competence in the targeting tradecraft. This factor appears primarily in three areas: target system analysis (TSA), weaponeering and capabilities analysis, and collateral damage estimation (CDE). Superior targeting personnel—through natural talent, higher quality training, experience, and strong targeting leadership—will give commanders both more, and better, options.

TSAs break down a target system, such as an integrated air defense system (IADS), and investigate the ways in which a targeting plan could affect it. For instance, an enemy headquarters may be identified in this step for neutralization because it is critical to the proper functioning of an air defense sector. Weaponeering and capabilities analysis entails an assessment of how friendly capabilities—weapons and platforms—will interact against a given target, with its inherent attributes. It is at this stage that planners would assess the probability of damage (PD) of a 2,000 pound Joint Direct Attack Munition (JDAM)

[9] Joffe 2003.

against a multi-story concrete building which is the enemy headquarters identified above in the TSA. CDE is the calculation of potential collateral damage of a weapon against items around a target, such as a hospital, mosque, or school, and the chance of harming non-combatants. In our example, targeting personnel, by conducting CDE, would know the possibility of damaging civilian objects in proximity to the headquarters, and the potential number of casualties. In sum, high tradecraft standards improve a targeting plan's chances for success; competency means hitting the right targets, identifying the appropriate amount of force to affect them, and avoiding damage to the wrong targets.

The last factor impacting targeting planning is the mental agility to change the plan as the environment evolves. Not every targeting effort has abundant time, good intelligence from the start or exceptional targeting tradecraft. In fact, the author has seen that the norm is often the opposite, at least at the beginning. But this can be corrected, either by adjusting the prior plans, getting the right people involved or shifting the intelligence effort to collect on the right things.

Two examples illustrate this effective reset. First, Operation Allied Force's targeting shift from purely military targets to targeting that included the cronies (and power brokers) of Serbian leader Milosevic proved highly effective at achieving campaign goals.[10] Second, at the outset of planning for Operation Odyssey Dawn (2011), US Africa Command planners found themselves very limited in the ability to accomplish basic targeting functions due to the fact that the command was staffed and focused for operations other than war, including peacekeeping and humanitarian operations. They wisely reached back to stateside targeting organizations, such as the newly established Air Force Targeting Center at Langley Air Force Base, Virginia.[11] These organizations were able to offer both capability and capacity, and enabled targeting success.[12]

4.3.3 Execution

The best planning, however, never guarantees positive results. The execution step of the targeting process is where planning meets the reality of combat, and a miscue can put campaign objectives at risk. For example, in 1986, the US executed Operation Eldorado Canyon, striking Libyan targets in retribution for a terrorist

[10]Clark 2001, pp. 265, 406.

[11]The author was the Commander at the Air Force Targeting Center (AFTC) at the time. The AFTC had approximately 120 personnel involved, including several individuals deployed at Ramstein Air Base, the home of the Air and Space Operations Center which executed the air operation.

[12]Major General Margaret Woodward, the 17th Air Force Commander, in Fontaine 2011. Also, Woodward acknowledged the central targeting role of the AFTC to several of its members who were deployed to Ramstein Air Base, Germany, during Odyssey Dawn.

attack against a Berlin discotheque, 'La Belle'. Tactically, the operation exacted very limited damage; multiple aircraft were unable to drop their munitions and others missed their targets. Operational planners were convinced the operation was unsuccessful, but ultimately the political objectives were achieved, at least temporarily. In another tactical execution gone awry, the Chinese embassy in Belgrade was struck because of a poor target vetting process, killing three individuals and wounding at least twenty, during Operation Allied Force.[13] Once again, this could have endangered campaign objectives, but the operation succeeded despite this blunder.

There are no magical solutions that ensure execution mistakes do not occur, for Von Clausewitz's concepts of the 'fog of war' and 'friction' are as prescient today as in his time. War and conflict carry risks that cannot be eliminated, but often can be mitigated. First, ISR effected just prior, during, and after execution enables more precise and less risky options. ISR can characterize activities with greater accuracy, clarify the intent of belligerents, and confirm the existence of critical targets, such as HVIs. These activities were commonplace in Afghanistan by 2012, as that theater saw an influx for over a year of every type of available sensor: imagery, Signals Intelligence (SIGINT), multi-spectral and hyper-spectral imagery (MSI and HSI), Full Motion Video (FMV), radar, Ground Moving Target Indicator (GMTI), and Laser Imaging Detection and Ranging (LIDAR).[14] Second, a flexible and adaptive combat execution system can make adjustments in real time, as the enemy and situation change. This was frequently seen in Afghanistan. Targeting options became increasingly more constrained in order to limit collateral damage and keep the Afghan population at least neutral.[15] Third, ROE must be drafted to be understood clearly by the lowest ranking soldier on point. Further, they must enable friendly forces to act decisively as the situation permits. If either of these conditions are not met, collateral damage will increase, friendly forces will suffer unnecessary casualties, and, HVIs will get away. All these results put campaign objectives at risk.

4.3.4 Assessment

The last step of the targeting process, and perhaps the most challenging, is assessment. Seemingly, one of the most notable 'lessons learned' of nearly all recent US operations is the failure of combat assessment.[16] Why is this case? First and fore-

[13]Myers 2000.

[14]Observations from the author's experience.

[15]This is a key element of "Karzai's Twelve," the nickname given to a dozen restrictions on NATO operations in Afghanistan required by Hamid Karzai, the Afghan president, as presented in Chivers 2011.

[16]Chivers 2011.

most, assessment is hard. The sensor must be positioned correctly, the timing must be right, and the targeting analyst must understand the weapon's dynamics, target characteristics, and how the weapon–target interaction actually occurred. If the weapon is non-lethal, such as a cyber attack, the assessment challenge grows exponentially. Did the attack work? How extensive was the damage? Whether lethal or non-lethal, assessing damage which you cannot see is a significant challenge to even the most experienced analyst. If this is hard for a single target, assessing an entire target system or multiple target systems is even more challenging.

Second, time constraints complicate assessment. In fast moving combat operations, there is tremendous pressure to assess rapidly at every level. Politicians want to report progress, senior military leaders must make resource decisions based on transitioning into the next phase, operational commanders have to consider branches and sequels at the first opportunity, and fielded forces want to make adjustments as necessary and as quickly as possible. This inevitably creates risk due to incomplete information and conflicting reporting. An analyst rarely has information that is both highly accurate and rapidly received. Given this dilemma, analysts must fill in gaps with lower confidence assessments.

The challenges do not end there. As military planners frequently say, the enemy has a vote—and his goal is typically to deny and deceive. A wide range of tools at the disposal of the belligerent. These include denial tools such as human shields, underground bunkers, caves in a mountainside and mobility, as well as deception tools like false allegations of killing civilians, accusations of bombing a 'baby milk factory', and inflated claims of their own effectiveness. Add in Von Clausewtiz's 'fog' and 'friction', and one can begin to understand the barriers the analyst must surmount to conduct effective assessment: incomplete and imperfect information, time constraints, demands for information from political leaders to the soldier in the field, and an uncooperative enemy.

Despite these challenges, assessment has been done effectively at the operational level. Three major factors have enabled success. First, a plan put in writing, clearly understood by all stakeholders, and adjusted as the situation dictates, has proven to be the most critical step for success. This step alone drove the relative success of the assessment effort during Odyssey Dawn.[17] Second, analysts have found great advantage with a prioritized assessment schema. This has enabled them to consider importance and timeliness to phase-specific assessments, making the process more manageable. Third and last, targeting practitioners have always understood that the best way to assess a target system is to thoroughly know that

[17]This is based on the feedback received by the author as Commander of the Air Force Targeting Center from senior officers at 17th and 3rd Air Forces, along with the Joint Staff, after Odyssey Dawn concluded. The AFTC was extensively involved with the combat assessment effort (see note 11). In fact, one of its members actually wrote the Combat Assessment plan.

system. A comprehensive, well-written and clear TSA has been key to this factor. Lacking that or augmenting it, planners have found success drafting the most qualified subject matter experts to the assessment effort. While these three elements have not guaranteed effective assessment, they have shown repeatedly that they dramatically increased the odds of success.

4.4 Dynamics Which Inform the Targeting Process

Today's targeting process cannot be simply explained by covering the four steps above. The author has identified six dynamics which exert significant influence on the process[18]:

- Tension between the art and science of targeting;
- Equal demands to both speed up and slow down the targeting cycle;
- High demand for precision;
- Avoidance or at least mitigation of collateral damage;
- Non-lethal capabilities, increasingly relevant in today's targeting operations;
- The cognitive approach as the bedrock targeting principle.

4.4.1 Tension Between the Art and Science of Targeting

Military professionals understand that their tradecraft blends art and science. In fact, the vital link between the strategic and tactical level is referred to as the 'operational art', which is 'the cognitive approach by commanders and staffs—supported by their skill, knowledge, experience, creativity and judgment—to develop strategies, campaigns and operations to organize and employ military forces by integrating ends, ways and means.[19] Yet, science remains equally vital to the military tradecraft; stealth and low observable technology, ICT architectures, logistics modelling for rapid resupply, etc.

The same can be said for targeting, except many believe that science trumps the art. After all, selecting targets to accomplish objectives should be based on objective scoring, which can be easily determined since a target's function is known and can be quantitatively tied to one or more objectives. Deriving precision coordinates, known as Precision Point Mensuration (PPM), for a target can be done

[18]These dynamics are derived from a combination of sources. Some sources are classified, the details of which cannot be identified or cited here. Other sources can be seen in the respective dynamic's section which follows. The foremost source of these dynamics is the author himself, drawing on his experience and his professional discussions with other subject matter experts.

[19]JCS, JP 1-02 2013, p. 194.

through any number of sensors, a sort of 'point and click' solution. A weapon–target interface is a physics equation which can be easily solvable. Assessment can be accomplished with a sensor that can readily detect the level of damage, or lack thereof. All of these assertions are at least partially true, but that is indeed the issue: they are only partially true, and therefore partially false.

The true function of a target is not always known. Sometimes the only thing clear about it is that it has some relevancy to a system. Even if it has a known function, the capacity and interrelationship to other parts of a system is rarely completely understood. The enemy seldom gives its blueprints away, and the analyst therefore is forced to make informed judgments and assessments. Deriving precision coordinates today is still labour intensive and prone to error if exacting procedures are not followed, even if it is done on special hardware/software systems. Weaponeering, the weapon–target interface, requires considerable judgment on most targets. Even when the size dimensions are identified, the interior of the target, the environment around it, the disposition of equipment and people, etc., are almost never known with absolute certainty, and any of these factors could affect how the weapon interacts with the target. Lastly, assessment is mostly art, as has been previously discussed. There are simply too many uncertainties: unclear imagery, ambiguous indications, unknown interior damage, etc.

Hence, a tension exists between the science and art of targeting. This has confounded targeting professionals for years since their superiors often do not fully appreciate this art/science dichotomy. After all, ICT has advanced the tradecraft unrelentingly for years. It may even conquer several of the challenges cited above, such as PPM and weaponeering, which lend themselves to quantitative solutions because they possess elements of hard data. But the science is still far from exact, and the author has seen many recent examples, even in 2013, in which the science element delivered poor operational planning results for field commanders. Yet, when human beings, particularly those long experienced in the tradecraft, were put in the equation, the results could be very positive due to their informed judgments of similar past events and scenarios. In this way, the tension can be made constructive, art combined with science or *vice versa*, to yield a better targeting result. But the tension remains, as the balance of each is constantly changing.

4.4.2 Equal Demands to both Speed Up and Slow down the Targeting Cycle

Today's targeting professionals deal with yet another tension—there are equal demands to both speed up and slow down the targeting cycle. From a US and NATO perspective, the argument for expediting the cycle goes something like this: we have an agile military, that is more capable than ever to respond to dynamic changes in the battlespace. We have IT tools that can rapidly recalculate weaponeering solutions, deliver a precise coordinate in less than ten minutes, and enable us to discover a new target's function in minutes. There is no reason why we cannot put at risk any target within our reach in minutes, not hours or days. However, this bumps up against the equally opposite forces slowing the process down.

The argument, again from the US and NATO perspective, for slowing the process down comes from the perspective that war is a complex undertaking which requires deliberate choices and actions. These must be informed by a consensus of the coalition, the command and control element and its commensurate situational awareness, the ground commander who has eyes on, and the risks involved with going after a target for which we do not have full clarity. In fact, an attack may threaten the good will (if there is any) of a local populace that has been cultivated for months or years, yet be jeopardized by one frivolous air strike against an insurgent laying an improvised explosive device … or was that a farmer who was simply digging an irrigation ditch? There are also the laws of armed conflict (LOAC) and ROE to consider, and the target must be validated by military lawyers. This argument therefore seeks more consensus and greater fidelity. Its supporters are willing to avoid military engagement (not striking the insurgent) if it could risk losing hard won gains (a cooperative farmer who tells the coalition who moves in and out of his fields).

How does this speeding up/slowing down dilemma get solved? In short, it does not. Within the same combat operation, the tempo may fluctuate widely. No one factor has ever dictated the speed of the process, but some have always played a part, such as the priority of the objective, specific ROE, the coalition environment and the urgency of the task at hand. It is this terrain that the targeting professional must understand and navigate. Only then can he or she understand how the speed of the targeting process may proceed. One thing that may help with briskly moving the process along is the availability of Precision Guided Munitions (PGMs). These weapons deliver a certainty of effects their predecessors did not. They are the weapon of choice in nearly all current operations.

4.4.3 High Demand for Precision

It is unclear exactly when the demand for precision reached its present level. Likely, it was sometime in the mid-1990s, post-Desert Storm and during the development of GPS-aided munitions. What is clear is that demand has been steadily building since the Vietnam War, when precision first came into widespread existence. As can be seen from Fig. 4.2, the percentage of PGM use has grown steadily. It must be noted that Vietnam lasted over a decade and the numbers of munitions employed far exceeded some of the shorter operations (such as Deliberate

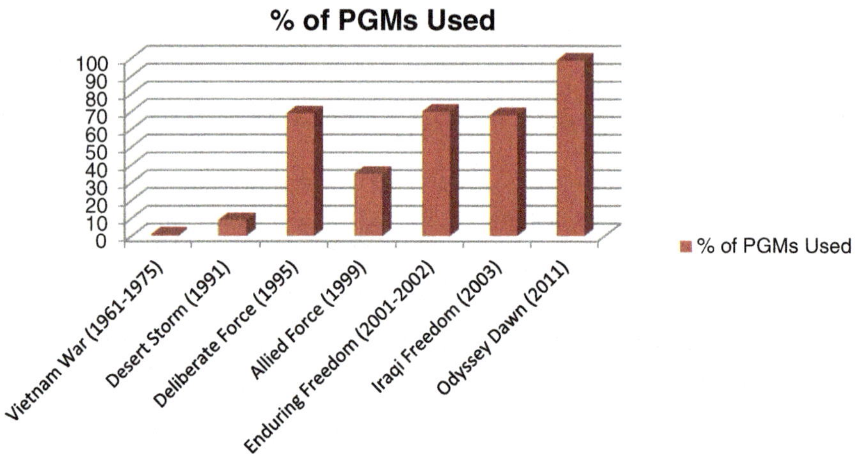

Fig. 4.2 Percentage Use of US and Coalition Air-Delivered Munitions in Operations, 1961–2013 (Sources for the table (Fig. 4.2) were as follows: Vietnam War: Loeb 2002, p. 7; Desert Storm: Lambeth 2000, as quoted by Murray 2007, p. 22; Deliberate Force: Sargent 2000, p. 257; Allied Force: Finn 2001 as quoted by Murray 2007, p. 26. Enduring Freedom: Fact Sheet 2011; Iraqi Freedom: Fact Sheet 2013; Odyssey Dawn: PBS 2013.)

Force).[20] Still, the trend line is undeniable. Further, when one considers the three most recent operations, Odyssey Dawn, Enduring Freedom, and Iraqi Freedom/New Dawn,[21] nearly every munition delivered today by US and NATO forces is a PGM of some sort.[22]

There are noteworthy drawbacks to PGMs. First, they are much more expensive than unguided munitions, especially the more standoff they provide. Second, they require much greater precision intelligence. This in turn demands more training, time, and resources from intelligence professionals. Yet, PGMs remain the munition of choice for three primary reasons: accuracy, economy of force and collateral damage avoidance.

[20]According to Loeb 2002, the US dropped 3.3 Million munitions during Vietnam from 1961–1975. Conversely, NATO dropped 1,026 precision munitions in the 22-day operation, according to Sargent 2000, p. 257.

[21]Operation New Dawn was the name of the operation in Iraq starting on 1 September 2010. Operation Iraqi Freedom officially concluded on 31 August 2010.

[22]Not on the table (Fig. 4.2) is the use of PGMs in the continued operations of Enduring Freedom (after major combat operations concluded, 2002-present) and Iraqi Freedom/New Dawn (after major combat operations concluded, 2003–2011). The author was unable to obtain that number. However, based on his two deployments and service in United States Air Forces Central Command in which he either participated in the planning or was aware of literally hundreds of munition releases from 2004–2013, the author estimates a nearly 100 % use of PGMs. Indeed, he cannot recall a single use of a non-PGM.

Contemporary PGMs have accuracies of single digit meters. Some even have a circular error probable (CEP)[23] of one meter. In combat, they routinely achieve direct hits against very small point targets. A number of GPS-aided weapons, such as the Joint Direct Attack Munition (JDAM), have the added feature of maintaining their high accuracy in bad weather, night, and smoke-obscured conditions. PGMs do not assure destruction nor the correct level of desired neutralization, since the weapon–target interface is a completely different challenge. But they nearly guarantee that the target is likely to be hit, and that makes their use extremely desirable.

With a high level of predictability, PGM employment also provides exceptional economy of force. Economy of force is defined as 'the judicious employment and distribution of forces so as to expend the minimum essential combat power on secondary efforts in order to allocate the maximum possible combat power on primary efforts'.[24] Instead of using four unguided bombs for one target, military forces can use four bombs for four targets with PGMs, depending on target vulnerabilities and damage requirements. More combat power can be applied to more primary efforts while saving munitions. The facts are clear: PGMs enable military planners to go after a greater number of targets with less force, ensuring the 'judicious employment' of forces.

Last, but certainly not least, PGMs assist military forces in avoiding and/or mitigating collateral damage. PGMs are so precise today that a military target can be attacked and heavily damaged while a school across the street remains nearly untouched. Thus, they continue to be a highly attractive option for planners. What PGMs cannot do is to know what type of target they are attacking. A PGM will go where it is directed, whether hitting a terrorist, a tank, an airplane, a non-combatant, a cultural site or a mosque. Indeed, during Allied Force, a PGM struck the target it was aimed at, the Chinese embassy in Belgrade, resulting in widespread international condemnation.[25] This was human error and does not obviate the many advantages PGMs have. After all, the desire to limit collateral damage is another dynamic that demands viable alternatives, such as PGMs.

4.4.4 Avoidance or at Least Mitigation of Collateral Damage

In some respects, the desire to limit collateral damage is as old as warfare itself, one embedded in the ancient idea of chivalry. Yet, the advent of the airplane, and the effects it could produce from the air, inspired the strategic bombing

[23]Circular Error Probable (CEP) is defined as the radius of a circle, centered about the mean, whose boundary is expected to include the landing points of 50 % of the rounds. It's not exactly an average, but rather a predictive tool for military planners based on empirical evidence and testing of the weapon.

[24]JCS, JP 1-02 2013 p. 81.

[25]Clark 2001, pp. 296–297.

philosophies of Giulio Douhet, Hugh Trenchard, and others. In many ways, these cast a blind eye towards limiting collateral damage. Instead, the idea was to inflict intolerable pain on the population, which would rise up and petition the government to bring a swift end to the conflict at hand. World War II signaled the death of this philosophy as a foundational approach, as the argument did not hold up by most measures. In addition, international law soon firmly established the principle of limiting unnecessary pain and suffering.[26]

As PGMs became a mainstay in the arsenals of the US and NATO, avoidance or at least mitigation of collateral damage became a high priority. And so it remains today. One of the key reasons for the elevated attention to collateral damage is the 24/7 globally interconnected world. With a never ending news cycle, any collateral damage event can be broadcast anywhere in the world repeatedly, and even threaten to 'go viral'. An undesirable event is therefore made sensational and its negative attributes amplified. ISAF missteps in Afghanistan are instructive in this regard. Accidental bombing of a wedding or funeral with civilian casualties, and many other similar events, have infuriated the Islamic world and put ISAF goals at risk. Given this environment, there is a discernable need to avoid such attention.

Minimizing collateral damage serves three purposes. First, it enables the attacker to claim a 'moral high ground'. This does not necessarily guarantee support, as both the US and Israel can attest. But what it does is to both limit potential international condemnation and allow the entity avoiding the damage a platform to condemn an indiscriminate opponent. Second, collateral damage avoidance supports proportionality, a key principle of the LOAC. Proportionality prohibits 'Launching an attack which may be expected to cause incidental loss of civilian life, injury to civilians, damage to civilian objects or a combination thereof, which would be excessive in relation to the concrete and direct military advantage anticipated, is prohibited'.[27]

Third, and perhaps most importantly, mitigating collateral damage provides for the possibility of a better peace. Warfare in the modern era demands this, perhaps more than conflicts in the past. Unconditional surrenders do not happen today. A vanquished opponent may fight for years and never give up the fight fully, as seen in Afghanistan and Iraq. The indiscriminate use of force does little to weaken this urge; instead, it may even intensify it. Avoiding and mitigating collateral damage contributes to peace by protecting non-combatants, keeping infrastructure intact, and lessening the enemy's desire to fight perpetual war.

[26]Powers 2013.

[27]Doswald-Beck and Henckaerts 2005, p. 46 (rule 14).

4.4.5 Non-lethal Capabilities, Increasingly Relevant in Today's Targeting Operations

Some of the same reasons for the collateral damage argument explain the increasingly significant role of non-lethal capabilities, which 'generate effects that limit collateral damage, diminish risk to civilians, and may reduce opportunities for adversary propaganda'.[28] Non-lethal operations are equally driven by declining defense budgets. Nearly all Western defense budgets have been cut over the last several years, a trend likely to continue.[29] Non-lethal capabilities do not have the high costs associated with complex weapon systems; indeed they are pennies on the dollar in comparison. When considered together, these advantages make non-lethal operations an attractive targeting option.

The author's experience provides further strength to this assertion. In the late 1990s, planned operations were largely focused on lethal, or kinetic, means. A bomb was the preferred capability in most cases. Non-lethal capabilities, somewhat embryonic at the time, were discussed, but these were only supporting efforts, and insular ones at that. Fast forward to 2013. By this time, planning included far more non-lethal capabilities and in many cases, these were the main operation, with lethal options actually playing a supporting role. Non-lethal options were far more mature, were 'executable' in many scenarios, and had developed a track record, albeit not one entirely well-developed or, for obvious reasons, well known. But these were viable options, and could provide effects on the battlespace that could directly contribute to fulfilling objectives.

Two examples of non-lethal capabilities are Computer Network Attack (CNA) and Military Information Support Operations (MISO).[30] CNA 'disrupts, denies, degrades, or destroys information resident in computers and computer networks (relying on the data stream to execute the attack), or the computers and networks themselves'.[31] An actor, either State or non-State, which can successfully conduct CNA possesses a capability with extensive applicability in the information age against a wide range of actors. The attacker almost always has plausible deniability, does not leave a blood trail, and can do severe damage to financial systems, infrastructure and military networks. And all of this may be done without even leaving the host nation. Perhaps most importantly, modern nation-States, like the US, are highly vulnerable to CNA.

Similar to CNA, MISO can work against a variety of actors as well. It seeks to 'convey selected information and indicators to foreign audiences to influence their emotions, motives, and objective reasoning, and ultimately induce or reinforce

[28]JCS, JP 3-0 2011, p. III-27. See Chap. 10, by Ducheine in this volume.

[29]Apps 2012.

[30]JCS, JP 3-0 2011 pp. III-26-27.

[31]JCS, JP 3-0 2011 p. III-26.

foreign attitudes and behavior favorable to the originator's objectives'.[32] Examples of MISO include print, audio, audiovisual, and electronic media, 'which can then be delivered by air, land, and sea-based means or through cyberspace to select target audiences'.[33] MISO is clearly not targeting in a traditional sense, but resembles it because it selects and prioritizes targets, and then matches an appropriate (MISO) response to them. The response is not a bomb, but perhaps a message sent on Twitter; the goal is to persuade and influence, albeit through a different means. This leads directly into the final dynamic of today's targeting process.

4.4.6 Cognitive Approach as the Bedrock Targeting Principle

Targeting remains a cognitive activity. It seeks to persuade the enemy to move towards your objectives, defeat the adversary's strategy, and find the right coercive means to make this happen.[34] In each of the three cases presented at the beginning of this chapter—the soldier in Afghanistan, planners in Germany preparing for Libyan operations, military strategists in Korea—a cognitive approach was used. If one goes back in time to the first strategic bombing efforts in World War I, the intent was clear: to coerce the enemy to submit to your will. This is evident in any form of targeting, whether deliberate or dynamic, an extended planning period or a compressed one, a counterinsurgency or a major combat operation.

This approach treats the fundamental nature of targeting as a cognitive activity incorporating the ends (the objectives), the ways (defeat the enemy's strategy), and the means (the force necessary to make it happen). In this way, targeting is also the intersection between intelligence, operations, and plans. The ends, ways and means—and the intelligence, operations and plans—must be congruent for mission success. Campaigns have often failed, or been severely at risk of failing, because of mismatches between these areas: unachievable objectives, poorly conceived targeting strategies, or too much or too little force for the task. Conversely, when the objectives are clear and achievable, the targeting strategy exploits the right enemy vulnerabilities, and the correct force, either lethal or non-lethal, is applied. The conditions for success are met.

But targeting efforts are rarely this smooth. The enemy always has a vote. Even if the initial blows are not in his favour, he can recover through denial and deception, persistence, striking blows of his own, etc. The cognitive approach nevertheless remains: developing the right objective focused on the right enemy vulnerability and employing the right force to accomplish it. And it also requires changing the ends, ways, and means as the enemy adapts.

---

[32] JCS, JP 3-0 2011 p. III-27.

[33] JCS, JP 3-0 2011 p. III-27.

[34] Personal interview with J. Glock 8 November 2013.

4.5 Conclusion: The Future of the Targeting Process through the Lens of Robotics

The steps of the targeting process, whether it be the formal six-step deliberate process, the F2T2EA dynamic, or the common four-step process advanced by the author, have survived the test of time because they are descriptive. Irrespective of the technology or type of conflict at hand, these steps are targeting's 'laws of physics'. They are immutable because they must occur in some fashion or form. Additionally, in the near future the dynamics that inform the targeting process addressed above are not likely to change significantly. There is perhaps one significant game-changer which could disrupt the balance of every one of these dynamics—robotics.

Robotics is defined as the 'the branch of technology that deals with the design, construction, operation, and application of robots'.[35] Robots are 'man made devices with three key components: "sensors" that monitor the environment and detect changes in it, "processors" or "artificial intelligence" (AI) that decide how to respond, and "effectors" that act upon the environment in a manner that reflects the decisions, creating some sort of change in the world around a robot'.[36] In the military, robotics can be seen in several broad ways: 'weapons that see, munitions that think, rolling and swimming robots that act autonomously …'.[37] In the targeting sphere, these US and NATO capabilities include: the Joint Direct Attack Munition (JDAM), the Joint Air-to-Surface Standoff Missile (JASSM), and the Tomahawk Land Attack Missile (TLAM). Soon enough, these weapons will be replaced by smarter capabilities with greater standoff range.

So, how will robotics change the equation? Clearly, these and future weapon systems may save lives and deliver decisive results on the battlefield. But they may also change war itself, such that it would become almost unrecognizable. Robotics 'might just make the way we have framed war, and rationalized the killing that takes place in it, fall apart.'[38] As applied to the six dynamics above, a few unnerving questions follow if robotics continues its march towards greater AI, increased precision, less need for human beings in the loop, and more isolation from the actual combat on the ground:

- Does the tension between the art and science of targeting go away, since science will always give the better targeting solution?
- Does the targeting cycle revert to high speed to keep up with robotics, with nothing to slow it down?

---

[35]Oxford Dictionaries 2013.

[36]Singer 2009, p. 67.

[37]Blackmore 2005, p. 9.

[38]Singer 2009, p. 432.

- If there is absolute precision in a nation-States' targeting—every target aimed at can be hit—does that take away the risk of going into war?
- Does an actor cede the responsibility of avoiding collateral damage to its robotics capabilities?
- Does a nation-State employ non-lethal capabilities more freely because its robotics can be more precise in achieving its intended effects?
- Most crucially, is it even necessary for the human being to employ the cognitive approach anymore, since robotics will better determine the ends, ways, and means of a given endeavour?

Any one of these factors could upset the fundamental way actors approach the targeting process. Robotics has had a positive effect on warfare, at least from the US and NATO perspective. It has enabled more precise targeting, less collateral damage, and relentless pressure on the enemy. Yet, it comes with the future risks alluded to above. For now, however, targeting remains focused on influence and coercion, leading one to the inescapable conclusion that it is a cognitive activity. And this cognitive activity, conducted by humans and focused on other humans, drives the current targeting process.

References

Apps P (2012) Western defense budget cuts may be unstoppable. Lux Libertas. http://www.luxlibertas.com/western-defense-budget-cuts-may-be-unstoppable/. Accessed 27 Nov 2013

Blackmore T (2005) War X. University of Toronto Press, Toronto

Chivers C (2011) Vantage point: restraint after dark. New York Times. http://atwar.blogs.nytimes.com/2011/03/02/vantage-point-restraint-after-dark/?_php=true&_type=blogs&_php=true&_type=blogs&_r=1. Accessed 29 March 2014

Clark W (2001) Waging modern war. Public Affairs, New York

Doswald-Beck L, Henckaerts J-M (2005) Customary international humanitarian law, vol I. Cambridge University Press, Rules 2005

Finn C (2001) The broader implications of the increasing use of precision weapons. Royal Air Force Air Power Rev 4(1):35–36

Fontaine S (2011) 17th Air Force chief: Trust growing in Africa. The Air Force Times. http://www.airforcetimes.com/article/20110515/NEWS/105150318/. Accessed 7 Jan 2014

Joffe L (2003) Obituary: Mordechai Hod, Israeli Air Force mastermind behind the six day war. The Guardian. http://www.theguardian.com/news/2003/jul/02/guardianobituaries.israel. Accessed 27 Dec 2013

Lambeth B (2000) The transformation of American air power. Cornell University Press, Ithaca

Loeb V (2002) Bursts of brilliance. Washington Post Magazine, 15 Dec 2002:6–27

Mann E (1995) Thunder and lightning: desert storm and the airpower debates. Air University Press, Maxwell Air Force Base

Murray S (2007) The moral and ethical implications of precision-guided munitions. Air University Press, Maxwell Air Force Base

Myers S (2000) Chinese embassy bombing: a wide net of blame. New York Times. http://www.nytimes.com/2000/04/17/world/chinese-embassy-bombing-a-wide-net-of-blame.html?pagewanted=all&src=pm. Accessed 27 Dec 2013

Oxford Dictionaries (2013) Robotics. http://www.oxforddictionaries.com/definition/english/robotics. Accessed 22 Dec 2013

Powers R (2013) The law of armed conflict. http://usmilitary.about.com/cs/wars/a/loac_2.htm. Accessed 18 Dec 2013

Priest D (2003) The mission: Waging war and keeping peace with America's military. W. W. Norton & Company Inc, New York

Sargent R (2000) Chapter 9: weapons used in deliberate force. In: Owen R (ed) Deliberate force: a case study in effective air campaigning. Air University Press, Maxwell Air Force Base, pp 257–277

Singer P (2009) Wired for war. Penguin Press, New York

Part II
Constraints

Chapter 5
Some Considerations Concerning the Role of the *Ius ad Bellum* in Targeting

Terry D. Gill

Abstract This contribution examines the influence of the *ius ad bellum* upon the targeting process. Specifically, it will examine how the rules of international law relating to the permissibility of the use of force can and do influence the targeting of both objects and persons which constitute military objectives under international humanitarian law and can, alongside other relevant rules and principles of international law and policy considerations, additionally influence the geographical and temporal scope of the targeting process.

Keywords *Ius ad bellum* · *Ius in bello* · Necessity · Proportionality · Immediacy military objective · Neutrality law · Non-intervention · Territorial scope of armed conflict temporal scope of armed conflict

Contents

T.D. Gill (✉)
Military Law, University of Amsterdam & Netherlands Defence Academy, Amsterdam, The Netherlands
e-mail: t.d.gill@uva.nl

P.A.L. Ducheine et al. (eds.), *Targeting: The Challenges of Modern Warfare*,
DOI 10.1007/978-94-6265-072-5_5

5.1 Introduction

The general relationship between the *ius ad bellum* and the *ius in bello* has been discussed extensively in the legal and ethical literature stretching back at least to the writings of Grotius and his immediate predecessors. These two bodies of law have distinct functions, with the *ius ad bellum* determining which reasons and purposes justify the recourse to armed force, while the *ius in bello* is primarily concerned with the actual conduct of hostilities, humane treatment of captured, and incapacitated combatants, and the protection of non-combatants and civilian objects from the effects of war to the maximum extent feasible once force has been resorted to.

The contemporary *ius ad bellum* consists of the prohibition of the use of force in international relations and provides for the recognized exceptions to this prohibition and the legal conditions pertaining to them. These exceptions are the use of force in the context of the UN Collective Security System and the right of self-defence. Any use of force outside national borders must be based on one or both of these recognized legal bases in order for it to be lawful under the UN Charter and customary rules of international law relating to the resort to force. Notwithstanding a certain degree of criticism of their separation and the tendency at times towards conflation of the two as a consequence of real or perceived considerations of morality or expediency, they are generally accepted as constituting distinct legal spheres or regimes, both historically and presently in practice and legal opinion. The separation of the two bodies of law is predicated upon the assumption that while any use of trans-boundary force must have a legal justification, the actual use of force must comply with the rules relating to the conduct of hostilities and humane treatment of persons irrespective of whether force has been lawfully resorted to.[1] This contribution is based on the assumption that the two branches of law are indeed separate, with their own distinct functions, rules, and

[1]The distinction between the *ius ad bellum* and the *ius in bello* can be traced back as far as late Mediaeval and Renaissance legal scholars and moral philosophers. Vitoria and Grotius, for example, argued that both sides in a conflict could believe they had a just cause and that a just war must also be waged with a degree of moderation. See e.g. de Vitoria 1991, pp. 314–326. By the eighteenth century the *ius ad bellum* and the *ius in bello* were viewed as separate bodies of law by such writers as Rousseau and Vattel. Some just war theorists question the morality of the distinction, but by and large most writers (including myself) and treaties accept it as a given. Nevertheless, there are always possible conflations on the basis of either perceived morality or expediency. Examples of such conflation, and in my view misapplication of *ad bellum* considerations, to justify ignoring *in bello* limitations include the arguments raised to justify area bombing of cities in WWII, the misapplication of IHL in relation to the treatment of suspected terrorists and the International Court of Justice's (ICJ's) controversial statement relating to the possible use of nuclear weapons in cases of 'extreme self-defence', after having concluded on the basis of a rather oversimplified reading of IHL that virtually any use of nuclear weapons would be incompatible with IHL. See Advisory Opinion, *Legality of the Use by a State of Nuclear Weapons in Armed Conflict, ICJ Reports* 1996, 66, pp. 262–263.

spheres of application. It does not purport to question or discuss this division at any length. Still less does it question the full applicability of the *ius in bello* (nowadays referred to as international humanitarian law, the law of armed conflict (or simply as IHL/LOAC) to all parties to an armed conflict, irrespective of their justifications for resorting to force under the contemporary *ad bellum* rules contained in the UN Charter and customary international law.

However, separation does not mean that once force is resorted to *ad bellum* considerations cease to influence questions relating to the employment of such force.[2] Aside from the obvious point that any use of force will have to conform to the rules laid down in both regimes or branches of the law to be fully legal under international law, it has been argued, and will be argued here, that *ad bellum* considerations, alongside the rules of humanitarian law, influence the actual employment of force. In particular, it will influence against what (or in some cases whom), where, and when (for how long) force may be employed. Put differently, it will impact upon the targeting process and in many cases pose limitations upon whether a military objective, which could otherwise be lawfully targeted under IHL/LOAC, may in fact be engaged as a consequence of *ad bellum* requirements. It should be pointed out that it is not a question of *ad bellum* considerations overriding or supplanting those of an *in bello* nature, but rather that even if a particular person or object constitutes a lawful military objective under IHL/LOAC, it may nevertheless be unlawful to engage the target under the law governing the use of force. This could be as a result of the scope of a UN mandate to use force for a particular purpose, or because the *ad bellum* self-defence prerequisites of necessity and proportionality restrict or preclude the targeting of a specific military objective or category of potential military objectives, such as leadership targets, industrial installations, or infrastructure, under the prevailing circumstances.[3]

The *ad bellum* conditions that most influence whether a particular military objective may be engaged are necessity, proportionality, and immediacy regarding the permissibility of the use of force. Necessity within the context of the exercise of self-defence relates to whether an armed attack has occurred or is imminent and to the lack of feasible alternatives to the use of force in self-defence. With regard to the exercise of force pursuant to a UN mandate, necessity would relate to the scope of the mandate and whether force is required to carry it out. Proportionality in relation to self-defence concerns the scale of the unlawful attack and what is required to ward off, or if need be, overcome the attack and forestall repetition of attack from the same source in the proximate future. When pertaining to the

[2] One of the (few) writers who has devoted attention to the impact of *ad bellum* considerations on the actual application of force in armed conflict is Greenwood 1983, pp. 221–234; Greenwood 1989, pp. 273–288.

[3] See Greenwood 1989, pp. 275–279, where he lists several of these categories (limitation on the type of target, geographical and temporal limitations) as well as others.

execution of a UN mandate, proportionality relates to whether the force employed is reasonable and necessary in relation to the scope of the mandate without exceeding its terms. Immediacy refers to the duty of a State to undertake defensive measures within a reasonable timeframe, taking all relevant circumstances into account, in order to distinguish defensive measures from punitive reprisals.[4]

In addition to restricting whether a specific target or category of military objectives might be lawfully engaged, *ad bellum* considerations will, alongside factors arising from IHL/LOAC and other relevant areas of international law, impact upon the geographical and temporal scope of where and when targets may be lawfully engaged. In relation to the geographical scope, *ad bellum* issues could limit the targeting of otherwise lawful military objectives under IHL/LOAC *within* the territory of the targeted State, due to the *ad bellum* elements of necessity or proportionality. This could occur in situations where targeting a specific military objective that is geographically removed from where an attack is in progress, would not contribute to warding off, or would be disproportionate in relation to, a relatively small-scale armed attack or imminent threat of such an attack, or one which was otherwise limited and local in scope. It could also limit or preclude the possibility of striking an otherwise lawful military objective on a *third State's* territory, alongside constraints arising from neutrality law and general international law rules, such as respect for territorial sovereignty and non-intervention. In temporal terms, *ad bellum* considerations could limit the time span in which lawful military objectives under IHL/LOAC might be targeted if, for example, other feasible options to using force became available that remove the necessity of continuing to conduct hostilities. This would be the case even if an armistice or ceasefire had not yet been implemented and targeting military objectives would still be lawful viewed from the perspective of IHL/LOAC.

It should be stressed again that the impact of *ad bellum* considerations in no way affects or weakens the equal applicability of IHL/LOAC to all parties to an armed conflict. Consequently, they cannot widen the scope of permissible targets under IHL/LOAC or any other body of the law. In other words, the fact that one party may have an undisputed legal basis to use force, while it is crystal clear that the other is engaged in the unlawful use of force that rises to the level of aggression, will not give the 'defending side' latitude to target persons or objects that may not be lawfully targeted under IHL/LOAC. Nor will the fact that one side has a right to use force under the *ius ad bellum* and the other does not give the defending side the freedom to employ means and methods of combat which are prohibited, or otherwise violate any other rule of IHL/LOAC in relation to either the conduct of hostilities or the treatment of persons. However, it is fair to say that the greater the scale of violation of the *ius ad bellum* by one side, the more latitude the *ius ad bellum* will give the 'defending side' to lawfully employ force to overcome

[4]For definitions of necessity, proportionality and immediacy *ad bellum*, see *inter alia*, Dinstein 2011, pp. 231–234; Gill 2010, pp. 195–197.

the unlawful use of force *within* the scope and confines of IHL/LOAC, including those relating to targeting. In other words, the larger the scale an unlawful attack is, the greater the scope of targeting military objectives under IHL/LOAC will be.

The above-mentioned influence of the *ius ad bellum* upon targeting will be given further consideration and illustration throughout this contribution. In the next section, the impact of *ad bellum* considerations upon the type of persons and objects that may be lawfully be targeted will be discussed. In the third section, the effect of *ad bellum*, and other relevant legal factors, upon the geographical scope of permissible targets will receive attention. In the fourth, the impact of *ad bellum* requirements upon the temporal scope of targeting military objectives will be treated. In the closing fifth section, these will be brought together to show how the two bodies of law form part of an overall system, and some brief consideration will be given to the possibility that policy considerations could pose restraints upon the targeting of lawful military objectives additional to those arising from legal constraints under both the law governing the use of force and the law of armed conflict.

Finally, it should be pointed out that this contribution does not pretend to treat the influence on and relationship between the two bodies of law in depth. It is limited to a brief illustration of a few ways in which the law governing the use of force can influence certain aspects of the targeting process. As such, it is primarily intended as a means to provoke further examination and discussion of this topic. It does not purport to comprehensively deal with, or definitively address, every aspect of the relationship between the two bodies of law, or even how this relationship may affect all parts of the targeting process.

5.2 The Potential Impact of *Ad Bellum* Considerations upon the Nature of the Target or upon Certain Categories of Targets: Who or What May Be Targeted?

Under IHL/LOAC a military objective is defined as a person or object which is not protected and is consequently subject to attack. Objects refer to those things that make an effective contribution to military action based upon their nature, use, purpose, or location, and whose destruction, capture or neutralization would confer a definite military advantage under the prevailing circumstances ruling at the time.[5] This can qualify a wide array of objects as military objectives, such as certain types of 'dual use' industrial and infrastructure targets. Examples that have been targeted frequently in both past and recent armed conflicts include oil storage facilities, electrical power stations and the electrical distribution grid, airfields, port installations, rail lines, communications facilities, and bridges and highways. The question of whether they may be targeted (in principle) under IHL/LOAC is

[5] Additional Protocol I of 1977 [hereinafter API], Article 52(2).

dependent upon the two-pronged test contained in the definition: first, does the object make an effective contribution to military action; and second, would engaging the target confer a definite military advantage. It is generally accepted that the first part of the definition would not automatically render a particular potential target a lawful military objective if it would not confer a definite military advantage.[6] But this is often seen as simply precluding the most obvious potential targets.[7] If, for example a bridge is, has recently been, or is likely to be used for military purposes, it is generally accepted that it would constitute a lawful military objective on the basis of use or purpose simply because its destruction, capture or neutralization would confer at least *some* definite military advantage. At a minimum, it would force the adversary to improvise another route and consequently delay or prevent the movement of its forces to or from a particular location. The fact that the bridge might be far removed from the 'zone of operations' does not rule this out, of course subject to other *in bello* considerations (in particular, the taking of precautions in attack and determining whether it can be attacked without causing excessive injury to civilians or damage to civilian objects in relation to the anticipated military advantage). Likewise certain objects, such as military headquarters, a ministry of Defence or a military installation like a barracks or air or naval base, would almost automatically qualify as military objectives by their nature, subject to the same *in bello* requirements.

With regard to persons, it is generally recognized under IHL/LOAC that any member of an adversary's armed forces who is not *hors de combat* (with the exception of medical and religious personnel) may be lawfully targeted (taking the aforementioned *in bello* conditions into account). In non-international armed conflicts this would, in principle, include members of an organized armed group (with a combat function).[8] In most States, it would also include certain members of the

[6]See ICRC Commentary to Article 52, p. 637. See also ICRC Customary IHL Database, Rule 8 available at http://www.icrc.org/customary-ihl/eng/docs/v1_rul_rule8.

[7]See, e.g. the discussion of targeting of industrial and infrastructure targets in the Desert Storm (Iraq, 1991) and Allied Force (Kosovo, 1999) air campaigns in Rogers 2004, pp. 71–78. For a recent and thorough treatment of targeting within IHL, see Boothby 2012. Dinstein sees certain infrastructure targets such as bridges as military objectives by nature in Dinstein 2004, pp. 92–93. Irrespective of whether one agrees or disagrees with all the positions taken by the authors of any of these works from an IHL perspective, it is worth pointing out (as an observation rather than a criticism) that none of them discuss whether or how *ad bellum* considerations might impact upon targeting. That illustrates how many authorities tend to view targeting exclusively from the perspective of the law of armed conflict.

[8]The ICRC Interpretive Guidance on the Notion of Direct Participation in Hostilities was published by the ICRC in 2009. Melzer 2009. There is a degree of controversy within IHL/LOAC regarding certain positions taken in the ICRC Interpretive Guidance on the Notion of Direct Participation in Hostilities. In particular, the possible restrictions on targeting of individuals on the basis of 'restrictive military necessity' and the targeting of members of armed groups in non-international armed conflicts are debated. I take no position here regarding these controversies as they do not directly relate to the question of whether or how *ad bellum* considerations could impact upon targeting. For examples of critiques, see Watkin 2009–2010, Schmitt 2009–2010, Boothby 2009–2010 and Parks 2009–2010.

government, such as heads of State or government, ministers of defence, and others who played a key role in exercising command over the armed forces in a real sense, rather than in a strictly titular or ceremonial capacity. As such, their elimination or incapacitation would almost always confer some degree of definite military advantage. This would be more than 'potential' or 'indeterminate' in most cases, since it is obvious that degrading the command function of an adversary will almost always confer a definite military advantage, and, in some instances, a very substantial advantage.[9] Consequently, in many, if not all, cases, attacking such objects and persons would be in conformity with IHL/LOAC, provided the other *in bello* prerequisites of precautionary measures and avoidance of excessive harm to civilians and civilian objects were respected.

Now we will turn to how the question of whether and how *ad bellum* considerations could, and in some cases would, influence whether objects and persons could not be lawfully targeted, even though they may constitute lawful military objectives under IHL/LOAC. This will use three possible scenarios as an illustration.

First, suppose the UN Security Council had issued a mandate to use all necessary force for a particular purpose and objective. This could be, for example, the use of force to protect civilians in a particular State from (imminent) threat of attack by that State's armed forces, or by a warring faction within that State. It cannot be ruled out that under certain circumstances attacks on the command and communications function or the logistical system of the force in question would provide a definite military advantage by decreasing the targeted force's capacity to carry out attacks upon the civilian population at some point in the future. As such, striking these functions and capabilities might well qualify as a lawful military objective under IHL/LOAC. But attacking such targets would, in principle, only be permissible under such a mandate if the targeted objects or persons were actually engaged in, or likely and able in the immediate future to engage in, or to provide a direct contribution to, such attacks, or had engaged in systematic attacks upon civilians in the recent past and continued to pose a direct threat of repeated attack in the proximate future. In the absence of credible evidence that any of these situations transpired, striking such targets would not fall within the given mandate and would be unnecessary to achieve the purpose of the mandate even though doing so might contribute to weakening the capacity of the designated force to conduct operations, including potential attacks upon the civilian population at some

[9] In both the Desert Storm (1991) and Iraqi Freedom (2003) aerial campaigns, 'leadership targeting' was engaged in on a systematic basis. This may well be permissible under IHL/LOAC provided the persons targeted are in fact either members of the armed forces or have a real command function over them. This should not be confused with assassination of persons by means of perfidious or treacherous attack which has long been prohibited under the law of armed conflict. See Boothby 2012, pp. 528–529. However, as pointed out above, it may not be permissible from an *ad bellum* perspective. Whether it was allowed in the context of those conflicts falls outside the scope of this contribution and is a determination I leave to the reader to make on the basis of the general considerations put forward here.

unknown and indeterminate point in the future. Consequently, unless there was a clear case of an ongoing, concrete and permanent threat to the lives and safety of the civilian population that could not be averted by other means, engaging such targets would not be permissible under the mandate, even if they were lawful military objectives under IHL/LOAC.

Second, suppose that State A sent troops across a frontier to occupy a relatively small disputed territory that had hitherto been under the jurisdiction of State B. This might be an island or a parcel of land territory, over which there had been a long-standing dispute as to which State actually had the best title to sovereignty. By crossing an international border or demarcation line and taking control of the contested territory, State A would not only be engaging in a violation of the prohibition of the use of force (in this case to resolve a territorial dispute), but also in a localized armed attack. This is because even if one takes the view that an armed attack must be of a significant gravity to trigger the right of self-defence, most States and legal authorities would consider such action as justifying counter force in self-defence to repel the attack and put an end to the (attempted) unlawful occupation of the disputed territory.[10] Hence, State B would have the right to exercise self-defence to achieve the recovery of the contested territory and, if necessary, to prevent renewed attempts by State A to re-enter the territory (the latter would depend upon whether State A continued to take concrete measures to maintain or regain control over the disputed territory once its initial attack had been repelled and actually had the capacity to pose an ongoing threat). State B would therefore have the right to engage in military operations which were necessary and proportionate to regain control and prevent direct threat of repetition.

This would not rule out attacks upon State A's overall military capability, transportation infrastructure (roads, bridges, etc.) and command capability if the war escalated. However, as long as the attack remained localized and relatively limited in scope, such targets would in most cases not constitute necessary objectives in terms of self-defence outside the immediate area in dispute. Moreover, they would likely be disproportionate in relation to the scale of the attack. Therefore, it would not be permissible to strike at these targets, even if their destruction or neutralization would confer a definite military advantage in IHL/LOAC terms and they were military objectives because of their nature, purpose or use. This would certainly

[10]Crossing a border, armistice line or other international demarcation can constitute a violation of the prohibition to use force and forcible attempts to expel the existing administering Power are also generally seen as armed attacks. See UNGA Res, 2625 (XXV) Declaration on Principles of International Law Concerning Friendly Relations and Cooperation Among States in Accordance with the Charter of the United Nations, 24/10/1970: Principle 1 relating to the duty to refrain from the threat or use of force. This was the reason why the forcible attempts to resolve territorial claims by Argentina *vis à vis* the Falklands/Malvinas, by Iraq, with regard to the invasion of Iran and later of Kuwait, and between Ethiopia and Eritrea have consistently been seen as violations of this prohibition and as providing a basis for the exercise of self-defence. See Eritrea-Ethiopia Claims Commission, Partial Award, *jus ad bellum*-Ethiopia's Claims 1–8 (19 December 2005). For a critical appraisal, see Ponti 2009 p. 267.

apply to attacks upon the political and military leadership of State A, or its strategic war-making capacity, such as its industrial installations and its overall military capacity (say its entire air force), unless the war escalated due to a massive response by State A to State B's self-defence actions aimed at regaining the disputed territory. Consequently, the categories of permissible targets would, in part, depend upon the scale of the unlawful attack; as long as the scale was restricted, the category of permissible targets would correspondingly be limited.

Third, suppose a group of State A's nationals (either civilian or military) had been taken hostage by an armed group located in State B, say by the latter crossing the border in a raid, taking them hostage, and removing them to State B's territory. Let us further assume that the armed group (Group X), while not under the direct control or substantial influence of State B, nevertheless operated openly and without hindrance by State B. This might be because of ideological sympathy, political instability inside State B, or the lack of capacity to suppress the group. In any case, there are no concrete indications that State B is in any way involved in the hostage-taking, even though it undertakes no measures to put an end to the situation. After negotiations aimed at ending the illegal situation have failed and with indications that the hostages are in imminent danger of being harmed, State A carries out a rescue operation aimed at freeing the hostages and removing them safely back to its territory.

This would be justified in *ad bellum* terms as a lawful act of self-defence (or for those who do not accept self-defence as a ground for the rescue of nationals, perhaps under the banner of 'state of necessity', or as a separate legal right).[11] Regardless of the legal basis, the conditions of necessity and proportionality *ad bellum* would limit the choice of permissible targets to those that were necessary and proportionate to achieve the purpose of rescue of the hostages. Consequently, neither Group X as a whole, nor State B's military forces would constitute lawful targets unless they intervened, or were clearly likely and capable of intervening, to interfere with the rescue operation. Only if Group X conducted such illegal incursions across the frontier on a regular and systematic basis would it be lawful to treat such a series of actions as a single phased larger scale armed attack. This, in turn, would justify a larger scale response aimed at weakening Group X's ability to continue such attacks, and thereby validate targeting its military capacity as such. Moreover, so long as State B remained outside the conflict, targeting its political leadership, military assets and personnel, and economic and communications infrastructure would in no way contribute to ending Group X's activities. As such, it would either be disproportionate or constitute an unnecessary punitive measure that would likely escalate the situation, and thus impermissible under the law of self-defence, even if some or all such potential targets constituted lawful military objectives under the law of armed conflict.

---

[11] For a treatment of the various views of the legality of rescue of nationals, either within the context of self-defence, or on other possible grounds, see Gill and Ducheine 2010, pp. 217–219 and accompanying notes.

All of the above examples point to the fact that even if certain categories of likely and potential targets constituted lawful military objectives under IHL/LOAC, the targeting of them could violate constraints imposed under the law governing the use of force (i.e., the *ius ad bellum*), taking into account the relevant circumstances. It is clear that if the scope of the use of force is restricted to a particular purpose, it will impact upon the nature of the targets that may be lawfully engaged if such action does not contribute to the achievement of that lawful purpose. Likewise, if the circumstances widen the scope of the permissible use of force, this will correspondingly expand the list of persons and objects constituting lawful military objectives under IHL/LOAC.

5.3 The Impact of *Ad Bellum* Considerations upon the Geographical Scope of Operations: Where May Targets Be Engaged?

We now turn to how *ad bellum* considerations, viewed together with other relevant areas or branches of international law, such as neutrality law and legal principles relating to respect for State sovereignty and non-intervention, can impact upon, and in some cases limit, *where* targeting can take place. The latter bodies of law will receive only passing attention in so far as they directly relate to the *ad bellum* requirements of necessity and proportionality, although they may pose additional constraints in their own right that go beyond the scope of this contribution.

The starting point for this examination is to set out a number of fairly broad issues of a general nature. I will also attempt to illustrate how these would apply in a limited number of potential scenarios. These will serve purely as possibilities and should not be considered as more than illustrative examples.

Our first general issue is related to the examples in the previous section. The smaller the scale of an armed attack, or the more restricted the mandate for using force for a particular purpose or within a specific geographical region, the narrower the geographical scope of targeting is likely to be. A relatively small-scale and localized armed attack will not, as a rule, permit the targeting of persons or objects that are not situated in the area in which the incident occurred, or reasonably proximate to it. An exception would be if there were clear indications that potential targets (say military assets) located outside the area of attack were likely to become directly involved in continuing or expanding the attack, or are being used (or would be used) to resist the lawful use of force in self-defence. Engaging targets which were geographically removed from the 'zone of operations' would not be in conformity with the *ad bellum* considerations of necessity and proportionality, even if such objects or persons might constitute lawful military objectives under IHL/LOAC, unless they were directly supporting military action.[12] The same applies, in principle, to the exercise of a mandate which has been given for a defined purpose, or within a given geographical area. If the mandate, for example, allowed 'all necessary means' to be employed to ensure the safety of civilians or humanitarian relief personnel against direct threats, the geographical scope of using such force as was necessary to implement it would, as a rule, be restricted to the area where the immediate threats manifested themselves. By the same token, if a UN, or UN-mandated, force is authorized to use force in a specifically named geographical region, it follows that, barring exceptional circumstances, the mandate only applies within that region.

Our second consideration of a general nature is that the territory of third States is inviolable, barring exceptional circumstances that would necessitate conducting attacks on targets located there. This flows from the *ad bellum* requirements of necessity and proportionality, as well as (in some cases) neutrality law and/or general principles and rules of international law relating to respect for territorial sovereignty, non-intervention, and other related rules relevant to the circumstances.[13] As a rule, within the context of an international armed conflict, IHL/LOAC applies in the territory of belligerent States and in international sea and airspace to the extent operations are conducted there.[14]

However, this does not always signify that such operations, including in particular targeting, may be conducted anywhere within these confines, much less on a third State's territory, simply because elements of the adversary's armed forces might be present there. If the scale of the conflict is geographically restricted, although hostilities might be intensive within that particular area, attacking targets located well outside the actual 'zone of operations' would likely be both unnecessary and disproportionate in most circumstances and would only exacerbate the conflict. If elements of one belligerent's armed forces were located on a third State's territory, those forces could only be targeted if they provided a direct contribution to military operations involving the conduct of hostilities directed against the other party from that third State's territory. For example, if a State had forces stationed on a third State's territory on the basis of prior agreement, it would be unlawful in the other party to an armed conflict which was taking place elsewhere to target the visiting State's forces unless those forces made a direct contribution to operations where the armed conflict was taking place.

[12]Greenwood 1989, pp. 276–278.

[13]Neutrality law is still valid under the UN Charter, albeit with certain modifications in relation to the duty of neutrals to not violate sanctions imposed under Article 41 of the Charter, and has been systematically relied upon by States since the Charter came into force, both in relation to military action mandated under the Charter to restore international peace and security and in relation to uses of force under the guise of self-defence. Other principles of general international law relating to territorial inviolability, exclusive jurisdiction over a State's territory and non-intervention likewise do not cease to be operative in relation to third States which are not directly involved in an unlawful use of force. For a treatment of neutrality law, see Bothe 2013, p. 549.

[14]See Kleffner 2013, pp. 56–59.

To use a hypothetical example based upon the context of the Vietnam War, US forces stationed in Germany would not have been lawful targets for a North Vietnamese airstrike (NVA) (assuming for the sake of the argument the NVA had possessed the means to conduct such a strike) unless those forces were directly contributing to the ongoing hostilities in South East Asia. This would have been an impermissible expansion of the scope of the conflict in *ad bellum* terms, as well as an attack on a neutral State's territory (Germany was not a party to the Vietnam conflict and was a neutral State in that regard, despite being a member of NATO).

If B52 bombers stationed on US bases in Germany had been used to conduct airstrikes on Vietnam, this would change the situation in our hypothetical example, since they would have directly contributed to operations in the theatre of war. Had Germany permitted the launch of such airstrikes from its territory, it would have forfeited its right to territorial inviolability under neutrality law. Likewise, the targeting of a North Vietnamese warship (or a US warship) in the North Atlantic by the opposing party, unless it had engaged in a hostile act or threatened such action, would not have been permissible, simply because there would have been no necessity to do so from an *ad bellum* perspective. Moreover, carrying out such an attack would have been disproportionate in *ad bellum* terms, despite the fact that such a vessel undoubtedly constitutes a lawful military objective under the law of naval warfare, which is part of IHL/LOAC. Although this point does not relate to respect for third State's territory or neutrality, it does serve as an additional illustration of the geographical restrictions upon targeting that arise from *ad bellum* considerations in a more general sense.

While neutrality law is not applicable in a non-international armed conflict, similar constraints would flow from other principles of general international law, alongside the previously mentioned *ad bellum* requirements of necessity and proportionality. Suppose a significant number of FARC fighters crossed the border into one of the neighbouring countries and buried themselves deep in the Amazonian jungles to escape capture. Assume that they continue with the illegal narcotics trade, but take no further part in the armed conflict in Colombia. Even if they were fugitives from justice inside Colombia and continued to call themselves 'FARC', no military operations by the Colombian armed forces against them would be justified. Only if they continued to mount attacks from their jungle sanctuary and the government of the State where they were located refused to, or was clearly unable to, put an end to such attacks, would a cross-border incursion by the Colombian armed forces targeting the source of the ongoing attack be justified.

A similar situation would arise if indications of some degree of contact and cooperation existed between the FARC and another guerrilla group located in a neighbouring State with a similar ideology and *modus operandi*. In such a circumstance, the Colombian armed forces would only be justified in targeting that second group if that group actually engaged in attacks, or provided direct support for attacks by the FARC that were directed against Colombia, and if no other means to counter that threat were available. This flows not only from the conditions relating to the exercise of self-defence (in particular, the principle of necessity *ad bellum*), but also from principles pertaining to respect for any State's sovereignty, and other rules of general international law.

The logical alternative for Colombia would be to demand remedial action by the State where the guerrilla group was located to halt and prevent further attacks by the 'FARC affiliate'. There is a clear duty of every State to prevent such action being undertaken from its territory. If the State failed to respond appropriately, or was clearly unable to prevent such attacks, this could justify a Colombian incursion targeting the guerrilla group, if and only if, that group was engaged in attacks itself, or provided direct and significant support for the FARC attacks being conducted from the third State's territory.[15] However, at the risk of stating the obvious, this is an *exceptional* situation, and by no means a *carte blanche* to conduct targeting anywhere an adversary's forces might be located, particularly if that happens to be on another State's territory. The fact that the targeting might otherwise conform to all rules governing the conduct of attacks under IHL/LOAC, simply means it does not violate the law of armed conflict. It does not signify that the attack is legal under international law in a broader sense.

In short, the scope of permissible targets can be limited in a geographical sense by the principles of necessity and proportionality *ad bellum* (alongside other relevant legal considerations), whether these are based on the scope and purpose of a mandate to use force for a particular objective or within a given geographical area, or from the right of self-defence. In relation to the latter, it is fair to say that the greater the magnitude of the attack, the wider the geographical scope of conducting self-defence action, including the targeting of lawful military objectives under IHL/LOAC will be, and *vice versa*.

Moreover, the territory of third States is inviolable unless a number of exceptional conditions are met. These include whether the adversary's forces located on a third State's territory actually (continue to) conduct operations constituting participation in ongoing hostilities, initiate a new attack or pose an immediate and manifest threat of a new attack, *and* whether exercising self-defence is the only feasible means available to justify violating another State's sovereignty and repel or forestall further attack from that source.

Even if this is the case, without clear indications that the third State is substantially involved with, or in control of, the force that is operating from its territory, the geographical scope of targets that may be engaged in self-defence will be limited to what is strictly necessary and proportionate (again in *ad bellum* terms)

[15]This duty has been stressed in numerous arbitral awards and judicial decisions including the *Island of Palmas* arbitral award, PCA, 4 April 1928, RIAA, Vol. II, p. 829 at 839; the *Corfu Channel* case, ICJ Rep. 1949, 4, at 32. Necessity as part of self-defence relates to the question whether the State possessing sovereignty over territory where an organized armed group is operating from autonomously in fact possesses the will and means to enforce this duty to preclude its territory being used as a base of operations to conduct attacks upon other States. Only if it fails to uphold this duty, does a necessity of self-defence potentially arise.

to halt such action and forestall repeated attack from the same source in the proximate future.[16] This would preclude engaging the third State's armed forces, or other military objectives other than the adversary's forces within the third State, unless providing direct support to the attack originating from its territory, or likely to resist the exercise of self-defence by the defending State.

Finally, it goes without saying that only persons and objects that constitute lawful military objectives under IHL/LOAC can be lawfully targeted within the above-mentioned restrictions of an *ad bellum* nature (including other relevant bodies of international law referred to previously). This is because the law of armed conflict is part of a broader legal system of which it forms only one component, albeit an important one. That legal system includes the law governing the use of force, rules relating to respect for State sovereignty and non-intervention, and, where relevant, neutrality law. This general conclusion applies across the board regarding the scope of permissible targeting, but has particular relevance to the geographical scope of targeting.

5.4 The Impact of *Ad Bellum* Considerations upon the Temporal Scope of Permissible Targeting: When May Targets Be Lawfully Engaged?

The law regulating the use of force (*ius ad bellum)* not only has influence on the type and location of targets that may be engaged, it also can impact on when (or how long) targeting may be carried out. There are no strictly defined temporal limits to the applicability of the law of armed conflict. As a rule, it applies in the context of an international armed conflict until one side is completely defeated, an armistice is concluded, or a general close of hostilities occurs. In relation to a non-international armed conflict, it generally remains applicable until a peace agreement is concluded, one side is defeated, or the qualitative threshold for the existence of an armed conflict is no longer met in terms of organization and intensity or duration, of the hostilities between the parties.[17]

However, these temporal limits on the applicability of IHL/LOAC must be seen in combination with other relevant legal factors, particularly those arising from the law governing the use of force. These considerations will, in principle, only pertain to trans-boundary uses of force, since the *ius ad bellum* has no direct bearing on uses of force that take place wholly within the confines of a State. While, in some cases, the Security Council may take action relating to wholly internal conflicts that have no spillover effects beyond a particular State, this latter point will not receive attention here as it is unlikely to have any significant impact on the

[16] Ducheine and Pouw 2012 p. 40.

[17] Kleffner 2013, pp. 60–70.

temporal scope of targeting under the *ius ad bellum*, beyond stating the obvious fact that if a ceasefire is implemented between warring factions, targeting may not occur thereafter, unless one side violates the terms of the agreement. This, however, is not related to the *ius ad bellum,* but to the fact that a ceasefire ends the right to engage in hostilities. In contrast, *ad bellum* requirements can impact upon the scope of permissible targeting as it pertains to trans-boundary force. This could occur in a number of situations, including where no ceasefire or armistice has come into force and no general close of hostilities has been otherwise acknowledged. We will have a look at how the *ad bellum* criteria can influence this aspect of targeting using several illustrative examples.[18]

The first and perhaps most important point to bear in mind is that any use of force in the context of self-defence is premised upon the principle of necessity. This means that self-defence is only permissible as long as an armed attack is either in progress or is clearly imminent and there are no other feasible alternatives to the taking of action in self-defence to halt the attack or forestall repeated attack in the reasonably proximate future. Hence, once the necessity to exercise self-defence ceases, there is no longer any right to target military objectives, even if doing so would be completely in conformity with IHL/LOAC. This applies to the existence of an armed attack, or a clear and unequivocal threat of attack in the reasonably proximate future, as well as to the existence of feasible alternatives to exercising self-defence. The latter could consist of adequate measures of law enforcement to forestall attacks by organized armed groups operating across an international border in situations where self-defence is invoked against attacks conducted by an autonomous armed group.[19] It could also take the form of negotiations leading to a peaceful resolution of the conflict, or it could entail any other non-forceful alternative which adequately terminates the need to resort to force.

The second consideration is that the scale of the attack, or series of attacks, will usually influence the temporal scope of permissible measures in self-defence. Just as this is the case with the other two categories addressed previously (what may be targeted and where may targeting take place), the smaller the scale of the armed attack, the shorter the scope of permissible self-defence action normally will be, and *vice versa*. This is linked to the first point relating to the existence of necessity to take action. It is evident that a small-scale armed attack will necessitate action to thwart the attack that normally will be limited in duration to a short period. This works the other way around as well. A large-scale invasion will necessitate a substantial armed response in the form of a war of self-defence—a war that, depending on the relative strength of the adversaries, could last months or even years until the parties conclude or accept an armistice, or hostilities cease. During that period, the targeting of military objectives under IHL/LOAC would likewise be lawful under the law regulating the use of force in self-defence.

[18]Greenwood 1989, pp. 275–276; Dinstein 2011, p. 232. For a fuller treatment of how long self-defence remains operative, see Gill 2015, pp. 737–751.

[19]Gill et al. 2013.

A third and final factor is the principle of immediacy, in the sense that an act of self-defence must be carried out within a reasonable timeframe following an armed attack, taking all relevant circumstances into account. These can include allowing for sufficient time to determine the author of the attack when this is not clear; deploying forces to the area under attack, or, in some cases, diplomatic contacts aimed at resolving the situation; and awaiting action by third States to assist in the exercise of self-defence. The key point is that action in self-defence must not be unduly delayed beyond what is reasonable under the circumstances. Action taken within this reasonable timeframe would be lawful, while action taken outside it would not.

A few examples will suffice to illustrate these considerations. In border skirmishes, aerial or naval incidents, and the like, self-defence will be limited in duration to repelling the attack, or clear threat of repeated attack, in the immediate future. There are many instances of such clashes, or potential threats of such clashes, in past and recent practice. Examples range from the situation on the Indian/Pakistan 'line of control' in Kashmir, through the Middle East, to the recurrent armed incidents between North and South Sudan. Likewise, the various disputes between China and its neighbours relating to sovereignty over islands and maritime space surrounding them could very possibly lead to such incidents. To the extent armed incidents occur, the scope of the right of self-defence is limited temporally to what is required under the circumstances to address the specific localized attack. Even if there are a series of such incidents spread over an extended period of time, it is not normally necessary to treat them as a single ongoing attack, rather than as discrete incidents, unless they are closely connected temporally and geographically and have the same author (e.g., the recurring incidents on the Indo-Pakistani 'line of control' in Kashmir are considered to constitute separate incidents and not one ongoing armed conflict). Consequently, the scope for permissible targeting will be correspondingly limited as well.

By contrast, larger scale unlawful uses of force, in the form of a closely related series of attacks by the same source over a period of time or a single large-scale use of force, will allow for a longer resort to force in self-defence, including obviously, the targeting of the attacking party's military objectives. The two World Wars, the Korean War, the Iran–Iraq War (1989), and the Desert Shield/Storm Kuwait conflict (1990–1991) are examples of hostilities conducted (partly) on the basis of self-defence over a longer period of time ranging from weeks to years. One area of controversy is whether the ongoing use of force by the US in self-defence against various armed groups sharing a common ideology and *modus operandi* in the Middle East and the Horn of Africa over a period of more than a decade remains a lawful response. The answer to this depends to a large extent on whether one sees this as a single act of self-defence in relation to the initial attack of '9-11' against the same actor, as a series of separate responses to ongoing and/or discrete threats, or, in some cases, as an overextension of reliance upon self-defence. However, that would require a separate chapter, if not an entire book, and cannot be answered here.

5.5 Concluding Remarks

Our examination of the impact of the *ius ad bellum* upon targeting leads us to a number of conclusions. First, while the determination of who or what constitutes a lawful military objective and the manner in which targeting must be conducted is wholly a matter which falls within IHL/LOAC in so far as that body of law is applicable, the question of whether the targeting may take place is not regulated exclusively by that body of the law. Other legal considerations that affect targeting include those of the law governing the use of force (*ius ad bellum*) and, in some cases, additional relevant legal rules and principles. These factors must equally be taken into account in determining whether specific types of targets may be attacked, where targeting may take place, and when and how long targeting is permissible, in addition to whether they constitute lawful military objectives under IHL/LOAC.

These requirements will generally be factored in at the strategic level of operations, but it would be a mistake for an 'operator' to conclude that they are wholly outside his/her realm of attention. It is quite possible that such considerations can impact targeting at the operational and even the tactical level. It would therefore be a mistake, and one with potentially far-reaching consequences, for military personnel involved in the planning and conduct of operations to be unaware of the influence of *ad bellum* requirements upon targeting and, where necessary, to (proactively) factor such considerations into the targeting process. This applies to virtually all levels of command and all branches of the armed forces, whether engaged in land, aerial, or naval operations. At the least, they must be aware of why there may be compelling legal reasons for not engaging certain targets on the basis of their nature, location or due to geographical or temporal constraints on permissible targeting that would otherwise constitute a lawful military objective in strictly IHL/LOAC terms. Consequently, not only policy-makers and senior officials, but all levels of command must be sensitive to of *ad bellum* influences upon the targeting process and must receive clear instructions on how these can affect what may be targeted and where and when targeting is permissible.

Second, it should also be pointed out that policy (and operational) considerations may act as an additional restraint above what the law (both *ad bellum* and *in bello*) strictly requires. That is, after all, the whole point of issuing Rules of Engagement, which often go well beyond what is required in a strictly legal sense in terms of restricting or prohibiting targeting.[20] A clear example of how such policy considerations affected targeting issues was in the Korean War. Chinese 'volunteers' massively intervened in the conflict. This led to the ensuing dispute between the UN Commander, General Mac Arthur and President Truman as to whether targets located in China, such as bridges and access routes in Manchuria should be attacked. While these could have been lawfully targeted from both an *ad*

[20]See Boddens Hosang on the influence of ROE upon targeting, Chap. 8 in this volume.

bellum and *in bello* perspective, considering the scale of the intervention and the potential targets' use and contribution to military action, it was deemed (rightly by most) unwise to do so from a policy perspective, in view of the very likely repercussions this could have had.[21]

Finally, it must be stressed again that international law is not just a collection of rules pertaining to one particular body or branch of it, or a collection of sets of rules in different legal 'boxes' which operate in isolation. It forms an interlocking system of rights and obligations, all of which must be taken into account, in particular when an activity such as targeting of persons or objects is concerned. Any use of force is subject to a whole range of legal (and other) considerations, including those discussed here.

References

Boothby WH (2012) The law of targeting. Oxford University Press, Oxford

Boothby WH (2009–2010) And for such time as: the time dimension to direct participation in hostilities. New York Univ J Int Law Policy 42:741–768

Bothe M (2013) The law of neutrality. In: Fleck D (ed) The handbook of international humanitarian law, 3rd edn. Oxford University Press, Oxford

Dinstein Y (2004) The conduct of hostilities under the law of international armed conflict. Cambridge University Press, Cambridge

Dinstein Y (2011) War, aggression and self-defence, 5th edn. Cambridge University Press, Cambridge

Ducheine PAL, Pouw EH (2012) Legitimizing the use of force: legal bases for Operation Enduring Freedom and ISAF. In: van der Meulen J, Vogelaar A, Beeres R, Soeters J (eds) Mission Uruzgan: collaborating in multiple coalitions for Afghanistan. Amsterdam University Press, Amsterdam, Chap. 3, pp. 33–46

Gill T (2010) Legal basis of the right of self-defence under the UN Charter and under customary international law. In: Gill T, Fleck D (eds) The handbook of the international law of military operations. Oxford University Press, Oxford

Gill T (2015) When does self-defence end? In: Weller M, Solomou A (eds) The Oxford handbook of the use of force in international law. Oxford University Press, Oxford

Gill T, Ducheine P (2010) Rescue of nationals. In: Gill T, Fleck D (eds) The handbook of the international law of military operations. Oxford University Press, Oxford

Gill TD, Ducheine PAL, F.H. Boddens Hosang JFH, Marchand C (2013) Report on the role of self-defence in multinational operations. In: Horvat S, Benatar M (eds) Recueil international society for military law and the law of war, Congress proceedings of the 19th international congress on the 'Legal Interoperability and Ensuring Observance of the Law Applicable in Multinational Deployments', Brussels, pp. 121–171

Greenwood C (1983) The relationship of the *ius ad bellum* and the *ius in bello*. Rev Int Stud 9:221–234

Greenwood C (1989) Self-defence and the conduct of international armed conflict. In: Dinstein Y (ed) International law at a time of perplexity: essays in honour of Shabtai Rosenne. Martinus Nijhoff Publishers, The Hague

[21]This led to General Mac Arthur being relieved of his command by President Truman. For an account, see Manchester 1978, p. 751.

Kleffner J (2013) Scope of application of international humanitarian law. In: Fleck D (ed) The handbook of international humanitarian law, 3rd edn. Oxford University Press, Oxford
Manchester W (1978) American Caesar: Douglas Mac Arthur 1880–1964. Dell Publishers, paperback edn
Melzer N (2009) Interpretive guidance on the notion of direct participation in hostilities under international humanitarian law, ICRC, Geneva. http://www.icrc.org/eng/assets/files/other/icrc-002-0990.pdf. Accessed 27 Jan 2014
Parks H (2009–2010) Part IX of the ICRC direct participation in hostilities study: no mandate, no expertise, and legally incorrect. New York Univ J Int Law Policy 42:769–830
Ponti C (2009) The Eritrea-Ethiopia Claims Commission on the threat or use of force and individual self-defence. In: de Guttry A, Post HHG, Venturini G (eds) The 1998–2000 war between Eritrea and Ethiopia: an international legal perspective. T.M.C. Asser Press, The Hague, pp 267–276
Rogers APV (2004) Law on the battlefield, 2nd edn. Manchester University Press, Manchester
Schmitt N (2009–2010) Deconstructing direct participation in hostilities: the constitutive elements. New York Univ J Int Law Policy 42:697–740
de Vitoria F (1991). *De Jure Belli* Reprinted. In: Pagden A, Lawrence J (eds) Vitoria political writings. Cambridge University Press, Cambridge
Watkin K (2009–2010) Opportunity lost: organized armed groups and the ICRC direct participation in hostilities interpretive guidance. New York Univ J Int Law Policy 42:641–696

Chapter 6
The Law of Targeting

Michael N. Schmitt and Eric Widmar

Abstract The law of targeting rests at the heart of modern warfare, as well as contemporary controversies over such matters as drones and autonomous weapons. While the weaponry and tactics of targeting continue to evolve with unprecedented advances in technology and innovation, the fundamental principles of targeting law will remain binding rules for the foreseeable future. This chapter examines the law governing who or what is a lawful target, which weapons are permissible, what precautions must be taken prior to an attack, how operations are limited by potential collateral damage and where targeting may take place. A firm understanding of these norms will enable military forces to carry out their missions effectively while minimizing harm to civilians, civilian property and other protected persons and objects.

Keywords Targeting · Proportionality · Means and methods · Direct participation in hostilities · Protected persons · Military object · Collateral damage · Weapons · Law of armed conflict · International humanitarian law

Contents

M.N. Schmitt (✉) · E. Widmar
Stockton Center, United States Naval War College, Newport, USA; Exeter Law School
e-mail: M.Schmitt@exeter.ac.uk; schmitt@aya.yale.edu

E. Widmar
e-mail: eric.w.widmar.mil@mail.mil

P.A.L. Ducheine et al. (eds.), *Targeting: The Challenges of Modern Warfare*,
DOI 10.1007/978-94-6265-072-5_6

6.1 Introduction

The law of targeting lies at the heart of the law of armed conflict (LOAC). It takes the form of treaty law binding on States party to the treaty or customary law, which is a unique type of international law that binds all States regardless of whether they are party to the treaty. Customary law emerges over time through a combination of State practice and *opinio juris* (the belief of States that they are engaging in an action or refraining from one out of legal obligation).[1] Much of the contemporary law of targeting is captured in the 1977 Additional Protocol I to the Geneva Conventions.[2] As of March 2014, 173 States were party to the instrument and are therefore bound directly by its terms.[3] Certain key States, most notably the United States and Israel, are not party thereto.[4] However, these and other non-party States consider most of the treaty's targeting provisions as reflective of customary international law.[5] Except as indicated, the references to AP I set forth in this chapter replicate accepted rules of customary law and therefore apply to targeting operations regardless of whether the State is a party to AP I.[6]

LOAC, also known as international humanitarian law (IHL) or the *jus in bello,* must be distinguished from the *jus ad bellum.* Whereas the latter addresses when States may resort to force (e.g., pursuant to a Security Council Resolution, consent or in self- or collective defence), the former governs how hostilities may be conducted during an armed conflict. They are entirely separate legal regimes. By the 'rule of equal application', LOAC applies to all sides of an armed conflict. Thus, even a State that finds itself embroiled in an armed conflict because it has been unlawfully attacked under the *jus ad bellum* by another State must comply fully with LOAC's dictates. Further, LOAC applies irrespective of the medium of conflict in which the targeting occurs, be it land, sea, air, space or cyberspace.[7] The key is to determine whether an 'armed conflict' exists as a matter of law, for such a conflict is a necessary condition for the applicability of LOAC targeting rules;

---

[1]Statute of the International Court of Justice, June 26, 1945, 59 Stat. 1055, 3 Bevans 1179, 33 UNTS 993, Article 38(1)(b); *Case Concerning the Continental Shelf* (Libyan Arab Jamahiriya v. Malta), 1985 ICJ 13 (June 3), paras 27, 34.

[2]Hereinafter AP I.

[3]International Committee for the Red Cross 2012, pp. 553–556.

[4]Other States not party to Additional Protocol I include Turkey, Iran, Pakistan, India, and Indonesia.

[5]See, e.g., Matheson 1987, p. 419 (also stating provisions the US does not consider customary). The authors will use the United Kingdom's *Manual of the Law of Armed Conflict* and the United States' *Commander's Handbook on the Law of Naval Operations* to illustrate guidance provided by States to their military forces by a party and non-party State respectively. UK Manual 2004; US Commander's Handbook 2007.

[6]See, e.g., Customary International Humanitarian Law Study; UK Manual, § 1.33.1; AMW Manual, commentary accompanying rule 1(s), para 4; Tallinn Manual, p. 6.

[7]AP I, Article 49(3); AMW Manual, p. xiv; Tallinn Manual, rule 20.

absent an armed conflict, international human rights law and domestic law govern any application of force.[8]

There are two forms of armed conflict to which different aspects of international humanitarian law apply—international armed conflict (IAC) between two or more States and non-international armed conflict (NIAC) between a State and an organized armed group or between multiple organized armed groups. Although AP I applies only to the former, most of its targeting rules are seen as expressing customary norms that equally control targeting during the latter.[9] Therefore, except as otherwise noted, the discussion of targeting law that follows applies to both international and non-international armed conflict.

In the language of LOAC, targeting is known as 'attack', which is defined as an act of 'violence against the adversary, whether in offence or defence'.[10] Despite the reference to 'adversary', attack is also understood as an act of violence against protected persons, objects and places. Reduced to essentials, international humanitarian law addresses five key aspects of attack: (1) target; (2) weapon; (3) execution of the attack; (4) collateral damage and incidental injury; and (5) location. The legality of an engagement depends on full compliance with the rules falling into each category. This chapter will address them serially.

6.2 Target

The keystone to the law of targeting is the principle of distinction. Recognized by the International Court of Justice as one of two 'cardinal' principles of international humanitarian law,[11] it has been codified in Article 48 of AP I:

> In order to ensure respect for and protection of the civilian population and civilian objects, the Parties to the conflict shall at all times distinguish between the civilian population and combatants and between civilian objects and military objectives and accordingly shall direct their operations only against military objectives.[12]

The fundamental principle of distinction, which is found in an array of specific LOAC rules discussed below, applies to all targeting operations. If, how and when those rules apply depends on whether a person or an object is being attacked.

---

[8]See Pouw 2013; Gill and Fleck 2010, Chap. 4 for a treatise on the subject.

[9]See generally, Customary International Humanitarian Law Study.

[10]AP I, Article 49(1).

[11]*Legality of the Threat of Use of Nuclear Weapons*, Advisory Opinion, 1996 ICJ 226 (July 8), para 78. The other is the prohibition on causing combatants 'unnecessary suffering'.

[12]See also Customary International Humanitarian Law Study, rule 1; UK Manual, §§ 15.8–15.9; US Commander's Handbook, § 5.3.2; OPLAW Handbook, p. 13.

6.2.1 Persons

LOAC affords certain categories of persons and the activities in which they engage special protection from attack. These include medical,[13] religious,[14] civil defence,[15] humanitarian relief personnel,[16] and civilian journalists performing professional functions.[17] However, the fulcrum of protection for persons is the principle of distinction between combatants and civilians cited above.

Article 51(2) of AP I operationalizes the principle with respect to persons: '[t]he civilian population as such, as well as individual civilians, shall not be the object of attack. Acts or threats of violence the primary purpose of which is to spread terror among the civilian population are prohibited'. A civilian is defined in the negative as 'any person who does not belong to one of the categories of persons referred to in Article 4 A(1), (2), (3) and (6) of the [1949] Third [Geneva] Convention and in Article 43 of this Protocol.'[18] These provisions have been the subject of significant controversy and confusion since their adoption, in part because Article 4 addresses prisoner of war status, not status for the sake of targeting. However, civilians are best understood as individuals who are not members of the 'armed forces' and who therefore enjoy protection from direct attack.

At the risk of oversimplification, the armed forces consist of two groups: traditional combatants and members of organized armed groups. The term 'combatants' refers to three types of individuals. First, members of the regular armed forces qualify as combatants.[19] For example, during the IAC in Iraq (Iraqi Freedom, 2003), members of the uniformed armed forces of Iraq and of all the Coalition States qualified as combatants on this basis. This category includes members of a paramilitary or armed law enforcement agency that has been incorporated into the armed forces.[20]

Second, members of militias or volunteer corps that 'belong to' a party to the conflict also qualify as combatants when they: (1) wear a fixed distinctive sign recognizable at a distance, (2) carry their arms openly, (3) abide by the laws of war,

---

[13]Convention (I) for the Amelioration of the Condition of the Wounded and Sick in the Armed Forces in the Field, Aug. 12, 1949, 75 UNTS 31[hereinafter GC I], Articles 24–26; Convention (II) for the Amelioration of the Condition of the Wounded, Sick, and Shipwrecked Members of Armed Forces at Sea, Aug. 12, 1949, 75 UNTS 85, [hereinafter GC II] Article 36; AP I, Article 15; Customary International Humanitarian Law Study, rule 25; US Commander's Handbook, § 8.10.2.1.

[14]AP I, Article 15; Customary International Humanitarian Law Study, rule 27; US Commander's Handbook, § 8.10.2.1.

[15]AP I, Articles 62, 67.

[16]AP I, Article 71(2); Customary International Humanitarian Law Study, rule 31.

[17]AP I, Article 79; Customary International Humanitarian Law Study, rule 34.

[18]AP I, Article 50(1); See also Customary International Humanitarian Law Study, rule 5.

[19]GC I, Article 13; GC III, Article 4A(1); Customary International Humanitarian Law Study, rule 3.

[20]AP I, Article 43(3).

and (4) operate under responsible command.[21] On the modern battlefield, few groups comply with all four criteria. For example, the Fedayeen Saddam, an Iraqi militia that took part in the fighting during the initial stages of the 2003 invasion of Iraq (Iraqi Freedom), generally carried their arms openly and were widely regarded as being under the responsible command of Saddam Hussein's eldest son Uday. Soon after the conflict began, they shed their uniforms to adopt irregular tactics against Coalition forces. Additionally, members of the group regularly violated LOAC by intermingling with and attacking civilians. Thus, they did not qualify as combatants in the legal sense.[22]

Third, the category of combatants includes members of a *levee en masse*. A *levee en masse* consists of '[i]nhabitants of a non-occupied territory, who on the approach of the enemy spontaneously take up arms to resist the invading forces, without having had time to form themselves into regular armed units, provided they carry arms openly and respect the laws and customs of war'.[23] Members of a *levee en masse* enjoy the benefits of combatant status, including combatant immunity and prisoner of war status upon capture, but are also subject to attack on the same basis as other combatants.

Combatants may be attacked based solely on their status; the extent of their involvement in the hostilities is irrelevant. There are several exceptions to this rule. In particular, it is unlawful to attack combatants *hors de combat*, that is, combatants who are wounded, sick, or shipwrecked; have unequivocally surrendered; have been captured; have parachuted from a disabled aircraft; or enjoy protected status, such as medical and religious personnel.[24]

Consensus has emerged in the past decade as to a second group of individuals who do not qualify as civilians *for the purpose of targeting*; members of 'organized armed groups'. To be considered 'organized', a group must be sufficiently structured to engage in military activities as a unit, albeit not to the extent of the regular armed forces.[25] Furthermore, to be 'armed', the purpose of the group must be to engage in hostilities. As an example, the Afghan Taliban maintains a tiered organization, loosely based upon tribal traditions, that enables Mullah Mohammad Omar and the Supreme Taliban Shura to exercise centralized decision-making and broadly direct decentralized execution through regional, local and village Taliban cells.[26] The Afghan Taliban's purpose is to expel anti-Taliban forces through vio-

---

[21]GC III, Article 4(A)(2).

[22]Note that sporadic violations by members of the group do not deprive other group members of their status as combatants. Additionally, an individual violation does not deprive the individual concerned of combatant status, although he or she may be prosecuted if the violation constitutes a war crime.

[23]GC III, Article 4(A)(6).

[24]GC I, Articles 24–25; AP I, Article 41; Customary International Humanitarian Law Study, rules 25, 87; US Commander's Handbook, §§ 8.2.3, 8.2.3.1, 8.2.4.1–8.2.4.2; UK Manual, §§ 5.6–5.7; AMW Manual, rules 15(b), 71.

[25]ICRC Interpretive Guidance, p. 32.

[26]Afsar, Samples and Wood 2008, pp. 64–68.

lence and regain its pre-9/11 status.[27] Thus, the Taliban qualifies as an organized armed group.

The lawfulness of targeting specific members of an organized armed group is the subject of on-going debate. According to the ICRC, treatment as a member of an organized armed group for targeting purposes depends on whether the individual has a 'continuous combat function' within the group.[28] Essentially, this means that the individual performs activities for the group that would amount to direct participation in hostilities (see below). Unlike individuals who do not belong to an organized armed group but directly participate, members of an organized armed group with a continuous combat function may be targeted even when they are not so participating because they are treated as analogous to members of the armed forces, rather than as civilians who are directly participating in hostilities.

While there is widespread consensus that members of an organized armed group with a continuous combat function are susceptible to direct attack at any time, some commentators take a broader approach by which all members may be targeted irrespective of their function in the group.[29] They argue that limiting attacks to members with a continuous combat function would create disequilibrium in the law because combatants, as described above, are targetable regardless of the role they play in their unit. Since the law recognizes protections for members of regular armed forces, such as their right to prisoner of war status and combatant immunity, it would seem incongruent to afford these combatants less protection from attack than similarly situated members of an organized armed group.

Some groups are composed of distinct military, political, and social wings, such as Hamas in the Gaza Strip and Hezbollah in Lebanon. Only members of the military component may be treated as members of an organized armed group for targeting purposes. Other members may be targeted pursuant to the rules regarding the targeting of civilians who directly participate in the hostilities set forth below. When a group does not have distinct wings, as in the case of the Afghan Taliban, the fact that members of the group may occasionally engage in activities that do not involve hostilities, such as performing judicial functions, does not deprive the group of its character as armed.

As noted above, civilians enjoy protection from attack pursuant to the principle of distinction. Those civilians who 'directly participate in hostilities' lose this protection 'for such time' as they so participate.[30] The International Committee of the Red Cross conducted a five-year project to elucidate the direct participation standard that culminated in its 2009 publication of the *Interpretive Guidance on the*

---

[27] Ibid., at pp. 64–65; See also Mapping Military Organizations.

[28] ICRC Interpretive Guidance, pp. 33–35.

[29] See generally the 42nd volume of the New York University Journal of International Law and Politics 2010.

[30] AP I, Article 51(3); AP II, Article 13(3); Customary International Humanitarian Law Study, rule 6; UK Manual, §§ 5.3.2–5.3.3; US Commander's Handbook, § 8.2.2.

Notion of Direct Participation in Hostilities under International Humanitarian Law.[31] In an approach that has been widely accepted, it suggested that acts of direct participation consist of three cumulative constitutive elements. First, the act in question 'must be likely to adversely affect the military operations or military capacity of a party to an armed conflict or, alternatively, to inflict death, injury, or destruction on persons or objects protected against direct attack.'[32] Second, there must be a direct causal connection between the act and the harm likely to result, or the act must be an integral part of a coordinated military operation that causes the harm.[33] Lastly, the act must have a belligerent nexus in the sense of being related to the ongoing conflict.[34]

Some activities clearly satisfy these criteria. There is broad agreement, for instance, that civilians who personally conduct attacks, such as those who emplace improvised explosive devices or snipe at passing convoys, are directly participating in the hostilities and are thus subject to attack. Additionally, civilians who directly support engagements, like those providing early warning for an impending ambush or transporting fighters to and from an attack, are also direct participants.[35]

The more difficult cases involve civilians who provide support without being directly involved in engagements. For instance, the *Interpretive Guidance* asserts that civilians who assemble and store an improvised explosive device, or those who purchase and transport components necessary for such weapons, do not lose their protected status and cannot be considered direct participants on the basis that causation is not direct enough.[36] Other international experts strongly disagree.[37] Such 'close cases' will have to be resolved on a case-by-case basis.

A notably controversial direct participation issue is the status of human shields. It is one of particular significance in light of the asymmetric tactics adopted by insurgents in Iraq, Afghanistan, Gaza and elsewhere. Facing overwhelming firepower, insurgents regularly shelter military objectives and activities through the use of involuntary and voluntary shields. The practical issue is not whether the human shields may be directly attacked; doing so would generally serve no military purpose. Instead, it is whether any expected harm to them during an attack on the military objective or activities they are shielding has to be factored into the proportionality and precautions in attack analysis (discussed below). If they are direct participants, such collateral damage can be ignored when performing the assessment; if not, it must be considered by the attacker.

[31] ICRC Interpretive Guidance.

[32] Ibid., at p. 47.

[33] Ibid., at p. 51.

[34] Ibid., at p. 58.

[35] Ibid., at pp. 54, 66.

[36] Ibid., at pp. 53–54 ('In the present context, direct causation should be understood as meaning that the harm in question must be brought about in one causal step.').

[37] Ibid., at p. 53, note 123. See e.g., Schmitt 2013a, p. 104.

While it sometimes may be tactically difficult to determine whether a human shield is participating voluntarily or involuntarily, legal understanding of the issue has developed along this fault line. Most experts agree that involuntary human shields do not lose their protected civilian status, and therefore any expected harm to them must be taken into account by attackers.[38] However, disagreement surrounds the treatment of voluntary human shields in the targeting decision. The *Interpretive Guidance* contends that they directly participate in hostilities only when creating a 'physical obstacle to military operations of a party to the conflict', as when they 'attempt to give physical cover to fighting personnel supported by them or to inhibit the movement of opposing infantry troops.'[39] Some experts counter that voluntary shields have willingly forfeited their protected status and do not count towards the proportionality assessment or factor into the requirement to take precautions in attack.[40] Another view adopts a middle ground approach and argues that while voluntary shields retain their protected status, their voluntary participation 'reduces the weight to be accorded to them' in the proportionality assessment.[41] Regardless of the position adopted, it is clear that the more remote a civilian's actions are from the actual hostilities, the more tenuous the argument that he or she has lost protected status and is subject to attack.

A further controversy surrounds the 'for such time' aspect of the direct participation rule. The *Interpretive Guidance* avers that participation begins with 'measures preparatory to the execution of a specific act of direct participation in hostilities, as well as the deployment to and the return from the location of its execution.'[42] For instance, a civilian who implants an IED is directly participating in hostilities while he travels to the location, buries the weapon, and returns home, in other words, throughout the course of the specific operation. At most other times, according to the *Guidance*, he is immune from attack. Many legal experts counter that the concept of 'for such time' includes all periods during which a definitive causal link to hostilities exists,[43] such that, for example, the acquisition and storage of improvised explosive device components, as well as the building of such devices for imminent use, would be considered sufficiently direct to allow those involved to be attacked while engaging in the activities.

The status of an individual can sometimes be unclear. When this is the case, LOAC requires the person in question to be treated as a civilian.[44] Note, however, that the mere existence of some doubt is insufficient to preclude attack on the basis that the individual is presumed civilian; after all, doubt is a persistent and

[38]See, e.g., Boothby 2012, p. 139.

[39]ICRC Interpretive Guidance, p. 56.

[40]Dinstein 2010, p. 153; US Commander's Handbook, § 8.3.2 (stating voluntary human shields 'may be excluded from the proportionality analysis').

[41]Boothby 2012, p. 139.

[42]ICRC Interpretive Guidance, pp. 65–68.

[43]Dinstein 2010, p. 148.

[44]AP I, Article 50(1); UK Manual, § 5.3.1; AMW Manual, rule 12; Tallinn Manual, rule 33.

pervasive factor in combat. Rather, the degree of doubt must be at a level that would cause a reasonable attacker in the same or similar circumstances to question the status of the individual. Thus, when General John Allen, former commander of International Security Forces-Afghanistan (COMISAF), reissued the COMISAF Tactical Directive and directed all coalition forces to 'presume that every Afghan is a civilian until otherwise apparent,'[45] he was reiterating a presumption that had long been ensconced in international law.[46]

LOAC's treatment of the status of persons during a NIAC is analogous to that in an IAC. Although the notion of combatancy is technically limited to the latter, LOAC does not prohibit the status-based targeting of a State's security forces or dissident armed forces during a NIAC. As to the targeting of members of an organized armed groups and civilians directly participating in hostilities,[47] the same rules generally apply—and the same disagreements appear—as in the case of IACs.

6.2.2 Objects

Article 52(1) of Additional Protocol I prohibits attacking civilian objects. The provision characterizes civilian objects as those that are not military objectives.[48] Article 52(2) defines the latter as 'objects which by their nature, location, purpose, or use, make an effective contribution to military action and whose total or partial destruction, capture or neutralization, in the circumstances ruling at the time, offers a definite military advantage'.[49] The prohibition and attendant definition are viewed by the United States and other non-parties to the treaty as reflective of customary international law.[50] If there is a question as to whether an object that is 'normally dedicated to civilian purposes, such as a place of worship, a house or other dwelling, or a school', is being used for military purposes, and thus subject

---

[45]Headquarters, ISAF-Afghanistan (2011b) COMISAF's Tactical Directive, p. 2.

[46]AP I, Article 50(1).

[47]Protocol Additional to the Geneva Conventions of August 12, 1949, and Relating to the Protection of Victims of Non-international Armed Conflicts, June 8, 1977, 1125 UNTS 609, Article 13.3 [hereinafter AP II].

[48]See also Customary International Humanitarian Law Study, rule 9. UK Manual, § 5.24.1; US Commander's Handbook, § 8.3.

[49]This is in accordance with other treaties and is seen to be reflective of customary international law. See, e.g., Protocol on Prohibitions or Restrictions on the Use of Mines, Booby-Traps and Other Devices (CCW Protocol II) (As Amended on 3 May 1996), 10 October 1980, Article 2(6) [hereinafter Amended CCW Protocol II on Booby-Traps]; Customary International Humanitarian Law Study, rule 8.

[50]US Commander's Handbook, § 8.2; 2013 OPLAW Handbook 2013, p. 22; AMW Manual, commentary accompanying rule 1(y), para 1; Tallinn Manual commentary accompanying rule 38, para 1.

to targeting, a presumption that the object retains its protected civilian status attaches until facts on the ground indicate otherwise.[51]

There are two cumulative criteria that must be satisfied before targeting an object; (1) it must make an 'effective contribution' to the adversary's military action; and (2) attacking the object must offer a 'definite military advantage'. The 'effective contribution' made by the object to the adversary's military action need not be critical or even significant, but it must in fact contribute to the enemy's military action.[52] At the same time, the military advantage that the attacker accrues from the engagement must be 'definite' in the sense that it may not be merely 'potential or indeterminate'.[53]

An object may make an effective contribution through its 'nature, location, purpose, or use'.[54] The 'nature' of a military objective refers to its 'inherent characteristic or attribute which contributes to military action.'[55] For example, tanks, artillery pieces, warships, submarines, fighter jets, military barracks, and ammunition depots are valid military objectives because they inherently make an effective contribution to military action.[56]

'Location' relates to 'selected areas that have special importance to military operations,'[57] regardless of how those areas are currently being used. For example, certain ancillary passes connected to the Khost-Gardez Pass in Afghanistan are well-known smuggling routes for the Haqqani network.[58] Assuming for the sake of analysis that the Haqqani network is a component of the same organized armed group led by the Afghan Taliban in the Afghanistan NIAC, targeting such passes in order to block or degrade their usefulness would be permissible based upon the location.[59]

---

[51]AP I, Article 52(3); UK Manual, § 5.24.3; AMW Manual commentary accompanying rule 22(d), paras 3–4.

[52]AMW Manual, commentary accompanying rule 1(y), para 4. See also US Commander's Handbook, § 8.9.1.

[53]Sandoz et al. 1987, para 2024.

[54]AP I, Article 52(2).

[55]AMW Manual, commentary accompanying rule 22(a), para 1. See also Sandoz et al. 1987, para 2020; Dinstein 2010, p. 96.

[56]Sandoz et al. 1987, para 2020; OPLAW Handbook 2013, p. 23. See also Dinstein 2010, pp. 96–97.

[57]AMW Manual commentary accompanying rule 22(b); Sandoz et al. 1987, para 2021.

[58]Afghan and Coalition Forces Disrupt Haqqani Operations in K-G Pass (Aug. 15, 2010). ISAF News. http://www.isaf.nato.int/article/isaf-releases/afghan-and-coalition-forces-disrupt-haqqani-operations-in-k-g-pass.html. Accessed 27 March 2014.

[59]The Haqqani network joined the Taliban in the 1990 s and its leader, Jalaludin Haqqani, was a member of the Supreme Taliban Shura. See generally Mapping Militant Organizations. The Haqqani network continues to receive orders from Mullah Mohammed Omar, the Taliban leader. S. Khan, The Afghan Taliban says it supports Haqqani, not Pakistan. (Sept. 29, 2011). CNN. http://www.cnn.com/2011/09/29/world/asia/afghanistan-taliban/. Accessed 26 March 2014.

'Purpose' denotes the intended future use of an object.[60] The criterion acknowledges that it is unnecessary for the attacker to wait until a civilian object is actually being used for military purposes before striking it. An object's purpose may be deducible using various forms of intelligence, such as observation with intelligence, surveillance and reconnaissance (ISR) assets (manned or unmanned), human intelligence or signals intelligence. However, when the intended future use of an object is not perfectly clear, the attacker must act reasonably given the information available at the time of the strike.[61] For example, in the Khost-Gardez Pass, it was common for insurgents travelling between Pakistan and Afghanistan to use specific small shelters along well-established mountain trails as safe-houses to store equipment, food, and other items necessary to make the mountain crossing by foot.[62] Provided an attacker has reliable and timely information that such shelters will be used by insurgents in the future for the same purposes, it would be permissible to target them in order to disrupt or degrade insurgent transportation routes.

Lastly, 'use' refers to how an object is currently being employed.[63] The criterion applies in the case of civilian objects that are being employed for military purposes during the period of use. It is important to note that a civilian object becomes a military objective regardless of the extent of military usage. Damage to distinct civilian components of the target must be considered in the proportionality and precautions in attack analyses and may therefore preclude attack on either or both of those bases, but the object nevertheless qualifies as a military objective once it is converted to military use, however slight.

The category of military objective by use is especially relevant on the contemporary battlefield because non-State actors often use civilian objects, such as residences, religious sites, hospitals, and schools, to support military operations. For instance, uninhabited residences in Afghanistan regularly serve as production factories for homemade explosives (HME).[64] It should be cautioned that insurgents frequently change locations to avoid detection by Coalition and Afghan forces. A residence used as an HME production factory remains a valid military objective

---

[60]Sandoz et al. 1987, para 2022.

[61]AMW Manual commentary accompanying rule 22(c), para 3.

[62]Author's personal experience as the senior legal adviser for a Joint Special Operations Task force in Afghanistan between 2010 and 2012.

[63]Sandoz et al. 1987, para 2022; UK Manual, § 5.4.4; OPLAW Handbook 2013, p. 23; AMW Manual commentary accompanying rule 22(d), para 3; Tallinn Manual commentary accompanying rule 38, para 8.

[64]ISAF Joint Command–Afghanistan Press Release (2010). In the author's own experience as the senior legal adviser for a Joint Special Operations Task Force he was regularly called upon to eliminate such factories. M. Mashal, Afghanistan's IED complex: inside the Taliban bombmaking industry (2 January 2013). Time World, http://world.time.com/2013/01/02/afghanistans-ied-complex-inside-the-taliban-bomb-making-industry/. Accessed 27 March 2014.

only for as long as it is so used. Once the materials and activities are moved, the residence regains protected civilian status and may not be targeted.[65]

There is universal agreement that war-fighting and war-supporting objects can qualify as military objectives on one of these four bases. A war-fighting object is one used for combat; such objects are typically military in nature and therefore almost always constitute military objectives. War-supporting objects are those used to directly buttress the war effort, as in the case of a facility used to produce improvised explosive devices. However, controversy surrounds whether so-called 'war-sustaining' objects are lawful military objectives, with the United States, and few other countries, taking the position that they do. The *U.S. Commander's Handbook on the Law of Naval Operations* defines war-sustaining objects as 'economic objects of the enemy that indirectly but effectively support and sustain the enemy's war-fighting capability.'[66] Supporters of this approach would, for instance, take the position that it is lawful to target the Afghan poppy crop because of the substantial funding the Afghan Taliban derives from opium production and trade.[67] However, most international legal experts would disagree because of the remoteness of the connection between those activities and military action.[68]

Certain types of military objectives are subject to either specific rules or merit particular care in application of the general rules. In the maritime environment, enemy warships are valid military objectives by nature and may be targeted subject to normal precautions in attack (discussed below).[69] Additionally, enemy and neutral merchant vessels may be targeted if they make an effective contribution to the enemy's military effort by their purpose or use and if targeting them yields a definite military advantage.[70] Conduct which renders them liable to attack includes being incorporated into an enemy's intelligence system, sailing under convoy of enemy warships, laying mines, minesweeping, cutting undersea cables, attacking friendly merchant ships, and acting as an auxiliary.[71] Additionally, enemy merchant vessels may be targeted if they refuse an order to stop or actively

[65]See e.g., UK Manual § 5.4.4(h) (providing a similar example of a divisional headquarters using a textile factory for operations, thus making the textile factory subject to attack, but only for so long as the headquarters remains present in the factory. If not, the textile factory would regain its protected status and not subject to lawful attack).

[66]US Commander's Handbook, § 8.2.5. See also AMW Manual commentary accompanying rule 24.

[67]See generally Peters 2009 (documenting how the Afghan opium trade supports the Taliban war-effort).

[68]See generally Schmitt 2009.

[69]UK Manual § 13.44; US Commander's Handbook, § 8.2.5; San Remo Manual, paras 65–66.

[70]UK Manual, §§ 13.40, 13.47; US Commander's Handbook, §§ 7.5.1–7.5.2, 8.6.2.2; San Remo Manual, para 40.

[71]UK Manual, § 13.5(d); San Remo Manual, para 13(h). (An auxiliary ship is a 'vessel, other than a warship, that is owned by or under the exclusive control of the armed forces of a State and used for the time being on government non-commercial service.'). See also, US Commander's Handbook, § 2.3.1.

resist visit, search or capture.[72] Neutral merchant vessels may be targeted, after prior warning, if they intentionally and clearly refuse to stop or actively resist visit, search or capture; however, the attacker must first have a reasonable belief the neutral merchant vessel is carrying contraband or attempting to breach a blockade.[73]

Military objectives in cyberspace can include computers, computer networks, and other tangible components of cyber infrastructure so long as they meet the definition set forth above.[74] Controversy exists over whether data *per se* can qualify as an object given its intangible characteristics.[75] However, it is clear that cyber infrastructure and other cyber related objects can be attacked by destroying, altering, or manipulating data; in such cases, the infrastructure constitutes the object of attack, not the data, and an assessment of whether the target qualifies as a military objective is made based upon the military use or nature of the infrastructure and objects. Additionally, military and civilian users often share computers, computer networks, and cyber infrastructure. As with other dual-use objects, such use for military purposes renders them military objectives.[76] When conducting attacks on dual-use cyber infrastructure, the attacker must of course take into account the principle of proportionality and the requirement to take precautions in attack (discussed below), a particular challenge in cyberspace.

In aerial warfare, military aircraft may be targeted based upon their nature, unless being used as a medical aircraft.[77] Non-military aircraft, except civilian airliners, may be targeted if they engage in activities that make an effective contribution to military action, such as conducting attacks, being integrated into the enemy's intelligence efforts, or providing troop or materiel transportation.[78] Additionally, non-military aircraft that fail to comply with the orders of military authorities for landing, inspection, and possible capture, or resist interception, may also be deemed military objectives.[79]

---

[72]San Remo Manual, para 60(e); US Commander's Handbook § 8.6.2.2.

[73]UK Manual, § 13.47; US Commander's Handbook, § 7.10; San Remo Manual, para 67(a).

[74]AP I, Article 52(2); Sandoz et al. 1987, paras 2007–2008; Tallinn Manual commentary accompanying rule 38, paras 3–10.

[75]Tallinn Manual commentary accompanying rule 38, para 5.

[76]Regulations Respecting the Laws and Customs of War on Land, annexed to Convention No. IV Respecting the Laws and Customs of War on Land, Oct. 18, 1907, 36 Stat. 2227, Article 27 [hereinafter Hague Regulations] (protecting civilian buildings 'provided they are not being used at the time for military purposes.'); Sandoz et al. 1987, para 2022; Tallinn Manual commentary accompanying rule 39, paras 1–3.

[77]AMW Manual commentary accompanying rule 1(u), para 4. A medical aircraft is 'any aircraft permanently or temporarily assigned—by the competent authorities of a Belligerent Party—exclusively to aerial transportation or treatment of wounded, sick, or shipwrecked persons, and/or the transport of medical personnel and medical equipment or supplies.' AMW Manual, rule 1(u).

[78]UK Manual, §§ 12.36–12.37; US Commander's Handbook, § 8.8; San Remo Manual, para 63; AMW Manual, rule 27(a)–(c).

[79]UK Manual, §§ 12.36–12.37; US Commander's Handbook, § 8.8; San Remo Manual, para 62(e); AMW Manual, rule 27(d)–(e).

Civilian airliners and aircraft granted safe conduct are subject to special legal requirements.[80] A civilian airliner that is being used for military purposes such as reconnaissance or transport of troops may only be targeted if: (1) diversion for landing, inspection and possible capture is not feasible; (2) no other method for exercising military control is available; (3) the actions that render the civilian airliner a military objective are sufficiently grave to justify an attack; (4) all feasible precautions have been taken[81]; (5) the strike will not violate the principle of proportionality, meaning the expected collateral damage will not be excessive in relation to the military advantage anticipated[82]; and (6) a warning has been issued whenever circumstances permit.[83] Aircraft granted safe conduct may be targeted if they violate the terms of agreement permitting that safe conduct or intentionally hamper movements of combatants, subject to these six requirements.[84]

Finally, a range of specific objects and facilities enjoy special protection under treaty or customary LOAC (or both) and may not be attacked unless they become military objectives. These include medical facilities and units[85]; areas specially established as civilian protective zones and for the care of wounded and sick[86]; humanitarian relief facilities, supplies and transports[87]; peacekeeping equipment and facilities[88]; cultural property[89]; works and installations containing dangerous forces, such as dams, dykes and nuclear electrical generating stations[90]; the natural

[80]UK Manual, § 12.7; AMW Manual, rule 1(i); Civilian airliner is defined as 'a civilian aircraft identifiable as such and engaged in carrying civilian passengers in scheduled or non-scheduled service.' Aircraft may be granted safe conduct by agreement between belligerent parties. UK Manual, § 12.28; US Commander's Handbook, § 8.6.3; AMW Manual, rule 64.

[81]AP I, Article 57; Customary International Humanitarian Law Study, rule 15.

[82]AP I, Article 51(5)(b) & 57(2)(a)(iii); Customary International Humanitarian Law Study, rule 14.

[83]AP I, Article 57(2)(a)(iii)(c); Customary International Humanitarian Law Study, Rule 20; UK Manual, § 12.32; San Remo Manual, para 57; AMW Manual, rules 68(a)–(d), 70.

[84]UK Manual § 12.30; San Remo Manual, para 55(c); AMW Manual, rule 65(a)(i).

[85]GC I, Article 19; AP I, Articles 12, 21–24; AP II, Article 11; Customary International Humanitarian Law Study, rules 28–29.

[86]GC I, Article 20; Convention (IV) Relative to the Protection of Civilian Persons in Time of War, Aug. 12, 1949, 75 UNTS 287, Articles 14–15 [hereinafter GC IV]; AP I, Article 60; Customary International Humanitarian Law Study, rule 36.

[87]GC IV, Articles 55, 59; AP I, Articles 69–70; AP II, Article 18(2); Customary International Humanitarian Law Study, rule 32.

[88]Convention on the Safety of the United Nations and Associated Personnel, 9 December 1994, 2051 UNTS 363, Article 7; Customary International Humanitarian Law Study, rule 33.

[89]Convention for the Protection of Cultural Property in the Event of Armed Conflict, 14 May 1954, 249 UNTS 240; Second Protocol to the Hague Convention of 1954 for the Protection of Cultural Property in the Event of Armed Conflict, 26 March 1999, 2253 UNTS 212; AP I, Article 53; AP II, Article 16; Customary International Humanitarian Law Study, rule 38.

[90]AP I, Article 56; Customary International Humanitarian Law Study, rule 42. The US does not consider this article to reflect customary international law. See Matheson 1987, pp. 419, 427.

environment[91]; and objects indispensable to the survival of the civilian population, such as food and drinking water supplies.[92]

6.3 Weapons

Even when a lawful military objective is the intended target, attacks using certain weapons are prohibited, a point confirmed in the Regulations annexed to the 1907 Hague Convention IV: 'the right of belligerents to adopt means of injuring the enemy is not unlimited'.[93] A number of the prohibitions apply to weapons generally. For example, Article 35(2) of Additional Protocol I prohibits the employment of weapons calculated or of a nature to cause superfluous injury or unnecessary suffering. A projectile containing fragments that cannot be detected using x-ray would, for instance, qualify on the basis that they complicate medical treatment when the same disabling or lethal effect can be achieved using metal fragments.[94]

A second general prohibition is that on the use of indiscriminate weapons (as distinct from the indiscriminate use of discriminate weapons).[95] Weapons that are incapable of being directed at a specific military objective are inherently indiscriminate and their use is accordingly prohibited.[96] The commonly cited historical example is the V-2 rocket employed by Germany in World War II. Its aiming mechanism was so inaccurate that any attempt to use it to attack a particular military objective, including large objectives such as military installations, would likely fail; successful attack was essentially the product of luck.

Weapons are also unlawfully indiscriminate if their effects cannot be controlled.[97] The paradigmatic examples are biological contagions or persistent airborne chemical agents that can easily spread to civilian populations, even if properly aimed at military objectives. In more modern times, particular types of malware in cyberspace may, by their very design, be either unable to discriminate

[91] AP I, Articles 35(3), 55. The US does not consider these articles to reflect customary international law. See Matheson 1987, p. 424. Customary International Humanitarian Law Study, rules 43–45.

[92] AP I, Article 54; AP II, Article 14; Customary International Humanitarian Law Study, rule 54.

[93] Hague Regulations, Article 22.

[94] Protocol on Non-Detectable Fragments (CCW Protocol I), 10 October 1980, 1342 UNTS 168; Customary International Humanitarian Law Study, rule 79; NIAC Manual, para 2.2.2; AMW Manual Commentary accompanying rule 5(b), paras 1, 3.

[95] The International Court of Justice has labelled the prohibition on indiscriminate weapons as one of two 'cardinal' principles, the other being the principle of unnecessary suffering. Nuclear Weapons Advisory Opinion, *supra* note 11, para 78.

[96] AP I, Article 51(4); Customary International Humanitarian Law Study, rule 12; UK Manual, § 6.4; US Commander's Handbook, § 9.1.2; AMW Manual, rule 5(a); Tallinn Manual, rule 43.

[97] AP I, Article 51(4); UK Manual, § 6.4; AMW Manual, rule 5(a); Tallinn Manual, rule 43.

between military and civilian cyber targets or have uncontrollable effects.[98] In most cases, however, such weapons would not be indiscriminate *per se* because they could be introduced into closed military networks.

Specific international treaties have prohibited particular weapons or restricted their use. These include poison,[99] explosive bullets,[100] expanding bullets,[101] biological and chemical weapons,[102] anti-personnel land mines,[103] booby-traps,[104] incendiary weapons,[105] blinding lasers,[106] cluster munitions,[107] naval mines,[108]

---

[98]Schmitt 2010, p. 256.

[99]Hague Regulations, Article 23(a); Protocol for the Prohibition of the Use in War of Asphyxiating, Poisonous or Other Gases, and of Bacteriological Methods of Warfare, 17 June 1925, 26 UST 571.

[100]St. Petersburg Declaration Renouncing the Use, in Time of War, of Explosive Projectiles Under 400 Grammes Weight, 19 November/11 December 1868, 18 Martens Nouveau Recueil (ser. 1) 474 (prohibiting the use of projectiles weighing below 400 grammes that are either explosive or charge with fulminating or inflammable substances).

[101]Hague Declaration (IV, 3) Concerning Expanding Bullets, 1899 (prohibiting the use of 'bullets which expand or flatten easily in the human body'). Note that the prohibition relates to use during armed conflict. Many States use such rounds for law enforcement purposes because of their significant stopping power. See Dinstein 2010, p. 70.

[102]Protocol for the Prohibition of the Use in War of Asphyxiating, Poisonous or Other Gases, and of Bacteriological Methods of Warfare, 17 June 1925, 26 UST 571; Convention on the Prohibition of the Development, Production, Stockpiling and Use of Chemical Weapons and on Their Destruction, 13 January 1993, 1974 UNTS 45; Convention on the Prohibition of the Development, Production and Stockpiling of Bacteriological (Biological) and Toxin Weapons and on Their Destruction, 10 April 1972, 1015 UNTS 163.

[103]Protocol II on Prohibitions or Restrictions on the Use of Mines, Booby-Traps and Other Devices, 10 October 1980 [hereinafter CCW Protocol II on Booby-Traps]; Amended CCW Protocol II on Booby-Traps, *supra* note 49; Convention on the Prohibition of the Use, Stockpiling, Production and Transfer of Anti-Personnel Mines and on their Destruction, 18 September 1997, 2056 U.N.T.S. 211.

[104]Amended CCW Protocol II on Booby-Traps, *supra* note 49. For a detailed explanation of the definition of booby- traps and the intricacies of international law concerning them, see UK Manual §§ 6.7–6.7.9; US Commander's Handbook, § 9.6.

[105]Protocol on Prohibitions or Restrictions on the Use of Incendiary Weapons, 10 October 1980, 1342 UNTS 171 [hereinafter CCW Protocol III on Incendiary Weapons].

[106]Protocol IV to the Convention on Conventional Weapons, Protocol on Blinding Laser Weapons, 13 October 1980.
Protocol on Blinding Laser Weapons (CCW Protocol IV), 13 October 1995, 1380 UNTS 370 (prohibits the use and transfer of laser weapons 'specifically designed, as their sole combat function or as one of their combat functions, to cause permanent blindness to unenhanced vision, that is to the naked eye or to the eye with corrective eyesight devices.')

[107]Dublin Convention on Cluster Munitions (opened for signature 3 December 2009), 48 ILM 357, 358 (2009).

[108]Convention No. VIII relative to the Laying of Automatic Submarine Contact Mines, 18 October 1907, 36 Stat. 2332, Articles 1(1)–(2) [hereinafter Hague Convention VIII]; UK Manual, §§ 13.52–13.64; US Commander's Handbook, §§ 9.2.2–9.2.3.

and torpedoes.[109] States party to the respective instruments are bound by their prohibitions and restrictions. Moreover, many of the provisions are now viewed as reflective of customary law, and as such, bind even non-parties.[110]

6.4 Execution of the Attack

Assuming a target qualifies as a military objective and the weapon used is lawful, an attacker (which in LOAC includes those who plan, approve or execute attacks), must nevertheless take 'constant care ... to spare the civilian population, civilians, and civilian objects'.[111] This general obligation, known as the requirement to take precautions in attack, is operationalized in a number of specific rules.

Before turning to those rules, a cautionary note is in order. LOAC only requires the taking of precautions that are feasible.[112] Feasibility is generally understood as referring to steps that are 'practicable or practically possible, taking into account all circumstances prevailing at the time, including humanitarian and military considerations'.[113] The ICRC *Commentary* sagely points out that what is practicable or practically possible entails 'common sense and good faith'.[114] Fundamentally, the 'feasible' standard requires attackers to take those measures to avoid civilian harm that a reasonable attacker would in the same or similar circumstances—based upon information 'reasonably available [to the commander] at the relevant time and place.'[115] In making the feasibility assessment, commanders may take into account military considerations, like risk to friendly forces, the availability of weapon systems, or other operational demands for surveillance resources, such as unmanned aerial vehicles.

---

[109]Hague Convention VIII, *supra* note 108, Article 1(3); UK Manual, § 13.51; US Commander's Handbook, § 9.4.

[110]Customary International Humanitarian Law Study, rules 72–74, 77–86.

[111]AP I, Article 57(1); Customary International Humanitarian Law Study, rule 15; UK Manual, § 5.32; US Commander's Handbook, § 8.3.1; Tallinn Manual, rule 52.

[112]AP I, Articles 57(2)(a)(i) & (ii).

[113]UK Reservation (b) to AP I, available at http://www.icrc.org/applic/ihl/ihl.nsf/Notification.xsp?action=openDocument&documentId=0A9E03F0F2EE757CC1256402003FB6D2 (last visited 18 March 2014) and repeated in Customary International Humanitarian Law Study, rule 15; CCW Protocol II on Booby-traps, *supra* note 49, Article 3(4); CCW Protocol III on Incendiary Weapons, *supra* note 105, Article 1(5); and, Amended CCW Protocol II on Booby-Traps, *supra* note 49, Article 3(10); Sandoz et al. 1987, para 2198.

[114]Sandoz et al. 1987, para 2198.

[115]UK Additional Protocol Ratification Statement, para (c); US Understanding Statement, para (1)(A) to CCW; US Commander's Handbook, § 8.3.1; Tallinn Manual, rule 38; AMW Manual commentary accompanying rule 1(q), para 3.

In terms of specific precautions in attack requirements, those who plan or approve attacks are obligated to 'do everything feasible to verify that the objectives to be attacked are neither civilians nor civilian objects … [or] subject to special protection …'.[116] For instance, the loiter capability and sophisticated sensor suite of unmanned aerial systems has significantly enhanced the capability of States fielding them to verify target status. As noted, however, the requirement to use them for this purpose is framed by the feasibility condition. In some cases, sufficient verification by other methodologies can render it operationally unwise to place them at risk of being downed. In others, higher priorities for employment elsewhere may make their use unfeasible operationally.

The level of certainty necessary for target identification is unsettled. Some observers demand near absolute certainty by positing a requirement that an attacker seek additional information even if there is a 'slight doubt' as to the status of a target.[117] However, the reality of contemporary combat—particularly in counterinsurgency operations—makes attainment of such a standard impractical. A more workable standard that is consistent with the concept of feasibility asks whether a reasonable attacker, having employed all reasonably available means of verification under the circumstances, would initiate the attack.

Attackers are also required to take feasible precautions in the choice of means (weapons) and methods (tactics) of attack in order to minimize 'incidental loss of civilian life, injury to civilians and damage to civilian objects'.[118] However, they need only select less harmful means or methods that do not involve sacrificing military advantage and that are feasible. As an example, an attacker does not have to use a less powerful bomb against an insurgent leader in a building in order to avoid civilian casualties if doing so would significantly lower the likelihood of success (assuming all other LOAC requirements are met).

Of particular note in this regard are precision weapons. The decision to employ a specific weapon system in a situation is highly contextual; categorical declarations that precision weapons must be used are simply incorrect. For instance, although precision weapons may be available for an operation, they may be more useful at later stages of the campaign and thus need to be preserved, or the employment of a precision weapon may be infeasible because it would require increased risk to ground forces in order to designate a target. Additionally, other systems may also avoid civilian harm without sacrificing military advantage. As an example, carbon filament bombs can be used to interrupt electricity with far less collateral damage than regular bombs, while cyber operations are especially useful in avoiding collateral damage.

---

[116] AP I, Article 57(2)(a)(i); Customary International Humanitarian Law Study, rule 16.

[117] See, e.g., Sandoz et al. 1987, para 2195.

[118] AP I, Article 57(2)(a)(ii); Customary International Humanitarian Law Study, rule 17; UK Manual, § 5.32.4; AMW Manual, rule 32(b); OPLAW Handbook 2013, p. 26; Tallinn Manual, rule 54.

Attackers are also required to use tactics or methods of attack, that will minimize the collateral damage, taking into account the risk to friendly forces. For instance, use of a 'tactical callout' became commonplace in Iraq and Afghanistan.[119] Once a compound was surrounded and secured, soldiers would call out the occupants and ask them to leave the premise. The occupants would then be separated and tactically questioned to identify who else was present in the compound.[120] Once a commander was reasonably certain based upon tactical questioning, any available overhead surveillance, and other sources of intelligence that civilians were on longer present in the compound (or were not going to leave and the attack would nevertheless be proportionate), he could launch the attack. It must be emphasized that tactical callout was possible only because resources were readily available and it was feasible to take such measures. An attacker without such assets and who reasonably concluded such actions were not feasible would not be required to engage in the tactic.

Beyond weapons and tactics choice, attackers must consider the full range of targets that, if attacked, would yield the same or similar military advantage. When options are available, the attacker has to select the objective that 'may be expected to cause the least danger to civilian lives and to civilian objects',[121] taking into consideration military factors, such as risk to friendly forces and assets available to conduct the attack. For example, consider an attack designed to disrupt the production of vehicle-borne improvised explosive devices (VBIED). Two facilities are used—one to structurally prepare the vehicle to carry the explosives and the other to install them. The former is located in a populated area, while the latter is in a remote location, but is heavily defended and significant friendly casualties will ensue in any attack against it. In this situation, targeting the heavily defended objective would not be required because it would be militarily unfeasible, even though its destruction would offer a 'similar military advantage' and cause less collateral damage.

Lastly, attackers are required to give advance warning if an attack may affect the civilian population, unless circumstances do not permit.[122] In particular,

[119] US Department of the Army Field Manual 3–24.2 (2009), paras 5–8; See also, Headquarters, ISAF-Afghanistan (2011a) COMISAF Night Operations Tactical Directive, p. 2, (directing commanders to 'initiate entry to the targeted residence by means of … an Afghan-led call-out in the appropriate Afghan language). In this respect, see also the Israeli Knock on the roof tactics. Schmitt 2013b, at 828.

[120] The United States defines tactical questioning as '[t]he field-expedient initial questioning for information of immediate tactical value of a captured or detained person at or near the point of capture and before the individual is placed in a detention facility. Tactical questioning is generally performed by members of patrols, but can be done by any appropriately trained DoD personnel. Tactical questioning is limited to direct questioning.' US Department of Defense Directive 3115.09 (2013), p. 32.

[121] AP I, Article 57(3); UK Manual, § 13.32; AMW Manual, rule 33; Tallinn Manual, rule 56.

[122] AP I, Article 57(2)(c); Customary International Humanitarian Law Study, rule 20; UK Manual, § 5.32.8; US Commander's Handbook, § 8.9.2; AMW Manual, rule 37; Tallinn Manual, rule 58.

advance warning that would result in a loss of operational surprise or increase of risk to friendly forces is not required. For instance, in the 2006 airstrike against al-Qaeda in Iraq leader Abu Musab al-Zarqawi, providing a warning to nearby civilians would have alerted him to flee.[123] Sometimes, specific warnings are not feasible, but an attacker may feasibly issue a general warning to the civilian population. To illustrate, coalition forces dropped hundreds of thousands of leaflets warning Iraqi civilians to avoid military sites prior to the initiation of ground combat in 2003.[124]

6.5 Collateral Damage and Incidental Injury

Even if an attack targets a lawful military objective and the attacker has taken every feasible precaution to minimize the harm to civilians and civilian objects, it must comply with the rule of proportionality. Regarded as a tenet of customary international law and codified in Articles 51 and 57 of Additional Protocol I, the rule prohibits 'an attack which may be expected to cause incidental loss of civilian life, injury to civilians, damage to civilian objects, or a combination thereof, which would be excessive in relation to the concrete and direct military advantage anticipated'.[125] The harm to civilians is technically labelled 'incidental injury', while that to civilian objects is 'collateral damage'. However, common usage generally fails to distinguish between the two and usually uses the latter term, as is done here, to refer to both.

Proportionality does not require a strict mathematical comparison, nor does it, as is often mistakenly believed, call for a balancing test; rather, likely collateral damage only precludes attack when it is 'excessive', that is 'when there is a significant imbalance between the military advantage anticipated, on the one hand, and the expected collateral damage to civilians and civilian objects, on the other'.[126] At its core, the rule is an acknowledgement that collateral damage may be unavoidable in order to successfully execute an attack.

As indicated by the terms 'expected' and 'anticipated', compliance with the rule of proportionality is assessed based upon the information reasonably available

---

[123] Burns 2006.

[124] P. Hess Propaganda leaflets dropped over Iraq, United Press International (18 March 2003), *available at* http://www.upi.com/Business_News/Security-Industry/2003/03/18/Propaganda-leaflets-dropped-over-Iraq/UPI-81231048022702/. Accessed 27 March 2014.

[125] AP I, Articles 51(5)(b), 57(2)(a)(ii), 57(2)(b); Customary International Humanitarian Law Study, rule 14; UK Manual, § 2.6; US Commander's Handbook, § 5.3.3; AMW Manual, rule 14; Tallinn Manual, rule 51.

[126] AMW Manual commentary accompanying rule 14, para 7.

to the attacker at the time the attack was planned, approved, or executed. It is not determined by the collateral damage or military advantage that actually resulted. However, it should be cautioned that those with the ability to control the engagement have a continuing duty to comply with the rule.[127] Thus, for example, if a soldier who is ordered to attack a building in which enemy forces have barricaded themselves becomes aware that, contrary to the intelligence available at the time the order was issued, civilians are unexpectedly present, the soldier must reassess the proportionality of the attack and either alter his means or methods of attack to avoid excessive collateral damage, or cease the attack altogether.

Consider, for example, the targeting of Taliban leaders in Afghanistan. In many instances, attacks are launched at night while the targeted individual is in a residence, presumably sleeping; family members may also be present. For operational reasons, it is often not feasible to attack at other times or places. When considering whether to proceed, those deciding on the operation must first identify the anticipated military advantage of eliminating the individual based upon his prior actions and function in the organization. They then estimate the expected loss of civilian life or damage to civilian property. In some instances, the leader may not be of sufficient stature to merit any significant loss of civilian life and the operation will be prohibited as a matter of law. In others, the balance may weigh in favour of targeting the leader, even though civilian deaths will result.

LOAC also imposes a number of restrictions on specific tactics. The two most significant are based on the broad prohibition on indiscriminate attacks. First, it is unlawful to engage in attacks 'which are not directed at a specific military objective' (as distinct from those which are aimed at an unlawful target).[128] In other words, the attacker employs force without heed to whether lawful or unlawful targets will be struck, as in the case of indiscriminately firing mortars into a city.[129] Second, '[a]ttacks which treat as a single military objective a number of clearly separated and distinct military objectives located in a city, town, village, or other area containing a similar concentration of civilians or civilian objects are prohibited'.[130] An example would be regarding an entire village as a target when it was possible to strike the specific building in which insurgents are located.

---

[127] AP I, Article 57 (2)(b); Customary International Humanitarian Law Study, rule 19.

[128] AP I, Article 51(4)(a); Customary International Humanitarian Law Study, rules 11–12; UK Manual, § 5.23.1; US Commander's Handbook, § 5.3.2; AMW Manual, rule 13(b); Tallinn Manual, rule 49.

[129] *Prosecutor v. Martic*, Case No. IT-95-11-T, ICTY Trial Judgment, 12 June 2007, paras 462–463; *Prosecutor v. Martic*, IT-95-11-A, ICTY Appeals Judgment, 8 October 2008, paras 239–240, 247, 250–252.

[130] AP I, Article 51(5)(a); Customary International Humanitarian Law Study, rule 13; UK Manual, § 5.23.2; US Commander's Handbook, § 5.3.2; AMW Manual, rule 13(c), Tallinn Manual, rule 50.

6.6 Location

During IACs, targeting may be conducted against valid military objectives within the territory of any of the belligerent States,[131] including their territorial sea and the airspace above it, as well as in international waters and airspace.[132] Belligerent military activities may not take place in the territory, territorial waters or territorial airspace of a neutral country.[133] However, in order to enjoy the protection afforded neutral States by the law of armed conflict, a neutral State must equally prohibit the use of its territory by any of the belligerents. If a belligerent attempts to use the territory of a neutral State in support of military activities, the neutral State has an obligation to take measures, including the use of force, to prevent or end that use.[134] Should the neutral State be either unable or unwilling to comply with that obligation, the opposing belligerent parties may conduct operations, including attacks, necessary to put an end to its opponent's misuse of neutral territory.[135]

The geographical limits of non-international armed conflict are less clear. During a non-international armed conflict attacks conducted on the State's territory with a nexus to the conflict are clearly governed by LOAC. However, there is an ongoing debate about whether LOAC applies outside the State involved in a NIAC. One view is that it does not, although that interpretation appears to be losing adherents rapidly. A second position, advocated by the ICRC, is that LOAC applies in cross-border areas into which a NIAC's hostilities have spilled over and thus would govern any targeting there.[136] A third view maintains that the reach of LOAC is dependent on party status, not on geography.[137] The distinction is critical, for if LOAC does not govern the conduct of targeting, norms contained in domestic law and human rights law will regulate the operation. The latter

[131] See Gill, Chap. 5 in this volume.

[132] International waters begin at the outer limits of a coastal State's territorial sea. US Commander's Handbook, § 1.9. International airspace is the airspace located above international waters, including the contiguous and exclusive economic zones. Agreement Relating to the Implementation of Part XI of the United Nations Convention on the Law of the Sea of 10 December 1982, 28 July 1994, 1836 UNTS 41, Article 2; UK Manual, § 12.14; US Commander's Handbook, § 1.9; AMW Manual commentary accompanying rule 1(b), para 8.

[133] Convention (V) respecting the Rights and Duties of Neutral Powers and Person in Case of War on Land, 18 October 1907; Convention (XIII) Concerning the Rights and Duties of Neutral Powers in Naval War, 18 October 1907, 36 Stat. 2310.

[134] Ibid, Article 5; Rules concerning the Control of Wireless Telegraphy in Time of War and Air Warfare, Drafted by a Commission of Jurists at the Hague, December 1922–February 1923 (Hague Rules on Air Warfare), Articles 42, 47; UK Manual, § 1.43; US Commander's Handbook, § 7.3; AMW Manual, rules 168(a) and 170(c).

[135] UK Manual, § 1.43; U.S. Commander's Handbook, § 7.3; AMW Manual, rule 168(b); Tallinn Manual commentary accompanying rule 94, para 4.

[136] International Committee of the Red Cross (2011).

[137] Schmitt 2014.

generally limits attacks to situations in which lethal force is necessary to prevent death or grievous bodily injury; it does not allow status based targeting.[138]

6.7 Conclusion

The law of targeting is designed to balance the military necessity of being able to conduct operations effectively with the goal of minimizing harm to civilians, civilian property, and other protected persons and objects. On the one hand, it sometimes allows harm to befall protected persons and objects in order to attain military goals. For instance, LOAC never requires the taking of precautions to avoid harming civilians and civilian objects when doing so is not operationally reasonable. It also allows an attack even in the full knowledge that innocents will be harmed so long as that harm is not excessive relative to the anticipated military advantage of the operation. On the other hand, militarily optimal operations are sometimes prohibited by LOAC. For instance, even when a military objective is being targeted in a manner that minimizes harm to civilians and civilian objects, the rule of proportionality prohibits attack if a certain level of collateral damage will be caused. This military necessity-humanitarian balance underpins virtually all of LOAC, but it is with respect to the law of targeting that it is at its apogee. Therefore, whenever the law appears uncertain in a particular engagement, the most reasonable approach is to analyse the situation through the lens of this balance.

References

Afsar S, Samples C, Wood T (2008) The Taliban: an organizational analysis, Mil Rev 2008(May–June):64–68

AMW Manual (2013) HPCR manual on international law applicable to air and missile warfare. Cambridge University Press, Cambridge

AP I—Protocol additional to the Geneva Conventions of 12 August 1949, and relating to the protection of victims of international armed conflicts, June 8, 1977, 1125 UNTS 3

AP II—Protocol additional to the Geneva Conventions of August 12, 1949, and relating to the protection of victims of non-international armed conflicts, June 8, 1977, 1125 UNTS 609

Boothby W (2012) The law of targeting. Oxford University Press, Oxford

Burns J (2006) U.S. strike hits insurgent at safehouse. (8 June 2006) The New York Times. http://www.nytimes.com/2006/06/08/world/middleeast/08cnd-iraq.html?_r=0. Accessed 27 March 2014

Henckaerts J, Doswald-Beck (2005) Customary international humanitarian law study. Cambridge University Press, Cambridge

[138] UN Basic Principles on the Use of Force and Firearms by Law Enforcement Officials, Adopted by the Eighth United Nations Congress on the Prevention of Crime and the Treatment of Offenders, Havana, Cuba, 27 August to 7 September 1990.

Dinstein Y (2010) The conduct of hostilities under the law of armed conflict. Cambridge University Press, Cambridge

GC I—Convention (I) for the amelioration of the condition of the wounded and sick in the armed forces in the field, 12 Aug, 1949, 75 UNTS 31, Articles 24–26

GC II—Convention (II) for the amelioration of the condition of the wounded, sick, and shipwrecked members of armed forces at sea, 12 Aug, 1949, 75 UNTS 85

GC III—Convention (III) relative to the treatment of prisoners of war, 12 Aug, 1949, 75 UNTS 135

GC IV—Convention (IV) relative to the protection of civilian persons in time of war, 12 Aug, 1949, 75 UNTS 287

Hague Regulations—Regulations respecting the laws and customs of war on land, annexed to convention no. IV respecting the laws and customs of war on land, 18 Oct, 1907, 36 Stat. 2227

Hashim A (2006) Insurgency and counterinsurgency in Iraq. Cornell University Press, Ithaca

Headquarters, ISAF-Afghanistan (2011a) COMISAF night operations tactical directive (1 Dec 2011). http://www.isaf.nato.int/images/docs/20111105%20nuc%20night%20operations%20tactical%20directive%20(releaseable%20version)%20r.pdf. Accessed 27 March 2014

Headquarters, ISAF-Afghanistan (2011b) COMISAF's tactical directive (30 Nov 2011). http://www.isaf.nato.int/images/docs/20111105%20nuc%20tactical%20directive%20revision%204%20(releaseable%20version)%20r.pdf. Accessed 27 March 2014

ICRC (2009) Interprative guidance—International Committee of the Red Cross, (Nils Melzer), Interpretive guidance on the notion of direct participation in hostilities under international humanitarian law

International Committee of the Red Cross (2011) International humanitarian law and the challenges of contemporary armed conflict. www.icrc.org/eng/assets/files/red-cross-crescent-movement/31st-international-conference/31-int-conference-ihl-challenges-report-11-5-1-2-en.pdf. Accessed 26 March 2014

International Committee of the Red Cross (2012) ICRC annual report 2012, vol I. www.icrc.org/eng/resources/documents/annual-report/icrc-annual-report-2012.htm. Accessed 27 March 2014

ISAF (2014) Joint command–Afghanistan press release: Taliban safe havens, explosives caches cleared in Arghandab. (Oct 7, 2010). NATO. http://www.isaf.nato.int/article/isaf-releases/taliban-safe-havens-explosives-caches-cleared-in-arghandab.html. Accessed 26 March 2014

Mapping Military Organizations. Stanford University (2014) www.stanford.edu/group/mappingmilitants/cgi-bin/groups/view/367. Accessed 27 March 2014

Matheson M (1987) The United States position on the relation of customary international law to the 1977 protocols additional to the 1949 Geneva Conventions. Am J Int Law Policy 2:419–436

Schmitt M, Garraway C, Dinstein Y (2006) NIAC Manual on the law of non-international armed conflict with commentary. International Institute of Humanitarian Law, San Remo

OPLAW Handbook—US Army International and Operational Law Department (2013) Operational law handbook. Judge Advocate General's Legal Center & School, U.S. Army, Charlottesville

Peters G (2009) How opium profits the Taliban (United States Institute of Peace, Peaceworks Series 62, Aug 2, 2009). www.usip.org/sites/default/files/resources/taliban_opium_1.pdf. Accessed 26 March 2014

Pouw EH (2013) International human rights law and the law of armed conflict in the context of counterinsurgency—with a particular focus on targeting and operational detention, PhD dissertation University of Amsterdam. www.uva.nl/binaries/content/documents/personalpages/d/u/p.a.l.ducheine/nl/downloads/downloads/assets%5B7%5D/asset?1404585556372

Sandoz Y et al (1987) (eds) Commentary on the additional protocols of 8 June 1977 to the Geneva Conventions of 12 August 1949. Martinus Nijhoff, Dordrecht

Doswald-Beck L (ed) (1994) San Remo manual on international law applicable to armed conflicts at sea. Cambridge University Press, Cambridge

Schmitt M (2009) Targeting narcoinsurgents in Afghanistan. Yearb Int Humanit Law 12:1–20

Schmitt M (2010) Targeting in operational law. In: Gill T, Fleck D (eds) The handbook of the international law of military operations. Oxford University Press, Oxford, pp 245–276

Schmitt M (2013a) Extraterritorial lethal targeting: deconstructing the logic of international law. Columbia J Int Law 52:79–114

Schmitt M (2013b) Military necessity and humanity in international humanitarian law: preserving the delicate balance. Va J Int Law 50(4):795–839

Schmitt M (2014) Charting the legal geography of non-international armed conflict. Int Law Stud 90:1–19

Schmitt M (ed) (2013) Tallinn manual on the international law applicable to cyber warfare. Cambridge University Press, Cambridge

UK Manual—United Kingdom Ministry of Defence (2004) The manual of the law of armed conflict. Oxford University Press, Oxford

US Commander's Handbook (2007)Department of the Navy & Department of Homeland Security, NWP 1-14 M/MCWP 5-12/COMDTPUB P5800.7A, The Commander's handbook on the law of naval operations

US Department of the Army Field Manual 3–24.2 (2009) Tactics in counterinsurgency, 21 April 2009. http://armypubs.army.mil/doctrine/DR_pubs/dr_a/pdf/fm3_24x2.pdf. Accessed 31 March 2014

US Department of Defense Directive 3115.09 (2013) DoD intelligence interrogations, detainee debriefings, and tactical questioning, 15 Nov 2013. http://www.dtic.mil/whs/directives/corres/pdf/311509p.pdf. Accessed 27 March 2014

Chapter 7
Ethical Issues in Targeting

Martin L. Cook

Abstract Decisions about targeting, since they involve the choice to destroy human lives and property, are inherently ethical decisions. This article reviews the ethical categories that have evolved in the Western tradition's philosophical and religious traditions. It discusses the ways in which these traditions both generate and on occasions diverge from the other major normative framework in which these decisions are evaluated—the legal tradition that became the Law of Armed Conflict (LOAC) and which is enshrined in International Law.

Keywords Ethics · Augustine · Kant · Walzer · Double effect · Just war · Discrimination · Proportionality · Drone · Close air support · Strategic bombing

Contents

7.1 The Perspective of Ethics

This volume addresses questions of targeting from a wide range of perspectives—political, legal, operational and strategic, to name only some. At the outset therefore, it is necessary to begin by articulating the perspective of ethics.

M.L. Cook (✉)
Stockdale Chair of Professional Military Ethics, US Naval War College, Newport, RI, USA
e-mail: martin.l.cook@usnwc.edu

P.A.L. Ducheine et al. (eds.), *Targeting: The Challenges of Modern Warfare*,
DOI 10.1007/978-94-6265-072-5_7

The first important point is that ethics is a *normative* enterprise. It is concerned with articulating what actions ought to be permitted, condemned and encouraged. This contrasts with *descriptive* approaches that give accounts of how things are, how they are practiced, and what attitudes individuals and groups might happen to have regarding them.

One immediate point of commonality and departure is between the ethical and the legal perspective. Both are normative. Both attempt to distinguish the permitted from the impermissible. Both are keenly aware of intricacy, ambiguity, and uncertainty in complex cases. An important distinction, however, lies in their normative sources. Since law deals with precedent and explicit legal requirements, it necessarily is backward looking and experiences some temporal lag when confronting novel challenges.[1] Further, most law dealing with military matters grew up in the specific legal regime that emerged in Europe following the Reformation and the subsequent wars of religion. It therefore is framed largely in terms of the Westphalian interstate system of organization, although it is adapting rapidly to the challenges posed by non-State actors in the modern context. By contrast, most of the ethics of war was forged far earlier. Thinkers in the Western Christian tradition began to develop an ethical framework for war—most importantly with Augustine in the fourth century. Challenges faced then were not matters of States acting on States, but of incursions by barbarians into the Roman Empire and rulers acting under the umbrella of papal authority in a notionally universal Christendom. Only after the erosion of Christendom following the Reformation did a secular just war tradition emerge and eventually evolve in the two parallel tracks of law and ethics.

Another important point is that ethics necessarily strives to be practical and provide useful guidance to moral choice and action. Inevitably therefore there will be no sharp division between ethical reflection and considerations of prudent statecraft. Although often caricatured as idealistic to the point of irrelevance, serious ethical reasoning applied to hard real world problems strives to be practical and relevant to decision makers. There will be, however, unavoidable overlap between sound ethical reflection and judgments arising from other perspectives.

Finally, it is common in some schools of international relations thought to dismiss ethical questions entirely as irrelevant to both normative guidance of State action and to what States do. Certainly, in the midst of complex decision making about military and international matters, it is difficult (as was indicated above) to point to the specific and unique contribution of the ethical amidst all the other factors at work. But the so-called Realist perspective, which dismisses all discussions of ethics, seems clearly false. All human beings, apart from sociopaths and nihilists, experience the moral as a palpable element of their interior worlds. Even leaders engaged in the most heinous of acts almost universally feel the need to use

[1] There are occasional exceptions to this. For example, Human Rights Watch has suggested a ban on autonomous weapons systems prior to their development and fielding. Human Rights Watch 2013.

moral language to describe and attempt to justify their actions. It is difficult to understand why that happens if there is not some recognition that human beings expect such an account. As Michael Walzer famously remarked, '[t]he clearest evidence for the stability of our values over time is the unchanging character of the lies soldiers and statesmen tell ... Where we find hypocrisy we also find moral knowledge'.[2]

To note all this is of course a normative point. It is a distinct and important question whether and to what degree actual leaders do incorporate ethical considerations into their targeting deliberations. That is an empirical question that goes beyond the scope of this essay.

7.2 Fundamental Ethical Principles

The fundamental ethical principle in targeting is presumptive immunity from attack. All human beings and objects are entitled to be left undisturbed and intact unless they have lost that immunity for a specific and morally weighty reason. From what moral considerations does this immunity arise?

The different ethical traditions of the West provide some variation in the answer to this question. Probably the oldest and most culturally foundational is the Western religious tradition, which holds that everything is a gift of God and that all human beings are equal creatures of God. That deep perception of the giftedness of the world and of life generates a strong sense of the wrongness of killing and gratuitous destruction. Indeed, so strong is that tendency that there has always been a solid pacifist minority, especially in the Christian tradition, which objects to use of force, sometimes even in clear cases of self-defence. For most of the Western tradition, reluctance to kill and destroy is a deep-seated but defeasible presumption, providing the foundation for just war exceptions and *jus in bello* restrictions on legitimate targets.

With the Enlightenment, other more secular versions arose. The most powerful are the Kantian/deontological emphasis on the inherent dignity and equal status of all rational beings ('always treat humanity ... as an end in itself, and never as a means only') and the emergence of a doctrine of universal human rights. These two outlooks share with the religious tradition the strong commitment to respecting the lives and property of other human beings, unless they have done something by their own actions to legitimate attacking and killing them in ways that, because of those acts, are still consistent with respecting their rights and dignity.

The one other major ethical tradition in the West, utilitarianism, poses a more complex case. Here the emphasis is on achieving the best possible outcomes. On some interpretations of utilitarianism, especially so-called 'act utilitarianism', in

[2]Walzer 1977.

which each decision is treated as *sui generis* and unique, the sacrifice of individuals for the achievement of good outcomes may indeed be viewed as legitimate. In military parlance, this is consistent with some interpretations of 'military necessity'. However, most serious defenders of utilitarianism are not 'act utilitarians', but 'rule utilitarians'. In rule utilitarianism, one generally acts in accordance with an agreed set of general rules. What makes this view utilitarian is that the rules themselves are justified with reference to utility maximizing (i.e., we are to choose that set of rules that, among possible alternatives, works to achieve overall utility). Unlike the religious and deontological traditions that ground their rules in the will of God, or the inherent dignity and rights of individuals, for the rule utilitarian the rules themselves are continually subject to reassessment in light of their utility maximizing consequences. Nevertheless, a rule utilitarian approach to targeting specifically, and the ethics of war generally, would still argue for the existence of rules, and would ask what set of rules regarding these matters, if generally observed, would reduce suffering and achieve good overall outcomes. Not surprisingly, therefore, rule utilitarian analyses are likely to result in rules not dissimilar to those emerging from the other ethical traditions.

From this general respect for the immunity of persons and objects, a number of specific moral considerations arise. Given the common lineage of ethics and law, these concerns track closely with their legal counterparts.

The first is that non-combatants (or 'innocents' in the Latin sense of the term, i.e., not engaged in harming) are always and everywhere immune from deliberate attack. By contrast, combatants have lost that immunity by virtue of the fact that they are not 'innocents' because they are (at least in principle) engaged in, or prepared to engage in, harming. For the overwhelming bulk of the tradition, there is a moral equality of soldiers on both sides of a conflict. Each side's forces are equally subject to deliberate attack and protected by the war convention, regardless of the *ad bellum* justice of their cause.[3]

For combatants some restraints remain. Because of the human status of even unjust combatants, there is an ethical constraint on force used against them. Attacks should not use weapons likely to cause suffering in excess of what is required to render them militarily ineffective. Occasionally in the history of the tradition, there have been endeavours to spell out restrictions on specific weapons in accordance with this general limitation. Examples include efforts to ban the crossbow, hollow point/dum-dum bullets, poison gas, and, recently, blinding lasers.

[3]It is worth noting that this 'moral equality' of combatants has come under considerable attack philosophically in recent years, especially by the work of Jeff McMahan and David Rodin. See Rodin 2003 and McMahan 2009. It is beyond the scope of this paper to assess that discussion. In general, they argue that in modern open societies, soldiers are indeed responsible to a degree for assessing the *ad bellum* justice of the cause, and therefore the soldiers on the unjust side are not morally equal to those fighting on the just side. Regardless of the philosophical merits of this argument, it is difficult to see how one could instrumentalize it as a practical matter without seriously undermining the law of armed conflict.

The two specific ethical requirements of legitimate targeting are discrimination (what the law usually calls 'distinction') and proportionality. Discrimination flows from the immunity of innocents and requires that all targets be assessed in terms of their military value at the time of the attack. Objects and personnel that are in no way involved in military operations and that serve no military purpose may not, in accordance with the requirement of discrimination, ever be the objects of deliberate targeting. We will return to the question of the sometimes inevitable and even foreseeable damage to non-combatants and non-military objects in the next section. For the moment, the goal is only to get the 'bright line' of the prohibition on deliberate attack clearly laid out.

Proportionality requires that the damage done to civilians and civilian objects as a result of a specific attack be in reasonable proportion to the military value of the object attacked. Proportionality is a somewhat inherently uncertain judgment, and the military value of a given object is not a fixed quantity based on the object's inherent properties. Rather, it depends of the nature of the object, its location, its role in ongoing military operations, and even the state of the conflict. For example, during the First Gulf War (1991), the Iraqi Air Force placed a number of its fighter aircraft in the open, but often next to cultural or religious sites. In general, they were not targeted, although they were clearly military objects. Why not? They could not be attacked without risking damage to significant non-military objects and the due to the Coalition's air supremacy the Iraqi Air Force was not flying. Because under these conditions the military value of the fighter aircraft at the time was essentially zero, any collateral damage would be disproportionate.

In short, the basic structure of the ethical requirements of targeting tracks closely with the law of armed conflict (LOAC) requirements. Only military personnel (or combatants in the case of irregular warfare) and objects of military value at the time are subject to deliberate targeting. Target selection must be made with a clear assessment of the ability of the attacker to attack the target in a discriminate way (i.e., one that aims as narrowly as possible at the object of military value). The target must be struck within the limits of practical considerations in ways that damage only the target itself and, to the extent possible, not other objects and personnel. Finally, even for attacks on legitimate military personnel, respect for humanity in the other (to put it in Kantian terms) requires minimizing unnecessary suffering. While there is clearly a legal requirement for combatants to observe LOAC restraints, in addition, part of the moral armour that protects the psyches of combatants from moral injury and assures them that, while they kill, they are not murderers, is precisely their ability to sustain a kind of Kantian respect for human dignity on all sides of the conflict.

7.3 Double Effect

In the previous section we laid out the basic ethical requirements for legitimate military targeting. Naturally, it is rarely possible to conduct targeting operations in ways that conform completely and neatly to those criteria. Specifically, it is often the case that legitimate targets are located amid civilian objects and persons and that the weapons available to the target planner simply do not allow complete precision to attack only the military target. This situation, in which a targeting planner foresees and understands that the attack will almost certainly involve damage to non-military objects and persons has been analysed in the ethical tradition through the lens of a principle traditionally called 'double effect'. It is a principle developed by Medieval Christian thinkers to provide ethical guidance when an act is being considered that foreseeably has both a 'good' outcome and, equally foreseeably, an 'evil' or bad one.

According to the principle of double effect, one may legitimately perform an act of this description if four criteria are met. First, the principle effect intended must itself be morally acceptable. In application to a targeting discussion, that principle effect would be a proportionate attack on a legitimate military target. Second, the 'evil effect' is not intended by the agent, but merely (regrettably) foreseen. That is, the actor sees that the effect is inevitable, but does not intend it and indeed would prefer that it not occur. Third, the 'evil effect' cannot be the means to achieving the good effect. This would rule out, for example, a bombing campaign aimed at stopping munitions production by 'dehousing the workers'—a euphemism in WWII for directly attacking housing areas because bombing was not precise enough to reliably hit the factories themselves. In this case, the 'good effect' of reducing or eliminating munitions production is being achieved by means of attacking the workers housing directly. By contrast, an attempted precision bombing attack on a factory would be acceptable even if (given the accuracy of the weapons) it is foreseeable that some bombs will fall off target and might hit civilian areas. The fourth criterion is that there must be an acceptable proportionality between the good effect achieved and the amount of undesired 'evil effects'. In other words, it must be 'worth it' in terms of the military value at the time of the primary target.

Double effect has been criticized on a number of grounds. One is that it bears the marks of its Christian origins in its emphasis on the inner intentional state of the agent—what Germans call the *Gesinnungsetik*, an ethic of intention. Some are sceptical about the ability of agents to fully understand their own internal States sufficiently to honestly assess those intentions.

On the other hand, removing those elements from double effect leaves straightforward utilitarian calculation in which 'military necessity' can justify almost anything that advances legitimate military objectives.

In targeting specifically, double effect is actually a practical means of assessing targeting decisions from an ethical point of view, especially for targeting precision weapons onto fixed targets in a relatively permissive air environment. Once targets have been vetted by intelligence and surveillance, the targeting staff has a great deal of discretion about choosing both the size of the weapon and the details of the attack profile. Weapon selection ranges from merely kinetic (i.e., no explosion whatsoever) to very large explosions. Attack profiles allow adjustment of time of day and angle of attack. Modern air forces such as the that of US go as far as running computer models of various attack profiles to determine the direction and distribution of blast effect. Taken together, these techniques allow for, and also measure, the sincerity of the intent to minimize 'evil effects' of an attack—often called somewhat euphemistically 'collateral damage'. For example, if a legitimate target is in a civilian commercial district which is busy during the day, but largely unpopulated at night, not selecting to attack it at night (assuming attack is not urgently required by military necessity) would indicate a lack of a serious intent to avoid the 'evil effect'. Similarly, assuming a range of ordinance is available to the planning staff, selecting a significantly larger weapon for the target than required for its destruction (and thereby deliberately creating a larger than necessary blast effect) would indicate a lack of sincere intention to minimize additional damage.

Michael Walzer famously has criticized the ordinary understanding of double effect as too permissive, since it relies on only a fairly imprecise and elastic proportionality judgment to restrain violence against non-combatants. He argues for a revision of the third requirement as follows:

> The intention of the actor is good, that is, he aims narrowly at the acceptable effect; the evil effect is not one of his ends, nor is it a means to his ends, and, aware of the evil involved, he seeks to minimize it, accepting costs to himself.[4]

The ground for Walzer's revision is that, because the combatants are responsible for all the risk to which the non-combatants are subjected (including using civilians as shields for combatants), the combatants should be expected to accept additional risks to themselves to protect the non-combatants. It is insufficient that the combatants do not intend directly to harm the non-combatants and then make a very subjective proportionality calculation. Rather, they should actively engage in actions to protect non-combatants, even if those actions increase their own risk. In addition, they should choose weapons and tactics that minimize risk to non-combatants. In practical terms, one assumes that if the political decision in the Kosovo air campaign (1999) to protect coalition aircraft by bombing from high altitude seriously diminished accuracy, it would be morally unacceptable on his revised version of double effect.

The moral force of Walzer's revision is strong. As a practical matter, however, it has yet to achieve anything like accepted normative status. As the Kosovo example shows, most normative thinkers still seem prepared to accept the moral legitimacy of political leaders weighing the costs of losses to their own forces and making a trade-off in targeting accuracy (short of deliberate targeting of civilians and civilian objects). That said, Walzer's concern that double-effect as traditionally understood may be too permissive is worthy of ongoing reflection with a view to possible future revision of normative understanding.

Furthermore, with the increased use of remotely piloted and possible future semi- or fully autonomous systems for bombing in the most contested air space, Walzer's revision may apply to increasingly rare circumstances, as highly technological air forces are capable of reducing the risks to their own forces to nearly zero.

[4]Walzer 1977, p. 155.

Double effect remains a very useful framework and one embedded in operational targeting procedures for modern high-technology air forces—especially when they are part of a carefully planned air campaign, conducted by modern air forces with precision munitions of widely varying explosive yield. The existence of those many variables in choosing a pattern of targeting makes realistic the ideal of targeting in ways that genuinely do strive to minimize collateral damage and sharpen the traditionally more imprecise proportionality calculation required to make good-faith claims regarding the intention of the targeting.

7.4 Targeting in Deliberative Planning Versus Close Air Support

So far we have discussed targeting in the context of a carefully planned air campaign against fixed targets that are nominated through a relatively rigorous vetting process. Such bombing campaigns are the core concept of US Air Force doctrine, although actual application of air power in recent conflicts has diverged from it considerably as close air support of ground forces has been an important requirement. Indeed, the commitment to the idea of the effectiveness of strategic bombing is the primary justification for an independent air force at all.[5]

As airpower has matured, the technology has evolved to enable such air campaigns to be conducted with impressive precision because of improvements in intelligence, reconnaissance and surveillance, and bomb guidance technologies (laser guided and global positioning system guided ordinance). On the other hand, the confidence in the effectiveness of airpower alone that inspired early airpower enthusiasts such as Douhet and Mitchell has generally proven to be excessive. Furthermore, the ethical assessment of targeting cannot be completely detached from a political context in which military planners may end up selecting and bombing targets well beyond what their planning doctrine and professional military judgment would support. Kosovo provides an excellent example. Political constraints placed on the air campaign forced the air forces to operate in ways well outside their doctrinal professional understanding in terms of altitudes from which weapons were dropped, the extension of 'strategic' bombing beyond well-vetted targets, and so forth. Consequently, comprehensive ethical assessment of targeting must include not only what military doctrine and practice would support as appropriate, but also the full picture of how all weapons are actually used in the midst of the messy political and military context of specific conflicts.

Recent uses of airpower in Iraq (after the initial stages of the invasion, 2003) and in Afghanistan (Enduring Freedom) have largely diverged from the model of

[5]Cook 2003, pp. 129–150 for a full discussion of the evolution of the theory of air power before World War II.

deliberative planning for strategic bombing. The exigencies of recent combat have forced an evolution of airpower to close air support (CAS) of ground forces—traditionally not a mission air forces have valued. The exception is, of course, US Marine aviation (both rotary wing and fixed wing) and Army rotary wing aviation. Indeed, one of the principle reasons for the Marine's insistence on maintaining their own aviation arm was their desire to insure that they have adequate CAS organically in Marine units.

Despite cultural resistance, necessity is the mother of invention and, as engagements in Iraq and Afghanistan wore on, airpower adapted to a dramatically different mode of targeting than its preferred and deliberative process. The objective requirements of the battlefield necessitated that rapidly responsive airpower be available to ground forces at virtually any time. This called for reinventing the method of identifying targets and controlling collateral damage on the fly in the midst of rapidly evolving and changing combat environments. In addition, new technologies such as drones for surveillance and vastly improved audio and communication technology, made real-time assessments highly accurate and timely.

Although operating in a very different context, the fundamental ethical principles guiding targeting were of course the same: discrimination/distinction and proportionality. But the fluid nature of the ground combat environment and the lack of uniforms, front lines or other traditional ways of clearly identifying combatants made implementing those core ethical requirements much more complex.

The system that ultimately evolved for the ground fight was to train Air Force and Navy personnel as 'Joint Terminal Attack Controllers' (JTACs).[6] JTACs were embedded with ground forces to serve as the liaison between the ground commander and all aviation assets in the vicinity. JTACs are equipped with a Remotely Operated Video Enhanced Receiver (ROVER) which allows them to see video feed from all air assets in the area, to communicate with pilots and remotely piloted vehicle (i.e., drone) pilots, and to direct air assets to move to provide surveillance of targets not accessible to ground forces.

Arguably, this process cannot be as thorough as the kind of deliberate planning possible for a strategic bombing campaign directed against fixed and largely stationary targets. On the other hand, as this integrated CAS system has evolved over the past decade, the interaction between the ground commander, the JTAC, and the surveillance capabilities of both piloted aircraft and remotely piloted aircraft has become quite precise, even in a 'troops in contact' (TIC) situation of urgency. It is certainly generally more precise than calling in unguided artillery strikes using unguided munitions or ground force operated weapons systems that can only be directed in the general direction of the target from which fire is being received. A particular attack can in effect be vetoed by the pilots, the remotely piloted vehicle

[6]Earlier conflicts had used Forward Air Controllers, of course, but usually by assigning a member of the ground forces that responsibility. Embedding airmen directly with ground units was innovative—as was most of the technology that allowed them to communicate with and indeed see the battlefield from the perspective of all air assets on station.

(RPV) pilots and sensor operators, the JTAC, and finally the ground commander, who bears ultimate responsibility for the decision to release a weapon. While no system can be guaranteed to be error free, this unique CAS combination makes possible a remarkable degree of discrimination and proportionality—especially in light of the long-loiter capabilities of RPVs.

7.5 Targeting with RPV's (Drones)

In recent years, the rapid growth in the number of strikes with RPVs has raised controversy regarding a number of aspects of their use. Since the technologies involved show evidence of quick improvement, ever-wider availability to many nations and non-State actors, and widening applicability to the air, land, sea surface, and underwater environments, it is worth a discrete section discussing them. Naturally, the fundamental ethical principles of their use remain the same as with any other technology: discrimination/distinction and proportionality.

So far, the most widespread use of drone technology for weapons delivery has been in the air environment, using RPVs such as the Predator and the Reaper. Insofar as they are employed to attack specific legitimate targets in a clear combat environment, there is really nothing novel about the ethical aspects of their use; they are simply another weapon system to be used in accordance with well-understood constraints limiting the use of all weapons systems. However, the unique combination of relatively low cost, expendability, long loiter time over possible targets, and the impunity of RPV operators combine to raise some novel issues.

One such issue is strictly a *jus ad bellum* rather than a *jus in bello* issue—their use inside the territories of nations where no state of armed conflict in the traditional sense exists. As part of its attempt to disrupt and destroy terrorist networks around the world, the US (both the military and intelligence communities) has attacked individuals, groups, and installations in Pakistan, Yemen, Somalia, and numerous other places.[7] In some cases, this has been at the request of, or with at least the tacit and sometimes explicit consent of, the State in which the attack is occurring.[8] These attacks raise obvious questions about the expansion of the concept of an on-going armed conflict. Moreover, if accepting military attacks inside the territory of sovereign States with whom one is not at war is thought to be establishing precedent in customary understandings of law and ethics, these attacks dramatically redefine the relationships of sovereign States—at least in the case where there is no permission for the attack.

There are also obvious ethical problems beyond the *jus ad bellum* ones. How good is the intelligence that indicates that a given individual, facility or group is a

[7]For a dataset on known US drone attacks, see The Bureau for Investigative Journalism at http://www.thebureauinvestigates.com/category/projects/drones/. Accessed 30 April 2014.

[8]See Murphy 2009, pp. 79–108.

legitimate target of attack? Examples range from the ethical relatively straightforward (leaving aside the *ad bellum* issue) case of a carefully targeted attack on a single individual known to a moral certainty to be an important member of a terrorist group, through groups obviously cooperating in the vicinity of one or more such individuals, to so-called 'signature strikes' in which the identity of the individual attacked is entirely unknown, but s/he is observed to be engaged in a pattern of what is deemed to be suspicious behaviour.[9] Needless to say, the farther one moves on this continuum in the direction of merely observed behaviour, the greater the risk of misjudging what one is witnessing and making an illegitimate or unwarranted attack. On the other hand, some observed activities are clear enough indications of active preparation for attack that one should not absolutely foreclose using them as indicators justifying attack.

Additionally, the proportionality calculation for such attacks is even more difficult than in more traditional battlefield targeting. Since the individuals and groups being attacked by a drone are almost always far removed geographically and temporally from active engagement in military activity, the decision to attack them at a particular moment is based on a past pattern of practice and predictions about their future activities. What they almost certainly are not is an immediate and imminent threat. Therefore their military value at the time of the attack is generally low or zero. This makes attacking them more morally problematic than attacking a target that is actively engaged in military operations, or even actively engaged in clear preparation for such operations. The fact that they are not 'combatants' in the ordinary sense complicates this calculation greatly because, if they were straightforwardly combatants, the issue would be reduced to a question of their status, rather than their present activities. That is, as ordinary combatants, they are liable to be attacked at any time, regardless of present activities, subject only to the rules limiting such attacks in terms of collateral damage to civilians and civilian objects. But for an individual (or group) who has in the past engaged in belligerent actions, the fact that s/he may no longer be engaging in such actions introduces the complicated issue of whether the participation is still ongoing. This entire question is further complicated, at least in the US case, because these attacks are carried out both by military forces and by intelligence agencies.

7.6 Conclusion

Although targeting decisions arise in a widely diverse range of contexts, the fundamental ethical principles governing targeting decisions are constant. All human beings (and by extension, property) possess a *prima facie* immunity from

[9]See Greenfield 2013 and Currier and Elliott 2013 for a discussion of signature strikes.

deliberate attack. The decision that they may legitimately be targets of deliberate attack, therefore, requires a 'showing' that they have done something to lose or compromise that immunity. In particular, they must be engaged in military action, or at least in relatively imminent preparation and planning for such action. Attacks against legitimate targets must be discriminate and all reasonable efforts must be made to insure that innocent individuals are not injured or killed in the process of attacking. If damage to innocent individuals or property is going to result as a by-product of a legitimate attack, that damage must not be intended, but only foreseen, and when choices are available (in weapon selection, time and angle of attack, etc.) the options least likely to cause that damage should be selected.[10] Lastly, foreseen but unintended damage must be in some reasonable proportion to the military value of the legitimate target at the time.

References

Cook ML (2003) The moral warrior: ethics and service in the U.S. military. State University of New York Press, Albany

Corn J, Blank L, Jenks C, Jensen E (2013) Belligerent targeting and the invalidity of a least harmful means rule. Int Law Stud 89:536–626

Currier C, Elliott J (2013) The drone war we still know nothing about (26 February 2013) ProPbulica. http://www.propublica.org/article/drone-war-doctrine-we-know-nothing-about. Accessed 1 May 2014

Greenfield D (2013) The case against drone strikes on people who only 'act' like terrorists (19 August 2013) The Atlantic. http://www.theatlantic.com/international/archive/2013/08/the-case-against-drone-strikes-on-people-who-only-act-like-terrorists/278744/. Accessed 1 May 2014

Human Rights Watch (2013) The need for new law to ban fully autonomous weapons. http://www.hrw.org/news/2013/11/13/need-new-law-ban-fully-autonomous-weapons. Accessed 20 Dec 2013

McMahan J (2009) Killing in war. Oxford University Press, Oxford

Murphy J (2009) Afghanistan: hard choices and the future of international law. In: Schmitt MN (ed) The war in Afghanistan: a legal analysis. Naval War Coll Int Law Stud 85:79–108

Rodin D (2003) War and self-defense. Oxford University Press, Oxford

Walzer M (1977) Just and unjust wars: a moral argument with historical illustrations. Basic Books, New York

[10]This requirement can be subject to unreasonable interpretation. For an excellent discussion of its limits see generally Corn et al. 2013.

Chapter 8
Rules of Engagement and Targeting

Hans Boddens Hosang

Abstract This chapter discusses the interaction between targeting (including applicable law) and the rules of engagement (ROE) for international operations. It begins with an examination of the nature, composition, and purpose of ROE in general. This includes the legal, policy, and military operational aspects of ROE, as well as their effect on ROE composition and application. In particular, the discussion explores how ROE can be used to control the conduct of an operation and its level of escalation. The following section considers how aspects of targeting are integrated into the ROE, as well as how targeting and ROE interact during the conduct of an operation. Specific areas of concern regarding targeting and ROE in relation to certain non-lethal methods and means of conducting operations are also analysed. The chapter concludes with the author's observations on targeting rules of engagement.

Keywords ROE · Rules of engagement · Targeting · LOAC

Contents

H. Boddens Hosang (✉)
Directorate of Legal Affairs, Netherlands Ministry of Defence, The Hague, The Netherlands
e-mail: JFR.BoddensHosang@mindef.nl

P.A.L. Ducheine et al. (eds.), *Targeting: The Challenges of Modern Warfare*,
DOI 10.1007/978-94-6265-072-5_8

8.1 Introduction

Military operations are governed by a number of interrelated documents that, in combination with applicable law, describe the objectives of the operation, the requisite conditions for its successful completion, and the tasks and duties to be carried out to achieve those objectives. This chapter focuses on the rules governing the execution of the assigned tasks and duties, referred to as the rules of engagement (ROE), and their interaction with targeting.

ROE are often assumed to relate exclusively to the use of force, including the commencement of combat engagement (reactive or proactive) and the exercise of the inherent right of self-defence.[1] To the extent that ROE address the use of force, it is clear that applying them requires clarity as to the relationship between the ROE and the law of targeting. However, as will be discussed, ROE also encompass a number of issues unrelated to the use of force. For example, ROE may cover interference (in the broadest sense of the word) with local civilian activities and information operations. In all cases in which ROE are applied, whether lethal or non-lethal, interaction between the ROE and the rules and laws governing targeting is inevitable. Understanding that relationship is essential to ensuring the legality of any such action.

This chapter will first examine the basic elements of ROE, including the definition, sources, purpose, and application of ROE in the operational context. Next, specific aspects of targeting in the context of ROE will be assessed. In particular, the interaction between ROE and targeting during non-lethal operations will be considered in order to discuss the complexities that can arise in that context. Finally, the chapter will analyse the interaction between ROE as an operational document and the other operational instructions, directives, orders, and rules that may apply in a given operation.

8.2 Rules of Engagement Basics

8.2.1 Definition and Sources

The term 'rules of engagement (ROE)' is understood and defined differently in various settings. It can be used to describe the numbered sets of rules issued by the political (command) authorities to senior military commanders, such as those authorized by the North Atlantic Council for implementation by the

[1]While almost all ROE include a phrase specifying that they do not limit or negate the inherent right of self-defence, many nonetheless contain guidance on the exercise of the right of self-defence. Conceptually, the two are distinct entities governed by separate elements of the applicable law. See Boddens Hosang 2008; Chairman of the Joint Chiefs of Staff 2000, pp. A-3–A-7.

Supreme Allied Commander Europe (SACEUR) during a North Atlantic Treaty Organization (NATO) operation. It may also refer to derivative instructions set forth in summarized cards ('soldiers' cards') or similar operational documents.

The United States Department of Defense defines ROE as '[d]irectives issued by competent military authority that delineate the circumstances and limitations under which United States forces will initiate and/or continue combat engagement with other forces encountered.'[2] The *San Remo Handbook* defines them as being issued to 'assist in the delineation of the circumstances and limitations within which military forces may be employed to achieve their objectives' and to 'provide authorization for and/or limits on, among other things, the use of force, the positioning and posturing of forces, and the employment of certain specific capabilities.'[3] The most commonly used, or paraphrased definition is that employed by NATO, which describes ROE as 'directives to military forces (including individuals) that define the circumstances, conditions, degree, and manner in which force, or actions which might be construed as provocative, may be applied.'[4]

The latter two definitions more accurately capture the fact that ROE not only deal with the use of force in the sense of employing weapons or other means of inflicting violence, but also govern actions or activities that may have an impact on the general situation in the theatre of operations. This aspect of ROE is important to bear in mind when considering the sources of ROE and the process by which they are developed. As regards the term 'directives' in the definitions, note that the legal status of ROE, that is their status as binding orders or as policy guidance, differs between countries.[5]

Roach's classic model of ROE composition[6] still applies. In this model, ROE are created in (or as a result of) the overlap of political policy, operational considerations, and the applicable law. For ease of understanding, the model is depicted as a Venn diagram consisting of three (or four)[7] equal circles, with ROE appearing in the overlap in the middle (Fig. 8.1).

In practice, however, the 'circles', or rather the sources or influences they represent, may not be equal in size (in the sense of influence exerted). The relative weight assigned to each depends on the nature and context of the operation for which the ROE are being issued.

The legal component of ROE generally reflects two key elements: the mission's mandate and the relevant law. It should be noted in this regard that ROE are not

[2]Department of Defense 2013, p. 243.

[3]Cole et al. 2009, p. 1.

[4]NATO 2010, p. 254.

[5]Cole et al. 2009, p. 1.

[6]Roach 1983, p. 48.

[7]Although the original Roach model differentiates between policy and diplomacy, it may be safely assumed that the two are synonymous in terms of underlying political considerations.

Fig. 8.1 ROE and its constituent elements

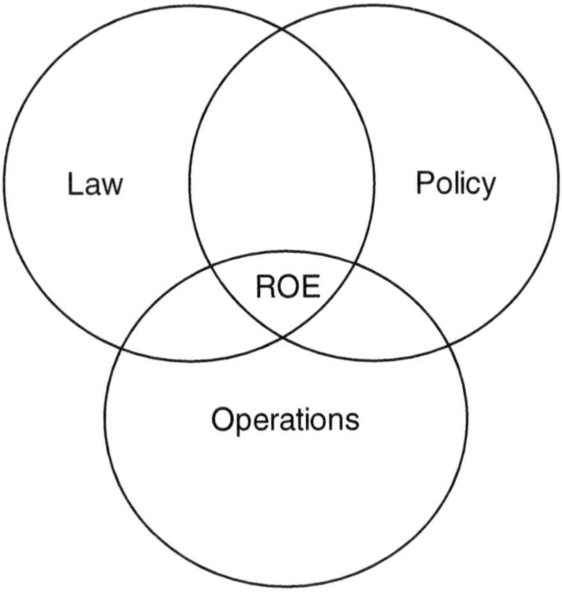

law.[8] The legal component of ROE is descriptive, not prescriptive. In other words, the legal constraints reflected in the ROE would apply even if the ROE had not been issued. Moreover, the legal component of ROE is, in and of itself (i.e., separate from the other ROE components), never more restrictive, nor more permissive, than the law. As will be discussed below, the restrictive effect of ROE is more commonly the result of the policy component of ROE. Any legal restriction imposed on the operation stems from the applicable law, not the ROE.

As ROE are issued primarily in order to regulate the use of force and other relevant actions in connection with mission accomplishment (and to delineate the right of self-defence),[9] they must also be compatible with the mission's mandate.[10] While generally containing only generic phrases regarding the use of force, such as 'all necessary means are authorized', the mandate provides the legal basis for, and sets forth the purpose and objectives of, the mission. The ROE must therefore give sufficient authorization to accomplish the mission, but cannot be more permissive than the mandate itself.

---

[8]Stafford 2000, p. 3. See also the comment mentioned above concerning the legal status of ROE in different countries. Regardless of their status, however, it is clear that ROE as such are not law in the sense of being issued or passed by a legislative body.

[9]See supra note 1.

[10]NATO 2010, p. 157; Boddens Hosang 2008, pp. 69–70. See also, however, the discussion of the policy element of ROE in this chapter. The word 'mandate' is used here as a generic term and may refer to either an authorizing resolution by the United Nations Security Council or any other source of international law, including the right of national self-defence.

In addition to the mandate, both national and international law govern military operations.[11] Applicable national law includes criminal law,[12] a component of which is military disciplinary law. Consequently, authorization for the use of force in ROE will typically be subjected to legal review to ensure they comply with national legal requirements.[13] Applicable international law contains elements of general (public) international law,[14] as well as either directly applicable (*de jure*) or applicable as a matter of policy (*de facto*) law of armed conflict (LOAC).[15] Given that ROE are intended to be succinct and easily understandable, they tend not to fully restate the law. Rather, ROE refer to those aspects of the law that are particularly relevant in the circumstances of the operation to which the ROE apply. In general, the key legal feature of ROE lies in the legal review that ensures they are consistent with the applicable law and mandate.

Policy considerations in ROE reflect the principle that all military operations, including armed conflict, are never a means unto themselves but are ultimately a political tool for achieving political policy objectives.[16] Accordingly, and despite the misperception that ROE restrictions are the fault of the legal advisors,[17] the constraints most commonly result from political considerations regarding the conduct of operations. Such restrictions may, for example, relate to (simultaneous) diplomatic efforts to resolve the situation,[18] seek to avoid spread of the conflict to neighbouring States,[19] or attempt to maintain (continued) support from the local population.[20]

---

[11]NATO 2010, p. 157; Chairman of the Joint Chiefs of Staff 2000, p. L-2.

[12]For example, based on Status of Forces Agreements, national contingents generally fall under the jurisdiction of their sending State. For a more extensive discussion of such agreements and sending State jurisdiction, see Voetelink 2012.

[13]The procedure in The Netherlands for legal review of military use of force in international operations is set forth in a letter from the Public Prosecutor's Office (*College van Procureurs-Generaal*) to the Chief Prosecutor (*Hoofdofficier*) of the Public Prosecutor's Office in Arnhem of 20 November 2006, published in the National Gazette of 2006, nr. 233.

[14]Such as, for example, elements of the law of the sea regarding the conduct of military operations in relation to the freedom of navigation on the high seas.

[15]While the LOAC applies *de jure* only during an armed conflict or situations of belligerent occupation, both NATO and its members States apply its principles in all operations. See, for example, Chairman of the Joint Chiefs of Staff 2000, p. A-2. See also the more detailed discussion on this issue, infra, Sect. 8.3.2.

[16]Von Clausewitz 1831, p. 99.

[17]Parks 2001, p. 35.

[18]Parks 1983, for example, describes the changes in the targeting authorizations in the air campaign over Vietnam following the breakdown of negotiations between the United States and North Vietnam in 1972, leading to wider authorizations for the Linebacker campaign as compared to the previous Rolling Thunder campaign.

[19]Milkowski 2001, for example, describes the geographical limits imposed on operations in the Korean war and restrictions on operations should Chinese or Soviet units be encountered.

[20]Cole 1995, for example, describes restrictions imposed on operations against the Rio Hato base during Operation Just Cause, imposed because it was feared that destruction of the base would lead to (increased) resistance among the Panamanian population.

Policy-related constraints frequently impose limitations on actions, including targeting choices, beyond those required by the law applicable to the given operation. However, because ROE are commonly formulated as authorizations or prohibitions, they are often mistaken as 'legal' rules. It is essential that the political nature of ROE restrictions be borne in mind at all command levels, since policy can change more frequently and easily than the law and ROE may need to be adjusted in accordance with such shifts.

The military-operational component of ROE consists of two aspects. The first relates to the nature of ROE. ROE are a military operational document; they are a military commander's tool for controlling and directing the execution of a given operation.[21] ROE influence the conduct of the operation both in terms of the use of force to achieve mission objectives and with respect to other actions that may impact on the behaviour of the opponent and various factions in the area of operations. The second aspect regarding the military element of ROE is that it may lead to certain restrictions on otherwise lawful actions. While rare, strategic concerns regarding unity of effort and rational allocation and expenditure of resources can lead to operational constraints. It should be noted in this regard that policy-based ROE restrictions can also serve military strategic concerns. The desire to maintain the support of the local population exemplifies such coinciding interests.

8.2.2 *Purpose and Development*

As was indicated above, the primary purpose of ROE is to control the level of violence or confrontation in the area of operations by setting limits on the actions authorized, including those that may be provocative. By controlling the use of force, ROE can influence the actions taken by other parties (including opposing forces). This is commonly referred to as 'escalation dominance',[22] and reflects the inherently military operational nature of ROE.

Secondary purposes of ROE derive from the other two constituent components. ROE can ensure that the forces to which they are issued comply with the overall policy goals of the operation. Similarly, because ROE may never be more permissive than the applicable law, they represent the 'maximum bandwidth' for lawful action, thereby serving as a useful means of gauging the legality of intended actions. However, given that ROE are typically drafted to apply in all circumstances within a given operation (and allow some degree of individual interpretation), they can never guarantee that every action is lawful.[23] In terms of targeting,

[21] Parks 2001, pp. 34–35; Duncan 1999.

[22] Boddens Hosang 2008, p. 66.

[23] A second reason for making this observation, apart from the generic formulation of the ROE themselves, is that the principles of necessity and proportionality must be applied to all actions undertaken, regardless of ROE authorization. Actions permitted by the ROE but failing the necessity and/or proportionality requirement(s) can consequently still lead to criminal prosecution.

some of the ROE can nevertheless significantly assist forces in making an initial estimation as to the legality of intended actions.

Finally, ROE do not assign tasks or specific missions,[24] nor do they limit the inherent right of self-defence.[25] Missions and tasks are assigned and authorized through the regular chain of command and cannot be justified by reference to the operation's ROE. Once the missions and tasks are assigned, however, the ROE provide the authorization for the use of force (or any action which may be considered provocative) that may become necessary to carry out those missions and tasks. Most ROE contain a statement indicating that they do not limit or negate the inherent right of self-defence. Nevertheless, the ROE should not be discounted too quickly as a result of this clause because they provide the overall policy, legal, and operational framework for the use of force during the operation.

Given the constituent parts of ROE as discussed above, it is clear that the process of developing ROE, as well as the authorization process, requires the involvement of each of the three disciplines described. However, military commanders (or their staff) must always play the central role in ROE development.[26] One approach to ensure that this occurs is to assign the primary responsibility for drafting ROE to the commander's staff, after which the staff legal and the policy advisers can review them.[27] Alternatively, ROE may be developed in an ROE planning cell composed of the operational experts and the staff legal adviser. Higher command levels and policy advisers then review the product.[28] Requests for ROE additions or changes generally follow the same process as was used to draft the initial ROE.

A number of international organizations have developed compendia setting forth basic ROE policy and standard ROE texts that can be adapted for a particular operation. These documents provide a useful tool, since they can serve to help ensure that the final ROE set addresses all relevant topics.[29] The *San Remo Rules of Engagement Handbook* is an especially useful document for this purpose and is available online.[30]

---

[24]Cole et al. 2009, p. 2; Cathcart 2010, p. 116.

[25]Chairman of the Joint Chiefs of Staff 2000, p. A-2; Cole et al. 2009, p. 4; Roach 1983, p. 49. For an extensive discussion on the interaction between ROE and self-defence, see Boddens Hosang 2008.

[26]Parks 2001, pp. 35–36.

[27]Chairman of the Joint Chiefs of Staff 2000, pp. L-1–L-2 and L-4.

[28]Ibid. While it is also theoretically possible to include a political policy adviser in a ROE planning or drafting cell, it is the author's professional experience that political review, to ensure compliance between the ROE and the policy objectives or political framework for an operation, usually takes place after the draft ROE have been formulated.

[29]Equivalent (or at least similar) documents within NATO, the EU and the UN contain the specific policy on ROE for each of those organizations, as well as considerable insight into the ROE structure and wording.The ROE compendia used by those organizations are unavailable to the general public.

[30]Cole et al. 2009.

8.3 Targeting and ROE

Although the wording may differ somewhat between the various operations for which they are issued, a number of ROE are always included in ROE sets issued to military personnel. Among these are specific ROE addressing targeting concerns. Furthermore, as ROE must conform to the applicable rules of international law, but international legal obligations may vary between nations, the interaction between the law on targeting and ROE must be examined carefully. Finally, certain specific types of non-lethal operations may lead to particular concerns regarding the interaction between the ROE and the applicable law on targeting.

8.3.1 Special Targeting (Elements of) ROE

The implementation of targeting considerations in the ROE takes two forms: a general form that applies to all ROE that authorize the use of force and a specific form that establishes the rules on target acquisition and positive identification.[31] While the first specifies the valid subjects of an engagement (lethal and non-lethal), the second more specifically prescribes the degree of certainty which must be achieved prior to engagement and the methods and means authorized or required to establish that certainty.

ROE authorizing the use of force or actions that may be provocative against a particular faction, (opposing) party, or category of targets are intrinsically mission-specific. ROE compendia entries usually contain an element to be filled in when drafting such ROE. In the *San Remo Handbook*, for example, the elements are indicated by '(SPECIFY…)',[32] while within NATO this component is indicated by the word 'DESIG'.[33] Identifying the permitted subjects essentially designates them as valid targets throughout the operation in question. Consequently, great care must be taken to ensure that the actions so authorized are permitted under applicable law. In some cases, it may be necessary to provide additional guidance as to specific circumstances (e.g., against DESIG subjects under DESIG circumstances).

During armed conflict, the DESIG element seldom poses problems with respect to authorizing action against enemy forces.[34] In operations other than armed con-

[31]The term 'positive identification' can mean various things in different contexts. For the purpose of this article, the term refers to a level of identification of an intended target that reaches the degree of certainty regarding its status, identity, location, etc., that allows an engagement decision.

[32]Cole et al. 2009.

[33]NATO 2010, pp. 26, 256.

[34]Bear in mind that any action undertaken pursuant to authorized ROE must still meet the requirements of applicable law. For instance, ROE authorizing the attack on enemy forces would clearly not justify attack on enemy units that have surrendered or have been (otherwise) rendered *hors de combat*.

flict, however, the DESIG component necessitates sensitive decisions on the legal and policy issues involved in targeting the designated subjects. For example, authorizing the use of force against persons who engage in a hostile act or demonstrate hostile intent[35] is less problematic[36] than authorizing pre-planned action against members of the local civilian population. Additionally, designation of the circumstances under which action is authorized is of greater importance when not involved in an armed conflict. In all cases, of course, the DESIG element must be suitable for the operation as a whole.

ROE normally also include rules containing specific guidance or instructions as regards targeting in individual cases. Such ROE can be used to prescribe the minimum requirements for establishing positive identification, as well as to specify, for example, which systems may or may not be used to identify them. It is important to note that where the ROE provide such rules, they apply equally to the implementation of the ROE authorizing actions against predetermined target categories. In other words, the ROE for which the DESIG element has been completed (e.g., authorizing attack on enemy forces) must be applied in conjunction with the specific ROE delineating the requirements for target identification.

Target identification ROE set forth the minimum (number of) required means for identifying a target. In the *San Remo Handbook*, they are found in the '31 series' ROE[37]; other ROE compendia follow a similar system. The most restrictive versions require visual[38] identification prior to engagement. Less constraining

[35]The terms 'hostile act' and 'hostile intent' provide a potential source of great confusion in the context of ROE. In the United States and in the San Remo Handbook, these terms are used to refer to an attack (hostile act) or an imminent attack (hostile intent) against one's own forces. See Chairman of the Joint Chiefs of Staff 2000, p. A-5; Cole et al. 2009, p. 82. Within NATO (and in the author's experience also within the context of EU military operations), the terms are used to refer to acts detrimental or prejudicial to the safety of own forces, but not rising to the level of an actual attack (hostile act) and to the identified intention to commit such acts (hostile intent); NATO 2010, p. 255. In the context of this chapter, the NATO definitions apply.

[36]Given the disparate definitions cited above, there is some debate as to whether hostile act and hostile intent ROE are inherently defensive in nature (in the sense of authorizing force in reaction to hostile behaviour by the other party or even in the sense of the inherent right of self-defence) or whether they are intended for (proactive) mission accomplishment by authorizing attack on the parties indicated. Since self-defence is not negated or limited by ROE and instead exists in its own right in parallel to ROE mission accomplishment engagement authority, the hostile act and hostile intent ROE are consequently, in a logical approach, not limited to the inherent right of self-defence. However, although the ROE in question do authorize 'attack on' the parties in question, their application requires a prior offensive act by the other party (obviously more so in the case of hostile act ROE than the hostile intent ROE). Consequently, the author is of the opinion that these specific ROE fall into a unique category lying between 'true' defensive ROE (such as those related to the right of self-defence) and 'true' offensive ROE (such as ROE authorizing proactive attacks on, or destruction of, specified categories of persons or objects).

[37]Cole et al. 2009, pp. 38–39.

[38]'Visual' in the sense of these ROE includes the use of image magnification devices, such as binoculars. It does not, however, include electro-optical systems such as Forward-Looking Infrared (FLIR) and (remote) camera systems. However, some debate surrounds the dividing line between image magnification and visual enhancement through electro-optical devices.

ones may authorize identification by a certain number of non-visual means (although obviously always permitting visual identification as well). Such non-visual means include systems requiring an active response from the target (e.g., an Identification Friend or Foe (IFF) transponder) and passive systems (e.g., radar, (passive) acoustic signature recognition, etc.). Additionally, the ROE may permit or restrict the use of certain devices for target identification or, more commonly, target designation.[39] These ROE are useful tools during operations in sensitive or politically complex contexts. They can serve either to reduce the chance of provocation (by prohibiting target designation by systems generating a warning or response in the target, such as certain fire control radars) or to demonstrate resolve or willingness to engage, by actively threatening the target.

A unit other than the one engaging the target may carry out target identification and designation. For example, a forward unit, whether ground-based (e.g., a forward air controller or joint terminal attack controller (JTAC)) or airborne (e.g., a drone equipped with cameras and relay system or a reconnaissance helicopter), may provide target data to an aircraft conducting close air support or to an artillery battery providing (long rage) fire support. In the case of pre-planned attacks, the targeting process is completed separate from the engagement both in time and geographically, since pre-planned targeting is generally conducted at the staff level.[40] The fact that the target identification and designation is carried out by a different unit or at a different level does not diminish the applicability of the ROE. All units or personnel that partake in targeting must apply the ROE for the given operation.[41] Of course, the use of other units to provide target identification and designation poses potential legal complications, a reality to be discussed.

8.3.2 Targeting as Reflected in ROE Application

The fact that ROE are applicable to the conduct of the operation as a whole by necessity precludes specificity as to the law of targeting. Consequently, ROE do not always indicate whether the intended target is a lawful one in the given circumstances. Even in the case of ROE in which the DESIG element has been completed, the validity of engagements based thereon will still depend on the

[39]For the purposes of this article, the distinction between target identification and target designation indicates the difference between identifying the target (that is, determining its characteristics in order to make further engagement decisions) and either designating a target for purposes of engagement status (for example, whether it is 'friendly' or 'hostile') or tracking it for engagement with available weapon systems (such as by means of fire control radars).

[40]For a detailed description of the targeting process related to pre-planned targeting, see Department of the Army 2010.

[41]Cole et al. 2009, p. 26; Corn and Corn 2011, p. 352; Department of the Army 2010, pp. 1–2.

circumstances of the situation.[42] ROE prescribing the required level of target identification further complicate the matter.[43]

In the absence of specific ROE authorizing engagement against the target type in question,[44] as well circumstance-specific engagement guidance, the validity of engaging a target must be determined separately from the ROE. The laws of armed conflict apply *de jure* to armed conflicts and occupation. Some nations, and NATO, have adopted a policy of applying them to situations not rising to the armed conflict thresholds set forth in the law.[45]

For nations Party to the First Additional Protocol of 1977 to the Geneva Conventions of 1949 (AP1), the definition of a valid military target is set forth in Article 52. Both in the targeting process and when applying the ROE in a given operation or situation, these nations must ensure that every target meets the criteria set out in the Article.[46] This requirement applies equally to targets identified and designated by other units; the engaging unit remains responsible for verifying the legality of the engagement.[47]

Problems may surface when a unit from a State Party to AP1 carries out an engagement in which target identification or designation was performed by units of a State which is not a Party to that treaty, and which may apply a different definition of a lawful military target. This is the case, for example, with the United States, which characterizes economic and infrastructural targets that indirectly contribute to the war-sustaining ability of the enemy as lawful.[48] In such circumstances, the ROE themselves provide no guarantee that an engagement is lawful, even when both the targeting and engaging units follow the specific targeting ROE.

There are two possible solutions to this dilemma. The first is to issue ROE that reflect the strictest legal obligations, thus ensuring adherence to the law even by those nations not normally subject to that law. Doing so will be unlikely to gain the approval of nations complying with a more permissive approach. The more

---

[42]See supra note 34, for an example of this observation.

[43]See supra, Sect. 8.3.1.

[44]As the 'attack on…' ROE are specifically offensive in nature, the authorization of such ROE is not always considered appropriate for all operations. Additionally, circumstances may require or render expedient the engagement of persons or objects not specified in the 'attack on…' ROE, thus requiring an ad hoc decision as regards such engagement.

[45]Letter by the Minister of Defence of The Netherlands to the First Chamber of Parliament, 25 November 2005, pp. 4–5 (Parliamentary Document number 30 300X, A). See also NATO 2010, p. 268 and supra note 15.

[46]It should be noted that this statement refers to engagement in the sense of attack. Non-lethal engagement is discussed elsewhere and is not necessarily subject to the criteria of Article 52 of AP1.

[47]While in the case of close air support it is common to apply the principle that the JTAC 'buys the bomb' (meaning that the JTAC is responsible for his or her targeting decisions and the aircraft 'merely' delivers the weapon), the pilot of the engaging aircraft is still under an obligation to verify that the target is at least *prima facie* a valid military objective prior to releasing the weapon.

[48]Dinstein 2002, pp. 145–146; Thomas and Duncan 1999, pp. 8–3.

commonly applied solution is for nations subject to a stricter legal obligation to issue national restrictions, essentially limiting the application of the ROE to fit within its legal obligations. Such national restrictions, or *caveats*, must be notified to the commander of the operation and to the other participating nations, in order that it can become clear that the forces from the nation in question may not carry out certain actions, regardless of the ROE for the operation as a whole.[49] For example, nations that are State Parties to AP1 could issue a *caveat* to the targeting ROE, specifying that their forces may only engage targets meeting the Article 52 criteria.[50]

Additionally, since the military personnel from non-AP1 nations cannot be expected to apply (or even to know) legal obligations to which they are not subject, measures must be taken to ensure that where target identification or designation is carried out by non-AP1 forces, engagement by AP1 forces satisfies the AP1 criteria. The *caveat* alone cannot achieve this end unless the nation in question restricts engagement to targets that have been identified and designated by forces with the same legal obligations. Doing so could lead to considerable interoperability problems. In particular, constraints on resource availability (including the limited availability of trained and certified JTAC personnel) and the division of tasks and capabilities between participating nations in a multinational operation may not allow all targeting to be carried out by the forces of States Parties to AP1. Furthermore, the approach would cause serious difficulties when rendering assistance to non-AP1 units that may need, for example, close air support to withdraw from (or in fact survive) a combat engagement.

An alternative, and more practical, solution to this problem is for the engaging unit to apply the targeting ROE (specifying the minimum requirements for target identification) in such a way that sufficient information is gathered to allow it to make its own determination as to the status of the target as a valid and lawful military objective. One method to achieve this, for example, is to require the engaging unit to pose additional verification or information questions to the targeting unit prior to weapons release.

As noted, policy and military operational concerns may impose restrictions on the conduct of operations by limiting otherwise lawful actions through the ROE. However, ROE may not always be the most useful or appropriate means by which to specify additional criteria for particular engagements. In 2009, for example, the commander of the International Security Assistance Force (ISAF) in Afghanistan issued a tactical directive setting certain restrictions on the use of air-to-ground weapons and indirect fire.[51] While it would, in theory, have been possible to issue separate and specific ROE for such weapon systems, doing so could have led to

[49] Boddens Hosang 2008, p. 74; NATO 2010, pp. 259, 261; Cathcart 2010, p. 118.

[50] While this discussion focuses on Article 52, it should be clear that the same principles, conflicts and potential solutions apply to other legal obligations as well.

[51] HQ ISAF 2009.

confusing ROE and negatively affected interoperability and joint operations.[52] Consequently, the document was issued in parallel to the ROE. While the targeting directive did not set aside or modify the ROE, it did affect the application of the ROE because compliance with the directive was required when applying the ROE. As this example illustrates, the ROE cannot be read in isolation; they must always be applied in combination with the other applicable documents and rules on targeting in the context of the given operation.[53]

8.3.3 Non-lethal ROE and Targeting

Contemporary operations increasingly involve the use of non-lethal methods and means of warfare intended to increase or maintain local support for the operation, contribute to post-conflict reconstruction, and foster local capacity development. These methods and means require a distinctly different approach to targeting. Because their use is so closely related to mission accomplishment (and because they may be construed as provocative), their inclusion in the ROE is necessary for the same reasons as apply to lethal methods and means.

The importance of engaging the local population and so-called 'key leaders' of local communities is well recognized in modern operations.[54] While the process of identifying these key leaders and determining the most effective means of engaging with them and their communities is not directly related to ROE, doing so may create a need to develop specific ROE for the operation. For instance, the ROE generally may restrict or clarify the geographical boundaries within which the forces may or should operate, as well as the positioning of forces relative to others.[55] In order to deal with local leaders or communities, the ROE may need to authorize entry into specific areas. Thus, geographic positioning ROE should not be drafted with only combat engagement in mind. The ROE may also have to

[52] While combat aircraft are normally issued 'Special Instructions' (SPINS) for the operation in question, such documents generally restate or summarize the ROE and do not in themselves have the status of separate ROE.

[53] See also Department of the Army 2006, p. 7, as regards the need to apply considerations on the use of force beyond the ROE themselves: 'Fires that cause unnecessary harm or death to noncombatants may create more resistance and increase the insurgency's appeal—especially if the populace perceives a lack of discrimination in their use. The use of discriminating, proportionate force as a mindset goes beyond the adherence to the rules of engagement. Proportionality and discrimination applied in COIN require leaders to ensure that their units employ the right tools correctly with mature discernment, good judgment and moral resolve.'

[54] Department of the Army 2006, pp. 5–29: 'Nonlethal targets are usually more important than lethal targets in COIN; they are never less important.' See also Hull 2009, pp. 15, 19.

[55] Cole et al. 2009 lists such ROE in the '50-series' ROE (geographic positioning) and in the '53-series' ROE (relative positioning).

specifically authorize such activities as a separate type of engagement.[56] Finally, targeted engagement of key local leaders can necessitate additional ROE addressing the gathering of the information required to effectively conduct such operations.[57]

A new form of operation that may pose considerable challenges vis-à-vis targeting and ROE is cyber operations. While no cyber-specific ROE have as yet been issued in multinational operations, advances in both defensive and offensive cyber operations will necessitate their development, as well as the formulation of specific guidance on targeting in the cyber context.[58] The nature of cyberspace, in which actions take place at great speed and that is characterized by the interconnection of systems and networks (including overlap between military and civilian systems and networks), will exacerbate the challenges for targeting and, concomitantly, ROE development. While the observations discussed above as regards the interaction between applicable law and implementing or applying ROE authorizations are equally valid in the context of cyber operations, future State practice may highlight a need for more custom-made ROE to ensure that cyber operations remain within legal, policy and operational parameters.

8.4 Conclusion

Rules of engagement provide operational commanders with a tool for regulating the use of force, and actions that may be construed as provocative, in order to manage escalation in the area of operations. As such, ROE supply the principal guidance and direction on the engagement of opposing forces and other persons and objects. The goal is to ensure that the actions undertaken by a commander's forces comply with the legal, policy, and operational interests underlying the operation. But ROE do not exist in splendid isolation; adherence thereto is usually insufficient to guarantee the legality or suitability of the actions undertaken.

Given the nature and purpose of ROE, it is unsurprising that targeting and ROE are closely related topics that form an almost symbiotic relationship. ROE cannot be successfully applied prior to the targeting process and the targeting process would yield unusable target lists absent proper implementation of ROE. This relationship is well reflected in specific target identification ROE and ROE authorizing particular actions to be taken (both lethal and non-lethal) against or towards

[56]NATO 2010, p. 256, refers to the '14-series' ROE regarding interference in non-military activities. Additionally, the '33-series' ROE referred to on the same page can be used for specific types of operations aimed more towards peacekeeping than combat operations.

[57]NATO 2010, p. 158. For ROE for psychological operations, see Cole et al. 2009, p. 60 ('132-series' ROE). While potentially carrying a more negative connotation, psychological operations are in essence a specific form of information operations, carried out for particular effect. Note that the '132-series' ROE refer to the ROE on the positioning of forces.

[58]Nakashima 2012, 2013.

specified targets. The interaction between ROE and targeting becomes even clearer in practice, but also yields a number of challenges.

Different legal obligations for nations participating in a multinational operation require both careful attention and constructive approaches to ensure the lawfulness of the actions taken in conformity with the ROE, as well as to maintain interoperability. Additionally, operational or policy considerations may dictate the promulgation of directives or orders that further delineate or restrict certain methods and means or provide more detailed guidance regarding specific types of targets. Although they do not nullify or necessarily modify the ROE, such considerations have the potential to significantly affect how the ROE must be applied in the operation in question.

Finally, certain types of operations or actions may require additional or specific ROE. Especially where the subjects of such operations or actions are non-combatants, both targeting and ROE must work in unison to ensure the legality of any action and its conformity with the operation's overall operational and policy objectives.

Ultimately, and despite their status as the capstone regarding the use of force and other actions affecting the conduct of an operation, the ROE are by themselves not completely definitive. In view of the symbiotic relationship between ROE and targeting, the ROE cannot even be said to be a *primus inter pares* in the panoply of operational guidance and operational directives for a given operation. Instead, they are an integral and essential part in a complex system, in which each of the parts must interact and be applied in proper cohesion with the others for the system to function as designed.

References

Boddens Hosang JFR (2008) Self-defence in military operations: the interaction between the legal bases for military self-defence and rules of engagement. Military Law Law War Rev 47:25

Cathcart B (2010) Force application in enforcement and peace enforcement operations. In: Gill TD, Fleck D (eds) The handbook of the international law of military operations. Oxford University Press, Oxford, p 115

Chairman of the Joint Chiefs of Staff (2000) Standing rules of engagement for US forces. CJCSI 3121.01A

Von Clausewitz C (1831) On war. In: Howard M, Paret P (eds and trans 1993) Everyman's library edition. Knofp, New York

Cole A, Drew P, McLaughlin R, Mandsager D (eds) (2009) Rules of engagement handbook. International Institute of Humanitarian Law, San Remo

Cole R (1995) Operation just cause: the planning and execution of joint operations in Panama February 1988–January 1990. Joint History Office, Office of the Chairman of the Joint Chiefs of Staff

Corn GS, Corn GP (2011) The law of operational targeting: viewing the LOAC through an operational lens. Tex Int Law J 47(2):337

Department of the Army (2006) Field manual FM 3-24 (MCWP 3-33.5) Counterinsurgency. Headquarters, Department of the Army

Department of the Army (2010) Field manual FM 3-60 (FM 6-20-10) The targeting process. Headquarters, Department of the Army

Department of Defense (2013) Dictionary of military and associated terms. Joint Publication 1-02, as amended through 15 April 2013

Dinstein Y (2002) Legitimate military objectives under the current jus in bello. U S Naval War Coll Int Law Stud 78:139

Duncan, JC (1999) The commander's role in developing rules of engagement. Naval War Coll Rev

Hull Jeanne F (2009) Iraq: strategic reconciliation, targeting, and key leader engagement. U.S. Army War College Strategic Studies Institute. http://www.strategicstudiesinstitute.army.mil/pdffiles/pub938.pdf. Accessed 27 Feb 2014

HQ ISAF (2009) Tactical directive. http://www.nato.int/isaf/docu/official_texts/Tactical_Directive_090706.pdf. Accessed 27 Feb 2014)

Milkowski SD (2001) To the Yalu and back. Joint Force Q 2001(Spring/Summer):38–46

Minister of Defence of The Netherlands, Letter to the First Chamber of Parliament on legal aspects of peace operations, 25 November 2005 (Parliamentary Document number 30 300X, A)

Nakashima E (2012) Pentagon proposes more robust role for its cyber-specialists. Washington Post, 9 Aug 2012

Nakashima E (2013) In cyberwarfare, rule of engagement still hard to define. Washington Post, 10 March 2013

NATO (2010) NATO legal deskbook. NATO Allied Command Transformation

Parks WH (1983) Linebacker and the law of war. Air Univ Rev 34:2

Parks WH (2001) Deadly force is authorized. Naval Inst Proc 127(1):33

Roach JA (1983) Rules of engagement. Naval War Coll Rev 36(1):46

Stafford WA (2000) How to keep military personnel from going to jail for doing the right thing. Army Lawyer 2000(Nov):1–25

Thomas AR, Duncan JC (eds) (1999) Annotated supplement to the commander's handbook on the law of naval operations. International Law Studies, vol 73. U.S. Naval War College, Newport

Voetelink JED (2012) 'Status of forces': strafrechtsmacht over militairen vanuit internationaalrechtelijk & militair-operationeelrechtelijk perspectief. Dissertation, University of Amsterdam, 20 Sept 2012

Part III
Special Issues in Targeting

Chapter 9
Means and Methods of the Future: Autonomous Systems

Jeffrey S. Thurnher

Abstract Autonomous systems will fundamentally alter the way wars are waged. In particular, autonomous weapon systems, capable of selecting and engaging targets without direct human operator involvement, represent a significant shift of humans away from the battlefield. As these new means and methods of warfare are introduced, many important targeting decisions will likely need to be made earlier and further away from the front lines. Fearful of these changes and coupled with other legal and moral concerns, groups opposed to autonomous weapons have formed and begun campaigning for a pre-emptive ban on their development and use. Nations intending to use these emerging technologies must grapple with how best to adjust their targeting processes and procedures to accommodate greater autonomy in weapon systems. This chapter examines these cutting-edge and controversial weapons with a particular emphasis on the legal impact on targeting during international armed conflicts. Initially, this chapter will explore the promising technological advances and operational benefits which indicate these weapon systems may become a reality in the not-so-distant future. The focus will then turn to the unique challenges the systems present to the law of armed conflict under both weapons law and targeting law principles. Next, the examination will shift to two key aspects of targeting most affected by autonomous systems: targeting doubt and subjectivity in targeting. The author ultimately concludes that autonomous weapon systems are unlikely to be deemed unlawful *per se* and that, while these targeting issues raise legitimate concerns, the use of autonomous weapons under many circumstances will be lawful.

The views expressed are those of the author and should not be understood as necessarily representing those of NATO, the United States Department of Defense, or any other government entity.

J.S. Thurnher (✉)
NATO Rapid Deployable Corps/1 (German-Netherlands) Corps, Muenster, Germany
e-mail: jeffrey.s.thurnher.mil@mail.mil

P.A.L. Ducheine et al. (eds.), *Targeting: The Challenges of Modern Warfare*,
DOI 10.1007/978-94-6265-072-5_9

Keywords Autonomy · Autonomous · Weapon system · Robot · Law of armed conflict · International humanitarian law · Artificial intelligence · Targeting · Drone · Means and methods

Contents

9.1 Introduction

The aim of this chapter is to explore the tremendous impact and legal ramifications that autonomous systems will have on the targeting processes of modern militaries. Increasingly, military systems are being fielded with embedded autonomous features, such as the ability to manoeuvre across the battlefield without a human controller. Yet, it is the potential advent of autonomous lethal targeting capabilities that is generating the most significant attention. If systems gain the autonomous ability to select and engage targets based upon pre-programmed criteria without direct human operator involvement, many key targeting decisions will likely need to be made in earlier phases of the targeting cycle and at locations further removed from the intended strike site. Nations desiring to use such autonomous systems will need to ensure that their targeting procedures nevertheless comply with international law, including all relevant law of armed conflict tenets. Thus far, no country has publically declared an interest in developing fully autonomous weapon systems,[1] but this will likely change in the future as the technology becomes more sophisticated and reliable and, as the operational benefits of autonomy become apparent.

[1]In fact, nations such as the United States and United Kingdom have declared they are not pursuing such weapons other than human supervised ones. House of Lords Debate 26 March 2013 (The UK Ministry of Defense 'currently has no intention of developing [weapon] systems that operate without human intervention'.); United States Department of Defense 2012a, p. 3 (The United States has no 'plans to develop lethal autonomous weapon systems other than human-supervised systems for the purposes of local defense of manned vehicles or installations'.).

A secondary aim of this chapter is to discuss some of the legal concerns and criticisms regarding these potential new means and methods of warfare. Although fully autonomous weapons have not yet been designed, a robust opposition to them has already formed. A coalition of non-governmental organizations, including human rights advocacy groups, is actively campaigning for the adoption of an international treaty to pre-emptively ban the development and use of autonomous weapon systems.[2] The coalition fears these weapon systems will be unable to comply with international law and would endanger civilians in a conflict area.[3] Similarly, a United Nations (UN) Special Rapporteur expressed reservations about autonomous weapon systems and proposed a moratorium on all related testing and development in an April 2013 report to the UN Human Rights Council.[4] In November 2013, the representatives of the UN Convention on Conventional Weapons agreed to discuss autonomous weapon systems as part of an intergovernmental meeting of experts in May 2014.[5] Although the chapter cannot fully address all of the various positions raised by opposition groups, the author will explain throughout why a ban on autonomous weapons is unnecessary and unjustified, and how the existing laws regulating international armed conflict provide sufficient protections and guidelines for these emerging means and methods of warfare.

To address these complex issues, this chapter is organized into the following subparts. Section 9.2 defines the levels of autonomy that future weapons may possess. Section 9.3 examines two key factors spurring nations toward increasing autonomy in their weapon systems. The first component is the recent, remarkable technological progress demonstrated in artificial intelligence and machine learning. The second is the immense operational advantages expected to be gained through greater autonomy. Section 9.4 explores the unique law of armed conflict issues raised by the potential deployment of autonomous weapon systems during international armed conflicts.[6] The discussion will focus both on whether the weapons themselves might be deemed lawful and under what circumstances the use of them might be lawful. Section 9.5 then delves into an analysis of targeting doubt and subjectivity in targeting. Those two facets of the targeting process will be most substantially impacted by the introduction of autonomous weapons.

---

[2]More than 40 non-governmental organizations have formed the *Campaign to Stop Killer Robots*, an umbrella organization dedicated to seeking a comprehensive and pre-emptive ban on the development, production, and use of autonomous weapons. Campaign to Stop Killer Robots 2013. http://www.stopkillerrobots.org/. Accessed 8 January 2014.

[3]Human Rights Watch is one of the founding organizations of the coalition. For a full description of their reservations and criticism of autonomous weapon systems, see Human Rights Watch 2012, p. 1.

[4]United Nations A/HRC/23/47, p. 21.

[5]Convention on Conventional Weapons CCW/MSP/2013/CRP.1, p. 4.

[6]Not all of the legal principles discussed below may apply during conflicts not of an international character, otherwise known as non-international armed conflicts. The use of fully autonomous weapons during non-international armed conflicts is outside the scope of this chapter.

Finally, Sect. 9.6 concludes with a discussion of why autonomous weapons are unlikely to be deemed illegal *per se* and how under many imaginable circumstances the use of such systems would be lawful.

9.2 Levels of Autonomy

A useful starting point for any examination of autonomous weapons is to define the term autonomy and to distinguish the various levels of autonomy that future weapon systems might employ. When discussing technology, the term autonomy describes the ability of a machine or computer system to perform certain functions without human assistance or direct input.[7] In the context of autonomous weapons, the crucial functions that a weapon system might be expected to perform independent of human operator involvement include the targeting actions of finding, fixing, and firing on an objective. The United States (US) Department of Defense (DoD) devised a definition for autonomous weapon systems that has become widely accepted and referenced. It defines an autonomous weapon system as 'a weapon system that, once activated, can select and engage targets without further intervention by a human operator'.[8]

The DoD has further attempted to stratify its systems based upon, in essence, three level of autonomy. First, its level of autonomy refers to 'semi-autonomous' systems or systems, which can only engage targets that have been specifically selected by a human operator. This level of autonomy includes weapons such as 'fire and forget' missiles, where the operator selects and fires the weapon at a target, but then the weapon autonomously hones in on and strikes the target.[9] The second level of autonomy under the DoD approach equates to 'human-supervised autonomous systems'. With human-supervised systems, a human operator retains the ability to override the system at any point, but the system can otherwise act independently to identify and strike a target. The third level applies to fully autonomous systems that can select and engage targets without human operator involvement. Human Rights Watch, among other groups, seemingly identifies three similar levels of autonomy, but they prefer to use the terms, 'human-in-the-loop', 'human-on-the-loop', and 'human-out-of-the-loop' respectively.[10]

A slightly more nuanced approach to the various levels of autonomy is proffered by Dr. Armin Krishnan in his book *Killer Robots*. Dr. Krishnan describes four levels as part of a spectrum or a sliding-scale of autonomy. In general, the more independently a system can perform its tasks, the greater the level of

---

[7]Krishnan 2009, p. 45.

[8]United States Department of Defense 2012, pp. 13–14.

[9]United States Department of Defense 2012, pp. 13–14.

[10]Human Rights Watch 2012, p. 2.

autonomy it possesses.[11] His starting point is with 'tele-operation', where a system is completely controlled by a human operator via a remote control and has no autonomy. Next, he describes 'pre-programmed' autonomous systems that are specifically programmed to conduct precise and non-varying missions. Then, Dr. Krishnan details an additional level of autonomy known as 'supervised autonomy', whereby a system autonomously controls the majority of basic functions, but not the most complex ones, such as those associated with targeting decisions. Those complex decisions would instead be made by human controllers. Dr. Krishnan's final level of autonomy is known as 'Complete autonomy'. Completely autonomous systems would theoretically receive human input on overall objectives, but could otherwise 'find solutions and handle' many complex targeting problems.

In general, unless otherwise specified, whenever this chapter refers to autonomous weapons it is intended to indicate a weapon system that falls under the fully autonomous weapon system level of autonomy as described by the DoD. It also equates to Dr. Krishnan's complete autonomy level, with one exception. Dr. Krishnan seems to imply that to reach this level of autonomy an autonomous system must be capable of operating 'without the need for any human input'.[12] The discussion of autonomous weapons in this chapter, however, does not anticipate that autonomous systems will operate devoid of human input in the foreseeable future.[13] Instead, a fully autonomous system will likely never be completely free of human input.[14] At a minimum, humans will decide under what parameters and frameworks it will operate, and when and where it will be deployed.

9.3 Drivers of Greater Levels of Autonomy in Weapon Systems

Despite the current absence of fully autonomous weapons in any nations' arsenal, numerous experts predict that the use of such systems in armed conflicts will become standard within a generation.[15] Many States are actively exploring ways to increase the use of autonomous features in their military systems. Two major factors help explain this growing interest. The first revolves around recent substantial leaps in technology and science that are making the possibility of these

---

[11]Krishnan 2009, p. 43.

[12]Krishnan 2009, p. 44.

[13]It is conceivable that advances in artificial intelligence technology in the future may allow systems to possess human-like reasoning. However, it is far from certain that the technology will successfully develop in such a manner, and even Dr. Krishnan contends that any such advances would be unlikely to materialize until well beyond the year 2030. Krishnan 2009, p. 44.

[14]Schmitt 2013a, p. 4.

[15]Singer 2009, p. 128.

futuristic systems more certain. The second involves shifting operational realities that will likely drive nations to develop autonomous targeting capabilities.

9.3.1 Advances in Autonomous Technology

Throughout history, scientific advances have led to remarkable improvements in weaponry and military tactics. The current pace of technological developments, however, has been unprecedented. Recent advancements in computer science and artificial intelligence have led some experts to conclude that it is technologically feasible today to design a fully autonomous weapon system.[16] Computer software innovations are at the heart of these successes, as scientists have found new ways of harnessing the increased computational power that is available. By converging complex 'high-level planning' computer algorithms,[17] scientists are enabling computerized systems to increasingly make independent decisions and perform independent actions.[18] Ground-breaking software is progressively incorporating machine learning and other learning models into its designs, allowing the systems to innovate and improve upon prior performance.[19] Tremendous strides have also been made in researching how to make human-system interaction more efficient and fluid. Many nations' militaries are eager to fully employ these advances.

Automatic and autonomous features have long been an aspect of weaponry. Decades ago, navies began using mines capable of responding automatically to 'acoustic, electromagnetic or pressure' signatures.[20] Since the mid-1970s, the United States Navy and others have placed defensive close-in weapon systems (CIWS) aboard its warships. These systems can detect the signatures of incoming missiles and rockets and automatically respond with lethal force to defeat them. Similarly, for many years, air defence weapon systems, such as the United States Army's Patriot Missile system and the United States Navy's Aegis combat system, have had the capacity to automatically defeat incoming artillery or missile attacks on ground and maritime forces.

Recent computing advances are making possible even greater leaps towards full autonomy. Newly designed military systems are showcasing this potential. For

[16]For example, the former chief scientist for the United States Air Force postulates that technology currently exists to facilitate 'fully autonomous military strikes'; Dahm 2012, p. 11.

[17]Guarino 2013.

[18]Poitras 2012.

[19]Guarino 2013. For a more general overview of machine learning capabilities and possibilities, see Russell and Norvig 2010, Chap. 18. For a discussion about how computer systems are learning, in approaches similar to how humans learn by examples, see Public Broadcasting Service 2011.

[20]Heintschel von Heinegg 2011, p. 184 (asserting that such mines are 'quite common and legally uncontested').

example, the latest developments in autonomous flight have been remarkable. The United States has demonstrated the ability to have a combat aircraft autonomously take off and land from an aircraft carrier. The aircraft, known as the X-47B, successfully performed these difficult manoeuvres without the help of a human controller during testing in 2013. For the past few years, the United States Marines have successfully used 'K-MAX' variant helicopters to autonomously fly and deliver supplies to forward operating bases across Afghanistan. The Taranis attack aircraft, a British Royal Air Force-led project, is expected to be capable of supersonic autonomous flight within the next several years. Furthermore, aircraft will likely soon be able to conduct autonomous mid-air refuelling. Maritime systems similarly show tremendous promise. Several nations have successfully developed underwater systems capable of autonomously adjusting themselves to maintain their position in the water for extended periods of time. These achievements have led the United States to begin exploring designs for a vessel capable of autonomously hunting enemy submarines for months at a time.[21] Even many land systems, such as sentry robots that South Korea has deployed along the Demilitarized Zone (DMZ), possess advanced autonomous features.

Perhaps the most dramatic advances, however, have been made in the cyber domain. Many cyber programs are now being designed to autonomously identify vulnerabilities in a target system and determine how best to infiltrate it.[22] Programs that will employ and 'react to countermeasures' autonomously are also being actively pursued.[23] Some commentators contend that autonomous cyber weapons not only exist today, but also have already been successfully employed as a means of warfare. They point to the use of the computer virus known as Stuxnet, which is believed to have caused damage to Iranian nuclear facilities in 2009, as an example of the potential and power autonomous cyber weapon systems hold.[24] Regardless of whether Stuxnet represents the world's first fully autonomous weapon system, it seems likely that cyberspace will continue to be a keen area of interest for autonomous systems research and development.

The exact path these advances in autonomous technology might take in the future is, however, uncertain. Many experts expect miniaturization to play a major role in future weapons development.[25] Based upon improvements in nanotechnology and other fields, future autonomous systems are envisioned to be more compact and able to operate over substantially increased distances and time. These systems also will be more expendable. Many of them will be designed to operate

---

[21]United States Defense Advanced Research Projects Agency 2013. Note, however, that at least initially the vessel is designed to require human approval before launching an attack. The United States Navy is developing similar underwater systems to conduct de-mining operations; Ackerman 2013.

[22]Guarino 2013.

[23]Ibid.

[24]Healey 2013.

[25]Guarino 2013.

collectively as part of a swarm, capable of quickly and overwhelmingly attacking an enemy force.[26] The computing power supporting future autonomous systems will unquestionably be more powerful and faster than existing capabilities. Future systems may increasingly be controlled with sophisticated forms of artificial intelligence, known as general or strong artificial intelligence. These systems will have an enhanced capacity to independently respond and adjust to their environment.[27] While the promise of future technological advances is bright, one should not expect major breakthroughs to be the norm. Instead, it is more likely that innovations in autonomy will occur incrementally and gradually over time.[28] As the technology slowly improves, the systems will begin assuming greater control over their own actions. Militaries are likely to accept and seek such moves towards autonomy because of the enormous operational advantages inherent with such weapons.

9.3.2 Operational Benefits of Autonomy

Operational benefits may propel nations to increasingly seek autonomous systems. First, current remotely controlled systems may prove to be prohibitive in terms of personnel. These systems require significant numbers of personnel to pilot and maintain them, as well as to constantly analyse the data they obtain. Militaries unable to meet the demand will instead turn to autonomous ones to fill the gap. As an example, the United States, in a recent roadmap on unmanned systems, pledged to 'take the "man" out of unmanned'.[29] Given that many of the duties will be performed automatically by computers, autonomous systems generally require far fewer human operators.[30] Additionally, the use of autonomous systems will also

[26]United States Air Force 2009, p. 16 (stating that '[a]s autonomy and automation merge, [systems] will be able to swarm … creating a focused, relentless, and scaled attack'). The United States Air Force's Proliferated Autonomous Weapons may represent an early prototype of future swarming systems. See Singer 2009, p. 232; Alston 2011, p. 43.

[27]Singer 2009, p. 74; Kellenberger 2011, p. 27. Note, consensus does not exist as to if and when general artificial intelligence might become available. Artificial intelligence has previously failed to live up to some expectations. Computer scientist Noel Sharkey doubts that artificial intelligence advances will achieve human-like abilities in even the next 15 years; Sharkey 2011, p. 140.

[28]Waxman and Anderson 2013, p. 2.

[29]United States Department of Defense 2013, p. 25. Under a heading labelled 'A Look to the Future' it explains: 'Currently personnel costs are the greatest single cost in (the Department of Defense), and unmanned systems must strive to reduce the number of personnel required to operate and maintain the systems. Great strides in autonomy, teaming, multi-platform control, tipping, and cueing have reduced the number of personnel required, but much more work needs to occur'.

[30]'Enable humans to delegate those tasks that are more effectively done by computer … thus freeing humans to focus on more complex decision making'; United States Department of Defense 2012b, p. 1.

likely offer an overall increase in capacity because, unlike human operators, autonomous weapons do not need to sleep or eat and do not become distracted.

Second, autonomous weapon systems are generally less susceptible to electronic or cyber-attacks. As adversaries increasingly become competent in jamming communications and attacking computer networks, communications links represent critical vulnerabilities. Remotely controlled systems are often completely dependent upon a satellite tether to a human pilot and are incapable of completing their mission if that communications link is severed. Autonomous systems, on the other hand, could conceivably continue operations unimpeded even in adverse and electronically contested areas. By not being reliant on a constant link with a human operator, autonomous weapons would also present less opportunity for cyber-attackers to hack into them. Future militaries may find such hardened systems particularly advantageous.

Third, only autonomous systems may be able to operate fast enough for the increased pace of combat in the future. Manned and tethered systems inherently suffer from communications and human operator reaction delays. These time lags may make such systems inferior to, ineffective against, an adversary's autonomous weapons.[31] Many commentators contend that future conflicts will be waged in an environment 'too fast [and] … too complex for humans to direct'.[32] To avoid facing a potential competitive disadvantage, nations will invariably seek to enhance their development of autonomous weapons.[33] Autonomous weapons will likely become an ever growing segment of their military arsenals.

9.4 A Law of Armed Conflict Analysis of Autonomous Weapon Systems

Assuming that technology will make autonomous weapon systems possible and operational realities will cause nations to clamour for them, it is important to closely consider what law would apply to these new means of warfare. If they were to be employed in armed conflict, then the law of armed conflict would apply. A State hoping to develop and deploy an autonomous weapon must analyse two separate facets of the law.[34] First, it must determine whether the weapon itself is lawful *per se*. Second, it needs to appraise whether the use of the weapon is

---

[31]Sharkey 2012, p. 110.

[32]Singer 2009, p. 128.

[33]For example, the United States has expressed an interest in seeking an expansion of autonomous features, albeit not lethal targeting capabilities, into its systems in the future; United States Department of Defense 2012b, pp. 1–3; United States Department of Defense 2013, p. 25.

[34]*Legality of the Threat or Use of Nuclear Weapons* (Advisory Opinion), ICJ Reports 1996, p. 226 (hereinafter *Nuclear Weapons*); Schmitt and Thurnher 2013, p. 243. Schmitt 2013a, p. 8.

prohibited. Only when a State confirms that the autonomous weapon fully complies with both facets of the law may the new weapon be employed.

9.4.1 The Lawfulness of the Weapon Itself

When determining the lawfulness of a new weapon, the first relevant inquiry is whether the new weapon violates the prohibition on means or methods of warfare that are of a nature to cause unnecessary suffering or superfluous injury. This rule is codified under Article 35(2) of *Additional Protocol I* and reflects customary international law.[35] As a customary rule, all States, including those that are not a party to the Protocol, are bound to observe this prohibition. The ban attempts to prevent inhumane or needlessly aggravating injuries to combatants. A classic example of an unlawful weapon under this prohibition is a bomb that contains glass bomblets. It violates the ban because the bomblets would be invisible to x-ray machines and may unnecessarily complicate medical treatment.

It is important to note that this prohibition focuses solely on the weapon's effects rather than its delivery method. The fact that a targeting decision might be made autonomously by the weapon system does not factor into the analysis. Nevertheless, to be lawful, autonomous weapon systems may only contain weapons and ammunition that do not cause unnecessary suffering or superfluous injury.

The second inquiry is whether the new weapon would breach the prohibition on means or methods of warfare that cannot be directed at a particular military object and are thus indiscriminate by their very nature. Weapons are unlawful when they cannot be specifically aimed, because they are as likely to strike civilians as they might strike combatants. Codified in Article 51(4)(b) of *Additional Protocol I*,[36] this rule is considered reflective of customary international law.[37] The focus of this analysis is solely on whether the system can be properly aimed. Whether the system engages a target based on an autonomous systems' determination versus that of a human is immaterial. As long as the autonomous weapon is capable of being directed at a specific military target, then the weapon would not be unlawful *per se* under this rule. It is therefore unlikely this prohibition will prevent the development of autonomous weapon systems.

There is an additional consideration when examining what constitutes an indiscriminate weapon, but it will similarly present few impediments to autonomous weapon designs. Codified in Article 51(4)(c) of *Additional Protocol I*, and

[35]Henckaerts and Doswald-Beck 2005, r. 70; *Nuclear Weapons*, *supra* note 34, para 78; Cadwalader 2011, p. 157.

[36]Protocol Additional to the Geneva Conventions of 12 August 1949 relating to the Protection of Victims of International Armed Conflicts (Protocol I), 8 June 1977, 1125 UNTS 3 (entered into force 7 December 1978) (hereinafter Additional Protocol I).

[37]Henckaerts and Doswald-Beck 2005, r. 71. See also Cadwalader 2011, p. 153.

reflective of customary international law, weapons are considered indiscriminate, and thus unlawful *per se*, if their strikes will produce uncontrollable effects.[38] Biological weapons are the classic example of a weapon that produces an effect that cannot be controlled. Clearly, an autonomous system could not be outfitted with such a weapon on-board without violating this prohibition. Otherwise, there is little concern that autonomous weapon systems would be considered unlawful *per se* for being indiscriminate by nature.

Any State intending to use a new weapon, like an autonomous weapon system, would need to confirm that the proposed weapon is not indiscriminate by nature and does not cause unnecessary suffering or superfluous injury. To confidently make such a pronouncement, the State would have to conduct a thorough legal review of the weapon. Given the unique nature of autonomous systems, the impact of these weapons reviews is significant.[39]

The requirement to conduct legal reviews on new means of warfare is codified in Article 36 of *Additional Protocol I* and considered reflective of customary international law. As such, all States, including non-parties to the Protocol, must carry out legal reviews prior to fielding any new weapons.[40] Any major modifications of an existing weapon system similarly would require additional legal review. Article 36 also contains a provision requiring reviews of new methods of warfare. In the context of autonomy, a new method of warfare might be akin to a novel approach to autonomously swarming an enemy or some other revolutionary technique for their use. There is, however, no consensus on whether the portion of Article 36 dealing with new methods of warfare reflects customary international law. In any case, parties to the Protocol would clearly be required to comply.[41] Autonomous weapons will unmistakably be sophisticated systems, and the legal review of any such system would invariably be complex. Nevertheless, the review focuses on whether the weapon itself is unlawful *per se*, and, as was discussed, autonomous weapons are unlikely to be labelled as such. The more challenging legal and targeting issues arise when one examines the potential uses of autonomous systems.

9.4.2 Rules Governing the Use of Weapons

Even if an autonomous weapon system is not deemed unlawful *per se*, its use may still be prohibited under international law. The use of a weapon is permissible only if it can comply with the law of armed conflict requirements of distinction,

---

[38]Henckaerts and Doswald-Beck 2005, r. 71.

[39]Some commentators even contend that autonomous systems require a new, more 'holistic' approach to weapons review procedures. See Liu 2012, p. 639.

[40]See for example Schmitt 2013b, commentary accompanying r. 48.

[41]Schmitt 2013b, commentary accompanying r. 48.

proportionality and precautions in the attack. Given that most criticism of autonomous systems focuses on the use (or 'conduct of hostilities') related issues, each warrants close examination.

Distinction is arguably the bedrock principle of the law of armed conflict.[42] It obliges a combatant to distinguish between combatants and civilians, and also between military objectives and civilian objects. Codified in Article 48 of *Additional Protocol I*, with accompanying rules in Articles 51 and 52,[43] the principle is also considered reflective of customary international law.[44] Undeniably, any autonomous weapon system must comply with this principle and accordingly be capable of attacking only military objectives.

Critics who charge that autonomous weapons will not be able to comply with the principle of distinction[45] fail to fully appreciate how the surrounding context and environment factor into this analysis. When examining the principle of distinction, it is critical to first determine the type of environment in which a State plans to use the autonomous weapon system. If, for example, an autonomous weapon is being deployed to a remote area generally devoid of civilians, such as underwater or a desert environment, the demands on the weapon to distinguish would be much lower. In fact, in circumstances such as these, an autonomous weapon system could possibly comply with the rule even if it possessed only a low level ability to distinguish. As the battlefield environment gets more complicated and interspersed with civilians, the demands on the system rise considerably. In urban or other populated areas, an autonomous weapon would likely need to have advanced sensor packages and recognition software. Even then, it is conceivable that the battlefield situation might be too cluttered for the system to accurately distinguish between military objectives and civilian objects or between combatants and the civilian population. In those cases, an autonomous weapon would be unlawful to use. Ultimately, autonomous weapons will only be an option in areas where the systems are able to reasonably distinguish between combatants and civilians and between military objectives and civilian objects given the particular battlefield circumstances ruling at the time.

The second requirement is proportionality. The principle of proportionality is codified in Articles 51(5)(b) and 57(2)(a)(iii) of *Additional Protocol I*.[46] Reflective of customary international law,[47] this complex principle prohibits an attack if it is 'expected to cause incidental loss of civilian life, injury to civilians, damage to civilian objects, or a combination thereof, which would be excessive in relation to

[42]The International Court of Justice has recognized distinction as a 'cardinal' principle of the law of armed conflict. *Nuclear Weapons*, *supra* note 34, paras 78–79.

[43]Additional Protocol I, Articles 49, 51–52.

[44]Henckaerts and Doswald-Beck 2005, r. 1; *Nuclear Weapons Case*, *supra* note 34, paras 78–79; Cadwalader 2011, p. 157.

[45]See for example, Human Rights Watch 2012, pp. 30–32.

[46]Additional Protocol I, Articles 51(5)(b), 57(2)(a)(iii).

[47]Henckaerts and Doswald-Beck 2005, r. 14; Cadwalader 2011, pp. 157–158.

the concrete and direct military advantage anticipated'.[48] The first component in this analysis is the expected amount of collateral damage. For the use of an autonomous weapon to be lawful, the weapon system would have to be able to produce an estimate of the number of civilians who may be harmed incidentally as a result of an attack. This step of the analysis is unlikely to be a challenge for autonomous systems because it is essentially a quantitative determination. The United States and other major militaries have developed a system to make such estimates called the Collateral Damage Estimation Methodology, which relies on scientific data and objective standards.[49]

The second step of the proportionality analysis involves more qualitative judgements and will present greater challenges for autonomous systems. If the collateral damage estimate reveals that civilian casualties or damage to civilian objects are expected from an attack, then the attacking force is obliged to consider the amount of harm to civilians or damage to civilian objects in relation to the anticipated military advantage of the attack. Determining the relative value of the military advantage of an attack is both subjective and contextual. It is unlikely an autonomous system will be capable of making independent value judgements as required by the proportionality principle. That is not to say, however, that the use of autonomous weapons would automatically be unlawful in such situations, as several critics contend.[50] To comply with this principle, nations might instead rely on pre-programing the acceptable values for the situations that an autonomous weapon might encounter. Military operators would thus establish a framework for the autonomous system to operate within. Essentially, the operator has pre-determined for the excessive amount of collateral damage any specific target. Although technologically challenging, it is conceivable that such a mechanism could be developed and embedded into an autonomous weapon. To ensure compliance with the principle, one can expect any predetermined values to initially be set conservatively. Moreover, militaries will likely resort to controlling autonomous weapons tightly with geographic boundaries or time limits as an additional compliance measure. While solving these dilemmas will pose difficulties, it is important to remember that proportionality decisions are complex even for human commanders. Autonomous weapons must at least meet the standard set by humans. If States can find a reasonable solution to these proportionality requirements, then their use of autonomous weapons should not be deemed unlawful.

The third requirement is one in which an attacker has a duty to take feasible precautions to minimize the harm to civilians and civilian objects. Considered a customary aspect of international law,[51] these precautions are detailed in Article

[48]Additional Protocol I, Article 51(5)(b).

[49]For a discussion of the collateral damage methodology used by the United States military, see Thurnher and Kelly 2012.

[50]For example, Human Rights Watch maintains that an autonomous weapon 'could not be programmed to duplicate the psychological processes in human judgment that are necessary to assess proportionality.' Human Rights Watch 2012, p. 33.

[51]Henckaerts and Doswald-Beck 2005, r. 15; Cadwalader, pp. 161–162.

57 of *Additional Protocol I*.[52] The series of precautions outlined in the article include many different attempts to safeguard civilians. One precaution requires a State to do everything feasible to verify that a proposed target is a military objective. Another focuses on the need to provide a warning before an attack if circumstances permit.[53] An additional requirement appears when a choice of targets exists. In such a situation, an attacker is obliged to choose the target, without sacrificing military advantage, that is expected to cause the least harm to the civilian population and damage to civilian objects. These and the other feasible precautions are just as applicable to autonomous weapon systems as they are for other weapons, and nations employing autonomous weapons must determine how best to fully comply with them.

The key is whether the attacker had taken all the steps that are feasible. Feasible steps mean those that are 'practicable or practically possible' given the existing circumstances.[54] Thus, a State is not required to attempt everything imaginable prior to an attack. Resolving how to perform all the practically possible measures before an autonomous attack will present a real challenge. As with other rules of the law of armed conflict, its actions will be assessed against a standard of reasonableness.

The precautions in attack rule plays a significant role in protecting the civilian population and civilian objects, and this is a point often overlooked or discounted by proponents of a ban on autonomous weapons. The rule already contains significant limiting factors on the potential uses of autonomous weapons. For example, part of the rule requires an attacker take all feasible steps to choose a means and method of attack with a view toward minimizing collateral damage.[55] To comply with this aspect of the rule, a State must assess which feasible system is better able to protect civilians and civilian objects without sacrificing military advantage and choose the means that presents a lower risk of harm to them. In many circumstances, a manned or remotely controlled system may prove to be the necessary choice. Under those circumstances, a ban on autonomous weapon systems would be unnecessary because the State would already be obligated under the law of armed conflict to use the different system. In fact, under the rule, the only time an autonomous weapon can lawfully be used is when it would be the better choice. In these situations, the outright prohibition of autonomous weapons might actually have a counter-productive effect. If a ban on autonomous weapons were enacted, then a State could be forced at times to rely on a human controlled weapon system that is comparatively less effective at protecting civilians. This showcases why an absolute ban would be unwise and how the existing law of armed conflict safeguards are sufficient to protect civilians.

---

[52]Additional Protocol I, Article 57.

[53]Additional Protocol I, Article 57(2)(c).

[54]Harvard Program on Humanitarian Policy and Conflict Research 2010, p. 38.

[55]Additional Protocol I, Article 57(2)(a)(ii).

9.5 The Impact of Autonomous Weapons on Targeting Processes

To properly account for the unique law of armed conflict challenges discussed above, nations will likely need to focus closely on refinements to their targeting processes. Although many facets of targeting may need to be adjusted, two, doubt and subjectivity, will be significantly affected by the introduction of autonomous targeting. This section will examine each in an attempt to decipher how doubt will need to be factored into autonomous targeting decisions and whether the numerous subjective value judgements required by the law of armed conflict can be made by autonomous systems.

9.5.1 Targeting Doubt

Doubt plays a major role in the targeting process and will factor prominently into autonomous targeting. Humans and machines alike may have difficulty determining with certainty whether a potential target is a civilian or a combatant. This situation is often exacerbated when the targeting decisions are being made on complex battlefields. Issues of doubt feature throughout law of armed conflict rules. For example, Article 50(1) of *Additional Protocol I* codifies the customary rule that any doubt regarding the status of a potential human target be resolved in favour of treating the person as a civilian.[56] Any State developing an autonomous weapon must carefully consider how it resolves these questions of uncertainty.

Doubt is a matter of degree. An attack is not prohibited under the law of armed conflict merely because some doubt exists. However, the precise amount of doubt required to trigger this prohibition is not specifically codified, and it is unclear whether any particular threshold is considered reflective of customary international law.[57] In general, if an attacker has enough doubt to reasonably hesitate to act, then the attacker is not legally allowed to continue with the action.[58] That threshold is met when the amount of doubt would cause a reasonable attacker in a similar situation to also hesitate. The fact that an autonomous system is making the decision complicates the analysis, and it is unclear exactly how these standards

[56]Additional Protocol I, Article 50(1); Henckaerts and Doswald-Beck 2005, r. 6. With regard to doubt involving the status of objects, Article 52(3) of Additional Protocol I requires Parties to presume an object is of civilian character in cases of doubt. Although it is unclear whether the rule is customary, States will nevertheless likely develop their autonomous systems to comply with such a rule. Henckaerts and Doswald-Beck 2005, r. 10.

[57]Schmitt 2013b, commentary accompanying r. 33. See also Henckaerts and Doswald-Beck 2005, r. 10, which describes an Israeli position that in situations of doubt as to the character of an object, the appropriate threshold is whether 'significant' doubt exists.

[58]See generally, CAVV 2013, p. 19.

might be determined in this context. Likely, one will examine whether a reasonable human attacker, who possessed the same information as the autonomous system, would decide to proceed with the attack. To help satisfy this requirement, nations may resort to imposing additional constraints through their Rules of Engagement for autonomous systems.

Developing a mechanism to accurately and reliably measure the amount of doubt in a particular situation will be a significant challenge when designing autonomous systems. Obviously an attacker uses a combination of many factors to assess whether a target is valid. Some basic considerations include evaluations about whether a target is armed, whether manoeuvring toward friendly forces, and how active the enemy has been in the general battlefield environment. To examine these factors, the suite of sensors used on any autonomous weapon would invariably need to be robust. More importantly, the data collected from those sensors would need to be able to be converted into or assigned some value of confidence. How exactly nations will enable this analysis is unclear, but computer programs could theoretically be developed to measure the likelihood that a potential target is valid.

Any such measurement of confidence for a particular attack would then need to be compared against what the State considers to be an unreasonable amount of doubt. Setting appropriate doubt thresholds will also prove difficult. Nations will need to pre-determine for a system the level of doubt that is acceptable under the circumstances. An autonomous system would then be prevented from conducting any proposed attack in which the likelihood of the target being valid falls below that threshold. States may devise techniques for reaching the appropriate doubt thresholds based upon tactical changes on the ground, such as allowing for an increased level of doubt in a more active battlefield environment. It is unlikely, however, absent significant technological advances, that autonomous systems will have the ability to adjust doubt thresholds based upon their own perceptions of the battlefield. Given the difficulties with autonomous targeting doubt, one can expect doubt thresholds to be cautiously established.

Although questions of doubt are challenging, autonomous systems offer a mitigating factor. The systems are not required to defend themselves. Without these self-defence constraints, a system could arguably assume greater risk to resolve issues of doubt. For instance, in some circumstances, an autonomous system could be programmed to basically sacrifice itself to further identify the intentions of the presumed enemy target.[59] By taking steps such as setting the system to engage initially only with nonlethal force or to use lethal force only in response to an attack, a nation employing an autonomous weapon system may have greater confidence and less doubt about the validity of an attack.

Ultimately, the test will be whether the commander was reasonably justified in using an autonomous system in that particular environment. A commander must know and understand the level of acceptable doubt embedded into the autonomous

[59] Arkin 2009, p. 46.

system he or she intends to use. Armed with that understanding, the decision to deploy the system into the specific situation will be evaluated for reasonableness. While mistakes of fact are allowed under the law of armed conflict, any error made must be reasonable. This requirement to act reasonably will apply to autonomous targeting doubt as well as subjectivity in autonomous targeting.

9.5.2 Subjectivity in Targeting

Subjective judgements are critical throughout targeting processes. When analysing distinction, proportionality and feasible precautions in attack, a military operator makes and relies on numerous value judgements. For instance, the operator must subjectively decide how valuable a target is in terms of military advantage and whether the expected collateral damage is excessive in relation to that anticipated military gain. Despite advances in artificial intelligence, fully autonomous systems are unlikely to make these inherently subjective judgements in the near term. This shortcoming has led many autonomous weapons critics and commentators to conclude that the systems are unlawful.[60] Such criticism is unjustified because the autonomous targeting process will, at its heart, still be controlled by humans who can ensure the systems fully comply with these legal requirements.

Nations will nevertheless have to make sure their targeting processes properly account for the changes autonomy introduces, particularly those involving the timing of the subjective decisions. Autonomy will alter the timing of many subjective targeting decisions. Humans must continue to make the required determinations, but many of the judgement calls will need to be made earlier in the targeting cycle than has been the case with more traditional human controlled systems. As opposed to human operated systems, where decisions about the lawfulness of an attack can sometimes be made up to the final moment before impact, subjective targeting decisions regarding the use of autonomous systems must be made while the human programmer retains the opportunity to adjust their parameters. If, for example, the autonomous system is being launched underwater or into area where communications jamming is prevalent, subjective decisions may need to be made prior to launch. Despite these differences from the traditional targeting process, autonomous targeting can be lawful if carefully managed.

To comply with the law, human operators will need to insert themselves into the targeting process at various points to make the required subjective decisions. Initially, a human will need to be intricately involved in programming the autonomous weapon for its mission. The operator will provide instructions to the autonomous system, in part, by subjectively determining values to assign to targets and establishing other attack criteria and thresholds. In essence, the controller is

[60] Herbach 2012, pp. 17–19; Wagner 2012, pp. 121–122. See generally Gillespie and West 2010, pp. 13–20; O'Connell, p. 7.

supplying the autonomous system with the answers to the subjective questions and building a framework for it to operate within. Rather than making subjective decisions itself, the autonomous system will follow strict guidelines to make objective decisions about when and how it may lethally engage a target. As an example, if the autonomous system objectively determines that an attack would result in a higher degree of harm to civilians or damage to civilian objects than the human operator has permitted, the weapon system would disengage or request additional guidance from the human controller.

The decision to order an autonomous weapon system into battle is another crucial subjective judgement that must be made by a human. A human controller must subjectively determine that an autonomous system is appropriate and lawful for a particular mission. He or she must therefore be familiar with the autonomous weapon system's specific capabilities and fully comprehend the embedded values, attack criteria and thresholds pre-programmed into the system. The operator needs to understand how an autonomous weapon would likely operate in a particular battlefield environment and whether it can be expected to be able to comply with the law of armed conflict in such circumstances. With such insight, a human operator can then make the critical subjective determination about whether an autonomous weapon is suitable for a specific mission.

These subjective targeting decisions will be made by humans before the actual lethal attack, often during an earlier phase of the targeting cycle than has traditionally been the case with manned systems. Many commentators have been critical of this fact, and some have even gone as far as to suggest there should be a temporal requirement limiting attacks to those where the human decision is made just prior to the actual lethal impact.[61] Not only does the *lex lata* contain no such rule, but that type of rule could have devastating effects. In some situations, such as in the cyber domain or on-board a warship, there may be precious little time to respond to an impending attack. Waiting for human approval could prove dangerous or impractical.

Rather than an arbitrary absolute time standard, these human subjective decisions will be examined under the standard of reasonableness. Without doubt, timing will be a key factor in any examination of reasonableness. The longer the time between the last human controller input and the autonomous attack itself, the greater the risk of changes on the battlefield resulting in an unanticipated action. The higher the risk, the less reasonable the order to deploy an autonomous system into that situation generally becomes. A State may be able to lower risk by enabling its autonomous systems to be regularly adjusted by human controllers based upon battlefield changes, although in some environments, such as underwater or in areas with persistent communications jamming, this may not be feasible. Ultimately, human controllers must reasonably assess these risk factors involved in deploying autonomous weapons.

[61] O'Connell 2013, p. 12 ('[T]he ultimate decision to kill must be made, therefore, by a human being at or very near the time of the lethal impact.').

Subjective judgements clearly play a major role in targeting. Despite an inability to make such qualitative decisions on their own, fully autonomous weapon systems can be lawfully employed on the battlefield. This can only occur if human controllers continue to make the critical qualitative decisions throughout the autonomous targeting process. States wishing to develop autonomous weapons will need to adapt their procedures to accommodate these unique challenges.

9.6 Conclusions

Whereas human judgement is often clouded by anger, revenge, fear, and fatigue, machines may offer the promise of removing those worries from the battlefields of the future. Nations are encouraged by this prospect and are actively seeking to embed autonomous properties into their military systems. This trend can be expected to continue. Technology may soon make possible the creation of autonomous weapon systems operating within tightly controlled parameters, but able to select and engage targets without human intervention. Such systems will both help protect a nation's own fighting forces from danger and also potentially provide better safeguards for civilian populations through more precise and accurate targeting.

As with any new means of warfare, some controversy is to be expected. Calls for bans on new weapon systems are common throughout history. From the crossbow to aerial bombers, critics have repeatedly argued that various new weapons undermine the existing laws of war. In this case, the proposed ban is unnecessary and unwise. The law of armed conflict properly represents a balance between the cardinal principles of military necessity and humanity. It contains sufficient protections for civilians, while allowing for the accomplishment of the military mission. The law will adapt and evolve as needed to the challenges autonomous systems present, but, in principle, the law of armed conflict and autonomy are not incompatible. This is one of the reasons the International Committee for the Red Cross has thus far not supported a ban on autonomous weapon systems. Instead, they wisely call on nations developing autonomous systems to remain mindful of the tenets of the law of armed conflict and only develop systems that fully comply with its provisions.[62] Proponents of a ban on autonomous systems seemingly fail to appreciate the significance of the law of armed conflict's existing protections.

When examining autonomous weapon systems from a law of armed conflict perspective, as this chapter has sought to do, they will likely be deemed lawful in many scenarios. Autonomous weapons are unlikely to be judged unlawful *per se*, as they are not indiscriminate, nor expected to cause unnecessary suffering or superfluous injury. The use of autonomous weapon systems may be limited in some complex battlefield situations because of the requirements of distinction,

[62] International Committee of the Red Cross 2013.

proportionality and precautions in attack. In other cases, however, autonomous weapons should be able to fully comply with those principles given the particulars of the battlefield environment. Moreover, as technology improves, one would expect the systems to be capable of being used in an increasing number of circumstances.

States are closely following the controversy surrounding autonomous weapon systems, and are sensitive to the concerns. They recognize the need to craft policies and targeting procedures that ensure full compliance with the law of armed conflict. A number of nations have already implemented some initial measures.[63] As the development of autonomous systems continues, nations will need to adjust their targeting procedures to properly consider the unique issues autonomy raises with respect to targeting doubt and subjectivity. Given the extraordinary potential benefits of these systems, they have huge incentives to work through these difficult challenges. Leading military armed forces should highlight, through actions and words, how their respect for the law of armed conflict is already constraining their development of these news weapons. If that begins to occur, it seems likely that nations will coalesce around the idea that the law of armed conflict meets the challenges of this emerging technology and, that a ban on autonomous weapons is unnecessary.

References

Ackerman S (2013) Navy preps to build a robot ship that blows up mines. www.wired.com/dangerroom/2013/01/robot-mine-sweeper/. Accessed 30 Dec 2013

Alston P (2011) Lethal robotic technologies: the implications for human rights and international humanitarian law. J Law Inf Sci 21:35–60

Anderson K, Waxman M (2013) Law and ethics for robot soldiers: why a ban won't work and how the laws of war can. Hoover Inst Policy Rev

Arkin R (2009) Governing lethal behavior in autonomous robots. Chapman & Hall, Boca Raton

Bar-Cohen Y, Hanson D (2009) The coming robot revolution: expectations and fears about emerging intelligent humanlike machines. Springer Science & Business Media, Pasadena

Barnes M, Jentsch F (eds) (2010) Human-robot interactions in future military operations. Ashgate Publishing Company, Burlington

Boothby W (2012) The law of targeting. Oxford University Press, Oxford

Cadwalader G (2011) The rules governing the conduct of hostilities in Additional Protocol I to the Geneva Conventions of 1949: a review of relevant United States references. Yearb Int Humanit Law 14:133–171

Campaign to Stop Killer Robots (2013) Who we are. http://www.stopkillerrobots.org/coalition. Accessed 30 Dec 2013

CAVV (Commissie Van Advies Inzake Volkenrechtelijke Vraagstukken) (2013) Advisory report on armed drones, Advisory Committee on Issues of Public International Law. Advisory Report 23, July 2013

---

[63]The United States issued a policy directive in 2012 establishing a strict approval process for any AWS acquisitions or development and mandating various safety measures be incorporated into future AWS designs. United States Department of Defense 2012.

Convention on Conventional Weapons (2013) Final report of the meeting of the high contracting parties to the Convention on Prohibitions or Restrictions on the Use of Certain Conventional Weapons which may be deemed to be excessively injurious or to have indiscriminate effects, CCW/MSP/2013/CRP.1

Coughlin T (2011) The future of robotic weaponry and the law of armed conflict: irreconcilable differences? Univ Coll Lond Jurisprudence Rev 17:67–99

Dahm W (2012) Killer drones are science fiction. Wall Str J, 15 January 2012

Fenrick W (2010) The prosecution of international crimes in relation to the conduct of military operations. In: Gill T, Fleck D (eds) The handbook of the law of military operations. Oxford Press, Oxford, pp 501–514

Gillespie T, West R (2010) Requirements for autonomous unmanned air systems set by legal issues. Int C2 J 4(2):1–32

Gogarty B, Hagger M (2008) The laws of man over vehicles unmanned: the legal response to robotic revolution on sea, land and air. J Law, Inf Sci 19:73–145

Graham D (2011) The law of armed conflict in asymmetric urban armed conflict. In: Pedrozo RA, Wollschlaeger DP (eds) International law and the changing character of war. International Law Studies, vol 87. US Naval War College, Newport, pp 301–313

Guarino A (2013) Autonomous cyber weapons no longer science-fiction. Engineering and Technology Magazine. http://eandt.theiet.org/magazine/2013/08/intelligent-weapons-are-coming.cfm. Accessed 27 Dec 2013

Harvard Program on Humanitarian Policy and Conflict Research (HPCR) (2009) Manual on international law applicable to air and missile warfare

Healey J (2013) Stuxnet and the dawn of algorithmic warfare. Huffington Post. http://www.huffingtonpost.com/jason-healey/stuxnet-cyberwarfare_b_3091274.html. Accessed 27 Dec 2013

Heintschel von Heinegg W (2011) Concluding remarks. In: Heintschel von Heinegg W, Beruto GL (eds) International humanitarian law and new weapon technologies. International Institute of Humantiarian Law, Sanremo, pp 183–186

Henckaerts J, Doswald-Beck L (eds) (2005) Customary international humanitarian law, ICRC. Cambridge University Press, Cambridge

Herbach J (2012) Into the caves of steel: precaution, cognition and robotic weapon systems under the law of armed conflict. Amsterdam Law Forum 4(3):3–20

House of Lords Debate 26 March 2013 (Lord Astor of Hever, Parliamentary Under Secretary of State, Defence). http://www.publications.parliament.uk/pa/ld201213/ldhansrd/text/130326-0001.htm#st_14. Accessed 30 Dec 2013

Human Rights Watch (2012) Losing humanity: the case against killer robots. www.hrw.org/sites/default/files/reports/arms1112ForUpload_0_0.pdf. Accessed 30 Dec 2013

IEEE (2012) Look ma, no hands. www.ieee.org/about/news/2012/5september_2_2012.html. Accessed 30 Dec 2013

International Committee for the Red Cross (2013) Autonomous weapons: States must address major humanitarian, ethical challenges http://www.icrc.org/eng/resources/documents/faq/q-and-a-autonomous-weapons.htm. Accessed 30 December 2013

Jenks C (2009) Law from above: unmanned aerial systems, use of force, and the law of armed conflict. North Dakota Law Rev 85:650–671

Jensen E (2013) Future war, future law. Minn J Int Law 22:282–23

Kellenberger J (2011) Keynote address. In: Heintschel von Heinegg W, Beruto GL (eds) International humanitarian law and new weapon technologies. International Institute of Humanitarian Law, Sanremo, pp 23–27

Krishnan A (2009) Killer robots: legality and ethicality of autonomous weapons. Ashgate, Burlington

Liu H (2012) Categorization and legality of autonomous and remote weapons systems. Int Rev Red Cross: New Technol Warf 94 No. 886:627–652

Melzer N (2013) Human rights implications of the usage of drones and unmanned robots in warfare. European ParliamentEXPO/B/DROI/2012/12

O'Connell M (2013) Banning autonomous killing. Notre Dame Legal Studies Paper No. 1445. http://www.ssrn.com/link/notre-dame-legal-studies.html. Accessed 27 Dec 2013

Pedrozo R (2011) Use of unmanned systems to combat terrorism. In: Pedrozo RA, Wollschlaeger DP (eds) International law and the changing character of war. International Law Studies, vol 87. US Naval War College, Newport, pp 217–270

Poitras C (2012) Smart robotic drones advance science. http://today.uconn.edu/blog/2012/10/smart-robotic-drones-advance-science/. Accessed 27 Feb 2013

Public Broadcasting Service (2011) Smartest machines on earth. (transcript) www.pbs.org/wgbh/nova/tech/smartest-machine-on-earth.html. Accessed 30 Dec 2013

Reeves S, Thurnher J (2013) Are we reaching a tipping point? How contemporary challenges are affecting the military necessity-humanity balance. Harvard Natl Secur J Featur 1–12. http://harvardnsj.org/wp-content/uploads/2013/06/HNSJ-Necessity-Humanity-Balance_PDF-format1.pdf. Accessed 27 Dec 2013

Russell S, Norvig P (2010) Artificial intelligence: a modern approach, 3rd edn. Prentice Hall, Upper Saddle River

Schmitt MN (2011) Investigating violations of international law in armed conflict. Harv Natl Secur J 2:31–84

Schmitt MN (2012) Discriminate warfare: the military necessity-humanity dialectic of international humanitarian law. In: Lovell DW, Primoratz I (eds) Protecting civilians during violent conflict: theoretical and practical issues for the 21st century. Ashgate, Farnham, pp 85–102

Schmitt MN, Thurnher J (2013) 'Out of the loop': autonomous weapon systems and the law of armed conflict. Harv Natl Secur J 4:231–281

Schmitt MN (2013a) Autonomous weapon systems and international humanitarian law: a reply to the critics. Harv Natl Secur J Featur. http://harvardnsj.org/wp-content/uploads/2013/02/Schmitt-Autonomous-Weapon-Systems-and-IHL-Final.pdf. Accessed 30 Dec 2013

Schmitt MN (ed) (2013b) Tallinn manual on the international law applicable to cyber warfare. International Group of Experts at the invitation of the NATO Cooperative Cyber Defence Centre of Excellence. Cambridge University Press, Cambridge

Sharkey N (2011) Automating warfare: lessons learned from the drones. J Law, Inf Sci 21:140–154

Sharkey N (2012) Drones proliferation and protection of civilians. In: Heitschel von Heinegg W (ed) International humanitarian law and new weapon technologies. International Institute of Humanitarian Law, Sanremo, pp 108–118

Singer P (2009) Wired for war: The robotics revolution and conflict in the twenty-first century. Penguin Press, New York

Stewart D (2011) New technology and the law of armed conflict: technological meteorites and legal dinosaurs? In: Pedrozo RA, Wollschlaeger DP (eds) International law and the changing character of war. International law studies, vol 87. US Naval War College, Newport, pp 271–300

Thurnher J, Kelly T (2012) Collateral damage estimation. US Naval War College video. www.youtube.com/watch?v=AvdXJV-N56A&list=PLam-yp5uUR1YEwLbqC0IPrP4EhWOeTf8v&index=1&feature=plpp_video. Accessed 30 Dec 2013

United Nations (2010) Interim report of the special rapporteur on extrajudicial, summary or arbitrary executions, UN Doc A/65/321

United Nations (2013) Report of the special rapporteur on extrajudicial, summary or arbitrary executions, Christof Heyns, UN Doc A/HRC/23/47

United States Air Force (2009) Unmanned aircraft systems flight plan 2009–2047. Headquarters Department of the Air Force, Washington, DC

United States Army (1956) The law of land warfare, Field Manual (FM) 27-10. Headquarters Department of the Army, Washington, DC

United States Defense Advanced Research Projects Agency (2013) DARPA's anti-submarine warfare game goes live. www.darpa.mil/NewsEvents/Releases/2011/2011/04/04_DARPA's_Anti-Submarine_Warfare_game_goes_live.aspx. Accessed 30 Dec 2013

United States Department of Defense (2009) FY2009–2034 unmanned systems integrated roadmap. Government Printing Office, Washington, DC

United States Department of Defense (2012) Directive 3000.09: autonomy in weapon systems. Government Printing Office, Washington, DC

United States Department of Defense (2012a) Directive 3000.09: autonomy in weapon systems: response-to-query talking points. Government Printing Office, Washington, DC (on file with author)

United States Department of Defense (2012b) Task force report: the role of autonomy in DoD systems. www.fas.org/irp/agency/dod/dsb/autonomy.pdf. Accessed 30 Dec 2013

United States Department of Defense (2013) FY2013-2038 unmanned systems integrated roadmap. Government Printing Office, Washington, DC

United States Joint Forces Command (2003) Rapid Assessment Process (RAP) Report No. 03-10, unmanned Effects (UFX): taking the human out of the loop, Headquarters Joint Forces Command, Suffolk

United States Navy, Marine Corps & Coast Guard (2007) The commander's handbook on the law of naval operations. Naval Warfare Publication (NWP) 1-14 M/Marine Corps Warfighting Publication (MCWP) 5-12.1/Commandant Publication (COMDTPUB) P5800.7A, Department of the Navy, Washington, DC

Van Tol J et al. (2012). Air sea battle: a point-of-departure operational concept. www.csbaonline.org/wp-content/uploads/2010/05/2010.05.18-AirSea-Battle.pdf. Accessed 30 Dec 2013

Vogel R (2010) Drone warfare and the law of armed conflict. Denver J Int Law Policy 39:101–138

Wagner M (2011) Taking humans out of the loop: implications for international humanitarian law. J Law, Inf Sci 21:1–11

Wagner M (2012) Autonomy in the battlespace: independently operating weapon systems and the law of armed conflict. In: Saxon D (ed) International humanitarian law and the changing technology of war. Martinus Nijhoff, Leiden, pp 99–122

Chapter 10
Non-kinetic Capabilities: Complementing the Kinetic Prevalence to Targeting

Paul A.L. Ducheine

Abstract Targeting is used in military doctrine to describe a military operational *way*, using (military) *means* to influence a *target* (or addressee) in order to achieve designated political and/or military *goals*. The four factors italicized are used to analyse non-kinetic targeting, thereby complementing our knowledge and understanding of the prevalent kinetic targeting. Paradoxically, non-kinetic targeting is not recognized as a separate concept; kinetic and non-kinetic are intertwined facets of targeting. Kinetic targeting refers to the targeted application of military force based on the release or concentration of kinetic energy against opposing forces or objects with (primarily) lethal effects in the physical domain, whereas non-kinetic targeting describes the targeted application of (other military and non-military) capabilities against addressees to generate (additional) non-kinetic effects in the non-physical and physical domain. This chapter attempts to provide a better demarcation between kinetic and non-kinetic targeting, first by reviewing recent developments in military operations and targeting and introducing a 'full spectrum approach'. It then enumerates and analyses a number of typical non-kinetic capabilities: information activities, key leader engagement, lawfare, criminal legal action, security detention, assets freezes, and cyber operations. The chapter concludes that although non-kinetic targeting does not exist as a stand-alone concept, it is vitally important in contemporary military operations. It provides opportunities to engage and affect additional target audiences (including supporters) with less devastating effects (including constructive effects) by

The author would like to thank Colonel (RNLAF) dr. Joop Voetelink, Lieutenant-Colonels (RNLA) Edwin de Ronde and Peter Pijpers LL.M. MA, Major dr. Eric Pouw LL.M. and Captain (RNLMC) Mark Roorda LL.M. for their suggestions.

P.A.L. Ducheine (✉)
Netherlands Defence Academy, Breda, The Netherlands
e-mail: pal.ducheine.01@mindef.nl

P.A.L. Ducheine et al. (eds.), *Targeting: The Challenges of Modern Warfare*,
DOI 10.1007/978-94-6265-072-5_10

offering additional means to conduct operations, stressing the crucial role of non-kinetic elements like information, perception, cohesion, understanding, and will.

Keywords Non-kinetic targeting · Non-lethal targeting · Information activities · Effect-based approach · Evidence-based targeting · Key leader engagement · Cyber operations · Lawfare · Detention

Contents

10.1 Noting the Kinetic Prevalence and Reinventing Non-kinetic Capabilities

Whether future conflict will involve another counterinsurgency campaign, a major combat operation, a stability operation or whatever (new) description fits operations to come, one of the great lessons learned from the last campaigns to which western armed forces have been committed is captured by David Kilcullen's characterizations Al Qaeda's 'main effort':

> In military terms, for Al Qaeda the 'main effort' is information; for us, information is a supporting effect.[1]

Whereas western armed forces tend to focus on kinetic action (and thus kinetic targeting) and support that action with other lines of action (e.g., information activities), irregular armed forces have reversed this practise. Groups like Al Qaeda, Hamas and to some extent Anonymous place more emphasis on information activities and use physical action to supplement them.

[1]Kilcullen 2009, p. 300.

Indeed, it may be easier, or even necessary, for irregular guerrilla forces to use information as their main 'weapon' if they lack the kinetic or physical resources possessed by western troops, or if they are less troubled by ethical, political, and legal constraints in exploiting their 'main effort' to the maximum extent possible.

Nevertheless, western forces have come to reappraise the value of information as a means to achieve desired effects. Moreover, they have recognized the importance of using non-physical or 'unorthodox' means in the operational process to pursue military goals—the use of other than 'traditional' kinetic (and lethal) military means in the operational process called targeting. Indeed, this is what Phillip Pratzner describes in Chap. 4 of this volume:

> In the late nineties, planned operations were largely focused on lethal, or kinetic, means: a bomb […]. Nonlethal capabilities, somewhat embryonic at this time, were discussed, but these were only supporting efforts and very insular ones at that. Fast forward to 2013. By this time, planning included far more nonlethal capabilities and in many cases, these were the main operation, with lethal options actually playing a supporting role.[2]

As used here, kinetic targeting refers to the targeted application of military force based on the release or concentration of kinetic energy against opposing forces or objects with (primarily) lethal effects in the physical domain, whereas non-kinetic targeting involves to the targeted application of (other military and non-military) capabilities vis-à-vis addressees to generate (additional) non-kinetic effects in the non-physical and physical domain.

Although the notion of (non-lethal and) non-kinetic targeting may sound rather unorthodox and new, particularly for generations of officers who grew up with traditional kinetic targeting, for those who have studied the classic strategists or have gained experience in recent counterinsurgencies, non-lethal targeting probably appears to reinvent the wheel. Sun Tzu noted centuries ago, that 'subjugating the enemy's army without fighting is the true pinnacle of excellence'.[3] This classic example of an 'effect-based approach' to military operations is well known, and its importance is accelerated by today's 'comprehensive approach', stressing the need for a coordinated, synchronized application of all available resources to achieve a defined end state. The notion is acknowledged in the US Army Field Manual referring to counterinsurgencies experiences: 'targets assigned to nonlethal assets are frequently more important than targets assigned to lethal assets'.[4] Although decades of kinetic prevalence have left their mark on military thinking, doctrine, and behaviour,[5] this prevalence is now officially countered, or complemented, by the reappraisal of non-kinetic capabilities.

Targeting can be defined as the application of capabilities (against targets) to generate effects to achieve objectives. While the regular military kinetic (and

---

[2]See Chap. 4, Pratzner, in this volume.

[3]Sun Tzu 1994, p. 177.

[4]US Army 2010a, p. B-1.

[5]Kitzen 2012b based on: Lynn 2003, p. xix; Hanson 1989, 2001; Smith 2005, p. 152.

lethal) capabilities and their contribution to these operations, including their input in the targeting process, are well covered, non-military, non-kinetic (and non-lethal) capabilities have attracted less attention. This chapter elaborates on the contribution of some typical non-kinetic capabilities to this operational process.

Paradoxically, non-kinetic targeting as such is not covered in doctrine and military literature. It is an integrated and intrinsic part of targeting. It nevertheless deserves our attention, as it has become increasingly important in recent decades. Non-kinetic targeting appears to provide opportunities to engage and affect not only opponents, but additional target audiences, including neutrals and supporters. It also generates less devastating effects (even adding constructive outcomes) by offering additional means to conduct operations, taking into account the crucial role of non-kinetic elements like information, perception, cohesion, understanding, and will.

This chapter sets off by briefly reiterating what targeting is, and is not, about (Sect. 10.2). It then continues in search of a demarcation between kinetic and non-kinetic targeting by reviewing recent developments in military operations and targeting (Sect. 10.3), introducing a definition of 'non-kinetic targeting' (Sect. 10.4) and stating the point of departure in doing so (Sect. 10.5). It continues to enumerate and analyse some of these typical modalities of non-kinetic targeting (Sects. 10.7, 10.8, 10.9, 10.10, 10.11, 10.12, 10.13), ending with conclusions (Sect. 10.14).

10.2 About Goals, Means, Targets, and Effects, as Well as Myths

Targeting is used in military doctrine to describe a military operational *way*, using (military) *means* to influence *targets* (or addressees) in order to achieve designated political and/or military *goals*.[6] It involves the focused and deliberate effort in (and prior to) military operations to determine goals, identify, acquire, engage, and assess specific targets that, when 'influenced' properly using all available means, contribute significantly to the success of military action. As stated in the Canadian Land Operations Manual:

---

[6]In its Allied Joint Doctrine for Joint Targeting, NATO defines joint targeting as 'the process of determining the effects necessary to achieve the commander's objectives, identifying the actions necessary to create the desired effects based on means available, selecting and prioritizing targets, and the synchronization of fires with other military capabilities and then assessing their cumulative effectiveness and taking remedial action if necessary.' NATO 2008, p. 1. See also US Air Force 2014, p. 3: 'Targeting is the process of selecting and prioritizing targets and matching the appropriate response to them, considering operational requirements and capabilities.'

> Targeting considers the entire range of targets and target audiences within an environment, and plans their engagement using the full range of capabilities and activities, that is, comprehensive operations, to create complementary effects on the physical and psychological planes. The targeting of fires and influence activities together may be viewed as comprehensive targeting. It should encompass all elements of power and agencies involved.[7]

Thus, four chronologically related elements come to mind: goals, means, targets and effects. Goals can be derived from the political and military-strategic defined ends or end states in which the military is deployed (alongside other instruments of power). Means, especially in modern operations that require an orchestrated and comprehensive use of all available instruments, refer to *all* available assets and capabilities—be they military, civilian, governmental, or private.[8] A target comprises physical (tangible) and non-physical elements that can be influenced. The NATO Allied Joint Doctrine for Joint Targeting defines a target as

> a selected geographic area, object, capability, person, or organization (including their will, understanding, and behaviour); which can be influenced as part of the military contribution to a political end-state. A target is normally not critical in and of itself but rather its importance is derived from its potential contribution to achieving the commander's military objective(s).[9]

Finally, effects are the direct and indirect consequences generated by influencing targets with the means available. They may be physical and tangible, but also virtual, digital, or otherwise non-physical in nature. In short, targeting is the systematic and effects-based process of matching appropriate responses to targets.

Four myths frequently complicate a proper understanding of targeting. First, targeting is not an exclusive air power or air force process. Instead, it refers to influencing actors with all (military) capabilities from all available armed services. Moreover, all services use targeting as an operational process.[10] Second, targeting is not a process solely used at the strategic level of command.[11] It occurs at all military command levels: strategic, operational, and tactical. Third, targeting is not

---

[7]Canada 2008, pp. 5–33.

[8]This element involves inter alia 'weaponeering', defined in the US Army Field Manual as 'the process of determining the quantity of a specific type of lethal or nonlethal weapons required to achieve a specific level of damage to a given target, considering target vulnerability, weapons characteristics and effects, and delivery parameters (JP 3-60).' US Army 2010a, pp. 2–17.

[9]NATO 2008, p. 1–1. See also US Air Force 2014, p. 4: 'A target is an entity or object considered for possible engagement or other actions.'

[10]See e.g. NATO (2005) Allied Joint Publication AJP-3.9.2 Land targeting.

[11]Operational process is used to refer to the application of this process in operations. This should not be mixed up with the command levels (strategic, operational and tactical).

an exclusive enemy-centric notion. Targets or, in more neutral terms, addressees, comprise not only opponents, but also supporters and neutral entities[12]:

> With respect to the term 'targets', a broader understanding the term must be used. Targets will include adversary elements, friendly and allied elements, and neutral audiences. Nothing nefarious is meant by the term, but it should be viewed in the sense of a business advertisement 'targeting' a particular audience. [...]. [13]

They can be humans, entities (groups or organizations), and objects.

The fourth, and main, myth is related to the subject of this contribution—targeting is not limited to the application of kinetic and lethal military force. Instead, it includes the use of *all* capabilities, military and otherwise, kinetic, lethal, non-kinetic, and non-lethal. The effects sought range from constructive to disruptive.

10.3 Setting a Myth Aside: Combining Lethal and Non-lethal Action

Contemporary military doctrine recognizes the fallacy of this fourth myth, by stressing that '[t]argeting is concerned with the creation of specific desired effects through lethal and nonlethal actions'.[14] This observation is the result of a period of adaption and evolution necessitated in operational environments around the world. Today, it is expressed in military doctrine, as illustrated by the US Army Field Manual 3-60 on Targeting:

> The targeting working group must always determine the weapon system for targets of opportunity, subject to the maneuver commander's approval. *All available attack assets* should be considered. Attacking targets should optimize the capabilities of: Light and heavy ground forces; Attack aircrafts; Field artillery; Mortars; Naval gunfire; Combat air operations (both close air support and air interdiction); Electronic Warfare; Military information support operations; Civil affairs teams.[15]

---

[12]See the Canadian Land Operations breakdown which distinguishes between allied, supportive, friendly, neutral, unsupportive, inactive hostile and enemy audiences:

'This approach requires a cultural understanding and stems in part from the need to engender support from local populations *and to engage* other elements of an environment. In order to support this approach the knowledge base must gain insight into the psychological plane and the intent, motivations, and relationships of elements in the battlespace in order to out manoeuvre them or to move them, through an effect of influence to a position of acceptance, cooperation, or even support. The assessment and analysis that leads to this categorization supports the targeting process, *for each of the audiences on the spectrum of relative interest is assessed with respect to how they may be influenced and moved to a position of support or acceptance.*'
Canada 2008, p. 43 [Emphasis added].

[13]Canada 2008, p. 43, footnote 99.

[14]US Army 2010a, pp. 1–2.

[15]US Army 2010a, pp. 2-8. [Emphasis added].

> Nonlethal targets are best engaged with civil-military operations, inform and influence activities, negotiation, political programs, economic programs, social programs, and other noncombat methods. In counter insurgency operations, nonlethal targets are just as important as lethal targets and the targeting is frequently directed toward nonlethal options.[16]

The contemporary targeting process, as noted by Lieutenant-General Mart de Kruif, is highly dynamic and adaptive:

> [t]he targeting process has evolved from having a primarily kinetic/lethal emphasis with hardly any consideration for collateral damage, to our current operational domain, characterized by operations amongst the people and heavily influenced by modern (social) media. In addition, targeting is no longer a process primarily focussing on air assets, but over the past two decades has come to incorporate a host of military engagement capabilities.[17]

As a result of this adaptation, targeting has advanced in a number of ways, thereby incorporating military doctrinal concepts such as the manoeuvrist approach, jointness, the comprehensive approach, and the effect-based approach to operations,[18] as well as societal views on warfare and technological changes. First of all, current practise utilizes all military assets and capabilities—land, sea, and air-power—as potential means to generate effects.[19] Non-military assets and capabilities such as diplomacy, money or supplies, and information also can be used to generate effects.[20] Likewise, targets to be influenced are not limited to combatants and military objectives,[21] but extend to other persons, tangible goods, and non-physical elements such as 'will', 'understanding' or 'information'.[22] Currently they also include cyber-objects and cyber-identities.[23] This supports the appreciation of the primacy of effects as the outcome of operations,[24] and

---

[16]US Army 2010a, pp. 2-1.

[17]See Kruif, in his Foreword to this volume.

[18]Not to be confused with 'effect based operations', see: US Department of Defence, US Joint Forces Command, 'Assessment of Effects Based Operations' (14 August 2008, Gen Mattis).

[19]See Chap. 4, Pratzner, in this volume.

[20]See the Strategic notion of DIME on the strategic level, and the Comprehensive Approach at the operational level, e.g. NATO, Lisbon Summit Declaration, Issued by the Heads of State and Government participating in the meeting of the North Atlantic Council in Lisbon, 20 November 2010. www.nato.int/cps/en/natolive/official_texts 68828.htm. Accessed 2 April 2014.

[21]As defined in the law of armed conflict.

[22]NATO 2008, p. 1. See also US Air Force 2014, p. 4.

[23]Ducheine and Haaster 2014.

[24]See NATO 2008, pp. 1–5, Targeting Principles: 'b. Effects. Targeting is concerned with supporting the creation of effects to achieve the JFC's objectives'; and NATO 2008, pp. 1–9, para 0119: 'The effects-based approach to operations (EBAO) is an evolving philosophy that is defined as 'the coherent and comprehensive application of the various instruments of the Alliance, combined with the practical cooperation along with involved non-NATO actors, to create the effects necessary to achieve planned objectives and ultimately the NATO end state.'

reinforces the notion that desired effects can be achieved in the physical as well as the non-physical realm.[25]

Targeting also has hugely benefitted from technological advances like precision weapons and intelligence-surveillance-reconnaissance (ISR) capacities. Furthermore, changes in the social appreciation of military intervention, and (the cost and consequences of) warfare have resulted in a high demand for precision, low levels of damage and casualties, and minimal risks for the military and warring parties.[26] In particular, legitimacy, real or perceived, is increasingly important, for military operations require public support.[27]

Not for the first time, these insights have resulted in renewed appreciation of the notion that warfare (and the use of military force in general) is a means to an end, and that the use of this blunt instrument should be as bloodless and painless as possible. Ideally, it would not have to be used at all.[28] However, military operations that utilize acts of force or the threat thereof to deter or coerce adversaries will likely remain necessary. Therefore, according to NATO, military forces must 'be able to employ and coordinate a complex integration of *lethal and non-lethal* actions in the midst of a variety of threat environments in a wide range of operations'.[29]

10.4 A Discourse on 'Defining' Non-kinetic Targeting

Despite their long preoccupation with kinetic force and the underrated value of information and non-physical effects on the battlefield and beyond, western armed forces have now explicitly supplemented regular (kinetic) with non-kinetic targeting. In doing so, however, they have resorted to a variety of descriptions and terms to explain what non-kinetic targeting means. Given the inconsistencies, it is useful to begin by framing the subject of this chapter definitionally.

NATO prefers to employ the term 'non-lethal' to describe non-lethal means (of attack), effects, force, capabilities, action, options, and weapons,[30] while using 'non-kinetic' only sporadically in relation to non-kinetic material and solutions.[31]

---

[25]NATO 2008, pp. 1–9, para 0119: 'At the operational level, an effects based approach involves the selective combination of actions, coordinated with the activities of other organizations to create lethal and non-lethal effects in order to achieve operational objectives in support of this end state.'

[26]See Chaps. 2, Coker, and 4, Pratzner in this volume.

[27]Ducheine and Pouw 2012, p. 33.

[28]See Sun Tzu 1994.

[29]NATO 2008, p. 1 [Emphasis added].

[30]NATO 2008 throughout.

[31]NATO 2008, pp. 3–6, A-10.

US Joint Doctrine on Targeting, JP 3-60, displays a similar approach, but adds 'nonlethal' assets and fires without reference to 'kinetic' or 'non-kinetic'.[32]

British Joint Doctrine Publication 3-00, Campaign Execution, also exclusively relies on the lethal–non-lethal dichotomy. It offers a comprehensive description of the terms, albeit without delineating their components, by introducing what it labels 'full spectrum targeting':

> If influence is the overall outcome, a holistic approach to targeting is required from the outset. This is enabled by a deep understanding of target systems and their critical vulnerabilities. With this understanding planners will be better able to select the most effective and appropriate activity, *lethal or non-lethal*, to apply.[33]

Through the combination of manoeuvre, information and outreach activities, and fires, effects are to be realized in the physical, virtual and cognitive domains.[34] Thus, 'fires' are defined as:

> the deliberate use of *physical and virtual* means to achieve the realisation of, primarily, *physical* effects. They can be both *lethal and non-lethal*, and conducted in both the *physical and virtual* domains. They are mainly focused on an actor's capability (through destruction and attrition) including that which enables his understanding. However, they may also be employed to directly, or indirectly, realise a wide range of psychological effects by shattering cohesion, degrading capability and thus impacting on will.[35]

The British holistic approach is acknowledged in the Netherlands Defence Doctrine, which provides, '[e]ffects can be achieved in *both* the physical and the psychological sphere'.[36] The Doctrine continues:

> It is not only the employment of armed force that produces these effects; influencing opponents by damaging their information and information infrastructure, their financial sources and their support base is a broader application. Other forms of fires are the targeted employment of assets to support favourably disposed actors and the provision of measured support to the local population. Fires are thus produced by bringing effectors to bear in the physical and psychological spheres. They are divided into firepower, which is used to achieve physical and psychological effects, and the capability of influencing the understanding of target groups or individuals. This influencing of understanding takes the form of [inter alia] information activities (key leader engagement, psychological operations, deception, electronic warfare, etc.) and the development or restoration of government functions (e.g., training of police and military capacities as part of security sector development), thus enabling the local population to provide its own security. Public affairs and other methods of enhancing the security situation can also contribute to this effect.[37]

---

[32] US Department of Defense 2013. See also US Air Force 2014 and US Army 2010a.

[33] UK Ministry of Defence 2009, p. iv [Emphasis added].

[34] UK Ministry of Defence 2009, pp. 3–5.

[35] UK Ministry of Defence 2009, pp. 3–6, para 317 [Emphasis added].

[36] Ministerie van Defensie 2013, p. 103. See also Canada 2008, pp. iii, 5-2 ff.

[37] Ministerie van Defensie 2013, p. 104.

In the same vein, the Canadian Doctrine for Land Operations states:

> The combination of physical and psychological effects in striking the adversary must be complementary. If not carefully considered in comprehensive planning and targeting, the effects of physical activities may undermine those of influence activities generated through information operations.[38]

These British, Canadian and Dutch full spectrum approaches demonstrate that a sharp demarcation between kinetic and non-kinetic targeting does not exist. Rather, most doctrines recognize the two are complementary. They refer to various distinct but interrelated facets in the application of military power or targeting[39]:

non-lethal and lethal activities, by using
physical (kinetic) and virtual (non-kinetic) means, to influence
physical (humans or objects) and non-physical targets (will, understanding, cohesion), to generate
lethal and non-lethal effects
in physical and non-physical domains.

The common denominator is that kinetic and non-kinetic targeting (whether or not the lethal/non-lethal dichotomy is used) jointly refer to a spectrum of means and methods employed to influence targets throughout the physical and non-physical dimensions by generating kinetic and non-kinetic effects. Hence, defining or describing non-kinetic targeting proves complicated. As used in this chapter, kinetic targeting refers to the targeted application of military force based on the release or concentration of kinetic energy against opposing forces or objects with (primarily) lethal effects in the physical domain. Non-kinetic targeting describes the targeted application of (other military and non-military) capabilities against addressees to generate (additional) non-kinetic effects in the non-physical and physical domains.[40]

10.5 Points of Departure and Reservations

Before embarking on the modalities of non-kinetic targeting, seven preliminary points should be made. First, this chapter will introduce a non-exhaustive list of typical forms of non-kinetic targeting. They use a variety of means against a

---

[38]Canada 2008, pp. 4–24.

[39]Cheng Hang 2010.

[40]Note the US reservation made to the NATO Allied Joint Doctrine for Information Operations: 'Kinetic and non-kinetic activities have no defined meaning in NATO doctrine. Kinetic is a scientific idea commonly applied to motion and energy related descriptions. Kinetic and non-kinetic (non-motion or non-energy activities) do not fit the context of the publication.' NATO 2009, p. xi.

variety of targets to generate either constructive or disruptive effects. Second, as all effects are designed to be advantageous to the applicant, the constructive and disruptive categorization is viewed from the target's or addressee's perspective.[41]

Third, it should be noted that not all means considered are military in nature given that the comprehensive approach is a point of reference.[42] It goes without saying that non-military means will primarily be employed to generate constructive or disruptive effects that can be taken into account during the targeting process. Financial support to key leaders, whether funded by military or non-military sources, serves as an example.

Fourth, reflecting on current (and future) conflict zones, this chapter also acknowledges that not only are adversaries potential targets and addressees, but so too are neutral parties and supporters, whether in a conflict zone or domestically.[43]

Fifth, the conflict environment, as well as the configuration of the military forces in that environment, will, to a large extent, define the availability, applicability, and feasibly of the various capabilities. In some cases, non-kinetic targeting in, for example, stability operations may significantly contribute to an overarching strategic purpose of enhancing the local rule of law, whereas in other situations kinetic solutions must prevail.

Sixth, this chapter refers specifically to the operational process called targeting that can be found on all levels of command, and within all services. It does not refer to the operational design of campaigns.

Finally, the reader should realize that by elaborating on non-kinetic targeting issues, and enumerating some of the modalities involved, his or her focus 'tends to move directly to [this enumeration] at the expense of the rest of the verbiage'.[44] To counter this risk, it should be stressed that the essence of targeting is to achieve designated effects and pursue stated goals, by whatever legitimate means: kinetic or non-kinetic.

10.6 Some Typical Non-kinetic Capabilities: Modalities

Contemporary military doctrine, research, and evaluations, as well as (other) publications dedicated to operational art and military strategy, reveal a wide range of non-kinetic capabilities. These include: (a) 'public affairs, key leader, engagement,

[41]It remains to be seen whether this dichotomy should be complemented with 'neutral' effects for the target/addressee.

[42]A comprehensive approach, as it is used within NATO, the EU and member States. See Allied Command Operations (NATO) 2010; European Commission 2013; Smith-Windsor 2008.

[43]See Canada 2008, p. 43 and also note 12 supra.

[44]Murphy 2009, p. 2.

civil-military operations, and military information support operations'[45]; (b) 'inform and influence activities, negotiation, political programs, economic programs, social programs, and other noncombat methods'[46]; (c) 'military deception, public affairs, EW activities'[47]; (d) 'presence, profile and posture, media, Psychological operations, deception, CIMIC [Civil-Military (relations)]'[48]; and, (e) political, economic, and social programs'.[49]

Enumerating these capabilities runs the risk of seeming to delineate the entire subset of means and methods. Doing so also draws too much attention to cataloguing and too little to the concept as such. It thereby limits commanders and their staff in the operational art of planning and executing military operations that contributes to the desired strategic and operational effects.[50] Rather, '[b]y explicitly excluding a laundry list of capabilities, the definition is no longer self-limiting since the tools available are now constrained only by the imagination of the commander and his staff'.[51]

It is nevertheless useful to present and discuss some general subcategories of typical non-kinetic courses of actions or means and methods:

- Information Activities (Sect. 10.7)
- Key Leader Engagement (Sect. 10.8)
- Lawfare (Sect. 10.9)
- Criminal Legal Action (Sect. 10.10)
- Deprivation of Liberty: Security Detention (Sect. 10.11)
- Asset Freezes (Sect. 10.12)
- Cyber Operations (Sect. 10.13).

The ultimate purpose of targeting is to create designated effects in pursuance of defined goals. Keeping this in mind, this chapter will define and analyse some of these capabilities. It will use, to the extent possible, a fixed set of parameters: goals, targets/addressees, means and methods, and desired effects.

10.7 Information Activities

While western armed forces generally use information operations to support regular kinetic actions, (modern) violent non-State actors use kinetic action to support their 'main effort', information (activities). Reflecting on recent conflicts in Afghanistan

[45] US Department of Defense 2013, p. II-16.

[46] US Army 2010a, p. 2-1.

[47] US Army 2010a, pp. 3–7.

[48] UK Ministry of Defence 2009, p. 3B-7.

[49] US Army 2010a, p. B-1.

[50] Matthijssen 2010, p. 521.

[51] Murphy 2009, p. 2.

and Iraq, Kilcullen notes, 'for Al Qaeda the "main effort" is information; for us, information is a supporting effect'.[52]

Western forces appear to have captured that idea to some extent as well. Recent operations have led to recognition of the increased importance of the informational dimension in human behaviour and social interaction, including violent behaviour and armed conflict.[53] This restatement of the value of the information environment is key to modern military doctrines, and is evidenced by emphasizing the process of 'influencing' actors as the heart of military operations.[54]

Information activities, covering a variety of actions and subsets, are described by NATO[55]:

> Information activities seek to degrade, disrupt, deceive, destroy or deny those capabilities that allow adversary decision-makers to increase their understanding; bolster, impose, apply and sustain their will and to exercise effective command. In concert with other military and governmental actions, information activities also seek to attack the source of the adversary decision-maker's power base, splitting internal and external groupings and alliances. The aim is to influence adversary decision-making processes, thereby preventing them from taking the initiative.
>
> Information activities also aim to protect those capabilities, for example friendly command, control and communication infrastructure, that allow us to exercise effective command, seize and maintain the initiative. NATO may seek to protect approved parties' capabilities directly by providing materiel and advice, or indirectly by targeting those adversary capabilities that could be used to attack an approved party's capability.[56]

The goal, as recognized by NATO, refers to three inter-related activity areas:

- changing, influencing or reinforcing perceptions and attitudes;
- preserving and protecting freedom of manoeuvre in the information environment by defending the data and information;
- countering command functions and capabilities by affecting data and information of others.[57]

---

[52]Kilcullen 2009, p. 300.

[53]Caldwell et al. 2009.

[54]See e.g. NATO 2008, pp. 1-2–1-3: 'From the strategic to the tactical level and across the range of military operations, information plays a vital role in the manner in which decisions are made. In military operations the ability to defeat adversaries or potential adversaries may rest on the perception of all actors involved, particularly the local population. There is therefore considerable benefit to be gained by affecting the flow of information through a decision-maker and his understanding of that information.'. See also US Department of Defense 2012, p. II-1 (stating, '[i]nfluence is at the heart of diplomacy and military operations'); UK Ministry of Defence 2009, pp. 3–5, 3A-2; Canada 2008, p. 2-2; Koninklijke Landmacht 2014, pp. 2–9 (in Dutch). For the ramifications and complications of effectively countering insurgents' information campaigns, see Pijpers 2014.

[55]Taking a slightly different (enemy centric) approach, the US defines it as: 'the integrated employment, during military operations, of [information-related capabilities] in concert with other lines of operation, to influence, disrupt, corrupt or usurp the decision making of adversaries and potential adversaries while protecting our own.' US Department of Defense 2012, p. iii.

[56]NATO 2009, p. 1-5.

[57]NATO 2009, pp. 1–7.

The target audiences are quite diverse. Depending on the designated goals, they could consist of opponents, neutral groups, and supporters (including leadership and cadre, as well as populations at home and abroad from various sectors of society). In the early days of Iraqi Freedom, Iraq's political and military leadership received messages via letters, faxes, phone calls, and emails 'urging them to stage coups, betray secrets, order troops to desert, and otherwise act in ways that would disrupt Saddam's political and military [command and control instruments]'.[58] In the same vein, supporters could be approached constructively.

The means and methods available could be 'any capability or activity that can exert influence, affect understanding or have a counter-command effect'; 'the extent is only limited by imagination, availability, policy, [...] and legal constraints'.[59] Basic capabilities are[60]: the use of force; electromagnetic and cyber assets; psychological operations; presence, posture and profile; deception; key leader engagement[61]; economic and diplomatic assets; and commercial, cultural and private enterprise assets.[62] Delegitimizing a non-State actor's campaign by communicating a counter-narrative could be one of the methods used. As explained by Wilner:

> 'Al-Qa'eda's use of suicide terrorism, for example, is legitimized by relying on religious decrees that justify and sanitize the taking of one's own life. [...] Of importance, however, is that suicide is an otherwise blasphemous act under Islamic law and Al-Qa'eda's objectives are refuted by a vast majority of those that share the Muslim faith'.[63]

The effects of information activities range from constructive (e.g. when the understanding of supporters is enhanced by providing assistance or information) to disruptive (such as when the target's understanding is troubled as a result of disinformation, deception or when public support is influenced). Wilner notes that al-Qa'eda, confronted with the counter-narratives, was compelled to expend half its airtime defending its legitimacy.[64]

Looking at the diversity in means and methods, and considering the various strategic and operational objectives involved, coordination between the comprehensive efforts deserves attention in order to prevent 'fratricide' between the different actions. This comprehensive effort is attained with, *inter alia*, strategic communication and a 'whole of government' approach. It is driven by interagency processes and integration of efforts in order to effectively communicate national

---

[58]Andres 2009, p. 74.

[59]NATO 2009, pp. 1–8 (maintaining that the enumeration also contains doctrine as a constraint for information activities). The present author rejects this reading, as doctrine is meant to provide guidance for commanders and staff officers/planners, not be a constraint.

[60]NATO 2009, p. 1-8.

[61]NATO 2009, pp. 1-8–1-9.

[62]NATO 2009, pp. II-3 to II-4.

[63]Wilner 2011, p. 26.

[64]Wilner 2011, p. 30.

strategy.[65] Strategic communication can be defined as the focused 'efforts to create, strengthen, or preserve conditions favourable for the advancement of national interests, policies, and objectives by understanding and engaging key audiences through the use of coordinated programs, plans, themes, messages, and products synchronized with the actions of all instruments of national power'.[66]

Considering modern complex, hybrid, multi-faceted, and multinational operations, synchronizing and reinforcing the various lines of actions is a complicated but essential process. Failure in this respect runs the risk of creating adverse or detrimental effects. Harsh kinetic actions generating severe collateral damage amongst local populations is difficult to reconcile with gaining trust and respect from the same villagers through humanitarian or economic aid programmes.

As the aforementioned means and methods are rather diverse, some of the subsequent and separately analysed non-kinetic capabilities also fit into the broad definition. This applies to key leader engagement, lawfare, cyber operations, and, to some extent, evidence-based operations.

10.8 Key Leader Engagement

Generally regarded as a subset of information operations, key leader engagement is frequently used in the context of stability and counterinsurgency operations.[67] However, engaging and affecting the 'attitudes of key local and/or regional leaders' is today considered to be fundamental for military effectiveness in general.[68] It can be defined as the 'deliberate and planned engagements between military (and civil) leadership and the leaders of foreign audiences'.[69]

The goals sought could be diverse, such as promoting change in current policy or stimulating a favourable attitude towards ongoing military operations, as long as they are supportive, or at least not detrimental.[70] Leader engagements can shape and influence the will, attitude, and understanding of the target audience—foreign leaders at the strategic, operational and tactical levels. Such operations may also be directed towards specific groups, such as religious, academic, or tribal leaders, to solidify trust and confidence in the operations involved.[71]

[65]NATO 2009, p. II-5; Matthijssen 2010.

[66]NATO 2009, p. II-5.

[67]US Joint Forces Command 2010, p. III-7.

[68]US Joint Forces Command 2010, p. III-7.

[69]NATO 2009, p. II-13.

[70]In general, Key Leader Engagement, entails generating constructive effects, although theoreticaly one could also aim at disruptive effects vis-avis selected stakeholders.

[71]NATO 2009, p. II-13. See also Andres 2009, p. 74.

As stated, the means comprise various forms of information, ranging from information (or message) that follows from the use of force to that following other engagements. One of the means available is the allocation of resources, financial, and/or material support to these key leaders.[72] Engagements could be initiated on grounds of diplomatic, governmental, economic, social, security, and military issues. In fact, they involve 'an effective collaboration strategy [...] focused on co-option of these [...] power-holders who traditionally command the high ground of the human terrain'.[73] The methods used to prepare and initiate engagements are conversation and communication.

Key leader engagement follows targeting procedures as described by Kitzen and amended by van Haaster: Defining end states and objectives; Identifying power-holders; Assessing key-leaders; Tailoring engagement profile; Decision making; and Evaluating.[74] This is supported in doctrine:

> The same process used to determine when a radar system should be attacked with the Army Tactical Missile System is also used to determine when building a new sewer system will influence local leaders to support friendly objectives.[75]

Conducting (and considering) key leader engagement clearly requires knowledge, skills, and competencies.

The desired effects resulting from key leader engagement are generally assessed as constructive. By backing, or even 'creating' key leaders, supporters can be gathered, generated, or assisted. In general, favourable conditions result that reinforce other lines of action, to ensure freedom of movement, support, and force protection. Such engagement is particularly useful in serving non-military lines of action, such as economic development, governance, and public security.

10.9 Lawfare

Lawfare, a concept introduced by Charles Dunlap,[76] can be defined as 'the strategy of using—or misusing—law as a substitute for traditional military means to achieve an operational objective'.[77] The goal of lawfare is to create effects that serve 'an operational purpose': the designated effects contribute to overarching

---

[72] US Army Center for Army Lessons Learned 2009, p. i. See also the role of CERP (Commander's Emergency Response Program) at p. 13 ff, arguably signalling particular advantages for this capability in counterinsurgencies, as it 'is defeating COIN targets without creating collateral damage'.

[73] Kitzen 2012a, p. 716.

[74] Kitzen 2012a, pp. 727–728; Haaster 2014. See also US Army 2010a, pp. 2–8, 2–1, and the text accompanying footnotes 15–16 supra.

[75] US Army 2010a, pp. 3–7.

[76] Dunlap 2001, 2009, 2010.

[77] Dunlap 2008, p. 146.

military or non-military goals, for instance delegitimizing participation in missions and operations at the strategic level or distracting military and political leadership from the primary processes of these missions and operations.[78]

The desired effects may vary from disruptive to constructive. Disruptive lawfare could be used to degrade the reputation of an opposing commander or force, thereby weakening his or its military power. The result could be that a commander is distracted from operations by responding to allegations, or that the public support for the operations or the military diminishes as a result of the allegations. As demonstrated by Dunlap, 'the mere perception of [law of armed conflict] violations can significantly impact operations'.[79] Constructive lawfare could be used to counter destructive lawfare, for example, by releasing to the public genuine information related to allegations voiced by others.[80] It is evident that lawfare, as well as counter-lawfare, coincide with information operations.

The target audience, or addressees, may include public opinion in general, judicial organs, and, in particular, the media as intermediate targets. The focal point, the target itself, is the perception of groups and individuals. Instead of addressing public opinion, one could also consider addressing 'key leaders' directly, such as members of parliament, politicians, military commanders, and other influential groups, organizations, and individuals. Therefore, the target audience not only includes direct targets (such as opponents, neutrals, and supporters), but also intermediate targets. Lawfare can be used to influence the perception (public support) of the population in troop-contributing countries, as well as in the conflict zones; 'Practitioners of lawfare try to destroy an opponent's will to fight by undermining the public support that is indispensable when democracies […] conduct military interventions'.[81] In some cases the target could be an individual, a group or a particular course of action, as was the case in the Gaza Freedom Flotilla (2011).[82]

The means are composed of pieces of information, false or true.[83] The content of that information can be about inappropriate behaviour in battle, such as (alleged) disrespect for elementary humanitarian or ethical rules, violations of the laws of war or rules of engagement, ordinary criminal behaviour, or undisciplined conduct in general.[84] It could refer to the (alleged) conduct itself, or to the

[78]The present author also rejects the neo-conservative view that even the legitimate use of (international) law by opponents qualifies as 'lawfare'. See, e.g. Goldstein and Meyer 2009; Goldstein 2014.

[79]Dunlap 2001.

[80]See NATO's response to questions from the UN's Human Rights Council related to Operation Unified Protector (Libya, 2011) in UN Human Rights Council 2012.

[81]Banks 2011.

[82]Wright 2011.

[83]For a manipulated impression of a battlefield situation, see the Valhalla incident in Iraq (2006) as described by Dauber 2009, p. 13 ff and Dungan 2008.

[84]For examples of the potential use of lawfare, see e.g. Shirbon 2014; Liljas 2014. See also UK House of Commons 2013.

responses of commanders and authorities involved. In addition to allegations of criminal or ethical misconduct, civil procedures may be applied to restrict the use of media, access to resources, or freedom of movement or speech.[85] In the Gaza Flotilla case, lawfare was used instead of another physical raid. The 'Israeli government and its front organizations, American Israeli Public Affairs Council (AIPAC) and the Shurat HaDin Law Center, us[ed] lawsuits filed against insurance and satellite telephone companies that may [have sold …] equipment to the flotilla organizers and against citizen activist groups that […] raised funds to purchase ships as strategies to attempt to stop the flotilla'.[86]

These methods may conversely be applied to enhance access to press and other assets or to enable freedom of movement and speech. Lawfare offers opportunities that, when seeking the initiative, force the side countering the charges to respond in defence.

10.10 Criminal Legal Action

Criminal legal action is distinguished from lawfare. As a specific branch of law, it is legitimately used to generate beneficial effects alongside other operations and activities. As such, its primary (operational)[87] goal is to generate disruptive effects. It generally reduces mobility, freedom of movement, resources, and ultimately (fighting) power of—most likely—opponents by initiating criminal procedures and engaging in enforcement powers (for instance by detaining individuals and removing them from the 'battlefield' using law). This type of targeting is also described as 'warrant-based targeting',[88] 'conviction-focused targeting',[89] or 'evidence-based operations'.[90] Such action might serve as an alternative to physical action or attacks, and be initiated for a variety of reasons, such as the illegality of physical attack because the target does not constitute a legitimate military objective under the law of armed conflict (LOAC).[91] As demonstrated in Iraq and Afghanistan,[92] the importance of criminal legal action as an alternative to kinetic targeting increases significantly in stability operations and occupation in general, and when sovereignty has been transferred to the indigenous government after an

[85] Haaretz 2014.

[86] Wright 2011.

[87] Operational or tactical goals are used in contrast to strategic goals (i.e. goals at strategic command levels in operations).

[88] Govern 2012.

[89] Berlin 2010.

[90] Voetelink 2013; Herrera 2013.

[91] See for instance the discussion on the legality to target (kill) individuals that could be related to the narcotic industry in Afghanistan: Pouw 2013, p. 288–289; Koelbi 2009; Schmitt 2009.

[92] Govern 2012, p. 477.

occupation in particular.[93] Yet, even during the early days of intervention in occupation,[94] law enforcement actions will be quite essential alongside kinetic actions, for instance when kinetic targeting (or attacking) with lethal capabilities would be illegal under domestic law or violate the law of armed conflict.[95]

In addition, a strategic secondary goal of criminal legal action is to generate constructive effects that promote the rule of law through the stimulation of host-nation judicial processes in post-conflict situations. This also contributes to State-building efforts during stability operations[96] and serves training purposes in military assistance, training, and advisory missions.[97]

The primary (operational) targets in criminal legal actions will, by definition, be 'suspects', particularly adversarial stakeholders. Criminal legal action is conditional on the availability of actionable and appropriate information related to criminal conduct or involvement of those targets. For example, criminal evidence that is eligible to be used in the (host-nation's) criminal process has to be gathered. Available intelligence may serve as a basis, although a complicated and delicate declassification process might be required. The secondary (strategic) target is the host-nation's judicial system, with a particular focus on the enhancement of various police and security organizations and different types of magistrates, such as public prosecutors, defence lawyers, courts and judges, and the detention system.[98]

A number of means and methods are available to initiate or undertake criminal legal action, including evidence, detention, searches, and seizure. By bringing forward relevant criminal information (evidence), legal action by appropriate host-nation authorities can be undertaken. This evidence might serve as the basis for criminal proceedings and investigations, which may ultimately result in the apprehension or conviction of suspects (targets). Cooperation with local security and law enforcement organisations can also have the additional effect of promoting the rule of law.[99] With an adequate legal basis, troops may also detain individuals, search places, seize evidence, gather evidence packages and transfer suspects and evidence to the appropriate national or international judicial authorities. The legal basis required to detain, search, and seize may stem from either LOAC, a UN

---

[93]Based on the consent by the sovereign Host Nation, as expressed in i.a. Status of Forces Agreements (SOFAs).

[94]Regulations Respecting the Laws and Customs of War on Land, annexed to Convention No. IV Respecting the Laws and Customs of War on Land, 18 October 1907, 36 Stat. 2227, Article 42 [hereinafter Hague IV Regulations].

[95]Based on the Hague IV Regulations, idem., Article 43. See e.g. Pouw 2013; Dinstein 2009.

[96]Chesney 2011, p. 477.

[97]Herrera 2013.

[98]Evidence-based operations 'are operations where Afghan law enforcement authorities, supported by ISAF, effectively investigate, apprehend, search and seize criminal suspects and affiliated property in accordance with Afghan law'. Voetelink 2013, p. 198.

[99]And *vice versa*.

Security Council authorisation, or an arrest warrant issued by host-nation authorities, international organizations (European Union),[100] or international tribunals (such as the ICC).[101]

Criminal legal action—as well as lawfare—is not without cost; it places strains on the regular forces. As noted by Voetelink, 'this particular approach requires military operations, which are generally intelligence driven, at some point to key in on the host state's criminal justice system'.[102] This will affect the military operations in various ways. Evidence-based operations and warrant-based or conviction-focussed targeting requires specific skills and competencies. As observed by Govern and Morris:

> These skills include the use of forensics prior to and during the apprehension; that is, the collection, preservation and analysis of evidence such as chemistry (for the identification of explosives), engineering (for examination of structural design) or biology (for DNA identification or matching).[103]

To enable prosecution, adjudication, and imprisonment of suspects, information related to the suspects and their criminal behaviour has to be secured and converted to make it admissible in the (host nation's) criminal legal system.[104] The 'package' may include personal data, data from communications (email, overview of telephone taps, text-messages, whatsapps), biometric evidence, thumbprints, witness statements, etc. Declassification of military intelligence may also call for additional procedures before it may be used as evidence in criminal procedures.

Because not all military forces have the skills and competencies required to gather and secure information of this kind, advisory teams from, or training by, law-enforcement officials can be beneficial.[105] As pointed out by Govern:

> Despite past military operations in which war crimes or other offenses were investigated after the fact, the practical challenge of applying warrant-based targeting oriented 'forensics' on the battlefield, especially with regards to building a case for prosecution, comes with the developing experience of military members outside of the military police and criminal investigative branches with regards to securing evidence.[106]

Of vital importance is the transfer of information (i.e., physical and forensic evidence). In this respect, it has become standard practise to equip troops with photo or video cameras and other specialized equipment to safeguard gathered and seized evidence.[107] Special attention is required to safeguard the chain-of-custody, as criminal evidence is only admissible if it is gathered and preserved in

[100] European arrest warrant: European Union 2002.

[101] Rome Statute of the International Criminal Court, 17 July 1998, 2187 UNTS 90, Article 58 Rome Statute (Statute of the International Criminal Court).

[102] Voetelink 2013, p. 195.

[103] Govern 2012, p. 484.

[104] See US Army 2010b; US Army Center for Army Lessons Learned 2010.

[105] Neuteboom 2014.

[106] Govern 2012, p. 484.

[107] See e.g. Voetelink 2013, p. 199 and Herrera 2013, pp. 94–108.

accordance with local (or international) criminal law and regulations.[108] This constraint applies not only to physical and forensic evidence, including electronic or digital information derived from modern communications, but also to that gathered from crime scenes. Safeguarding *locus delicti* may require troops to extend their presence for law enforcement purposes, whereas they would normally return to their bases or continue their operations elsewhere.

Some of these operations, particularly those that aim to apprehend or arrest suspects,[109] require an amended logistical and organizational footprint. Specialists may be called on to conduct arrests, search places and objects, and process and guard detainees, as well as evidence or investigate crimes scenes. Apart from detention facilities, one would also need medical examination capabilities, appropriate transportation, translators (with criminal law expertise), biometrical expertise, and advisors with knowledge of criminal law, forensics, and biometrics.[110]

10.11 Deprivation of Liberty: Security Detention

In designated circumstances outside the framework of criminal legal action, the liberty of individuals may be restricted for security reasons.[111] The prisoner of war is perhaps the best-known illustration of 'security detention',[112] although it is limited to situations of international armed conflict.[113] In non-international armed conflict and other situations of violence, 'detention' in the form of internment (or administrative detention) has also become routine for the military. Internment is defined as the deprivation of liberty of individuals, initiated or ordered by (organs of) the executive branch of government outside the law enforcement framework, in order to protect the security (of the State) or public order in designated circumstances.[114]

The primary goal of security detention—in designated circumstances—is disruptive. It prevents individuals from participating in activities that may pose a threat to public safety, public order, or the security of (local or international) personnel of governmental organs and international (military and civil) forces that are

---

[108] Herrera 2013, p. 94.

[109] These are often referred to as 'detention' operations. This term however, will be reserved for 'security detention' (see infra).

[110] Berlin 2010, pp. 2, 8 (referring to 'prosecution support teams' that should be established).

[111] Pouw 2013, p. 18.

[112] The term 'operational detention' is also used.

[113] See Convention (III) relative to the Treatment of Prisoners of War (Geneva, 12 August 1949) 75 UNTS 135.

[114] See Pejic 2005, p. 375. For 'operational detention', see Kleffner 2010, p. 465.

present in conflict areas.[115] Security detention offers an alternative to lethally targeting individuals in specific situations. This may serve secondary goals, such as a favourable public perception toward the legitimacy of military operations in both the host and home nations. The need to consider this option may be found in legal, diplomatic, or operational reasoning. Civilians who do not directly participate in hostilities may not be physically attacked. However, even when they lose their protection as a civilian, and so are targetable for that time (due to their direct participation in hostilities),[116] diplomatic or operational considerations may prevent a State from conducting physical attacks.

The primary target is an individual that poses a designated threat. The secondary target for detention operations is public opinion, as it can promote the legitimacy of the military operation by lowering the number of casualties because the number of physical attacks can be reduced.

'Arrests' or 'detention operations' that deprive persons of their liberty can be seen as a method of targeting individuals. Human rights obligations and/or customary LOAC necessitate that a lawful ground exist for this type of targeting.[117] In military operations, detention is based on either the Security Council's authorisation 'to use all necessary means', on LOAC, on Status of Forces Agreements, or on host nation legislation. In all cases, dedicated Rules of Engagement (ROE) will be formulated to provide guidance. Combined and interagency detention operations are commonplace, as are operations undertaken in coordination with indigenous civil or military forces. The latter offers additional opportunities to enhance the rule of law in post-conflict environments, an advantageous side effect.

10.12 Asset Freezes

Using the authority provided for by appropriate (international) bodies such as the Security Council or host nation institutions, operations with the aim of depriving individuals of (their) assets can be mounted in the financial realm, for instance by seizing or freezing (financial) assets and resources.[118] The primary goal is to incapacitate or control individuals by blocking or restricting their access to resources. The secondary goal is the reduced availability of resources for warring parties or violent non-State actors in post-conflict zones, thereby undermining the logistic and financial support that is necessary to prolong conflict or violence.

---

[115]In general, see: Cole et al. 2009; Gill and Fleck 2010, p. 465. For a specific operation: Innenriks 29 January 2004.

[116]Or when s/he fulfils a 'continuous combat function', resulting in a loss of protection from attack throughout that period.

[117]Kleffner 2010, pp. 469–470, mentioning a Security Council Resolution, LOAC, self-defence, the prevention of breaches of international (criminal) law; and Agreements with the Host Nation.

[118]Noorda 2014.

The targets are (members of) rebel groups and non-State actors or selected individuals participating in conflict and violence.[119] The means/methods are the freezing, seizure, or revelation of financial assets and resources.[120] As such this also serves law enforcement and information operations purposes. More specifically, the method has been used in the sphere of counter-terrorism sanctions after the 9/11 attacks.[121]

This route, at least when asset freezing is involved, requires the application of a comprehensive approach at the (inter)national level given that international approval is generally necessary. Disclosure and seizure as a method are available at the operational level as soon as authorization through ROE is available.

The effects generated are disruptive in nature, as the 'freedom of movement' of groups, organisations, and individuals is restricted, and resources are restrained. The backlash of asset freezing lies in reduced information, as financial transactions can be monitored and thereby provide valuable information. In addition, the addressees might be forced to resort to other—less traceable—resources.[122]

10.13 Cyber Operations

Military cyber operations can be defined as 'the employment of cyber capabilities with the primary purpose of achieving military objectives by influencing actors in or by the use of cyberspace'.[123] The goal of cyber operations is to influence actors constructively or disruptively. Opponents will most likely have to face effects aimed at disruption and reduction of their resources, including information. Neutral and supportive actors can be engaged in a constructive manner, enhancing their sources of power.

Targets are found in particular layers of the digital domain (or cyberspace).[124] Cyberspace contains—apart from the physical layers of geographic locations, persons and tangible objects—two virtual layers. First, the cyber persona layer consists of cyber identities, i.e., the virtual reflection of persons (e-mail addresses,

[119] See the model presented by Brooks 2002, p. 19; Drezner 2011.

[120] See the activities of the UK based NGO Global Witness, www.globalwitness.org/campaigns/corruption/oil-gas-and-mining/Afghanistan. Accessed 25 May 2014.

[121] See UK Government, Current List of Designated Persons, Terrorism and Terrorist Financing (update 11 April 2014). www.gov.uk/government/publications/current-list-of-designated-persons-terrorism-and-terrorist-financing. Accessed on 25 May 2014.

[122] See Barrett 2012, p. 723; Basile 2004.

[123] Ducheine 2015, based on Schmitt 2013, p. 258, referring to this notion as 'cyber warfare': 'employment of cyber capabilities with the primary purpose of achieving [military] objectives *in or by* the use of cyberspace' [Emphasis added].

[124] Ducheine and Haaster 2014, pp. 309–310.

Facebook-accounts). Second, the logical network layer contains so-called cyber objects, in contrast to tangible objects in the physical dimension. Examples of cyber objects include applications (software or code) and IP-addresses. By addressing (or targeting) cyber identities and cyber objects, disruptive and constructive effects can be achieved.[125] The physical layers of cyberspace (i.e., tangible objects and persons) can be affected indirectly through the intermediate activities against the cyber identities and cyber objects.[126]

Taking into account diplomatic and operational limitations, the means and methods for cyber operations are only restricted by one's imagination and skill in developing tools for use in cyberspace. Cyber capabilities employed to conduct operations can be rather basic, as in denial of service activities, or advanced, such as Stuxnet. Although often suggested otherwise, disruptive cyber operations can be repeatedly used, even against the same targets. This may be due to innovative changes by the 'targeteers', or because the victim (target) fails to fix vulnerabilities. Constructive cyber operations, assuming that the target (audience) is approved, may be repeated until further notice.

Generic targeting procedures are also applicable to the planning and execution of cyber activities.[127] Moreover, cyber operations may be used to accelerate information operations and to conduct counter-lawfare operations. As demonstrated by Dauber, modern media covering military operations abroad relies heavily on footage provided by a variety of actors: the local population (bystanders), the military (through social media), and violent non-State actors involved in the conflict. In fact, Dauber observes that 'American television networks, unable for a variety of reasons to obtain usable combat footage on a regular basis, depend on insurgents for visual products'.[128] Footage of insurgent attacks, staged, filmed and posted by them is used as news footage 'as if it had been filmed by Western photojournalists'.[129] For procedural and bureaucratic reasons, it then proves extremely difficult for western governments to counter the perception that was created by the use of this footage.

Apart from the fact that investigations into alleged misconduct should be completed as soon as possible, armed forces may need to act in a more proactive way to prevent this course of events by engaging in 'rapid response or, if at all possible, to get out ahead of stories that are predictable'[130]:

> It is not about satisfying the press, an annoyance that interferes with the mission. If the story has the potential to erode public support, either domestically or internationally, then it is, in fact, mission critical.[131]

---

[125] Ducheine 2015. See also Andres 2009, p. 74.

[126] Ducheine and Haaster 2014, pp. 313–314.

[127] Ducheine and Haaster 2014, pp. 320–323.

[128] Dauber 2009, pp. v–x.

[129] Dauber 2009, pp. v–x.

[130] Dauber 2009, pp. v–x.

[131] Dauber 2009, pp. v-x.

In this respect, cyber operations could be used to pre-empt opposing information operations or lawfare. By releasing footage, information, or statements as soon as possible after actions, or when possible even before operations are launched, the initiative can be seized.

10.14 Conclusions

This chapter set out to complement discussions of the kinetic targeting in previous chapters by introducing some of the non-kinetic capabilities available in modern military operations. The four elements of targeting (a military operational *way* that uses military *means* to influence a *target* or addressee in order to achieve designated political and/or military *goals*) served as a red line throughout the chapter. It should be cautioned that non-kinetic targeting as such does not exist as a standalone concept. There is only targeting, which refers to a spectrum comprising kinetic and non-kinetic elements.

Kinetic targeting is about the targeted application of military force based on the release or concentration of kinetic energy against opposing forces or objects with (primarily) lethal effects in the physical domain. Non-kinetic targeting refers to the targeted application of (other military and non-military) capabilities against addressees to generate (additional) non-kinetic effects in the non-physical and physical domain.

Non-kinetic targeting complements the (existing) kinetic arsenal and capabilities. It is limited only by our imagination, political, ethical, and legal norms, and operational policy. In the context of complex modern operations, whether taking the comprehensive approach in a counterinsurgency operation, stabilization operation or during classic interstate warfare, it is evident that all available (and legitimate) capabilities can be used as means to influence other actors. The targets potentially comprise opponents, neutral groups, and supporters. The means and methods (and targets) used will depend on the effects sought; they should contribute to the strategic and military goals set out.

Non-kinetic targeting thus offers some definite advantages. It opens up the classic target audience for military operations. Additional opposing forces that are somehow protected from direct kinetic (lethal) attack may also be affected. The same is true for supporters and neutrals, whether in the battlefield at home or abroad. Non-kinetic targeting also offers alternatives to kinetic means and methods, and supplements the legitimate arsenal available to commanders and forces. The effects generated complement traditional kinetic and disruptive effects, including constructive ones. Moreover, even when causing detrimental effects for the addressees/targets, the damage or disruption might be less severe than kinetic targeting, offering preferable options and minimizing collateral damage. Non-kinetic targeting can also provide favourable options for avoiding the negative (physical or psychological) backlash of kinetic action, and for facilitating freedom of movement, public support, and force protection. In some situations, therefore, non-kinetic targeting could be more effective, efficient, and opportune. As stated in the US Joint Publication on targeting:

> Nonlethal capability use can also influence adversary decision maker's choice of actions, local public condemnation of adversary actions, and directly impact domestic and international support of the adversary. [...] The scalability, selectability, and responsiveness of nonlethal capabilities provide the JFC the means to engage all target types: facilities (e.g., to clear a facility of personnel, thus stopping its function), individuals (e.g., detaining an individual), virtual targets (through cyberspace), equipment (e.g., through seizure), and organizations (e.g., revoking a license to engage in commerce).[132]

When using these various assets and lines of actions—kinetic and non-kinetic—it is essential to harmonize and synchronize all output at all levels in order to prevent detrimental effects from one course of action affecting another. In military headquarters this is commonplace. In multidimensional operations using a comprehensive approach, the need to synchronize becomes even more relevant. Special attention is needed to harmonize all full spectrum efforts, especially the 'message' accompanying these actions. Strategic communication is therefore key, particularly in full spectrum operations and if and when western forces stress the importance of information alongside physical action.[133]

The various non-kinetic targeting modalities may require different legal bases and are governed by a variety of legal regimes. Warfighting may find its basis in international self-defence and the law of armed conflict, whereas other actions, such as asset freezing, may require additional legal grounds at the strategic level. The different modalities also require the military to apply the various applicable legal regimes. For instance, criminal law, law of armed conflict, and human rights apply to detention, which also necessitate sufficient knowledge of local regimes when cooperating with domestic authorities.

In order to make full use of the entire arsenal, true comprehensive approaches will be required, as some of the means and methods needed are not available within the military chain of command. Multinational and joint operations are necessary in order to benefit from the potential of full spectrum operations. Looking at the modalities and capabilities needed, much of non-kinetic targeting focuses on the human domain, physical as well a psychological.[134] The human social and cognitive element is essential, whether for influencing physical behaviour or affecting understanding. This has consequences for the force composition and

[132]US Department of Defense 2013, p. II-16.

[133]It goes beyond the focus of the chapter to elaborate on the notion of strategic communication. See e.g., NATO Military Concept for Strategic Communications 2010, p. 1, defining strategic communication as 'the coordinated and appropriate use of NATO communications activities and capabilities—Public Diplomacy, Public Affairs, Military Public Affairs, Info Ops and PsyOps—in support of Alliance policies, operations and activities, and in order to advance NATO's aims'.

[134]Cyber operations, however, are partially different.

footprint. Additional expertise and knowledge may be required; this will not necessarily result in fewer numbers of deployed (military and civilian) staff. The experts will most often deploy with land forces and joint headquarters in general.

It has not, however, been analysed whether the targeting procedures used for kinetic targeting are also suitable for non-kinetic avenues. This seems to be the case with key leader engagement and cyber operations, considering that the targeting process is adaptive in nature, and essentially about achieving goals with allocated means. The composition of targeting boards will differ, depending on the modality of non-kinetic targeting considered. Yet, while means and effects may vary, the ultimate goals remain the same.

When evaluating the western prevalence of kinetic targeting, it should be noted that some actors have developed better skills and gained more proficiency in non-kinetic targeting than have western armed forces. Although specific guidance is on the rise, the conclusion that '[a]t present, weaponeering is more developed to support munitions than nonlethal actions' is probably still valid.[135] However, considering the latest military doctrine, a shift in thinking appears to be emerging; instead of classically addressing (attacking) enemy forces and objects, modern publications now acknowledge that targeting also very much focuses on will (psyche), situational awareness, choices, mental resilience, understanding, and behaviour. More recently, cyber identities and cyber objects could be added to this list.

For westerners, it is worth noting that our non-kinetic efforts quite often are in support of kinetic action. In other parts of the world, the reverse is true.

References

Allied Command Operations (NATO) (2010) Comprehensive Operations Planning Directive (COPD). V1.0 Mons: Supreme Headquarters Allied Power Europe, 7 Dec 2010

Andres RB (2009) Deep attack against Iraq. In: Mahnken TG, Keaney TA (eds) War in Iraq: planning and execution (strategy and history). Routledge, London, pp 69–96

Banks WC (2011) New battlefields/old laws: critical debates on asymmetric warfare. Columbia University Press, New York

Barrett R (2012) Preventing the financing of terrorism. Case West Reserv J Int Law 44(3):719–736

Basile M (2004) Going to the source: why al qaeda's financial network is likely to withstand the current war on terrorist financing. Stud Confl Terror 27(3):169–185

Berlin SD (2010) Conviction-focused targeting: targeting violent extremists while developing rule of law capacity. Small Wars J

Brooks RA (2002) Santions and regime type: what works, and when? Secur Stud 11(4):1–50

Caldwell WBI, Murphy DM, Menning A (2009) Learning to leverage new media: the Israelian Defense Forces in recent conflicts. Mil Rev 89(3):2–10

Canada ND (2008) B-GL-300-001/FP-001 Land Operations

Cheng Hang T (2010) Non-kinetic warfare: the reality and the response. Point J Singap Armed Forces 36(1):45–57

[135]US Department of Defense 2013, p. II-15.

Chesney R (2011) Iraq and the military detention debate: firsthand perspectives from the other war, 2003–2010. Va J Int Law 51(3):549–636
Cole A, Drew P, McLaughlin R, Mandsager D (eds) (2009) Rules of engagement handbook. International Institute of Humanitarian Law, San Remo
Dauber C (2009) YouTube war: righting in a world of cameras in every cell phone and photoshop on every computer. Strategic Studies Institute, U.S. Army War College, Carlisle
Dinstein Y (2009) The international law of belligerent occupation. University Press, Cambridge
Drezner DW (2011) Sanctions sometimes smart: targeted sanctions in theory and practice. Int Stud Rev 13(1):96–108
Ducheine PAL (2015) The notion of cyber operations in international law. In: Tsagourias N, Buchan R (eds) Reseach handbook on international law and cyber space. Edwar Elgar Publishing, Cheltenham, pp 211–232
Ducheine PAL, Haaster Jv (2014) Fighting power, targeting and cyber operations. In: Proceedings of the 6th International Conference on Cyber Conflict, CCDCOE, Tallinn, pp 303–327
Ducheine PAL, Pouw EH (2012) Legitimizing the use of force: legal bases for Operation Enduring Freedom and ISAF. In: Meulen Jvd, Vogelaar A, Beeres R, Soeters J (eds) Mission Uruzgan: collaborating in multiple coalitions for Afghanistan. Amsterdam University Press, Amsterdam, pp 33–46
Dungan P (2008) Fighting lawfare at the special operations task force level. Spec Warf 21(2):10–15
Dunlap CJ (2001) Law and military interventions: preserving humanitarian values in 21st conflicts. Humanitarian Challenges in Military Intervention Conference, Carr Center for Human Rights Policy, Kennedy School of Government, Harvard University Washington, D.C., 29 Nov 2001
Dunlap CJ (2008) Lawfare today: a perspective. Yale J Int Aff (Winter):146–154
Dunlap CJ (2009) Lawfare: a decisive element of 21st century conflicts? Joint Forces Q 54:34–39
Dunlap CJ (2010) Does lawfare need an apologia? Case West Reserv J Int Law 43:121–143
European Commission (2013) Joint Communication to the European Parliament and the Council. The EU's comprehensive approach to external conflict and crises. JOIN (2013) 30 final, Brussels, 11 Dec 2013
European Union (2002) Council Framework Decision 2002/584/JHA of 13 June 2002 on the European Arrest Warrant and the Surrender Procedures Between Member States, 2002 O.J. (L 190/2) 1 (EU)
Gill TD, Fleck D (2010) The handbook of the international law of military operations. Oxford University Press, Oxford
Goldstein B (2014) What is lawfare? www.thelawfareproject.org. Accessed 15 April 2014
Goldstein B, Meyer AE (2009) Legal jihad: how Islamist lawfare tactics are targeting free speech. ILSA J Int Comp Law 15:395–410
Govern KH (2012) Warrant-based targeting: prosecution-oriented capture and detention as legal and moral alternative to targeted killing. Ariz J Int Comp Law 29(3):477–516
Haaretz (2014) Twitter suspends account of Hamas' military wing (14 January 2014)
Haaster Jv (2014) Key-leader engagement in or through cyberspace. Essay, Netherlands Defence Academy (on file with the author)
Hanson VD (1989) The western way of war—infantry battle in Classical Greece. Hodder & Stoughton, London
Hanson VD (2001) Why the west has won: carnage and culture from Salamis to Vietnam. Anchor Books, New York
Herrera P (2013) Evidence based operations: a guide for intelligence professionals to operate in conjunction with the rule of law in Afghanistan. NATO Operational Headquarters (on file with author)
Innenriks (2004) The rules of engagement: stridsreglene. http://www.nrk.no/nyheter/innenriks/3462304.html. Accessed 22 April 2014

Kilcullen D (2009) The accidental guerilla. University Press, Oxford
Kitzen M (2012a) Close encounters of the tribal kind: the implementation of co-option as a tool for de-escalation of conflict: the case of the Netherlands in Afghanistan's Uruzgan Province. J Strateg Stud 35(5):713–734
Kitzen M (2012b) Western military culture and counter-insurgency, an ambigious reality. Sci Mil S Afr J Mil Stud 40(1):123–134
Kleffner J (2010) Operational detention and the treatment of detainees. In: Gill TD, Fleck D (eds) The handbook of the international law of military operations. Oxford University Press, Oxford, pp 465–479
Koelbi S (2009) Battling Afghan drug dealers: NATO High Commander issues illegitimate order to kill (28 January 2009). Der Spiegel
Koninklijke Landmacht (2014) Doctrinepublicatie Landoptreden. www.defensie.nl/binaries/defensie/documenten/publicaties/2014/02/11/militaire-doctrine-voor-het-landoptreden/DP+3.2.pdf. Accessed 29 April 2014
Liljas P (2014) Top U.K. defense officials accused of war crimes: International Criminal Court receives huge dossier of allegations relating to British conduct during war in Iraq (13 January 2014). Time. http://world.time.com/2014/01/13/top-u-k-defense-officials-accused-of-war-crimes/. Accessed 16 May 2014
Lynn J (2003) Battle: a history of combat and culture from ancient Greece to modern America. Westview Press, Boulder
Matthijssen CJ (2010) Strategic communication. Mil Spect 179(10):517–531
Ministerie van Defensie (2013) Netherlands defence doctrine. http://www.defensie.nl/binaries/defensie/documenten/publicaties/2013/11/20/defence-doctrine-en/defensie-doctrine_en.pdf. Accessed 16 March 2014
Morris VR (2010) Battlefield forensics: dynamic adaptation of the company-level task force. Infantery 99(Nov/Dec):6
Murphy DM (2009) Talking the talk: why warfighters don't understand information operations. Issue Paper, Center for Strategic Leadership, US Army War College
NATO (2008) Allied joint doctrine for joint targeting (AJP-3.9)
NATO (2009) Allied joint doctrine for information operations (AJP-3.10)
NATO (2010) NATO military concept for strategic communications (27 July), enclosure 1 to MCM-0085-2010 revised, dated 11 August 2010. http://www.docstoc.com/docs/136613988/NATO-Military-Concept-for-Strategic-Communications
Neuteboom P (2014) Beyond borders: the role of the Netherlands Army in public security during crisis management operations (diss. University of Tilburg). Wolf Legal Publishers, Nijmegen
Noorda H (2014) Preventive deprivations of liberty: asset freezes and travel bans. Amsterdam Law School Research Paper No 2014-20. http://papers.ssrn.com/sol3/papers.cfm?abstract_id=2400390. Accessed 25 May 2014
Pejic J (2005) Procedural principles and safeguards for internment/administrative detention in armed conflict and other situations of violence. Int Rev Red Cross 87(858):376
Pijpers PBMJ (2014) De twitterende tegenstanders: een discours over de rol van mediaculturen in het conflict (org. Dutch). Mil Spect 183(6):300–314
Pouw EH (2013) International human rights law and the law of armed conflict in the context of counterinsurgency—with a particular focus on targeting and operational detention (diss. UvA)
Schmitt MN (2009) Targeting narcoinsurgents in Afghanistan: the limits of international humanitarian law. Yearb Int Humanit Law 12:301–320
Schmitt MN (ed) (2013) Tallinn manual on the international law applicable to cyber warfare. Cambridge University Press,
Shirbon E (2014) Campaigners ask ICC to investigate alleged UK war crimes in Iraq (12 January 2014). Reuters
Smith-Windsor B (2008) Hasten slowly: NATO's effects based and comprehensive approach to operations. NATO Research Paper 38 (NATO Defence College)

Smith R (2005) The utility of force. Allen Lane, London
Sun Tzu (1994) The art of war (trans: Sawyer R). Westview Press, Boulder
UN Human Rights Council (2012) Report of the International Commission of Inquiry on Libya (UN Doc nr. A/HRC/19/68)
UK House of Commons DC (2013) UK armed forces personnel and the legal framework for future operations. Twelfth Report of Session 2013-14, HC 931, Published on 2 April 2013
UK Ministry of Defence (2009) Joint doctrine publication 3-00 (JDP 3-00), 3rd Edn. Campaign Execution. Development, Concepts and Doctrine Centre (DCDC). https://www.gov.uk/government/uploads/system/uploads/attachment_data/file/33697/20111130jdp001_bdd_Ed4.pdf. Accessed 17 March 2014
US Air Force (2014) Annex 3–60 Targeting https://doctrine.af.mil/download.jsp?filename=3-60-Annex-TARGETING.pdf. Accessed 6 April 2014
US Army Center for Army Lessons Learned (2009) Commanders Guide to Money as a Weapon System. Handbook 09-27 (March)
US Army, Center for Army Lessons Learned (2010) Forensics and Warrant-Based Targeting, pp 10–35 (March)
US Army (2010a) Field manual (FM 3-60) the targeting process (November 2010), Department of the Army
US Army (2010b) Site exploitation operations ATTP No. 3-90.15 (FM 3-90.15)
US Department of Defense (2012) Joint publication information operations (JP 3-13). Joint Chiefs of Staff. http://www.dtic.mil/doctrine/new_pubs/jp3_13.pdf. Accessed 6 April 2014
US Department of Defense (2013) Joint publication targeting (JP 3-60). Joint Chiefs of Staff. http://cfr.org/content/publications/attachments/Joint_Chiefs_of_Staff-Joint_Targeting_31_January_2013.pdf. Accessed 6 April 2014
US Joint Forces Command (2010) Commander's handbook for strategic communication and communication strategy. U.S. Joint Warfighting Center, Suffolk
Voetelink JED (2013) Evidence-based operations: how to remove the bad guys from the battlefield. J Int Law Peace Armed Confl 4:194–201
Wilner AS (2011) Deterring the undeterrable: coercion, denial, and delegitimization in counterterrorism. J Strateg Stud 34(1):3–37
Wright A (2011) Lawfare: Israeli-AIPAC attack on the Gaza Freedom Flotilla (13 June 2011). http://sabbah.biz/mt/archives/2011/06/13/aipac-israel-attack-gaza-flotilla/. Accessed 29 April 2014

Chapter 11
Targeting in Coalition Operations

Chris De Cock

Abstract In this paper, the author examines the normative framework in coalition operations with respect to the concept of targeting. He considers the complexity of the legal framework, including the mandate and the interplay between international human rights law and the law of armed conflict. The author then considers the implications of the mandate and the use of force used pursuant to it for the applicability of the *jus in bello* laws regulating the conduct of hostilities. In the second half of the paper, the author examines some legal interoperability problems by reference to the *jus in bello* laws of targeting, demonstrating the complexity of the targeting decision making process. Finally, he considers the issue of accountability of coalition commanders under the doctrine of command responsibility.

Keywords Coalition operations · Legal interoperability · Legal framework · Targeting · Command responsibility

Contents

The views expressed in this paper are those of the author in his personal capacity and do not intend to reflect the views of the DG or of the Ministry of Defense.

C. De Cock (✉)
Lieutenant-Colonel (GS), Head Operational Law Section, DG Legal Support & Mediation, Belgian Ministry of Defense, Brussels, Belgium
e-mail: Christian.DeCock@mil.be

P.A.L. Ducheine et al. (eds.), *Targeting: The Challenges of Modern Warfare*,
DOI 10.1007/978-94-6265-072-5_11

11.1 Introduction

The complexity of contemporary military operations requires armed forces of different States to be able to operate as partners. Based on their national interests, States may conclude political and/or military partnerships in order to achieve their strategic aims. Such partnerships can take the form of ad hoc coalitions,[1] in which case they are created for specific purposes and a limited timeframe, or can consist of institutional partnerships or alliances, such as the European Union (EU)[2] or the North Atlantic Treaty Organization (NATO).[3] They are usually referred to as coalition operations, multinational operations,[4] or combined operations.[5] In this chapter, the term 'coalition operations'[6] will be used in a generic way and as synonymous with the other terms. The exact role of the armed forces in such operations will vary according to each political and military situation.

---

[1]An example of such military cooperation is Operation Apollo, in which US and Canadian infantry units conducted combat operations in Afghanistan. See the Canadian Forces' Contribution to the International Campaign Against Terrorism, cited in Walsh 2005, p. 316.

[2]EU operations are based on Council Decisions, pursuant to Articles 42(4) and 43 of the Treaty of the European Union. Treaty on European Union (Lisbon Consolidated Version) OJ C 83/13, 30 March 2010.

[3]North Atlantic Treaty, Washington D.C., 4 April 1949, 34 UNTS 243, see in particular Article 5.

[4]Multinational is the adjective used to describe activities, operations and organizations in which elements of more than one nation participate.

[5]Combined operations should be distinguished from joint operations. The former are operations in which two or more States are involved, whereas the latter are operations in which at least two components or services of a single State participate. When different services or branches of at least two States are involved, those forces are usually referred to as Combined Joint Task Forces (CJTF).

[6]According to NATO, 'coalition operations' are operations conducted by forces of two or more nations, which may not be allies, acting together for the accomplishment of a single mission, whereas 'coalition actions' are multinational actions outside the bounds of established alliances, usually for a single occasion, or for longer cooperation in a narrow sector of common interest. NATO APP-13 Coalition Operations Handbook.

One of the key factors for success in coalition operations is to ensure compatibility at all levels between the different partners.[7] Achieving political and military objectives will depend primarily on the ability of the coalition partners to ensure unity of command or at least unity of effort.[8] This will require specific understandings and agreements with the other partners and the Joint Force Commander (JFC).

The fact that States participating in a coalition operation will be subject to different legal obligations, or have different interpretations on a variety of legal issues, may give rise to friction and, ultimately, undermine the desired unity of effort. Confronting contemporary issues of the law of armed conflict can be challenging for both State parties to Additional Protocol I to the Geneva Conventions and non-State parties, such as the United States.[9] Consequently, legal interoperability becomes crucial in order to allow coalition commanders to achieve their strategic and operational goals.[10] As stated by one observer:

> The capability of legal interoperability is necessary in combined operations no matter whether led by an international organization or in the efforts of an ad hoc coalition. The capability of legal interoperability offers a Command and Control solution to the challenge of managing the diversity of authority that grows exponentially when each new troop-contributing nation adds its forces to the fight. Legal interoperability requires recognition of issues related to language, cultural expectations, organization and working practices that vary from country to country. Effective legal interoperability offers a means to resolve differences in legal principles, and priorities of law to be addressed.[11]

Military legal advisors are essential to the process of achieving interoperability. They are able to identify potential points of friction, such as differences in Rules of Engagement (ROE) or employment of weapons, and resolve these differences

---

[7]As stated by one observer: 'Multinational operations pose unique challenges, as the respective capabilities, political will and national interests of each partner will impact on its role in the coalition. The challenge of the commanders is to synchronize the contributions of coalition partners so as to project focused capabilities that present no seams nor vulnerability to an enemy for exploitation.' Center for Law and Military Operations 2004, p. 110.

[8]Unified action is the synergetic application of all instruments of national and multinational power; it includes the actions of non-military organizations as well as military forces. This concept is applicable at all levels of command. In a multinational environment, unified action synchronizes and/or integrates multinational operations with the operations of intergovernmental and nongovernmental agencies in an attempt to achieve unity of effort in the operational area. JP 3-16 2007 p. III-12, para 9(a).

[9]It should be recalled that substantial portions of AP I have been recognized as being reflective of customary international law.

[10]'Force interoperability' is '[t]he ability of the forces of two or more nations to train, exercise and operate effectively together in the execution of assigned missions and tasks.' AAP-6 2013, p.2-F-5. Compare with: US DoD, Joint Chiefs of Staff, Dictionary of Military and Associated Terms: 'Interoperability is the ability to operate in synergy in the execution of assigned tasks.' JP 1-02 2010 (As Amended Through 2014), p. 133.

[11]Mosquera and Haussler 2008, p. 1.

during the planning of the operation.[12] Sensitive to the complexity of modern military operations, several States have created 'operational law' departments within their military legal system to fulfil this responsibility.[13]

Because international law affects all phases of the targeting cycle, planners must apply the basic principles of the law of armed conflict (LOAC)[14] to targeting discussions.[15] This is particularly true during the target development, validation, nomination, and prioritization phases, mission planning, and force execution. In general, the LOAC is binding on the Troop Contributing Nations (TCNs). The issue at stake here is not so much the existence of the basic rules and principles, such as the principles of distinction, proportionality and unnecessary suffering. Rather, the question is how to implement them in the conduct of a coalition operation.[16]

11.2 The Legal Framework

Military operations will always be conducted within a legal framework. This includes the legal basis for the operation itself and the way in which the operation is conducted.[17] The applicable law may also be constrained by policy. This combination of law and policy will influence many aspects of the operation, including the ROE. Consequently, all aspects of the operational planning, orders, standing operating procedures (SOP), and instructions must be in accordance with the law and extant policy. The legal framework is comprised of international law (treaty and customary international law), the mandate, the domestic law of the TCN, and the domestic legislation of the host nation (HN) (if and when applicable).

[12] The requirement to incorporate legal advisors to advise military commanders is set forth in Article 82 of Additional Protocol I to the Geneva Conventions. AP I, Article 82. On the role of the military legal adviser, see Rogers and Stewart 2010, pp. 538–564. On ROE: see Chap. 8 in this volume, by Boddens Hosang.

[13] 'Operational law' is defined as 'the body of domestic, foreign and international law that impacts specifically upon the activities of U.S. Forces in war and operations other than war … It includes military justice, administrative and civil law, legal assistance, claims, procurement law, national security law, fiscal law, and international law.' OPLAW Handbook 1994, p. A-1.

[14] The term 'law of international armed conflict' (LOAC) is used in a generic way and is synonymous with other terms such as 'international humanitarian law' and 'law of war'.

[15] Targeting is the process of selecting and prioritizing targets and matching the appropriate response to them, considering operational requirements and capabilities. JP 1-02 2010 (as amended through 2014), p. 252.

[16] International Tribunal for the former Yugoslavia, Final Report to the Prosecutor by the Committee Established to Review the NATO Bombing Campaign Against the Federal Republic of Yugoslavia, 13 June 2000, para 48. Available at: http://www.icty.org/sid/10052.

[17] Gill and Fleck 2010, pp. 8 10.

11.2.1 International Law

In whatever capacity troops are employed, as organs of the TCN they will always have to operate under the appropriate international law binding on their State. This means that the LOAC has to be followed when an armed conflict exists.[18] In other situations of violence, where the threshold of armed conflict has not been reached, such as situations of internal disturbances and tensions, the LOAC will not apply and international human rights law (IHRL) will have an impact on the operation.[19]

It should also be recalled that the applicable legal framework could change during the military campaign. Situations of internal disturbances and tensions may escalate to a non-international armed conflict, non-international armed conflicts can internationalize, and international armed conflicts can internalize.[20] Therefore, the tactics, techniques, and procedures that are permissible in one operation may be prohibited in another or, perhaps, even during the same operation if the legal framework changes.

Finally, participating States in coalition operations can have differing obligations under both the LOAC and IHRL. Particularly relevant in the framework of targeting is the diversity of respective obligations arising out of Additional Protocol I to the Geneva Conventions,[21] the Ottawa Convention on anti-personnel mines,[22] and the Oslo Convention on cluster munitions.[23]

11.2.2 LOAC Versus IHRL

The conduct of military operations is governed by international law, in particular IHRL and/or the LOAC. As stated previously, the legal framework will determine the applicable law.[24] For instance, it would be illegal for troops, when responding to domestic riots, to establish ambush positions with a view to killing those attempting to leave the area. On the other hand, when the situation has developed to the point it has become an armed conflict, then such action would be legal so

[18]See Chap. 6 in this volume, by Schmitt & Widmar.

[19]Protocol Additional to the Geneva Conventions of 12 August 1949, and Relating to the Protection of Victims of Non-International Armed Conflicts (Protocol II), 1977, 11125 UNTS 609, Article 1(2).

[20]Solis 2010, pp. 154–155. See also Milanovic and Hadzi-Vidanovic 2013, pp. 292–302.

[21]Protocol Additional to the Geneva Conventions of 12 August 1949, and Relating to the Protection of Victims of International Armed Conflicts (Protocol I), 1977, 16 ILM 1391 [hereinafter AP I].

[22]Convention on the Prohibition of the Use, Stockpiling, Production and Transfer of Anti-Personnel Mines and on Their Destruction, 1997, 36 ILM 1507.

[23]Convention on Cluster Munitions, opened for signature, 3 December 2008, 48 International Legal Materials 357 (2008) [hereinafter Oslo Convention].

[24]Pouw 2013.

long as those targeted were identified as enemy combatants or civilians taking a direct part in hostilities, and fell within the approved target set.

The growing focus on human rights law has significantly impacted the way military operations are conducted. No State has been immune from this development, especially the States party to the European Convention on Human Rights (ECHR). Not all coalition partners are necessarily bound by the same IHRL obligations. Additionally, coalition partners may take different views on whether IHRL norms apply extraterritorially (if and when applicable).

Finally, the possible application of human rights in times of armed conflict has been the subject of much debate and criticism. The International Court of Justice (ICJ) stated in its *Wall Advisory Opinion* that with regard to the relationship between the LOAC and IHRL, 'there are three possible situations: some rights may be exclusively matters of humanitarian law; others may be exclusively matters of human rights law; yet others may be matters of both these branches of international law'.[25] In other words, the ICJ provided that human rights law continues to apply in times of armed conflict.[26] However, how those human rights provisions are interpreted will depend upon the applicable LOAC as *lex specialis*.[27]

These interoperability problems are not confined to the (extra-) territorial application of human rights,[28] but also impact on detainee operations,[29] situations of belligerent occupation,[30] and the conduct of hostilities. Consequently, considerable cooperation among the coalition partners is needed to resolve such interoperability matters. The main IHRL issue with respect to targeting relates to the applicability of the right to life provision during coalition operations. Indeed, IHRL allows the use of lethal force against individuals only on the basis of their personal threat or dangerousness. The LOAC, by contrast, is governed by the principle of distinction allowing the targeting of enemy combatants on the sole basis

[25]Advisory Opinion on the Legal Consequences of the Construction of a Wall in the Occupied Palestinian Territory, [2004] ICJ General List No. 131, 9 July 2004, para 112.

[26]See also the position of the Human Rights Committee on the applicability of the ICCPR in the West Bank and Gaza in UN Doc. CCPR/CO/78/ISR and UN Doc. CCPR/C/79/Add.93, para 10.

[27]On the relationship between humanitarian law and human rights law, see also Dinstein 2010, pp. 19–26; Martin 2001, pp. 347–396.

[28]See Coomans and Kamminga 2004; Dennis 2005, pp. 119–141; Tondini 2005, pp. 175–242. According to Naert, 'there seems to be a growing consensus that effective control over territory and effective control over persons (especially detention) constitute jurisdiction in this sense and lead to the applicability of human rights. Beyond this, including in combat situations and in cases of the exercise of limited authority, the matter is not settled.' Naert 2010, p. 567. See also Ducheine 2008, p. 413; Orakhelashvili 2013, pp. 598–637.

[29]Pouw 2013, pp. 154–168.

[30]See Al Skeini v. United Kingdom, N° 55721/07, Grand Chamber, Judgment, 7 July 2011; Al Jedda v. United Kingdom, N° 27021/08, Grand Chamber, Judgment, 7 July 2011; Al-Sadoon and Mufdhi v. United Kingdom, ECtHR, N° 61489/08, Judgment, 2 March 2010.

of their status (unless they become '*hors de combat*').[31] Moreover, under the LOAC, the principle of proportionality grants States more 'flexibility' in launching attacks which are likely to result in incidental damage to civilians than is found under IHRL. If coalition partners take different positions on the classification of the conflict by characterizing an operation as being outside of an armed conflict, this will affect coalition legal interoperability because coalition partners might be applying different bodies of law.

Considering the extensive jurisprudence of the European Court on Human Rights (ECtHR), it is fair to say that whenever European States participate in coalition operations, the implications of their adherence to the ECHR may give rise to legal interoperability problems. This is illustrated by the *Ysayeva, Yusupova and Bazayeva* case, in which the Russian armed forces engaged enemy insurgents in Chechnya with high-explosive bombs.[32] The violence clearly amounted to a non-international armed conflict, although Russia denied the existence of such a conflict in the region. Consequently, the ECtHR observed that this military operation was carried out in peacetime and thus had to be judged against a normal legal background.[33] Such an approach is not without risk in the context of coalition operations.[34] Commanders and legal advisors should be aware of the legal basis of the operation and policy decisions defining the framework of the mission they will support, including the characterization of the conflict by coalition forces under their command and control, as well as the other law (such as the ECHR) affecting TCN forces.

11.2.3 Domestic Law (TCN and Host Nation)

The domestic legislation of the TCN remains applicable when its troops operate extraterritorially. But to what extent are they bound by the domestic legal system of the State on whose territory they operate? The domestic legislation of the HN will bind the troops of the TCN, depending on the arrangements between the TCN and the HN. This could give rise to interoperability issues if the coalition consists of HN and TCN forces. The applicable arrangements will be set out in international agreements, such as Status of Forces Agreements, Memoranda of Understandings, or Exchange of Letters. If an agreement is reached that each TCN retains national responsibility, the position among the different coalition partners may differ. In

---

[31] AP I, Article 41.

[32] Isayeva, Yusupova and Bazayeva v. Russia, App. N° 57950/00, 57948/00, 57949/00, Judgment, 24 February 200541.

[33] See also Pouw 2013, p.172.

[34] See also Esmukhambetov and Others v. Russia, Case N° 23445/03, ECtHR, Judgment, 29 March 2011; Kerimova and Others v. Russia, N° 171170/04, 20792/04, 22448/04, 23360/04, 5681/05 and 5684/05, ECtHR, Judgment, 3 May 2011; Khamzayev and Others v. Russia, N°1503/02, ECtHR, Judgment, 3 May 2011.

order to avoid discrepancies between the different TCNs, it is advised that these arrangements be concluded by the lead nation or the framework nation on behalf of the other coalition partners, or by the international organization.

11.2.4 The Mandate

The legitimacy of a coalition operation is based on a mandate recognized under international law. In general, the decision to use force will be founded in the inherent right of self-defence under Article 51 of the UN Charter, a UN (Chap. 7) Resolution by the Security Council (UNSCR), or HN consent. A sound and clear understanding of the legal justification is required at all levels because it may limit the scope of the operation. Unless the situation amounts to the use of force in self-defence, the first requirement is a clear and unambiguous mandate. However, in some situations the UNSCR lacks the precise scope of the mandate. States may also have divergent views on the interpretation of the mandate, which can influence the applicable legal framework or restrict the ability of military forces to use force in particular circumstances. The impact of the mandate can be illustrated by two case studies—Libya (Unified Protector) and Afghanistan (ISAF).

When NATO launched operation 'Unified Protector' pursuant to UNSCR 1973,[35] this raised some legal issues as to what extent NATO and NATO-led forces were authorized to use force in order to implement the mandate.[36] Acting under Chapter VII, NATO was authorized to use all necessary measures to protect civilians and civilian populated areas under threat of attack in Libya, establish a ban on all flights in the airspace of Libya, and enforce an arms embargo on the high seas. Two issues arose out of the wording of this Resolution. Firstly, how was the conflict in Libya to be qualified, and, secondly, what exactly was NATO authorized to do under this mandate?[37] The classification of the conflict would have caused major interoperability issues if one accepted the viewpoint that this operation was an enforcement action under Chapter VII, not triggering the applicability of the law of international armed conflict. However, it became clear to all partners that the conflict was an international armed conflict between Libya and the States participating in operation 'Unified Protector'.

Assuming that the situation amounted to an armed conflict between Libya and NATO/NATO-led States and a non-international armed conflict between the rebels

[35]UN Security Council Resolution S/RES/1973, 17 March 2011.

[36]The mandate defines the political end state for the operation. Taking the strategic level as starting point, the JFC derives his military strategic campaign objectives from the mandate of that particular operation. Consequently, political objectives and political end states should be unambiguously clear and well defined in order to facilitate the development of feasible military strategic objectives. On the mandate provided by UNSCR 1973, see also Henderson 2011, p. 767.

[37]See also Bartolini 2012, pp. 242–279.

and the Libyan governmental forces, other issues arose with regard to the conduct of hostilities. What was the status of the rebel forces? Were they 'civilians' within the meaning of the LOAC, and thus only targetable for such time as they were directly participating in the hostilities, or did they qualify as an organized armed group? Was NATO authorized to target rebel forces if they attacked or threatened to attack civilians and civilian populated areas? Was NATO authorized to attack governmental forces once they retreated? Was NATO authorized or even obliged to enforce the no-fly-zone vis-à-vis rebel flights? Fundamental questions such as these must be clarified from the outset of the military operation.

The second case relates to the ongoing operations in Afghanistan. Three different operations are currently conducted in the same theatre: a non-international armed conflict between the Afghan and ISAF-led forces and the insurgents (ISAF-operation); a non-international armed conflict between US-led forces and Al Qaeda (Operation Enduring Freedom); and a counter-narcotic (law enforcement) operation between the Afghan authorities and narcotic traffickers. Some ISAF-Sates participate in all these operations, while others will not allow their forces to be actively involved in Operation Enduring Freedom and/or the counter-narcotic operation. Additionally, certain States consider that the counter-narcotic operation is part of the counter-insurgency operation and that, consequently, narcotic infrastructure and narcotic traffickers may be subject to targeting under the law of non-international armed conflict, while other States consider that this is a purely law enforcement operation under human rights law. In the context of the ongoing military operations in Afghanistan, it goes without saying that the disparity between, on the one hand, the more expansive position and, on the other hand, those States that consider the nexus between the narcotics industry and the insurgency too remote, inevitably gives rise to coalition interoperability issues, such as the (positive) identification of military objectives in the targeting process.[38] This challenge can be illustrated by the following example. A Ground Force Commander (GFC) identifies a narcotics production facility and requests Close Air Support (CAS) in order to neutralize the facility. Pilots from TCNs that do not adhere to the more expansive interpretation will be prohibited from providing fire support, unless the ground forces find themselves in a situation of self-defence.

11.2.5 Standing Operating Procedures

In order to ensure coalition cohesion, there will be an Operational Plan (OPLAN) agreed between the coalition partners. The OPLAN sets out the command relationships for the units participating in the intended operations, the role planned for the troops, the ROE, and other responsibilities. In well-established military structures, there will also be a wide range of policy documents with which to comply.

[38]De Cock 2011, pp. 111–112; Schmitt 2009, pp. 301–320.

More detailed guidelines on the use of force are usually contained in SOPs. They define what is meant by force and the principles governing its use, explain in detail the circumstances in which force may be used, and establish the level of responsibility for taking the decision to use it. In principle, coalition operations will be governed by mission-specific SOPs in the fields of joint fires, collateral damage, CAS, and other relevant domains. More detailed procedures are developed on component level, such as the Special Instructions (SPINS).

11.2.6 Rules of Engagement

Rules of Engagement are designed to ensure that the application of force is carefully controlled.[39] ROE are directives to military forces that define the circumstances, conditions, degree, and manner in which force, or actions that might be construed as provocative, may or may not be applied.[40] Although commanders can delegate authority for operations, they remain responsible for the conduct of the forces under their command. Multinational commanders exercise command and control over foreign contingents through the mechanism of Transfer of Authority (TOA). The TOA message details the exact scope of the C2 transfer, generally restricted to operational command or operational control. TOA may occur in the early planning stages of the operation, but should ideally be realized before the contingents deploy into the area of operations. Ideally, there should just be one common set of ROE, agreed by the competent coalition authority and all TCNs. In general, the OPLAN contains the approved ROE and the political policy indicators governing the operation.[41] However, national imperatives often result in additional national limitations, also known as 'caveats', which may be more restrictive than the coalition's ROE.[42] National caveats will be a major concern for the JFC and his subordinate commanders and can have major implications in the assignment of troops to task.[43] Divergent or even contradictory ROE for national contributions may derive from domestic legal reasons (restrictions of national law), political sensitivities about the subordination of units to foreign military commanders, or even cultural reasons.[44] The coalition commander must ensure that the interpretation and application of implemented ROE within his chain of command are consistent with his own. Simplified versions of the ROE may be issued to the soldiers in the form of a soldiers' card.

---

[39]See Chap. 8 in this volume, by Boddens Hosang.

[40]Cole et al. 2009, p. 1. See also Boddens Hosang 2010.

[41]Additional amplifications on the ROE are to be found in the ROE Implementation Message. Legal definitions and guidance are contained in the Legal Affairs Annex of the OPLAN.

[42]It should be kept in mind that ROE can never authorize actions that would contravene the State's obligation under IHRL/LOAC. Dinstein 2010, p. 30.

[43]Williams 2013, p. 24.

[44]Cathcart 2010, p. 202.

One of the domains where different national interpretations exist relates to the notions of self-defence, hostile act (HA), and hostile intent (HI).[45] For some States, HA and HI are included in the notion of self-defence, while other States require an explicit ROE in order to justify the use of force in those specific circumstances.[46] Such differences are unavoidable, but it is crucial for the coalition commander to understand how the forces under his C2 may or may not take action in self-defence. Further complicating the use of force issue is the right of a unit or individual to use force, including deadly force, to protect property. Indeed, States have different views in this regard.[47] The US and some nations consider that force may be used to defend certain designated property. Other nations hold the opposite view, that deadly force may never be used for the sole purpose of defending property, no matter how sensitive that property may be.[48] In the UK, Canada, and a number of others nations, a third position exists, one that distinguishes between operations within the nation's own territory and those undertaken elsewhere. These countries do not permit deadly force to be used domestically in defence of property.[49]

11.3 Targeting and Interoperability

The integration of joint fires is a complex process, especially when operating in a coalition. On one hand, modern operations require an effective tempo to engage the enemy in these complicated environments. On the other hand, commanders must be aware of the fact that ROE and a low tolerance for collateral damage and civilian casualties will restrain their actions. Targeting is the process through which joint fires will be coordinated, taking into consideration national caveats, ROE, political constraints, and other legal issues.[50] This process results in what is known as the Joint Prioritized Target List, which includes both kinetic and non-kinetic targets.[51]

---

[45]Hostile intent is defined in the Rules of Engagement Handbook as 'the threat of the imminent use of force. A determination of hostile intent is based on the existence of an identifiable threat recognizable on the basis of both the following conditions: i. Capability. ii. Intention.' Cole et al. 2009, Appendex 4 to Annex A, para 4.1.

[46]See also Boddens Hosang 2010, pp. 429–430; and Cole et al. 2009, Part II, para 9: 'For the purpose of this Handbook, the right to use force in *self-defense* arises in response to a *hostile act* (*attack*) and/or demonstrated *hostile intent* (*threat of imminent attack*).'

[47]Boddens Hosang 2010, p. 436, Rule 23.09.

[48]Walsh 2005, pp. 328–330.

[49]NATO Legal Deskbook, 2010, p. 257.

[50]See Chap. 4 in this volume, by Pratzner. See also FM 6-20-10 1996, Chap. 2.

[51]In NATO, targeting is part of an effects based approach to operations (EBAO). COPD INTERIM V1.0 2010, Annex A, pp. A-11–A22. See specifically ibid., Annex A, p. A-15: 'Effects play a crucial role because they provide a focus of actions and contribute to the accomplishment of objectives and the end state. Actions are designed to create effects that contribute to changes in the capabilities, behaviour or opinions (perceptions) of actors within the operations environment.'

11.3.1 Intelligence

In coalition operations, good intelligence is key, both in deciding which target to hit in time and space and in relation to battle damage assessment and measurement of effects. Technology in surveillance has significantly improved in recent decades and commanders should take full advantage of coalition surveillance and imagery systems, not only to find the right target and accurately determine its proximity to civilian infrastructure and people on the ground, but also to monitor the patterns of life around each target to further minimize the risk to civilians. Intelligence sharing nevertheless remains a major interoperability challenge, including the establishment of intelligence-sharing policies and defining procedures for sharing data. In general, coalition partners tend to rely upon their own national assets for intelligence collection and strive to protect the security of both intelligence and the sources and methods used to acquire it. However, coalition operations require some level of trust and intelligence-sharing. The use of liaison officers to share mission-critical intelligence in a less formal setting and common guidelines on intelligence-sharing may overcome these problems.

11.3.2 Principle of Distinction

Targeting requires identifying potential targets that when affected through targeting (kinetic or non-kinetic) generate effects that contribute to the goals of the operation; detecting and establishing their geographical location; and verifying whether these targets are military objectives in accordance with the LOAC.[52] During the execution phase of coalition operations, identification essentially refers to the geographical location of the target, while PID can be defined as the reasonable certainty that a functionally and geospatially defined object of attack is a legitimate military target in accordance with the LOAC and the ROE.[53] One of the difficulties is to determine who bears the responsibility for the PID during coalition operations, especially when partners are not bound by the same treaty provisions—the pilot, the ground force commander (GFC), or the Forward Air Controller (FAC)? Both the pilot and the GFC have a role to play. The primary responsibility lies with the GFC unless the mission was pre-planned. In that case

[52]PID can be achieved visually or by other means, e.g., by querying the Forward Air Controller (FAC).

[53]It should be noted that identification is not solely confined to their geographical location, but also includes the identification of potential targets, which when affected through targeting (kinetic or non-kinetic) 'generate' effects that contribute to the overall goals of the coalition operation. Increasingly, the term Combat Identification (CID) is used by tactical units. CID is the capability to differentiate potential targets—mobile and fixed, over large areas with corresponding long distances—as friend, foe or neutral in sufficient time, with high confidence, and at the requisite range to support engagement decisions and weapon release.

the target is preselected (by the targeting cell) and the pilot establishes PID during execution. The GFC close air support missions will be flown when ground forces act in self-defence, when confronted with enemy HA/HI, or in offensive operations. Under these circumstances, the GFC has the primary responsibility to conduct both ID and PID. The pilot, however, based on the intelligence reasonable available to him, will also PID the target before the attack in order to be reasonably sure that the target meets the requirements of a military objective. The question is relevant when the pilot and GFC/FAC are not bound by the same treaty provisions. Consider the case where the pilot is bound by AP I, while the GFC and FAC are not. Can the pilot rely solely on the intelligence provided by the GFC/FAC, even in cases where there is (reasonable) doubt surrounding the classification of the target as a military objective within the meaning of AP I? Can the pilot strike the target if he has no 'eyes-on-target' (e.g., in bad weather conditions)? In such cases, the pilot has a duty to actively pursue the necessary information that allows him to make this determination.

11.3.2.1 Military Objectives

An area where there is substantial difference in interpretation is the definition of military objectives in relation to what (objects) and who (persons) are targetable in times of armed conflict. Coalition commanders should be aware of these legal differences, as stated by Lt Gen M. Short, NATO Air Commander during Operation Allied Force, in a description that is still relevant today:

> So every day I put together what was called the air task order which is sent out to the thousand or more NATO airplanes indicating what targets they were going to strike the next day. I had to wait for the individual nations to answer back, having gone to their capitals and asked whether they should accept that target. And, indeed, in many capitals the answer was no—we do not define that as a valid military target. Now if I could get that answer back in a timely fashion, I could assign that target to a nation that had a less restrictive view of the law of armed conflict, but if I got that information late, and the aircraft were already airborne, then I ended up cancelling the strike[54]

Concerning objects, the issue at stake is the phrase 'effective contribution to military action' found in Article 52(2) of AP I,[55] compared to 'war-sustaining capabilities' proposed by the US. State parties to AP I are bound by the strict definition of Article 52(2), while other States may accept a broader interpretation.[56]

---

[54]Short 2002, p. 25.

[55]Article 52(2) of AP I reads as follows: 'In so far as objects are concerned, military objectives are limited to those objects which by their nature, location, purpose or use make an effective contribution to military action and whose total or partial destruction, capture or neutralization, in the circumstances ruling at that time, offers a definitive military advantage.' AP I, Article 52(2).

[56]According to Watkin, 'the Canadian approach of looking at the effect of the attack as a whole is broad enough to include as military objectives targets which indirectly make an effective contribution to an opposing party's military war effort.' Watkin 2005, p. 308.

Other points that might surface in coalition warfare relate to so-called 'dual use targets'. These are objects that are primarily civilian in nature, but have some military uses in armed conflict, such as lines of communication, bridges, railway stations, TV stations, etc. Coalition partners may have different opinions as to whether such objects may be targeted. Ideally, States should make clear their limitations, restrictions, or constraints on their military forces when they participate in coalition operations.

11.3.2.2 Individuals and Direct Participation in Hostilities (DPH)

According to the principle of distinction, belligerents must always distinguish between combatants and civilians. Consequently, the civilian population and individual civilians shall not be the object of attack. Acts or threats of violence the primary purpose of which is to spread terror among the civilian population are prohibited as indiscriminate attacks.[57] While the legality of killing of enemy combatants in situations of armed conflict remains undisputed, much debate has arisen in the context of killing members of organized armed groups.

As a matter of law, civilians are protected from attack, unless and for such time they take a direct part in hostilities. According to the Interpretive Guidance on the Notion of Direct Participation in Hostilities (DPH Guidance), members of organized armed groups may only be attacked if they perform a 'continuous combat function'.[58] Additionally, the DPH Guidance states that attacks to kill can only exceptionally be justified and capture should be the standard procedure.[59] However, when persons may legitimately be attacked, the legality thereof should be determined by the *lex specialis*, that is to say the LOAC. In practice, it is permissible to kill members of organized armed groups based on group status.[60] For coalition commanders, it is imperative to understand what the different national positions of the TCN are in relation to these issues and to take them into consideration when planning for the use of those coalition forces.

---

[57] AP I, Article 51(4).

[58] Melzer 2009, p. 70. For a comprehensive critique of this aspect of the DPH Guidance, see Watkin 2010. Other contributions include Schmitt 2010; Boothby 2010; Parks 2010; Rogers 2009, pp. 143–160.

[59] Melzer 2009, p. 85.

[60] An example of a 'declared hostile' ROE provision is given by Solis:

> DECLARED HOSTILE FORCES. CDR, CENTCOM [Commander-in-Chief, Central Command] has designated certain Iraqi military and paramilitary forces (former regime security forces, conventional and/or unconventional air, ground, and naval forces) as declared hostile forces. Since the end of major combat operations, these forces have transitioned from overt conventional resistance to insurgent methods of resistance. This declaration continues to apply to Former Iraqi Military and Paramilitary personnel who are operating as insurgent individuals or groups that continue hostilities against the Iraqi Government and MNF [Multi-National Forces]. These individuals and/or groups may be engaged and destroyed. [...].

Solis 2010, p. 508.

11.3.3 Collateral Damage

In attacking legitimate military objectives (persons and objects), constant care should be taken to spare the civilian population.[61] Consequently, everything feasible must be done to choose means and methods of warfare with a view to avoid or, in any event, minimize collateral damage and to determine whether the collateral damage to be expected from the attack is excessive in relation to the concrete and direct military advantage anticipated.[62] The methodology used to approve each deliberate target should include a mandatory collateral damage estimation process based on a three-part checklist. The checklist has to prove that (1) the right weapon can be delivered with enough accuracy; (2) against a valid target; and (3) under the right conditions in terms of the proximity of civilian life and infrastructure. Approving the checklist and authorizing the strike must be done by Coalition commanders. During this process, the commanders should use a wide range of civilian and military experts from multiple allied States, encouraging their concerns and recommendations.

The higher the collateral damage estimation, the more senior the approving officer, up to the JFC himself.[63] During Operation 'Unified Protector', pilots dynamically striking regime weapons that were either attacking or that represented a threat to the civilian population used a similar, predetermined collateral damage estimation.[64] If the pilot had any reservations about the target, he could refer the decision to higher authorities using a predetermined set of procedures. In order to streamline this process, a standardized collateral damage estimation methodology should be used throughout the military campaign. It provides a logical framework applicable to joint targeting that describes and enables a process to estimate and mitigate collateral effects. Operation specific ROE will dictate decision authorities and collateral damage thresholds.

Although the term 'feasible precautions' is generally understood as 'those precautions which are practicable or practically possible taking into account all circumstances ruling at the time, including humanitarian and military considerations',[65] it should be noted that coalition partners may have different interpretations of what exactly is required to ensure that innocent civilians are spared in the attack. But who is to say what is feasible and what is not? The refusal of a coalition partner to strike

---

[61] AP I, Article 57(1).

[62] AP I, Article 51(5)(b).

[63] The Target Engagement Authority identifies the level of command required to authorize an engagement at each collateral damage level.

[64] Planned targets are those known to exist in the operational area and are attacked in accordance with an air tasking order (ATO), mission-type order or fire support plan. Immediate targets are not identified (or selected for attack) soon enough to be included in the normal targeting process. See also Turns 2013, pp. 372–373.

[65] UK Ratification Statement to Additional Protocol I, para (c). Available at: http://www.icrc.org/applic/ihl/ihl.nsf/Notification.xsp?action=openDocument&documentId=0A9E03F0F2EE757CC1256402003FB6D2 (last visited 1 May 2014).

a target does not automatically lead to a coalition no-strike. Other coalition partners may validate the strike if they consider the parameters to be within the confines of the law. However, the final decision remains with the coalition commanders. They will not authorize any engagement that may be expected to breach the LOAC principles of necessity and proportionality.

11.3.4 Weapons

Aspects of the law of armed conflict—treaty or customary—will be binding on certain members of the coalition, while others may be bound by other legal instruments. This is particularly the case with Additional Protocol I of 1977 to the Geneva Conventions of 1949, the Conventional Weapons Convention of 1980 and its five Protocols,[66] the Ottawa Convention of 1997,[67] and the Oslo Convention of 2008.

11.3.4.1 Precision Guided Munitions (PGM)

The choice of weapons used for particular attacks is relevant to increasing or decreasing the scale of collateral damage. Under the LOAC, there is no legal obligation to use PGM.[68] However, there may be situations where the mission cannot be fulfilled without the use of PGM.[69] Collateral damage concerns have driven coalition commanders to increasingly rely on them. Consequently, the ability to contribute to coalition operations will largely depend on the capabilities of coalition partners for employing these weapons. When only a few coalition partners can employ PGM in sufficient numbers, or at all, the overall requirement for strikes may lead to a capability shortfall, and affect the ability to operate as an effective coalition.

11.3.4.2 Anti-personnel Mines

According to Article 1 of the Ottawa Convention, each State party 'undertakes never under any circumstances [...] to use anti-personnel mines'. Additionally, it

---

[66]Convention on Prohibitions or Restrictions on the Use of Certain Conventional Weapons Which May Be Deemed to Be Excessively Injurious or to Have Indiscriminate Effects, 10 October 1980, 1342 UNTS 137.

[67]Convention on the Prohibition of the Use, Stockpiling, Production and Transfer of Anti-Personnel Mines and on Their Destruction, 17 September 1997, 2056 UNTS 211 (entered into force 1 March 1999), Article 1(1)(c) [hereinafter Ottawa Convention].

[68]Solis 2010, p. 275.

[69]AMW Manual 2013, Rule 8. *See also* Solis, stating that 'Precision-guided munitions are not a LOAC/IHL requirement, but a failure, or inability, to discriminate may be inherently disproportional. Solis 2010, p. 275.

is prohibited to assist, encourage, or induce, in any way, anyone to engage in any activity prohibited to a State party under this Convention.[70]

This raises some questions in relation to the obligations of States, bound by the Ottawa Convention, when their forces engage in coalition operations with non-States parties. The Convention does not define what constitutes use of anti-personnel mines. In order to cope with this issue, several States clarified their national positions through interpretive declarations when depositing their instrument of ratification, such as Canada,[71] Australia,[72] and the United Kingdom.[73] Other States, such as Norway, clarified their position before ratification in Parliament.[74]

Controversy still exists on the definition of the terms 'assist', 'encourage', and 'induce', none of which are defined in the Convention. According to the United Kingdom, 'assisting' includes the following activities: 'planning with others for the use of anti-personnel mines ...; training others for the use of APM; agreeing Rules of Engagement permitting the use of APM; agreeing operational plans permitting the use of APM use in combined operations; ... [and] providing security or

---

[70]Ottawa Convention, Article 1(1)(c).

[71]Canadian Understanding to Article 1(1)(c) of the Ottawa Convention. Available at http://www.icrc.org/applic/ihl/ihl.nsf/Notification.xsp?action=openDocument&documentId=93A8C30465E5CBC54125658500490529 (last visited 25 April 2014). Canada declared that:

> in the context of operations, exercises or other military activity sanctioned by the United Nations or otherwise conducted in accordance with international law, the mere participation by the Canadian Forces, or individual Canadians, in operations, exercises or other military activity conducted in combination with the armed forces of States not party to the Convention which engage in activity prohibited under the Convention would not, by itself, be considered to be assistance, encouragement or inducement in accordance with the meaning of those terms in Article 1, paragraph 1(c).

[72]Australian Declaration to Article 1(1)(a) of the Ottawa Convention, available at: http://www.icrc.org/applic/ihl/ihl.nsf/Notification.xsp?action=openDocument&documentId=C94AC352BD44A2494125658500442880 (last visited 25 April 2014):

> It is the understanding of the Government of Australia that, in the context of operations, exercises or other military activity authorized by the United Nations or otherwise conducted in accordance with international law, the participation by the Australian Defense Force, or individual Australian citizens or residents, in such operations, exercises or other military activity, conducted in combination with the armed forces of States not party to the Convention which engage in activity prohibited under that Convention would not, by itself, be considered to be in violation of the Convention.

[73]UK Declaration to Article 1(1)(c) of the Ottawa Convention, available at: http://www.icrc.org/applic/ihl/ihl.nsf/Notification.xsp?action=openDocument&documentId=8E616974F39078BC41256586004AB729 (last visited 25 April 2014):

> It is the understanding of the Government of the United Kingdom that the mere participation in the planning or execution of operations, exercises or other military activity by the United Kingdom's Armed Forces, or individual United Kingdom nationals, conducted in combination with the armed forces of States not party to the [said Convention], which engage in activity prohibited under that Convention, is not, by itself, assistance, encouragement or inducement for the purposes of Article 1, para (c) of the Convention.

[74]Dahl 2013, p. 350.

transport for APM'.[75] Other States have a more liberal interpretation of the Convention, such as Norway, which of the view that it is not contrary to the Convention 'that mines are transported over Norwegian soil in connection with rotation of the stocks, or if Norwegian forces are protected by minefields laid by others'.[76] Additionally, Norway considers that the definition of the term 'use' in the Convention 'will not include pure participation in combined military operations where use of mines that are contrary to the Convention can be relevant for non-Convention parties'.[77] Insofar as the planning phase is concerned, Canada holds the position that 'while Canadians may participate in operational planning as members of a multinational staff, they may not participate in planning for the use of anti-personnel mines'.[78]

Whereas the restrictions of the Convention are clear during the planning phase of combined operations, problems may still arise during execution of the operation, especially when the ground forces of a State party request or receive CAS from a non-State party. Most commentators would agree that State parties may not (actively) request the use of anti-personnel mines. Canadian forces, for example, may not use AP-Mines and cannot solicit, even indirectly, the protection of those mines (or encourage the use of such mines by others).[79] This is certainly true for CAS in case of deliberate targeting, but remains hard to sustain in dynamic targeting. In the latter case, ground forces will probably require CAS when under attack or imminent attack. It would be unreasonable or even impossible to verify the payload of the aircraft. Another issue that may arise on the battlefield is the problem of mixed units, such as an embedded FAC in a foreign unit. Is the FAC authorized to request CAS from an aircraft carrying anti-personnel mines if both the aircrew and the supported ground forces are not bound by the Convention?

11.3.4.3 Cluster Munitions

Cluster bomb units are bombs, that, when dropped, spin while in flight, opening at a predetermined height and rate of spin. Each canister disperses many, sometimes hundreds, of smaller sub-munitions, over a long and wide area of ground. One of the problems with cluster bombs is their so-called 'dud' rate, namely the

[75] Ottawa Standing Committee on the General Status and Operation of the Convention, 16 May 2003, United Kingdom intervention on Article 1. Available at http://www.apminebanconvention.org/fileadmin/pdf/mbc/IWP/SC_may03/speeches_gs/UK_Art_1.pdf (last visited 25 April 2014).

[76] Dahl 2013, p. 350.

[77] Ibid.

[78] B-GJ-005-104/FP-021, Annex A, para A002(11)(d).

[79] Watkin 2005, p. 288.

number of sub-munitions that fail to detonate because of fuse or detonator failure. These weapons obviously present problems of distinction and proportionality and continue to cause many civilian casualties after the end of the hostilities. The use of cluster munitions and the subsequent humanitarian concerns about the effects thereof on the civilian population led to the 2008 Oslo Convention on Cluster Munitions.

According to Article 1(c) of the Convention, '[e]ach State party undertakes never under any circumstances to assist, encourage or induce anyone to engage in any activity prohibited to a State party under this Convention.'[80] This provision must be linked with Article 21 on interoperability. According to Article 21(2), State parties shall make their 'best efforts to discourage States not party to the Convention from using cluster munitions'. This raises questions pertaining to the joint planning of coalition operations and the establishment of ROE for that particular operation. When permissible ROE on the use of cluster munitions are developed, States party must issue national restrictions.

Article 21(3) of the Oslo Convention provides:

> notwithstanding the provisions of Article 1 of this Convention and in accordance with international law, States Parties, their military personnel or nationals, may engage in military cooperation and operations with States not party to this Convention that might engage in activities prohibited to a State Party.

In other words, States party can engage in coalition operations with non-State parties, provided they do not 'assist', 'encourage' or 'induce' others to engage in activities prohibited under the Convention. At this stage, it remains unclear what activities are precisely covered by the term 'engage' in Article 21(3).

Article 21(4) of the Convention provides:

> '[n]othing in paragraph 3 … shall authorize a State Party:
>
> (a) To develop, produce or otherwise acquire cluster munitions;
> (b) To itself stockpile or transfer cluster munitions;
> (c) To itself use cluster munitions; or
> (d) To expressly request the use of cluster munitions in cases where choice of munitions used is within its exclusive control'

It therefore follows that any activity falling outside the scope of Articles 1 and 21(4) of the Convention is permissible. In practice, when the armed forces of a State party request CAS from a non-State party, this would not result in a breach of the Convention as long as they do not exercise exclusive control over the decision following such request.

[80] Compare with Article 1(1)(c) of the Ottawa Convention.

11.4 Responsibility

11.4.1 Command and Control Arrangements

The command structure of a multinational force should ensure that the capabilities of the TCN can be brought to bear decisively in order to achieve the desired outcome in the most effective way. Unity of command will generally be achieved by vesting the authority to direct and coordinate the actions of all the available military forces in a single military commander. To ensure this unity of command, the JFC will in most cases have operational control over all troops in his area of operation. It is important for him to understand what kind of C2 has been delegated to him because this will directly impact his ability to issue orders, request ROE or identify the appropriate target engagement authority.[81] His competency in understanding and integrating the capacities of each TCN in his coalition is a key factor in this regard. In coalition operations conducted under the authority and control of international organizations, States will transfer at least some degree of C2 to the organization. However, they will never delegate full command to the JFC.[82]

According to the Model Agreement between the United Nations and Member States Contributing Personnel and Equipment to the United Nations Peacekeeping Operation, the personnel of the TCN remain under their national service, but shall be under the command of the UN.[83] Indeed, the chain of command for UN operations runs from the Security Council through the Secretary-General (and his representatives) to the troops supplied by the TCN. According to Article 47 of the UN Charter, the Security Council is responsible for the command and control of military forces put at its disposal. Whereas the C2 structure is clear for peacekeeping operations, one cannot disregard the UN practice for peace enforcement operations in which the Security Council basically outsources the C2 of the operation to

[81]Command and control arrangements for coalition action are specific to the particular operation. Coalition partners may operate independently in separate areas of operations, they may act under the tactical and operational control of a lead nation, or some arrangements in-between. See Cathcart 2010, pp. 235–244.

[82]NATO defines 'full command' as the 'military authority and responsibility of a commander to issue orders to subordinates. It covers every aspect of military operations and administration and exists only within national services. AAP-6 2013, p. 2-F-7. States that assign forces to a NATO operation will always retain full command of those forces and will only delegate operational command or operational control. Ibid.

[83]Model Agreement between the United Nations and Member States Contributing Personnel and Equipment to the United Nations Peacekeeping Operation, UN Doc. A/46/185, 23 May 1991, Annex. In UN operations, UN Command 'involves the full authority to issue operational directives within the limits of (1) a specific mandate of the Security Council; (2) an agreed period of time, with the stipulation that an earlier withdrawal requires adequate prior notification; and (3) a specific geographical range (the mission area as a whole)'. Comprehensive Review of the Whole Question of Peacekeeping Operations in All Their Aspects: Command and Control of United Nations Peacekeeping, UN Doc. A/49/681, 21 November 1994, para 6.

Member States, individually or collectively (through regional organizations).[84] For each operation, the Secretary General appoints the Head of Mission and the JFC to lead the military component. In theory, the Secretary General has command authority over the JFC. In practice, however, States will never delegate full command to the UN.[85] It is appropriate to speak of 'dual control' in such situations.

During NATO operations, States shall only delegate operational command,[86] tactical command,[87] operational control,[88] or tactical control to the JFC.[89] During Operation Allied Force, States had the capacity to abstain from participating in any

[84]According to Greenwood, three different models can be identified: (1) Operations under UN command and control, in which a force is composed of national contingents placed under UN command and control pursuant to agreements between the Participating States and the United Nations; (2) Operations conducted under national command and control but authorized by the Security Council; and (3) Operations in which a force under United Nations command has operated alongside other forces under national command and control. Greenwood 1998, pp. 12–13.

[85]In general, States will never delegate more than Operational Command. Needless to say that peace operations are generally conducted under a complex command structure combining both UN authority and Member State powers, in which case it cannot be said that the Organization exercises exclusive control. Porretto and Vité 2006, p. 28.

[86]According to NATO, 'operational command' is '[t]he authority granted to a commander to assign missions or tasks to subordinate commanders, to deploy units, to reassign forces, and to retain or delegate operational and/or tactical control as the commander deems necessary.' AAP-6 2013, p. 2-O-3.

[87]NATO defines 'tactical command' as '[t]he authority delegated to a commander to assign tasks to forces under his command for the accomplishment of the mission assigned by higher authority.' AAP-6 2013, p. 2-T-1. UN 'tactical command' means '[t]he authority delegated to a Military or Police Commander in a United Nations Peacekeeping Operation to assign tasks to forces under their command for the accomplishment of the mission assigned by higher authority.' United Nations Department of Peacekeeping Operations 2008, para D(10).

[88]According to NATO, 'operational control' is '[t]he authority delegated to a commander to direct forces assigned so that the commander may accomplish specific missions or tasks which are usually limited by function, time, or location and to deploy units concerned, and to retain or assign tactical control to those units.' AAP-6 2013, p. 2-O-3. The United Nations defines UN 'operational control' as '[t]he authority granted to a Military Commander in a United Nations Peacekeeping Operation to direct forces assigned so that the Commander may accomplish specific missions or tasks which are usually limited by function, time, or location (or a combination), to deploy units concerned and/or military personnel, and to retain or assign Tactical Command or Control of those units/personnel. Operational Control includes the authority to assign separate tasks to subunits of a contingent, as required by operational necessities … in consultation with the Contingent Commander and as approved by the United Nations Headquarters.' United Nations Department of Peacekeeping Operations 2008, para D(9).

[89]NATO defines 'tactical control' as '[t]he detailed and, usually, local direction and control of movements or manoeuvres necessary to accomplish missions or tasks assigned.' AAP-6 2013, p. 2-T-2. UN 'Tactical Control' means '[t]he detailed and local direction and control of movement, or manoeuvre, necessary to accomplish missions or tasks assigned. As required by operational necessities, the Head of the Military Component (HOMC) and the Head of the Police Component (HOPC) may delegate the Tactical Control of assigned military/police personnel to the subordinate sector and/or unit commanders.' United Nations Department of Peacekeeping Operations 2008, para D(11).

bombing phases they did not agree with. NATO policy permitted Member States to refuse bombing assignments if they regarded a particular target as being illegitimate.[90] As a result, a NATO commander will always be faced with national authorities that can limit his prerogatives, including his ability to execute the mission. Thus, if there is a clash between national direction and the approved OPLAN and ROE, national rules will control the actions of a national commander, even if he is under the operational command and control of a NATO commander. Nearly all States contributing forces to NATO operations provide those forces subject to national 'caveats' that may restrict where the force may operate, when lethal force may or may not be used, and the types of operations in which their national forces may participate.[91]

In the context of EU operations, the Council will set out the mission and mandate, designate the commanders and the headquarters, specify the C2 arrangements, and determine the duration of the operation. While the Council is vested with the power to select the objectives of the operation, the Political and Security Committee is authorized to decide on amendments to the planning documents, including the OPLAN and the ROE. Finally, since the EU has no standing military headquarters, a distinct chain of command has to be agreed for each EU operation. The highest level of command in EU military operations rests with the Operation Commander, who will receive operational control over the forces assigned to him. The next level of command is the Force Commander.[92]

11.4.2 State Versus International Organization Responsibility

As a general rule, it should be noted that the armed forces of a State and its members are State organs wherever they perform their functions.[93] When carrying out tasks and missions in its name, their actions remain attributable to that State. According to the *Manual on International Law Applicable to Air and Missile Warfare*, the legal obligations of a State participating in combined operations do not change when its armed forces are operating in a multinational force under the command and control of a military commander of a different nationality.[94]

[90] Kelly 2005, p. 163.

[91] As far as EU military operations are concerned, the Operation Commander will be vested with the appropriate command authority, allowing him sufficient flexibility over the required forces. EU Council Doc. 11096/03 EXT 1, 26 July 2006.

[92] Naert 2012, pp. 373–404.

[93] Regulations Respecting the Laws and Customs of War on Land, annexed to Convention No. IV Respecting the Laws and Customs of War on Land, 18 October 1907, 36 Stat. 2227, Article 3; AP I, Article 91.

[94] AMW Manual 2013, Rule 162.

However, when members of the armed forces are placed at the disposal of another State or an international organization (IO), their conduct will be attributable to that State or IO insofar as that entity exercises effective control over the conduct in question. In coalition operations, the responsibility can thus rest solely upon the international organization or on both the international organization and the State for internationally wrongful acts committed by members of the armed forces.[95] In order to determine each other's share in the responsibility, it will be necessary to analyse the command and control arrangements on a case-by-case basis.[96] In general, three different situations can be distinguished: the act is only attributable to the State, the act is only attributable to the IO, or the act is attributable to both the State and the IO. As stated by the International Law Association:

> If operational command rests with the IO, the responsibility of the IO will result from non-observance of the same rules, while States have the special responsibility to ensure respect for international humanitarian law by the IO. In cases where strategic control formally rests with the IO but where in practice national commanders choose the targets, both the State and the IO share responsibility for a violation of international humanitarian law. In other words, primary responsibility is always accompanied by independent, secondary obligations.[97]

Before NATO assumed command over the operations against Libya (pursuant to UNSCR 1973), it was clear that States exercised effective control over their own air assets. Once NATO assumed command, the question arose to what extent NATO exercised effective control over these national aircraft. Were these aircraft still subject to national sovereignty or did NATO, as a separate legal entity, assume responsibility? Transferring authority of national assets to an IO is in and of itself

---

[95]For peacekeeping operations, the responsibility of the acts and omissions of the members of the Force remains with the United Nations. See UN Doc. A/46/185 (23 May 1991), para 7 of the UN Model Contribution Agreement:

> During the period of their assignment to [the United Nations peace-keeping operation], the personnel made available by [the Participating State] shall remain in their national service but shall be under the command of the United Nations, vested in the Secretary-General, under the authority of the Security Council. Accordingly, the Secretary-General of the United Nations shall have full authority over the deployment, organization, conduct and direction of [the United Nations peace-keeping operation], including the personnel made available by [the Participating State].

See also ibid, para 9:

> The functions of [the United Nations peace-keeping operation] are exclusively international and the personnel made available by [the Participating State] shall regulate their conduct with the interests of the United Nations only in view. Except on national administration matters, they shall not seek or accept instructions in respect of the performance of their duties from the authority external to the United Nations, nor shall the Government of [the Participating State] give such instructions to them.

However, in practice, States intervene in daily decisions and by doing so they create a parallel chain of command. In such case, the State engages its responsibility if it continues to exercise effective control over its troops.

[96]Different situations are possible. The C2 rests with the international organization, but it is not excluded that C2 is delegated to a coalition of States.

[97]ILA 2004, p. 24.

not sufficient to sustain the claim that only the IO bears responsibility for the acts of TCN put at its disposal.[98]

Although States transfer some form of command and control to international organizations, such as NATO, the fact is that States will always retain power over their national contingents. This national 'interference' is not restricted to issues of prosecution and disciplinary actions, but extends to the core activities of combat operations, including the decision on whether to strike military objectives. This is also known as the 'red card holder' procedure, according to which the use of military assets remains subject to national approval in relation to combat missions.[99] The impact of this 'red card holder' procedure on coalition commanders was described as follows by LTG M. Short:

> I expected that I would be the targeteer, and so the advice of my lawyer would be extraordinarily important to me because everything I struck had to be a valid military target for all coalition members. Concern for the law of armed conflict was absolutely paramount in my mind. However, as I said to you earlier, those target decisions were taken out of our hands. Target decisions were made by the president of the United States, the prime minister of Great Britain, the president of France, and the president of Germany, and targets were just issued to me.[100]

The final responsibility to engage national air assets to strike military targets rests with the national 'red card holder'. As national approving authority, he will approve or deny the use of national assets in deliberate and dynamic missions, in accordance with national policy and caveats.[101] Obviously the State will be responsible if its forces act pursuant to national instructions. This must be assessed on a case-by-case basis. In order to affirm effective control by States over their troops, it is necessary to analyse the C2 arrangements and the role of the State in the decision-making process, particularly the possibility of accepting or denying the IO's C2 requests.

---

[98]According to the Venice Commission:

> [n]ot all acts by KFOR troops which happen in the course of an operation 'under the unified command and control' ... of a NATO Commander must be attributed in international law to NATO but they can also be attributed to their country of origin [...]. Thus, acts by troops in the context of a NATO-led operation cannot simply all be attributed either to NATO or to the individual troop-contributing states. There may even be difficult intermediate cases, such as when soldiers are acting on the specific orders of their national commanders which are, however, themselves partly in execution of directives issued by the KFOR commander and partly within the exercise of their remaining scope of discretion.

Opinion No 280/2004, Opinion on Human Rights in Kosovo: Possible Establishment on Review Mechanisms, CDL-AD (2004)033, 11 October 2004, para 79.

[99]See Cerone 2001, p. 486.

[100]Short 2002, p. 25.

[101]See also Zwanenburg 2005, pp. 47–48.

11.4.3 Command Responsibility

In modern conflicts, such as Operation Allied Force (1999), the Gulf Wars (1991 and 2003), or Operation Unified Protector (2011), air assets have been used in coalition operations. In the context of a Combined Joint Task Force, this not only raises legal questions on the responsibility of States, but also regarding the criminal responsibility of military superiors for war crimes committed by subordinate units. Whereas the subordination link(s) in the framework of national operations conducted by a State's regular armed forces are generally quite clear, difficulties may arise on the exact scope of the command structure in combined operations. As stated previously, a variety of command and control subordination links between a unit, units, or organizations are feasible. The authority vested in an individual of the armed forces for the direction, coordination and control of (other) military forces varies from full command, tactical command, operational command, and operational control to tactical control. The issue of responsibility becomes even more difficult when operations are conducted within the framework of international organizations, such as NATO or the United Nations.[102]

The responsibility of the IO or the TCN, as the case may be, for IHRL/LOAC violations does not affect the individual criminal responsibility of the people involved. Commanders incur individual criminal responsibility when they participate in the commission of war crimes (as author, co-author, or accomplice),[103] when they order the commission thereof (direct command responsibility),[104] or when they fail to take the necessary and reasonable measures to prevent or repress crimes they knew or should have known their subordinates were about to commit or had committed (indirect command responsibility).[105] The concept of command responsibility may trigger the prosecution of those superiors holding the required level of control for crimes committed by subordinates.

---

[102]In particular, see the difficulties raised in Kosovo and the relationships between the UN, NATO and the TCN in the *Behrami and Saramati* case before the ECtHR. Behrami and Saramati v. France, Germany and Norway, ECtHR, N. 71412/01 and 78166/01, Decision as to the Admissibility, 2 May 2007. Rowe states that 'the acts of a military group organized into a military structure may be attributed to a European Convention of Human Rights State where that State keeps its own armed forces within its borders but wields overall control over the group, not only by equipping and financing [it], but also by coordinating or helping in the general planning of its military activity.' Rowe 2005, p. 197.

[103]See Statute of the International Criminal Tribunal for Rwanda, S.C. Res. 955 annex, U.N. Doc. S/RES/955, (8 November 1994), *reprinted in* 33 International Legal Materials 1598 (1994), Article 6(1); Statute of the International Criminal Tribunal for the former Yugoslavia, S.C. Res. 827, U.N. Doc. S/RES/827 (25 May 1993), adopting The Secretary-General Report Pursuant to Para 2 of Security Council Resolution 808, Article 7(1);
Rome Statute, 17 July 1998, 2187 UNTS 90, Article 25.

[104]Ibid.

[105]API, Articles 86 and 87.

Extending the doctrine of command responsibility to coalition commanders raises some practical issues. The major obstacle relates to their status as commander, meaning that they must exercise effective control in order to qualify as a military commander under international criminal law. Coalition commanders will usually lack the requisite level of (effective) control because nations will never delegate disciplinary or criminal authority to them.[106] Although coalition commanders can create the necessary conditions for a LOAC compliant environment, such as adopting adequate reporting and inquiry mechanisms, the final responsibility for ensuring that members of the Force respect the LOAC rests with the TCN. If coalition commanders lack the required level of effective control in the strict sense, the question arises as to what extent their ability to influence national decisions may be equated to effective control in a more general sense. According to the jurisprudence of the International Criminal Tribunal for the former Yugoslavia (ICTY), (substantial) influence does not constitute a sufficient degree of control to establish command responsibility.[107]

11.5 Conclusion

In an ideal world, all TCNs participating in coalition operations would adopt and abide by the same legal standards. However, practice has demonstrated that different partners, bound by different legal regimes, cannot change the legal framework they bring to a coalition force. Only to the extent that treaty provisions are regarded as customary in nature, can these differences be resolved. Because nations do not adhere to the same treaties, and since maintaining the unity of effort in a coalition is one of the key factors to achieving success, it is imperative to improve legal interoperability. One solution is the adoption of common ROE and standardized procedures for training. Although this chapter has illustrated that interoperability has multiple and complex legal dimensions that may manifest themselves at each level (strategic, operational and tactical), and that strategic problems can have operational and tactical implications, legal interoperability problems are not unsurmountable, provided that they are considered in the context of all three levels.

References

AMW Manual (2013) HPCR manual on international law applicable to air and missile warfare. *Cambridge University Press*, Cambridge

Bartolini G (2012) Air targeting in operation *Unified Protector* in Libya. jus ad bellum and IHL issues: an external perspective. In: Horvat S, Benatar M (eds) Legal interoperability and ensuring observance of the law applicable in multinational deployments, international society for military law and the law of war. 19th international congress, Recueil XIX

---

[106] Fenrick 2010.

[107] ICTY, Prosecutor v. Delalic et al., IT-96-21-T, Trial Chamber, 16 November 1998, para 377.

Boddens Hosang JFR (2010) Force protection, unit self-defence, and extend self-defence (Chapter 22) and Personal Self-defence and its relationship to rules of engagement (Chapter 23). In: Gill TD, Fleck D (eds) The handbook of the international law of military operations. Oxford University Press, Oxford, pp 415–444
Boothby W (2010) 'And for such time as': the time dimension to direct participation in hostilities. NY Univ J Int Law Politics 42:741–768
Cathcart D (2010) Command and control in military operations. In: Gill TD, Fleck D (eds) The handbook of the international law of military operations. Oxford University Press, Oxford, pp 235–244
Cerone J (2001) Minding the gap: outlining KFOR accountability in post-conflict Kosovo. Eur J Int Law 12:469–488
Cole A, Drew P, McLaughlin R, Mandsager D (eds) (2009) Rules of engagement handbook. International Institute of Humanitarian Law, San Remo
Coomans F, Kamminga T (eds) (2004) Extraterritorial application of human rights treaties. Intersentia, Antwerp
Dahl AW (2013) Observance of international humanitarian law by forces under the command of international organizations. In: Horvat S, Benatar M (eds) Legal interoperability and ensuring observance of the law applicable in multinational deployments. Recueil XIX, Printing House of Defense, Brussels
De Cock C (2011) Counter-insurgency operations in Afghanistan: what about the '*jus Ad bellum*' and the '*jus in bello*': is the law still accurate?. T.M.C Asser Press, The Hague
Dennis MJ (2005) Application of human rights treaties extraterritorially in times of armed conflict and military occupation. Am J Int Law 99:119–141
Dinstein Y (2010) The conduct of hostilities under the law of international armed conflict. Cambridge University Press, Cambridge
Ducheine P (2008) Krijgsmacht, geweldgebruik en terreurbestrijding. Een onderzoek naar juridische aspecten van de rol van de strijdkrachten bij de bestrijding van terrorisme. Nijmegen, Wolf Legal Publishers
Fenrick WJ (2010) The prosecution of international crimes in relation to the conduct of military operations. In: Gill TD, Fleck D (2010) The handbook of the international law of military operations. Oxford University Press, Oxford, pp 501–514
Gill TD, Fleck D (2010) The handbook of the international law of military operations. Oxford University Press, Oxford
Greenwood C (1998) International humanitarian law and United Nations military operations. Yearb Int Humanit Law 1:3–34
Henderson C (2011) International measures for the protection of civilians in Libya and Côte d'Ivoire. Int Comp Law Q 60:767–778
International Law Association (2004) Final report on the accountability of international organizations. Available at: http://www.ila-hq.org/download.cfm/docid/6B708C25-4D6D-42E2-8385DADA752815E8 (last visited 28 April 2014) [ILA 2004]
Kelly M (2005) Legal factors in military planning for coalition warfare and military interoperability, some implications for the Australian Defence Force. Aust Army J II(2):161–172
Martin F (2001) Using international human rights law for establishing a unified use of force rule in the law of armed conflict. Saskatchewan Law Rev 64(2):347–396
Melzer N (2009) Interpretive guidance on the notion of direct participation in hostilities under international humanitarian law. ICRC, Geneva
Milanovic M, Hadzi-Vidanovic V (2013) A taxonomy of armed conflict. In: White ND, Henderson C (eds) Research handbook on international conflict and security law, *jus ad bellum, jus in bello* and *jus post bellum*. Edward Elgar, Cheltenham, pp 256–314
Mosquera A M, Haussler U-P (2008) An approach to legal interoperability. NATO Legal Gazette, p 1
NATO (2013) Glossary of terms and definitions, AAP-6 [AAP-6]
Naert F (2010) International law aspects of the EU's security and defense policy, with a particular focus on the law of armed conflict and human rights. Intersentia, Antwerp

Naert F (2012) Observance of international humanitarian law by forces under the command of the European Union. In: Horvat S, Benatar M (eds), Legal interoperability and ensuring observance of the law applicable in multinational deployments. ISMLLW, 19th international congress, Recueil XIX, pp 373–404

NATO (2008) Allied joint doctrine for joint targeting, AJP-3.9 [NATO AJP-3.9]

NATO (2010) (2d ed) Legal deskbook. Office of the Legal Adviser, Allied Command Transformation Staff Element Europe, Mons [NATO Legal Deskbook 2010]

Parks HW (2010) Part IX of the ICRC 'direct participation in hostilities' study: no mandate, no expertise, and legally incorrect. NY Univ JIL & Pol 42:769–830

Porretto G, Vité S (2006) The application of international humanitarian law and human rights law to international organizations. University Centre for International Humanitarian Law, Research Paper Series N°1, 105

Pouw E (2013) International human rights law and the law of armed conflict in the context of counterinsurgency—with a particular focus on targeting and operational detention (PhD dissertation University of Amsterdam), Breda. www.uva.nl/binaries/content/documents/personalpages/d/u/p.a.l.ducheine/nl/downloads/downloads/assets%5B7%5D/asset?1404585556372

Rogers APV (2009) Direct participation in hostilities: some personal reflections. Mil Law Law War Rev 48:143–160

Rogers APV, Stewart D (2010) The role of the military legal advisor. In: Gill TD, Fleck D (eds) The handbook of the international law of military operations. Oxford University Press, Oxford, pp 537–564

Rowe P (2005) The application of the European Convention on Human Rights during an international armed conflict. In: Burchill R, White ND, Morris J (eds) International conflict and security law, essays in memory of Hilaire McCoubrey. Cambridge University Press, Cambridge, pp 185–208

Schmitt MN (2009) Targeting narco-insurgents in Afghanistan: the limits of international humanitarian law. Yearb Int Humanit Law 12:301–320

Schmitt MN (2010) Deconstructing direct participation in hostilities: the constitutive elements. NY Univ J Int Law Politics 42:697–739

Short M (2002) Operation Allied Force from the perspective of the NATO Air Commander. In: Wall AE (ed) Legal and ethical lessons of NATO's Kosovo campaign. United States Naval War College International Law Studies 78:19–26

Solis GD (2010) The law of armed conflict, international humanitarian law in war. Cambridge University Press, Cambridge

Supreme Headquarters Allied Command, Europe (2010) Allied command operations comprehensive operations planning directive (COPD INTERIM V1.0), 17 Dec 2010 [COPD INTERIM V1.0]

Tondini M (2005) UN peace operations: the last frontier of the extraterritorial application of human rights. Mil Law Law War Rev 44(1–2):175–242

Turns D (2013) Targets. In: White ND, Henderson C (eds) Research handbook on international conflict and security law, *jus ad bellum, jus in bello* and *jus post bellum*. Edward Elgar, Cheltenham, pp 342–374

United Nations Department of Peacekeeping Operations (2008) Authority, command and control in United Nations peacekeeping operations. Policy, Ref. 2008.4

United States Army, Center for Law and Military Operations (2004) Legal lessons learned from Afghanistan and Iraq, vol I—Major combat operations (11 Sept 2001–1 May 2003)

United States, Department of the Army (1996) Tactics, techniques and procedures for the targeting process, FM 6-20-10, 8 May 1996 [FM 6-20-10 1996]

United States, Department of the Army International and Operational Law Department (1994) Operational law handbook. Judge Advocate General's Legal Center & School, U.S. Army, Charlottesville [OPLAW Handbook 1994]

United State Joint Chiefs of Staff (2007) Multinational operations. Joint Publication 3-16, 7 March 2007 [JP 3-16 2007]
United States Joint Chiefs of Staff (2010) (as amended through 15 March 2014) DOD dictionary of military and associated terms. Joint Publication 1-02 [JP 1-02 2014]
Walsh G (2005) Interoperability of United States and Canadian Armed Forces. Duke J Comp Int Law 15:215–331
Watkin K (2005) Canada/United States military interoperability and humanitarian law issues: land mines, terrorism, military objectives and targeting. Duke J Comp Int Law 15:281–314
Watkin K (2010) Opportunity lost: organized armed groups and the ICRC 'Direct participation in hostilities' interpretive guidance. NY Univ J Int Law Politics 42:641–695
Williams WS Jr (2013) Multinational rules of engagement: caveats and frictions. Army Lawyer, pp 24–28
Zwanenburg M (2005) Accountability of international peace support operations. International humanitarian law series. Martinus Nijhoff, Leiden

Chapter 12
Evaluating the Effectiveness of Leadership Decapitation Tactics Against Terrorist Groups

Bryan Price

Abstract This chapter examines the effectiveness of leadership decapitation as a counterterrorism tool. Several States have put decapitation tactics—those that seek to kill or capture the leader of an organization—at the forefront of their counter-terrorism efforts. However, most of the scholarly work on decapitation suggests it is ineffective at best and counterproductive at worst. Using survival analysis to measure decapitation effectiveness against an original dataset, this chapter shows that decapitation significantly increases the mortality rate (the rate at which groups end) of terrorist groups. The results indicate that the effect of decapitation on terrorist group mortality decreases with the age of the group, even to a point where decapitation may have no effect on the group's mortality rate, which helps explain the previously perplexing mixed record of decapitation effectiveness. Additionally, this work puts forth a theoretical justification for why terrorist groups are especially susceptible to decapitation tactics and challenges the conventional wisdom regarding terrorist group durability, showing that politically relevant terrorist groups last significantly longer than previously believed.

Keywords Leadership decapitation · Counterterrorism · Targeted killings · Al-Qaeda · Durability

---

This is an updated version of the article, Price B (2012) Targeting Top Terrorists: How Leadership Decapitation Contributes to Counterterrorism. *International Security* 36(4):9–46 (reprinted and edited with permission of the author and the publisher).
The views expressed in this chapter do not necessarily reflect those of the US Army or the Department of Defense.

B. Price (✉)
Combating Terrorism Center, Department of Social Sciences,
US Military Academy, West Point, NY 10996, USA
e-mail: bryan.price@usma.edu

P.A.L. Ducheine et al. (eds.), *Targeting: The Challenges of Modern Warfare*,
DOI 10.1007/978-94-6265-072-5_12

Contents

12.1 Introduction

Decapitation tactics which are designed to kill or capture the key leader or leaders of a terrorist group[1] feature prominently in the counterterrorism strategies of many States, including Israel and the United States.[2] These tactics may be prevalent, but are they effective? The death of Osama bin Laden captured the world's attention, but what will it mean for al Qaeda as an organization? This chapter attempts to answer these questions using the empirical evidence of leadership decapitation as a counterterrorism tool from 1970 to 2008.

The scholarly record on leadership decapitation is mixed. Some scholars believe targeting the group's leadership reduces its operational capability by eliminating its most highly skilled members and forcing the group to divert valuable time and limited resources to protect its leaders.[3] Decapitation tactics are also intended to disrupt the terrorist group's organizational routine and deter others from assuming power.[4] Scholars have credited these tactics with creating intra-organizational turmoil and even organizational collapse, most notably, the demise of the Kurdistan People's Party (PKK) and the Shining Path following the arrest of their leaders.[5] Despite questions about the legality and moral legitimacy of tar-

[1]For this study, I defined terrorist groups as organizations consisting of more than one person that engaged in violence with a political purpose that is aimed at evoking a psychological reaction in an audience that extends beyond the targeted victims. My definition does not include 'lone wolf' terrorists (e.g., Ted Kaczynski) because my focus is on the organizational dynamics of terrorist organizations.

[2]E.g. Colombia (FARC), Turkey (PKK), Russia (Chechyan groups), France (FLN in Algeria).

[3]David (2002, pp. 1–26), David (2003, p. 120), Hafez and Hatfield (2006, pp. 359–382), Ganor (2005, p. 128), Byman (2006, pp. 102–104).

[4]Byman 2006, pp. 103–104.

[5]Jordan 2009, p. 721; Pape 2003, p. 14.

geted assassinations,[6] the United States has expanded, rather than contracted, its targeted killing program during President Obama's two terms in office.[7] In early 2010, the US government even authorized the lethal targeting of Anwar al-Awlaki, a US citizen living abroad in Yemen. This unprecedented decision was fraught with constitutionality concerns about due process.[8] Less than a month after the bin Laden operation and amid criticism about the United States' disregard for international sovereignty, an American drone fired a Hellfire missile at al-Awlaki in a remote region inside Yemen, killing him instantly.[9]

Leadership decapitation is often an appealing counterterrorism tactic to domestic audiences for a variety of reasons.[10] Most scholars, however, argue it is ineffective at best and counterproductive at worst.[11] While proponents of decapitation highlight cases where the tactic has contributed to the organizational collapse of terrorist groups, critics counter with examples in which decapitation has increased and intensified terrorist activity.[12] These critics argue that targeted killings are both morally and ethically wrong and warn that they may produce a backlash effect. Rather than reducing the terrorist threat, leadership decapitation is likely to increase the number of willing recruits for terrorist groups to exploit, allowing them to grow in size and popularity.[13] Decapitation tactics may be prominent in Israel and the United States, detractors say, but that does not mean they are necessarily effective. Israel arguably has the most liberal and robust targeted killing policy of any State,[14] yet one scholar concluded that 'no compelling evidence exists that targeted killings have reduced the terrorist threat against Israel'.[15]

I argue that leadership decapitation significantly decreases the survival rate of terrorist groups, even after controlling for other factors. I used an original database, the largest and most comprehensive of its kind, to analyse the effects of leadership decapitation on the survival rate of 207 terrorist groups from 1970 to 2008. The analysis differs from previous quantitative analyses because it evaluates the effects of decapitation on the duration of terrorist groups as opposed to the number, frequency, or lethality of attacks after a group experiences leadership decapitation.[16] In doing so, it challenges the conventional wisdom regarding terrorist group duration and addresses some of the most pressing questions about decapitation

[6]David 2003; Byman 2006 p. 101.

[7]Miller 2011.

[8]Shane 2010.

[9]Mazzetti 2011.

[10]Byman 2006, pp. 102–103.

[11]Jordan 2009, p. 723; David 2003; Pape 2003, pp. 1–19.

[12]Kaplan et al. 2005, pp. 225–235; Ganor 2005, pp. 129–130.

[13]Kaplan et al. 2005, p. 230; Cronin 2006, p. 22.

[14]For a review of Israel's long history of targeted killings, see Byman 2006 and David 2002.

[15]David 2002, p. 8.

[16]Langdon et al. 2004, pp. 59–78; Mannes 2008, pp. 40–49.

effectiveness. Ultimately, this study illustrates the importance of evaluating the long-term effects of counterterrorism policies in conjunction with the short-term metrics more commonly used today.

The chapter is structured as follows. First, I briefly survey the literature on leadership decapitation and show why new metrics are needed to accurately evaluate its effectiveness. I then use concepts from leadership studies, organizational ecology, and terrorism to provide a theoretical explanation for why terrorist groups are particularly susceptible to decapitation tactics. I argue terrorist groups have unique organizational characteristics that amplify the importance of their top leaders and make leadership succession more difficult. Next, I identify the covariates most likely to influence terrorist group duration and then explain how I estimate them. Following a review of the main findings, I conclude with a discussion of Usama bin Laden's death and recommendations for policymakers.

12.2 Leadership Decapitation, Succession, and Organizational Characteristics of Terrorist Groups

According to Audrey Kurth Cronin, the field's most noted scholar on how terrorist groups end, work on the effectiveness of leadership decapitation remains in its infancy. She writes, '[p]ast experience with the decapitation of terrorist groups … is just beginning to be studied in a systematic way and, as we shall see, the relationship between decapitation and a group's demise is not straightforward'.[17] Although several scholars have evaluated the effectiveness of decapitation tactics, few have done so systematically.[18] The vast majority of analyses use case studies to support a specific conclusion.[19] Others examine the effectiveness of decapitation tactics within a particular country, of which Israel seems to be the most popular.[20] Although these country- and region-specific case studies help policymakers and scholars understand more about this controversial tactic, the findings from these studies cannot be generalized across all terrorist groups.

The track record for leadership decapitation in other policy arenas is not promising. Several scholars have concluded that targeted assassinations are ineffective for ending insurgencies,[21] disbanding drug cartels,[22] and changing State behaviour.[23] The conclusions from these analyses cast doubt on the likelihood that

[17]Cronin 2008, p. 27.

[18]Exceptions include (Langdon et al. 2004; Mannes 2008; Jordan 2009).

[19]Cronin 2006; Turbiville 2007.

[20]Gupta and Mundra 2005, pp. 573–598; Kaplan et al. 2005; Byman 2006.

[21]Staniland 2005/2006, pp. 21–40. For an opposing view, see Johnston 2009.

[22]Kenney 2007; Hyder 2004.

[23]Hosmer 2001; Pape 1996. For an opposing view, see Jones and Olken 2009, pp. 55–87.

leadership decapitation can work against terrorist groups. Terrorist groups, however, are different. I argue they have unique organizational characteristics that amplify the influence and importance of their leaders and make leadership succession more difficult.

For leadership decapitation to work as a counterterrorism policy, two conditions must be met. First, leaders need to be important to the overall success of the organization. If they are not, there is no reason to expect organizational performance will suffer in their absence. Second, leadership succession must be difficult. If leaders are easy to replace, the benefits of targeting high-ranking leaders may not be worth the costs.

Replacing terrorist group leaders is more difficult than replacing leadership in other organizations. Leadership succession is important in all organizations, and scholars have studied its effects on sports teams,[24] economic firms,[25] and political organizations.[26] Scholarly consensus on the effects of leadership succession, however, is non-existent. Succession can improve, decrease or have no discernible impact on organizational performance.[27] Glenn Carroll attributes this lack of agreement to the 'untenable implicit assumption of homology'[28]—the idea that one can treat all kinds of leadership succession in the same way, regardless of differences in organizational type. In other words, scholars who liken managing a baseball team to leading a manufacturing firm fail to consider organizational aspects such as organizational structure, control and coordination mechanisms, and the external environment.[29] Similar problems exist in the study of leadership succession in terrorist groups,[30] despite their unique organizational features. I argue that leadership succession is especially difficult for terrorist groups because they are violent and clandestine organizations that are values-based.

12.2.1 Leadership and Leadership Succession in Violent Organizations

Violent organizations are more cohesive than their nonviolent counterparts and are often led by charismatic leaders, two features that make their leaders more consequential and leadership succession more difficult. First, like military units, police

[24]Grusky 1960, pp. 105–115, 1963, pp. 21–31.

[25]Gouldner 1954, pp. 93–113; Lieberson and O'Connor 1972.

[26]Zald 1965, pp. 52–60.

[27]For an excellent review of the literature on this subject, see Carroll 1984.

[28]Ibid., p. 96.

[29]One notable exception is Carroll 1984.

[30]Langdon et al. 2004, for example, lump terrorist groups, religious organizations, guerrilla, and revolutionary movements into the same study.

departments and gangs, terrorist groups commit violence and risk being victims of violence, which makes them naturally more cohesive.[31] Extremely close-knit organizations are more likely to experience instability during a change in leadership.[32]

Second, leaders in violent organizations are dependent on charisma, and charismatic leaders are more difficult to replace. Leaders in nonviolent organizations can readily depend on conventional forms of authority to ensure compliance from their subordinates,[33] but these forms of authority often prove inadequate for leaders in violent organizations. Instead, the latter use charisma to motivate subordinates into committing violent acts in the face of danger. As John Bahnsen argues, 'charisma is the warrior's basis of authority'.[34] Because they head organizations with no legal standing and therefore have no source of legal authority, terrorist leaders are inordinately dependent upon charisma to attract, control and keep followers.[35] In violent organizations, replacing charismatic leaders is difficult, which can significantly affect organizational survival.

12.2.2 Leadership and Leadership Succession in Clandestine Organizations

The clandestine nature of terrorist groups also increases dependency on leaders; complicates leadership succession; and negatively affects organizational learning, performance, culture, and decision-making.[36] To maintain operational security and avoid detection from outsiders, leaders of terrorist organizations have a disincentive to institutionalize their operations, which makes leadership succession difficult. There are two distinct reasons behind this disinclination. First, leaders in terrorist organizations do not want to codify how they operate because doing so makes them more susceptible to State infiltration. Bureaucratization may enhance organizational learning, performance, and efficiency, but it may also provide the State with the knowledge necessary to destroy the organization.[37] Some terrorist

[31]Pedahzur discusses how violent organizations such as terrorist groups and militaries share this unique cohesion built around dangerous missions, in his book, Suicide Terrorism. Pedahzur 2005, pp. 41–42.

[32]Grusky 1960, pp. 105–115.

[33]Max Weber referred to these means of authority as the rational (legal or formal) and traditional forms. See Weber 1947.

[34]Bahnsen 2001, p. 274.

[35]Chasdi 1999.

[36]McCormack 2003, pp. 473–507; Eilstrup-Sangiovanni and Jones 2008, pp. 7–44.

[37]For an example, consider the Sinjar records about al-Qaeda that were found in Iraq in 2007. See Blanche 2008; Combating Terrorism Center 2014.

groups do have formal hierarchies, but not all members are likely to understand them.[38] Individual cells often maintain independence from one another and remain ignorant of other cells so captured individuals, or even cells, cannot compromise the entire group. This lack of formalization and institutionalization increases the level of uncertainty, which in turn complicates leadership succession and produces organizational instability. While this characteristic holds true for all organizations, including legitimate organizations such as State governments following the assassination of the head of State,[39] its consequences are more significant for terrorist groups.

The second reason terrorist leaders are disinclined to institutionalize their organizations may be more selfish and more personal. Not only do terrorist leaders fear being captured or killed by the State or rival groups, but they also worry about being removed from power by their own group. Similar to other illicit, violent and clandestine organizations, leadership succession in terrorist groups is often based on Hobbesian principles rather than on institutionalized processes. It is common for terrorist leaders to suffer from paranoia,[40] a personality disorder worsened by a clandestine existence. The condition can produce 'burn syndrome' or a 'pervasive fear that other people know what they're doing.'[41] Sabri al Banna (a.k.a. Abu Nidal),[42] the head of the Abu Nidal Organization, believed that his group was plotting against him and on a single night ordered the murder of 170 followers he suspected were traitors.[43] Abimael Guzman, the leader of the Shining Path in Peru, was so paranoid about coups within his organization that he 'surrounded himself with female lieutenants but readied none to command in his absence'.[44] Because terrorist leaders know that they live and die by the sword, they hesitate to provide subordinates with the knowledge and skills to run the organization in their place. This disinclination to institutionalize not only centralizes power in the hands of the terrorist group's leader, but it also injects an air of uncertainty when a top leader is removed, making it more difficult for a successor to understand and run the organization effectively.[45]

Because of their clandestine nature, terrorist groups are often composed of culturally and ideologically like-minded members. Although this can be extremely useful for developing cohesion, trust, loyalty and strong social bonds among

---

[38]As one former Navy intelligence analyst noted, '[t]errorist organizations do not have organizational charts. They have relationships, and if you can understand those relationships you have gained valuable intelligence'. See Bender 2007.

[39]Iqbal and Zorn 2008, pp. 385–400.

[40]Galanter and Forest 2006.

[41]Kenney 2007, p. 145.

[42]Seale 1992.

[43]Clarridge 1997, p. 336.

[44]Harmon 2007, p. 57.

[45]This affects other clandestine organizations such as drug cartels as well. See Hyder 2004, pp. 40–46, specifically for the description of Pablo Escobar's tenure.

members, it can also allow leaders to frame the group's sense of reality. Depending on how deeply underground the group is, the leaders may be its only source of information, which makes the group highly susceptible to group think.[46] As terrorist groups become more clandestine and the social bonds of group members intensify, the likelihood of members opposing the group leaders' decisions decreases even further. This can often inhibit organizational learning and result in poor decision-making.[47]

12.2.3 Leadership and Leadership Succession in Values-Based Organizations

Values-based organizations such as religious cults, social clubs and terrorist groups have greater difficulty replacing their leaders than do profit-based organizations, including drug cartels. Three reasons explain why. First, values-based organizations require their leaders to possess unique skill sets that not every leader has, namely the ability to provide transformational leadership. Finding successors with these requisite skill sets is not easy. Second, the monetary incentives of holding power in profit-based organizations are usually sufficient to attract a steady stream of successors, even when leading involves tremendous risk, which makes leadership succession less difficult. The incentives for holding power in values-based organizations can be more complex and abstract. Third, articulating the vision, mission and strategy in values-based organizations can be difficult, especially when these elements are created from scratch and are hard to conceptualize.

Leaders of terrorist groups must possess a particular set of skills to attract and maintain membership. In his seminal work on leadership, Burns draws a distinction between transactional and transformational leadership.[48] Transactional leadership involves relationships that appeal to people's self-interests. For example, a shop owner pays a salary to an employee in return for work, and a politician may pass laws that attract a certain constituency in return for votes. Transformational leadership, on the other hand, goes beyond personal self-interest incentives by appealing to the values and emotions of followers. Transformational leaders, therefore, seek to create significant change in the behaviour and belief systems of their adherents, often encouraging personal sacrifice to achieve goals that benefit the team, group, or organization.[49] Although some recruits join terrorist organizations for financial or other reasons of self-interest, I argue that terrorist leaders need transformational leadership to expand and maintain their organizations.

---

[46]Janis 1972.

[47]McCormack 2003.

[48]Burns 1978.

[49]Ibid., at p. 20.

Transformational and charismatic leaders are thought to be more effective in ideological organizations than they are in non-ideological organizations.[50] In the former they must articulate 'a vision that draws an emotional and enthusiastic response,'[51] since that the group's goals may not always be 'specific, tangible, and calculable'.[52] Thus, leaders in ideological organizations must have more than expertise in their field or be competent managers if they want to recruit and maintain members; they must also be able to communicate, evoke confidence, and serve as role models for their followers.[53]

Similar to clandestine organizations, values-based organizations operate under more uncertainty than profit-based organizations, which amplifies the importance of their leaders. As a result, '[w]hen follower's efforts are directed toward implementation of ideological goals and values, or when their efforts are directed toward creating or delivering some social good,' followers are more dependent on their leaders' vision and framing.[54] In contrast, many profit-based organizations generally do not lend themselves to this type of transformational leadership. In profit-based organizations with 'roles requiring highly routine, non-thinking effort in institutions directed exclusively to economic ends,' charismatic leaders would theoretically be less effective.[55] In these organizations, the demands for leadership are more performance based than value based, where the image of the leader as a role model is considerably less important than, and may even be irrelevant to, her managerial competency.

In values-based organizations, leadership succession can be difficult because successors may have ideological differences with the outgoing leadership. Ideological salience in these organizations differs across group leaders and followers, and ideology is generally more salient in first-generational members than with younger, nth-generational members. For example, Jacob Shapiro argues that lower-level terrorist group members are less committed than their leaders.[56] Martha Crenshaw writes that in terrorist groups, 'the leadership may possess more complex and differentiated belief structures than do followers'.[57] In fact, in some values-based organizations, 'the basis for the authority of leaders may lie precisely in the ability to articulate beliefs held implicitly by followers. Or authority may derive from the relevance of the leader's background to the general belief system'.[58] When Andreas Baader, leader of the German Red Army Faction, was

[50]Etzioni 1961; House 1977, House and Singh 1987, pp. 669–718; Mumford et al. 2007, pp. 217–235.

[51]Aminzade et al. (2001, p. 152).

[52]House and Singh 1987, p. 686.

[53]House 1977.

[54]House and Singh 1987, p. 691.

[55]House 1977, p. 204.

[56]Shapiro 2007.

[57]Crenshaw 1988, p. 19.

[58]Ibid.

arrested and jailed, second-generation leaders with less impressive ideological credentials tried to assume power, but could not, even though they may have had better organizational and managerial skills. Baader's capture marked the end of the first-generation's grip on the organization. As Crenshaw noted, 'no subsequent leaders possessed their degree of control, and the organization was divided by rivalries between managerial and ideological leadership styles.'[59]

Leaders in values-based organizations are responsible for framing the groups' ideology, and in certain cases, for creating it, as they have in some terrorist groups and religious cults. Because charismatic and transformational leadership is usually required in forming a purely ideological and values-based group, removal of the leader may cause more instability than it would in a non-ideological, profit-based organization. This is especially the case if the successor lacks transformational leadership skills or if the former leader has not succeeded in what Max Weber termed the 'routinization of charisma' prior to the changeover.[60] Removing a leader can have serious implications if followers have not internalized his or her ideological/values-driven goals, particularly if they are abstract and difficult to understand. Two groups, the Solar Temple and Aum Shinrikyo, exemplify this type of values-based organization. Both were founded on complicated belief systems that required significant framing and explanation from their leaders. The Solar Temple melded neo-Christian mystical beliefs of the Holy Grail and the Knights Templar with Egyptian thanatology, oriental folk medicine and ecological apocalypticism.[61] The Japanese group Aum Shinrikyo combined Indian and Tibetan Buddhism with Christian apocalypticism and New Age medical practices, none of which are easily compatible with one another.[62] Both groups lost direction in the absence of their leaders. Once its leader committed suicide, the Solar Temple ceased to exist. Following the arrest of Aum Shinrikyo's leader, the group changed its name to Aleph and its membership dropped by more than 90 % during the 1990s.[63]

The fact that terrorist groups are violent, clandestine, and values-based makes them particularly vulnerable to leadership decapitation. All three organizational characteristics amplify the importance of leaders and make leadership succession problematic. This helps explain why leadership decapitation has failed against other organizational types that may have one or more of these characteristics, but lack all three. For example, drug cartels are violent and clandestine organizations, but they are profit-based. Leaders in these organizations are important, but they are easily and quickly replaced. Leadership decapitation has been a central feature in US counterdrug strategy since the early 1990s through the 'kingpin strategy', but it has failed to produce meaningful results, and may even be counterproductive.

---

[59] Ibid. See also Crenshaw 1996, p. 263.

[60] Weber 1947, pp. 363–373.

[61] Dawson 2002, p. 83.

[62] Ibid.

[63] Terrorist Organization Profiles (TOPS) database available at: http://www.start.umd.edu/tops/.

A leaked 2010 US Customs and Border Protection report concluded that removing key cartel leaders has had no effect on the drug trade.[64] When a US/Colombian counterdrug operation killed Pablo Escobar, head of the powerful Medellin cartel, in 1993, the cocaine industry did not suffer a catastrophic blow. Instead, Hyder writes that 'eliminating Escobar made things worse'.[65]

In the next section, I discuss some of the problems associated with analysing terrorist group behaviour and provide an alternative method to examining the effectiveness of leadership decapitation as a counterterrorism tactic.

12.3 A New Way of Evaluating the Effectiveness of Leadership Decapitation

There are a number of challenging data limitations associated with measuring common terrorist group performance variables such as attack frequency and fatalities.[66] As a result, I chose an alternative approach and studied the mortality rate of terrorist groups. Organizational theorists in fields outside of terrorism research sometimes prefer studying organizational mortality rate over other dependent variables because 'organizational death is a fundamental standard of organizational performance' and 'has the advantage of relatively unambiguous measurements and interpretation, which is often not the case with performance variables.'[67]

12.3.1 Criteria

Because of the issues associated with available terrorism datasets, I created an original dataset[68] consisting of 207 terrorist groups from 65 countries that were active from 1970 to 2008.[69] Among quantitative analyses that have examined leadership decapitation and terrorist groups, it is the largest dataset of its kind. It includes 204 observations where the leader or leaders were either killed or captured. Additionally, I recorded 95 other incidents where the leader or leaders (1) were thrown out or expelled from their groups, (2) died of natural causes or accidents, (3) voluntarily stepped down from their organization, or (4) accepted a

---

[64] U.S. Customs and Border Protection 2010.

[65] Hyder 2004, p. 45.

[66] Price 2012.

[67] Carroll 1984, p. 6.

[68] The dataset, as well as all of the tables, figures, and appendices associated with this article, can be found at http://www.bryancprice.com/Data.html.

[69] Some of these groups were founded prior to 1970, but all were active for at least part of the period from 1970 to 2008.

cease-fire agreement with the government and formally entered the political process. In total, the dataset contains 299 observations of leadership change.

I used only groups that posed a credible threat to the target State. Terrorist groups that commit a few (if any) minor attacks that result in superficial damage may never make it onto the State's 'radar' and could conceivably remain active for decades. Or more likely, these groups end soon after carrying out one or two attacks, never to be heard from again. As a result, I considered only groups that had committed at least four attacks, including one or more causing fatalities.[70] Because this study is interested exclusively in the organizational decline of consequential terrorist groups, this criterion ensured that only groups that could genuinely be defined as terrorist organizations pursuing a systematic campaign of violence were taken into account.[71]

Additionally, the dataset excluded the killing or capture of high-ranking or upper-echelon leaders who were not the primary leaders or co-leaders.[72] It also disregarded groups created by States to counter oppositional groups within their borders. I included only umbrella organizations if attacks were conducted under their name. Individual groups that joined umbrella organizations were not coded as ending after they joined the group. Instead, I recorded these individual organizations as surviving as long as the umbrella organization.[73] Finally, groups that appeared on the terrorism lists of the major State powers were incorporated, even if the groups did not meet my initial attack/fatality criteria.[74] A table of the terrorist groups and dates used in this study can be found on my website.[75]

---

[70]My initial criterion consisted of five attacks. Although my results were consistent with the finding using four attacks, my sample size was much larger when I lowered the attack threshold to four.

[71]Several datasets in political science employ similar filters. For example, many scholars studying civil wars use coding criteria that include conflicts featuring at least 1000 total deaths and 100 deaths per year. I felt that limiting my dataset to groups that have killed at least one person and have conducted four attacks would be a fair demonstration of organizational capability.

[72]Including leaders at all levels would be an improvement over this study, but it is too difficult to accomplish using open source material. I encourage other researchers, particularly those with access to classified information, to include all levels of leadership.

[73]For example, the Armed Forces of National Liberation (FALN) was one of several terrorist groups in El Salvador that joined forces to form the Farabundo Marti National Liberation Front (FMLN) in 1980. Because the FMLN conducted attacks under its umbrella name, I included it as a separate group in the dataset with a start date of 1980 and an end date of 1991, when it signed a peace agreement with the government. Instead of coding the FALN's end date at the time of the merger in 1980, I gave it the same end date as the FMLN in 1991.

[74]Two examples of these groups include the Libyan Islamic Fighting Group and the Moroccan Islamic Combatant Group. Both groups are on the 2005 US Foreign Terrorist Organizations list and the United Kingdom's Proscribed List of terrorist organizations, but they did not have at least four attacks recorded in the Global Terrorism Database (GTD) or MIPT Terrorism Knowledge Base (TKB). Additionally, I utilized left-censoring for any groups with start dates prior to 1970.

[75]Supra note 68.

To verify the number of attacks, I used the Global Terrorism Database (GTD), which includes domestic and international terrorist incidents from 1970 to 2004,[76] as well as the MIPT's TKB, which contains international terrorist incidents from 1968 to 2007 (but is no longer maintained).[77] Open source research served as a supplement as well as additional validation of the information found in these datasets.[78]

12.3.2 The Variables

In order to determine whether leadership decapitation increases the mortality rate in terrorist groups, I included several variables and controlled for numerous factors that might influence terrorist group behaviour. In addition to leadership decapitation—the main explanatory variable—I controlled for the presence of allied and rival terrorist groups, the counterterrorism capacity and regime type of States targeting each group, other forms of leadership turnover, and the organizational structure, size, and ideology of the group. I also examined whether the method of leadership decapitation had any effect on the group's mortality rate.

To increase the robustness of my findings, I varied the duration of leadership decapitation's effects on terrorist groups in three different ways. I measured the dependent variable, terrorist group mortality, in years. To determine the start time of each group, I used the date of its first attack, not its purported founding date.[79] Because all of the groups in the Terrorism Organization Profiles (TOPS) database[80] are clandestine organizations, accurate information about when each group officially formed is often unavailable or unverifiable. Thus, it made practical sense to use the group's first attack as the start date. Likewise, determining when a group 'dies' was equally problematic. Groups can exist for months or years without committing violence. This lack of activity can result from extended planning cycles, reconsolidation efforts, effective counterterrorism campaigns by the State, and, of course, patience, as a group bides its time until a more advantageous opportunity presents itself. I considered a group inactive if 2 years passed without a violent

76 The Global Terrorism Database (GTD) is available at http://www.start.umd.edu/gtd/.

77 The MIPT Terrorism Knowledge Base (TKB) can be found at the TOPS database at http://www.start.umd.edu/tops/.

78 Websites operated by the South Asia Terrorism Portal, www.satp.org, and the Northern Ireland Conflict Archive on the Internet (CAIN), http://cain.ulst.ac.uk, as well as the dataset created by RAND scholars Jones and Libicki, were also consulted and cross-checked for accuracy. See Jones and Libicki 2008.

79 It is important to note that starting in 2008, I assume the State knows about the group and therefore targets it even though the group may not have met all of the criteria for inclusion into the dataset in this first year (i.e., conducted at least four attacks and killing at least one person). Some, of course, do meet this criterion. I thank Kenneth Schultz for bringing this to my attention.

80 Supra note 63.

attack, with the year of the group's last attack serving as the end date. For a list of all groups and dates, see the online appendix.[81]

Other covariates that help explain terrorist group mortality include the presence of allied and rival groups. Terrorist groups allied with other groups should have greater longevity because they can pool resources and information and coordinate attacks against the State; all of which may improve their chances of achieving their political goals. In addition, if these allied groups operate within the same State, they may force the State to divide its counterterrorism resources in an effort to combat multiple threats. The TOPS database contains allied groups in its description of each terrorist organization, and I included these groups in my database.

Rival groups, even if they espouse different ideologies, may increase one another's survivability by distracting the State from focusing on one particular group. Moreover, the 'Red Queen' theory from the literature on organizational ecology suggests that organizations facing intense competition from other groups are better equipped to learn, adapt, and thus survive.[82] There are also cogent arguments, however, for why rivals might reduce the survivability rate of terrorist groups. For example, rivals present a legitimate decapitation threat to other terrorist groups. They also compete for limited resources, especially when it comes to replenishing their ranks. Therefore, although groups with allies should be more resilient than groups with none, the predicted relationship between group longevity and the presence of rival groups is less obvious.

Organizational structure—whether the group is hierarchical or decentralized—is another covariate that scholars believe influences terrorist group behaviour.[83] Many scholars make the claim that decapitation has greater success against groups that are more hierarchical and less decentralized.[84] Because verifying the organizational structure of terrorist groups is often impossible, determining the degree to which a group is hierarchical or decentralized is difficult.[85] In a self-admittedly weak attempt to measure this, I included co-leader, a dichotomous variable indicating whether a group was led by a single leader or multiple leaders.[86]

---

[81]Supra note 68.

[82]Barnett and McKendrick 2004, pp. 535–571.

[83]Jackson 2006, pp. 241–262.

[84]Hutchinson and O'Malley 2007.

[85]Brian Jackson's work on the difficulty of characterizing terrorist organizations as purely hierarchical or purely decentralized speaks to this point. Ultimately, it is a question of degree; rarely can one label a group as being purely hierarchical or purely decentralized. Instead, Jackson recommends examining the quality and quantity of a group's command and control linkages to better understand the structure. This, however, is often difficult to accurately determine as well. For more information, see Jackson 2006.

[86]In addition to coding leaders and co-leaders, I coded founders and follow-on leaders in previous work (Price 2009). Although terrorist groups are 70 % more likely to survive when one or more of their founders lead the organization, there is no statistically significant difference between the mortality rates of groups with founders at the helm and those with successor leaders in charge.

The dataset also includes information about each group's ideology and estimated size. Some scholars argue that ideology and size are important factors for explaining group strategy, resiliency and longevity.[87] Cronin contends that terrorist groups with a predominantly religious ideology are more dangerous, because these groups may launch attacks to please a certain deity and are seemingly unconstrained by secular laws and norms.[88] This commitment to a non-secular ideology may lead them to frame their goals with a longer time horizon, which allows them to overlook short-term failures, a combination that may increase the group's longevity. Bruce Hoffman disagrees and argues that ethno-nationalist/separatist terrorist groups are more resilient and ultimately more successful given their ability to 'draw sustenance and support from an already existing constituency,' and because they benefit from 'the clarity and tangibility' of their stated goals.[89] In other words, ethno-nationalist/separatist groups will continue to fight because they believe they are on the right side of history. Along similar lines, Louise Richardson contends that ethno-nationalist terrorist groups survive longer because they have closer ties to their communities than do other types of groups.[90]

Identifying a group's ideology can be problematic, however, leading some scholars to have less confidence in its ability to explain terrorist behaviour. Jerrold Post has quipped that 'the cause is not the cause'.[91] When discussing the relationship between ideology and the motivation behind terrorist group behaviour, Crenshaw asserts that cultural influences can be as strong, if not stronger, than ideological influences. Instead of blindly following ideological ambitions, terrorist leaders may first develop a set of beliefs and 'then seek justification for them through the selection of fragments of compatible theories'.[92] To confuse matters further, groups are not necessarily beholden to one ideology.[93] Finally, ideologies may change over the course of a group's lifecycle, as can the importance of ideology to the organization and its goals.

Nevertheless, because ideology can play an important role in explaining longevity in certain types of terrorist groups, I included ideology as a variable in the dataset. Although several of these terrorist groups could be considered hybrids—groups featuring elements of several ideologies—I used the same ideological types as coded by Seth Jones and Martin Libicki in their RAND study.[94] The authors

---

[87]Hoffman 2002; Cronin 2002/2003, pp. 30–58; Jordan 2009; Mannes 2008.

[88]Cronin 2002/2003, pp. 41–42.

[89]Hoffman 2002, p. 171.

[90]Richardson 2006, p. 48.

[91]Post 1990, p. 35.

[92]Crenshaw 1988, p. 27.

[93]For example, one could argue that the Popular Front for the Liberation of Palestine (PFLP) advocates both nationalist/separatist and Marxist-Leninist ideologies. Hamas is both nationalist and Islamist.

[94]Jones and Libicki 2008.

classified ideology into a common set of four types: right wing, left wing, nationalist, and religious.[95] While all four types are in some ways values-based, and thus especially prone to organizational death following leadership decapitation, religious groups may be more susceptible to mortality given the leader's important role in framing and interpretation.

Some scholars use the size of a group to explain mortality rates in organizational ecology. Additionally, several large-*n* terrorism studies use size as a proxy for group capability based on the idea that larger groups have access to more resources than smaller groups. This, in turn, makes them better equipped to conduct attacks and withstand a State's counterterrorism efforts, including successful leadership decapitation.[96] Research in anthropology suggests, however, that leaders of groups with fewer than 150 members are more influential. Groups of this size are optimal for the cognitive capacity of humans to establish genuine social relationships, which increase the group's trust, cohesion and transactive memory.[97] Thus it is not clear how a group's size will affect its mortality rate following leadership decapitation. Instead of assessing a group's size down to the individual member as some scholars have,[98] I used the less ambitious, but probably more accurate, estimates from the RAND study of how terrorism ends.[99] These approximations placed terrorist group size in one of four 'buckets': fewer than 100, 100–999, 1000–10,000, and more than 10,000 members.[100]

Because States may be in a position to determine the longevity of terrorist groups, I included control variables that might influence their ability to combat such groups. This required estimating State counterterrorism capacity and regime type. States, like terrorist groups, are hesitant to make their capabilities part of the public record, mainly because doing so would reveal their sources and methods of intelligence gathering. Although reliable data on State counterterrorism budgets and the size of their counterterrorism bureaucracies are not readily available, it is still possible to approximate their counterterrorism capabilities by employing the same logic used to measure a terrorist group's capacity to attack—the more resources that are available, the more robust a State's capability to wage its counterterrorism campaign. In other words, wealthier States are better equipped to create, resource and maintain counterterrorism agencies than poorer States. I used the

[95]As a robustness check, I also ran a Cox model with the ideologies as they were coded in the TOPS dataset. Ideology in this dataset was coded as nine types: anarchist, anti-globalist, socialist/communist, environmental, leftist, nationalist/separatist, racist, religious, right-wing conservative, right-wing reactionary, and other. Because the results exhibited no major changes and because the RAND typologies are easier to comprehend, I used the RAND ideologies.

[96]Jordan 2009; Asal and Rethemeyer 2008.

[97]Gladwell 2002, p. 180.

[98]Jordan 2009; Asal and Rethemeyer 2008.

[99]Jones and Libicki 2008.

[100]This type of bracketing is a common feature in several academic studies on terrorism. See Mannes 2008; Jones and Libicki 2008.

Penn World Tables to obtain the gross domestic product (GDP) per capita of the target State to measure this capacity.[101] This variable becomes tricky to measure, however, when transnational terrorist groups are involved and thus wage violence against more than one State. To measure the counterterrorism capacity of the target States of transnational groups,[102] I took an average of the top three target States' GDP per capita estimates.[103]

Regime type served as another control variable given that many scholars believe democracies are at a greater disadvantage than autocracies in combating terrorism within their borders.[104] According to this line of thought, politicians in democracies are constrained by commitments to civil liberties and accountability to electorates, and thus cannot use the heavy-handed tactics and tools that many authoritarian regimes rely on to fight terrorism. Therefore, one could argue that terrorist groups are more likely to have shorter life spans in autocratic States than they do in democracies. Another argument for using regime type as a control variable, and one that comes to a different conclusion, centres on the initial motivation for groups that resort to terrorism in the first place. The logic here is that terrorist organizations in democratic governments may not last as long, because these groups have more options to achieve their political ends than they do in authoritarian governments.[105] As a result, I included Polity IV scores for each group-year in the analysis.[106]

---

[101]This method is consistent with other works in political science. See, for example, Fearon and Laitin 2003, pp. 75–90. While admittedly an imperfect measure, because no other studies of leadership decapitation have attempted to control for a State's counterterrorism capability, I felt that using an imperfect measure was better than ignoring the issue. Fortunately, averages were only needed for 37 groups in my dataset (17 %), 11 of which include averaging the counterterrorism capacities of Ireland and the United Kingdom for many of the terrorist groups operating in Northern Ireland.

[102]As an example, for al-Qaeda, I used the GDP per capita of the United States, United Kingdom and Pakistan.

[103]In Resolution 1373, the UN developed evaluation criteria for State counterterrorism capacity, which obligated member States to revise laws and enhance their law enforcement capability. Additionally, the UN encouraged States to sign and ratify twelve counterterrorism conventions. UNSC Res. 1373, 28 September 2001. The UN's counterterrorism program, however, suffers from several weaknesses. The resolution contains vague language (e.g., the resolution states that a member State must have 'the administrative capacity to enforce various counter-terrorism mandates') and no mechanism for evaluating compliance. According to a report, '[e]valuating whether states are actually implementing these conventions and complying with the requirements of Resolution 1373 is a difficult challenge. There are no agreed criteria for evaluating implementation capabilities, or determining what additional steps a state should take to achieve compliance'. See Cortright 2005. Therefore, I did not find compliance with these conventions to be a better measure than GDP per capita.

[104]Art and Richardson 2007; Lesser et al. 1999; Wilkinson 2000; Cronin 2006; Zimmerman and Wenger 2007; Enders and Sandler 2006.

[105]I thank Martha Crenshaw for pointing this out.

[106]Polity IV: Regime Authority Characteristics and Transitions Datasets, Integrated Network for Social Conflict Research (INSCR). Available at: http://www.systemicpeace.org//inscr/inscr.htm.

I conducted several tests on whether killing or arresting the terrorist leaders hastens the group's demise in order to address the debate between proponents and critics of decapitation. Some scholars believe that arresting the leader is more beneficial for several reasons.[107] First, there are more legal and moral issues involved with targeted killings than with capturing and incarcerating terrorist leaders.[108] Second, not only can the State interrogate the leader and obtain useful information about the organization, but a leader in State custody damages the psyche of the group. According to Cronin, the incarceration of the group's leader is 'an implicit answer to the illegitimacy of terrorism, and demonstrates the authority of the rule of law'.[109] Steven Hutchinson and Pat O'Malley note that 'the demoralization that accompanies seeing a leader captive and under control of the enemy appears highly relevant to group perseverance'.[110]

In contrast, some scholars argue that decapitation acts as a deterrent. First, killing the leader sends a message that successors will face a similar fate.[111] Second, when the leader is killed, the operational routine of the organization is interrupted, and the group must invest resources in finding a suitable successor. Moreover, knowing that the State is targeting the leadership means that the organization will probably invest resources in protecting successors, a move that ultimately detracts from its ability to conduct terrorist attacks. Boaz Ganor argues that interruptions in the organizational routine are 'liable to have ongoing consequences, rather than merely a short-term effect'.[112]

To provide some empirical evidence into this debate, I coded each decapitation according to whether a terrorist group's leader was killed or captured. I also coded a dummy variable (*Both*) for when the leader is captured and then killed by the State at a later date. The logic here is that the State has an opportunity to interrogate a captured leader and obtain information about his or her organization in hopes of destroying it. Killing the leader afterward may provide the deterrent that Ganor describes above.[113] Therefore, the decapitation method of *Both* includes cases where death was a result of execution or death from wounds suffered at the hands of the State often during brutal interrogation sessions.

Tables 12.1 and 12.2 offer descriptive statistics about the terrorist groups in this dataset. Table 12.1 shows the status of the 207 groups in the dataset and denotes whether they experienced leadership decapitation. Seventy percent of the groups that experienced such an event from 1970 to 2008 are no longer in existence. Table 12.2 shows the sizes and ideological types of all groups in the dataset, and indicates which have experienced leadership decapitation and their current status.

---

[107]Cronin 2006; Hutchinson and O'Malley 2007.

[108]Lotrionte 2003, pp. 73–86; Ganor 2005; Shane 2009; Mazzetti and Shane 2009.

[109]Cronin 2008, p. 30.

[110]Hutchinson and O'Malley 2007, p. 6.

[111]Ganor 2005.

[112]Ibid., at p. 128.

[113]Ibid.

Table 12.1 Terrorist mortality and leadership decapitation, 1970–2008

		Group ended	
		No	Yes
Experienced decapitation	No	32	44
	Yes	38	93

Table 12.2 Descriptive statistics of politically relevant terrorist groups & leadership decapitation

					Decapitated		Not Decapitated	
		N	Decap	Not Decap	Alive	Dead	Alive	Dead
Number of Members	Fewer than 100	48	37	11	1	36	3	8
	100–1000	87	63	24	24	39	11	13
	1000–10,000	52	25	27	11	14	14	13
	More than 10,000	20	6	14	2	4	4	10
Ideology	Left-wing	74	55	19	6	49	4	15
	Nationalist	74	36	38	13	23	15	23
	Right-wing	6	4	2	0	4	0	2
	Religious	53	36	17	19	17	13	4
Total		207	131	76	38	93	32	44

12.3.3 The Model

I used survival models to analyse the effect leadership decapitations have on terrorist group duration. Scholars employ such models to understand the causes and consequences of change over time in a particular population, for example in evaluating the effect of medical treatment on different patient populations or understanding the failure rates of machine components. In this study, my 'patients' were terrorist groups and leadership decapitations were the 'treatments'. One of the more attractive features of these models is their ability to account for censored-data, which is more difficult to do with linear regression models.[114] In other words, these models are capable of using data on mortality rates from past terrorist groups to predict

[114]The Cox proportional hazards model is the most widely used model in survival analysis, not only because it can accommodate censored data and time-varying covariates, but also because it is a semi-parametric model that allows researchers to use event history analysis without knowing the exact distribution function of failure times. If a researcher knew that the risk a terrorist group endures from a decapitation event would always increase or decrease with time, then parametric models such as the Weibull model or the exponential model would be preferable. If, however, there is any doubt as to what the distribution function of failure times is, as is the case with terrorist groups and decapitation events, the Cox model is a better choice. See Box-Steffensmeier and Jones 2004, p. 21.

what to expect from terrorist groups that remain active beyond 2008, the last year of this study's observation period. Central to all survival models is the hazard rate, defined as the 'rate at which units fail (or durations end) by t (a predetermined period of time) given that the unit has survived until t'.[115] For Cox models, which I used in my study, 'the hazard rate for the ith individual [or terrorist group in this case] is: $h_t(t) = h_0(t)\exp(\beta' x)$, where $h_0(t)$ is the baseline hazard function and $\beta' x$ are the covariates and regression parameters.'[116] The models seek to explain how certain covariates affect the survival rate of terrorist groups. They identify which variables increase or decrease the mortality rate or have no effect at all.

If the hazard ratio is greater than '1', then that variable increases the hazard rate for a terrorist group and places them more at risk of 'dying'. A hazard ratio of less than '1' means that the variable decreases the hazard rate for the terrorist group and makes it more resilient to organizational death. If the hazard ratio is '1', then the variable neither increases nor decreases the risk to the terrorist group. For example, if the hazard ratio for the dummy variable *ally* ('1' indicated the presence of an ally, '0' otherwise), is 0.5, this can be interpreted as a 50 % decrease in the mortality rate for terrorist groups with allies. Another way of saying this is that terrorist groups with allies are 50 % less likely to end than terrorist groups without allies.[117]

To control for *ideology*, a variable with four factors in my model, I had to omit one ideological type to serve as a comparison group.[118] In a Cox model, it is customary to drop the most prevalent factor and use it for comparison. The choice, however, is ultimately up to the researcher. I chose nationalist/separatist groups as my comparison group for two reasons. Not only were these groups the most prevalent in my dataset, but I wanted to see how they compared to religious groups. As previously mentioned, there is a debate among scholars about which type of terrorist group is more resilient, so I wanted to determine if there was a statistically significant difference between religious and nationalist/separatist groups.

12.4 Results

The null model, in which I treated all of the terrorist groups as a single population without including any of the covariates, can be graphically depicted by a survival curve using the Kaplan-Meier (K-M) estimates.[119] The curve in Fig. 12.1 is the

[115]Ibid., at pp. 13–14.

[116]Ibid., at p. 48.

[117]The standard errors reported below the hazard ratios are for the coefficients from which the hazard ratios were derived, not the hazard ratios themselves.

[118]This is because Cox models do not have an intercept term. All results are interpreted relative to the baseline hazard rate. For more information, see Therneau and Grambsch 2000.

[119]Kaplan=Meier (K-M) estimates are maximum likelihood estimators that allow researchers to approximate survival functions of populations over time, even when individual subjects drop out of the study. In this case, it computes the number of terrorist groups that have ended at a certain point, divided by the number of terrorist groups still remaining in the study.

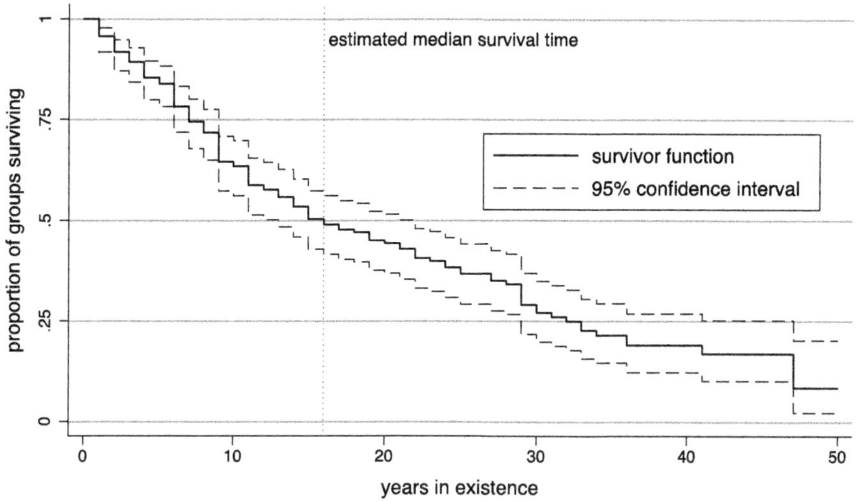

Fig. 12.1 Terrorist group survivorship, 1970–2008

K-M curve along with its 95 % confidence intervals. The confidence intervals widen at the longer periods, because there are fewer observations at these higher group ages (i.e., fewer groups 'die' in those particular years of group age). The dotted vertical line that intersects the K-M curve represents the estimated mean survival time for all 207 groups in the sample. It is approximate because 76 of these groups were still active when the study ended in 2008. The estimated mean group survival time is 16.2 years. Of the 131 groups that ended from 1970 to 2008, the mean survival time is 13.9 years.[120]

Beyond the null model, I conducted tests on 16 Cox models that evaluated terrorist group mortality using a variety of variables. The detailed statistical results can be found elsewhere, but below are the primary findings from this study.

First, this analysis showed that decapitated terrorist groups have a significantly higher mortality rate than non-decapitated groups. Regardless of how I specified the duration of the effect from leadership decapitation (i.e., whether I limited it

[120]The mean survival time for terrorist groups in this study differs drastically from David C. Rapoport's widely cited claim that 90 % of all terrorist groups survive less than a year, with nearly half of the remaining groups unable to survive more than a decade. See Rapoport 1992, p. 1067. Many scholars, including top names in the field, have referenced this estimate so much that it has become the conventional wisdom. Rapoport did not include any empirical evidence to support his claim, however. In his defence, his sentence reads: '*Perhaps* as many as 90 % last less than a year' (emphasis added), which leads me to believe he never intended it to be taken as a bold empirical fact. Although it is possible that his estimate is correct if one considers the overly inclusive number of politically inconsequential groups that have committed few, if any attacks, or in some cases, only threatened attacks, this does not give policymakers an accurate assessment of the durability of politically relevant terrorist groups.

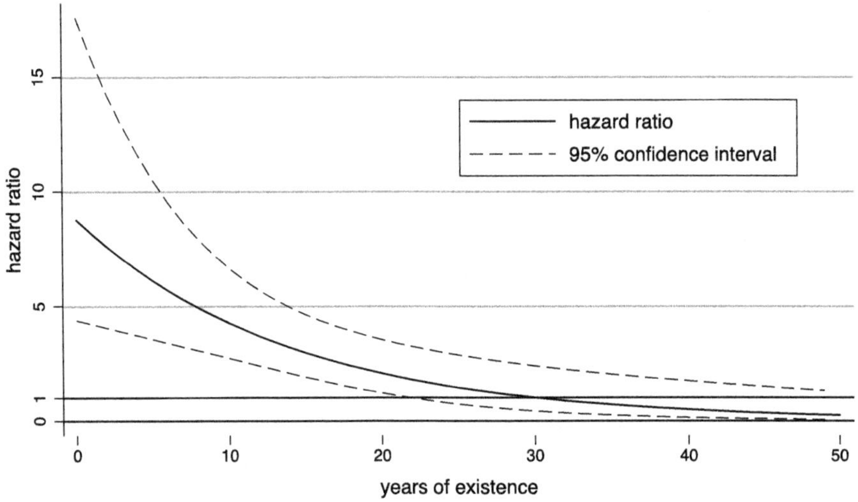

Fig. 12.2 Effect of decapitation over time on the hazard ratio of terrorist group survival

to the year in which it occurred, restricted it to two years, or allowed it to linger indefinitely), killing or capturing a terrorist leader increased the mortality rate of the group. There is no guarantee, however, that organisational death will be immediate; only 30 % of decapitated groups (40 of 131) ended within two years of losing their leader.

Second, the earlier leadership decapitation occurs in a terrorist group's life cycle, the greater effect it will have on the group's mortality rate. Additionally, the magnitude of this impact decreases over time. Killing or capturing a terrorist leader in the first year of the group's existence makes the group over 8 times more likely to end than a non-decapitated group. The effects, however, diminish by half in the first ten years, and after approximately twenty years, leadership decapitation may have no effect on the group's mortality rate. This finding is in line with others who have argued that a terrorist group's organizational capacity increases with age, making it more durable with time (Fig. 12.2).[121]

Third, all three methods of leadership decapitation in this study—killing, capturing, or capturing then killing the leader—significantly increase the terrorist group's mortality rate. The relative ranking of each method differs according to how one specifies the duration of the decapitation effect, but even then, the impact of these methods are statistically indistinguishable from one another.

Fourth, the results from this study show that any type of leadership turnover, not just decapitation, will increase the mortality rate of terrorist groups. This is an important finding because States may not have to kill or capture a leader to hasten the group's demise.

[121]Horowitz 2010.

Fifth, group size does not affect terrorist group duration. The results show that smaller groups are just as durable as smaller groups, and groups of different sizes react similarly after losing a leader.

Sixth, contrary to conclusions in other studies,[122] I found that religious terrorist groups were less resilient and easier to destroy than nationalist groups following leadership decapitation. Although religious groups appear to be 80 % less likely to end than nationalist groups based on ideology alone, they were almost five times more inclined to end than nationalist groups after experiencing leadership decapitation. I believe this is because of the important role leaders of religious terrorist groups play in framing and interpreting organizational goals and strategies.

Based on these findings, States willing to employ leadership decapitation as part of their counterterrorism strategy should target terrorist group leaders as early as possible, and allocate their resources accordingly. As terrorist groups age, especially as they approach the twenty year mark, States might consider reducing their resources towards killing and capturing the group's leadership and investing in other counterterrorism initiatives. States that are unwilling to use decapitation tactics, whether for moral or legal reasons, or fear of the retaliatory 'boomerang effect,'[123] can still achieve similar effects with non-lethal or non-kinetic targeting the terrorist leader. The findings suggest States can accelerate the group's demise by exploiting intra-organizational rifts and removing the leader through shaming or by pitting one faction within the group against another.[124] It is unclear, however, how long it would take for these internal processes to succeed in removing the leader, not to mention how difficult it is to implement this type of strategy in the first place. Ultimately, States must weigh the costs and benefits associated with implementing decapitation strategies.

12.5 Implications for al-Qaeda and Concluding Thoughts

In the introduction, I asked what effect Usama bin Laden's death would have on al-Qaeda. Given that the organization was widely considered to be more than twenty years old when he died, bin Laden's death will most likely increase the group's chances of organizational death, but not nearly at the rate that it would have if it had occurred during the group's early years. Preliminary reports, however, indicate that leadership succession within al-Qaeda may lead to organizational instability.[125] Three points deserve mentioning.

First, it was a month and a half before the group ended a long silence regarding the group's response to bin Laden's death and named long-time deputy Ayman

122 Jordan 2009, p. 727.

123 Ganor 2005; Hafez and Hatfield 2006.

124 Brachman and McCants 2006; Shapiro 2007; Felter 2007.

125 Sheridan 2011.

al-Zawahiri his successor.[126] This was odd for an organization that is known for its media savvy and aware that bin Laden was the number one target for the US after the 9/11 attacks.

Second, prior to bin Laden's death, scholars and pundits believed that al-Qaeda's decentralized and amorphous organizational structure—a structure many failed to acknowledge was implemented out of necessity rather than choice—made the group more dangerous in the long run. Much of the evidence gleaned from the bin Laden compound since, however, indicates that he was still very much in charge of the organization, still heavily involved in operational planning, and potentially took part in the tactical planning of future attacks. Inconsistent with the 'leaderless jihad'[127] theories that were popular before bin Laden's death, but in keeping with a leader of a violent, clandestine and values-based organization, bin Laden was centralizing power and maintaining information at the highest levels. As a result, the bin Laden operation landed what is considered to be the largest single intelligence find in the post-September 11th era.[128]

Finally, bin Laden was a charismatic and transformative leader who will be very difficult to replace. Although al-Zawahiri is now acting as bin Laden's successor, he is thought to lack the charisma that made bin Laden so beloved and revered.[129] The recent infighting between two al-Qaeda affiliates fighting in Syria, Jabhat al-Nusra and al-Qaeda in Iraq and the Levant (ISIL), despite al-Zawahiri's best attempts to put the leaders of both groups in their place, serves as further evidence that he leads without the influence bin Laden enjoyed.[130] In his book *The Looming Tower*, Lawrence Wright includes a story that sows doubt about al-Zawahiri's ability to effectively lead the organization. Prior to al-Zawahiri leaving al-Jihad, his old terrorist organization, for al-Qaeda, one of his closest friends and mentors gave him the following advice: 'Remember, if you are a member of any group, you cannot be the leader.'[131]

Leaders play important roles in organizations, and especially so in terrorist groups. The organizational characteristics of terrorist groups make replacing their leaders very difficult. Previous scholars have called leadership decapitation 'a misguided strategy', 'an ineffective means of reducing terrorist activity',[132] and even 'counter-productive'.[133] Strategies and tactics aimed at removing terrorist leaders may have negative consequences in the short term, but they increase the mortality rates of the groups they lead, a factor that policymakers should include in their decision calculus.

---

[126]Ibid.

[127]Sageman 2008.

[128]Gorman and Entous 2011, p. 1.

[129]Sheridan 2011.

[130]Lahoud 2013.

[131]Wright 2006, p. 217.

[132]Jordan 2009, p. 754.

[133]Ibid., at p. 723.

References

Aminzade RA, Goldstone JA, Perry EJ (2001) Leadership dynamics and dynamics of contention. In: Aminzade RA, Goldstone JA, McAdam D, Perry EJ, Sewell WH, Tarrow S, Tilly C (eds) Silence and voice in the study of contentious politics. Cambridge University Press, New York, pp 126–154

Art RJ, Richardson L (2007) Democracy and counterterrorism lessons from the past. United States Institute of Peace Press, Washington DC

Asal V, Rethemeyer RK (2008) The nature of the beast: organizational structures and the lethality of terrorist attacks. J Polit 70(2):437–449

Bahnsen JC (2001) Charisma. In: Kolenda C (ed) Leadership: the warrior's art. Army War College Foundational Press, Carlisle, pp 259–276

Barnett WP, McKendrick DG (2004) Why are some organizations more competitive than others? Evidence from a changing global market. Adm Sci Q 49(4):535–571

Bender B (2007) Antiterrorism agency taps Boston-area brains. Boston Globe, 28 Mar 2007

Blanche E (2008) An Al Qaeda rolodex. Middle East 387:6

Box-Steffensmeier JM, Jones BS (2004) Event history modeling: a guide for social sciences. Cambridge University Press, Cambridge

Brachman JM, McCants WF (2006) Stealing Al-Qa'ida's playbook. Combating Terrorism Center, West Point

Burns JM (1978) Leadership. Harper and Row, New York

Byman D (2006) Do targeted killings work? Foreign Affairs 85(2):95–111

Carroll G (1984) Dynamics of publisher succession in newspaper organizations. Administrative Sciences Quarterly 29(1):93–113

Chasdi RJ (1999) Serenade of suffering: a portrait of Middle East terrorism, 1968–1993. Lexington, Lanham, Md

Clarridge DR (1997) A spy for all seasons. Scribner, New York

Combating Terrorism Center (2014) Harmony program. http://www.ctc.usma.edu/programs-resources/harmony-program. Accessed 20 Jan 2014

Cortright DA (2005) A critical evaluation of the UN counter-terrorism program: accomplishments and challenges. In: Global enforcement regimes transnational organized crime, international terrorism, and money laundering. Transnational Institute, Amsterdam

Crenshaw M (1988) The subjective reality of the terrorist: ideological and psychological factors in terrorism. In: Slater RO, Stohl M (eds) Current perspectives on international terrorism. Macmillan, Hong Kong, pp 12–46

Crenshaw M (1996) Why violence is rejected or renounced: a case study of oppositional terrorism. In: Gregor T (ed) A natural history of peace. Vanderbilt University Press, Nashville, pp 249–272

Cronin AK (2002/2003) Behind the curve. Int Secur 27(3):30–58

Cronin AK (2006) How al-Qaida ends: the decline and demise of terrorist groups. Int Secur 31(1):7–48

Cronin AK (2008) Ending terrorism: lessons for defeating al-Qaeda. Routledge, London

David S (2002) Fatal choices: Israel's policy of targeted killings. Mideast Secur Policy Stud 51:1–26

David S (2003) Israel's policy of targeted killings. Ethics Int Aff 17(1):111–126

Dawson LL (2002) Crises of charismatic legitimacy and violent behavior in new religious movements. In: Bromley DG, Melton JG (eds) Cults, religion, and violence. Cambridge University Press, Cambridge, pp 80–102

Eilstrup-Sangiovanni M, Jones C (2008) Assessing the dangers of illicit networks: why al-Qaida may be less threatening than many think. Int Secur 33(2):7–44

Enders W, Sandler T (2006) The political economy of terrorism. Cambridge University Press, New York

Etzioni A (1961) A comparative analysis of complex organizations. Free Press, New York

Fearon J, Laitin D (2003) Ethnicity, insurgency, and civil war. Am Polit Sci Rev 97:75–90
Felter J (2007) Cracks in the foundation: leadership schisms in al-Qa'ida 1989–2006. In: Felter J (ed) Harmony project. Combating Terrorism Center, West Point
Galanter M, Forest JJF (2006) Cults, charismatic groups, and social systems: understanding the transformation of terrorist recruits. In: Forest JJF (ed) The making of a terrorist: recruitment, training, and root causes. Praeger, Westport, Conn
Ganor B (2005) The counter-terrorism puzzle: a guide for decision makers. Transaction Press, New Brunswick
Gladwell M (2002) The tipping point: how little things can make a big difference. Back Bay Books, New York
Gouldner A (1954) Patterns of industrial bureaucracy. Free Press, Glencoe, Ill
Gorman S, Entous A (2011) Massive intelligence haul. Wall Street J, 4 May 2011
Grusky O (1960) Administrative succession in formal organizations. Soc Forces 39(2):105–115
Grusky O (1963) Managerial succession and organizational effectiveness. Am J Sociol 69:21–31
Gupta D, Mundra K (2005) Suicide bombing as a strategic weapon: an empirical investigation of Hamas and Islamic Jihad. Terrorism Polit Violence 17(4):573–598
Hafez M, Hatfield J (2006) Do targeted assassinations work? A multivariate analysis of Israeli-counter-terrorism effectiveness during Al-Aqsa uprising. Stud Conflict Terrorism 29(4):359–382
Harmon CC (2007) The myth of the invincible terrorist. Policy Rev 142:57
Hoffman B (2002) Inside terrorism. Columbia University Press, New York
Horowitz MC (2010) Diffusion of power: causes and consequences for international politics. Princeton University Press, Princeton
Hosmer ST (2001) Operations against enemy leaders. RAND, Santa Monica
House RJ (1977) A 1976 theory of charismatic leadership. In: Hunt JG, Larson LL (eds) Leadership: the cutting edge. Southern Illinois University Press, Carbondale
House RJ, Singh JV (1987) Organizational behavior: some new directions for I/O psychology. Annu Rev Psychol 38:669–718
Hutchinson S, O'Malley P (2007) How terrorist groups decline, vol Vol. 2007–1. Canadian Centre for Intelligence and Security Studies, Norman Paterson School of International Affairs, Carleton University, Ottawa
Hyder VD (2004) Decapitation operations: criteria for targeting enemy leadership. School of Advanced Military Studies, Fort Leavenworth
Iqbal Z, Zorn C (2008) The political consequences of assassination. J Conflict Resolut 52(3):385–400
Jackson B (2006) Groups, networks, or movements: a command-and-control-driven approach to classifying terrorist organizations and its application to Al Qaeda. Stud Conflict Terrorism 29(3):241–262
Janis IL (1972) Victims of groupthink: a psychological study of foreign-policy decisions and fiascos. Houghton Mifflin, Boston
Johnston PB (2009) Does decapitation work? Assessing the effectiveness of leadership targeting in counterinsurgency campaigns. Int Secur 36(4):47–79
Jones BF, Olken BA (2009) Hit or miss? The effect of assassinations on institutions and war. Am Econ J Macroecono 1(2):55–87
Jones SG, Libicki MC (2008) How terrorist groups end: lessons for countering al Qa'ida. RAND, Santa Monica
Jordan J (2009) When heads roll: assessing the effectiveness of leadership decapitation. Secur Stud 18(4):719–755
Kaplan E, Mintz A, Mishal S, Samban C (2005) What happened to suicide bombings in Israel? insights from a terror stock model. Stud Conflict Terrorism 28(3):225–235
Kenney M (2007) From Pablo to Osama: trafficking and terrorist networks, government bureaucracies, and competitive adaptation. Pennsylvania State University Press, University Park

Lahoud N (2013) Jihadi discourse in the wake of the Arab Spring. Combating Terrorism Center, West Point
Langdon L, Sarapu AJ, Wells M (2004) Targeting the leadership of terrorist and insurgent movements: historical lessons for contemporary policy makers. J Public Int Aff 15:59–78
Lesser IO, Hoffman B, Arquilla J, Ronfeldt D, Zanini M (1999) Countering the new terrorism. RAND, Santa Monica
Lieberson S, O'Connor JF (1972) Leadership and organizational performance. Am Sociol Rev 37(2):117–130
Lotrionte C (2003) When to target leaders. Wash Q 26(3):73–86
Mannes A (2008) Testing the snake head tragedy: does killing or capturing its leaders reduce a terrorist group's activity? J Int Policy Solutions 9:40–49
Mazzetti M (2011) Drone strike in Yemen was aimed at Awlaki. New York Times, 7 May 2011
Mazzetti M, Shane S (2009) CIA had plans to assassinate Qaeda leaders. New York Times, 14 July 2009
McCormack GH (2003) Terrorist decision making. Annu Rev Polit Sci 6:473–507
Miller G (2011) Under Obama, an emerging global apparatus for drone killing. Washington Post, 27 Dec 2011
Mumford MM, Espejo J, Hunter S, Bedell-Avers KE, Eubanks DL, Connelly S (2007) The sources of leader violence: a comparison of ideological and non-ideological leaders. Leadersh Q 18(3):217–235
Pape R (1996) Bombing to win: air power and coercion in war. Cornell University Press, Ithaca
Pape R (2003) The strategic logic of suicide terrorism. Am Polit Sci Rev 97(3):343–361
Pedahzur A (2005) Suicide terrorism. Polity, London
Post JM (1990) Terrorist psycho-logic: terrorist behavior as a product of psychological forces. In: Reich W (ed) Origins of terrorism. Woodrow Wilson Center Press, Washington, pp 25–42
Price B (2009) Removing the devil you know: unraveling the puzzle behind leadership decapitation and terrorist group duration. Ph.D. dissertation, Stanford University, Stanford
Price B (2012) Targeting top terrorists: how leadership decapitation contributes to counterterrorism. Int Secur 36(4):9–46
Rapoport DC (1992) Terrorism. In: Hawkesworth M, Kogan M (eds) Encyclopedia of government and politics. Routledge, London, pp 1049–1080
Richardson L (2006) What terrorists want: understanding the enemy, containing the threat. Random House, New York
Sageman M (2008) Leaderless jihad: terror networks in the twenty-first century. Pennsylvania State Press, Philadelphia
Seale P (1992) Abu Nidal: a gun for hire. Hutchinson, London
Shane S (2009) Government hit squads, minus the hits. New York Times, 19 July 2009
Shane S (2010) U.S. approves targeted killing of American cleric. New York Times, 6 Apr 2010
Shapiro JN (2007) The terrorist's challenge: security, efficiency, and control. Ph.D. dissertation, Stanford University, Stanford
Sheridan MB (2011) Zawahiri named new al-Qaeda leader. Washington Post, 16 July 2011
Staniland P (2005/2006) Defeating transnational insurgencies: the best offense is a good fence. Wash Q 29(1):21–40
Therneau TM, Grambsch PM (2000) Modeling survival data: extending the Cox Model. Springer, New York
Turbiville, GH Jr (2007) Hunting leadership targets in counterinsurgency and counterterrorist operations: selected perspectives and experience. Joint Special Operations University Report, No. 07-6 Joint Special Operations University, Hurlburt Field
U.S. Customs and Border Protection (2010) Drug trafficking organizations adaptability to smuggle drugs across SWB after losing key personnel. info.publicintelligence.net/CBP-NoChangeDTOs.pdf. Accessed 5 Jan 2011
Weber M (1947) The theory of social and economic organizations. Free Press, New York

Wilkinson P (2000) Terrorism versus democracy. Frank Cass Publishers, London
Wright L (2006) The looming tower: al-Qaeda and the road to 9/11. Knopf, New York
Zald MN (1965) Who shall rule? A political analysis of succession in a large welfare organization. Pac Sociol Rev 8(1):52–60
Zimmerman D, Wenger A (2007) How States fight terrorism: policy dynamics in the west. Lynne Rien Publishers, London

Annex: Table of Operations

Operation (& Alias)	Period	Actor	Addressee/ target state	Description
Allied Force (Kosovo-war)	1999, March 24–June 10	NATO	Serbia	Kosovo-war, NATO-operation against Serbia
Anaconda	2002, March 2–16	USA	Taliban and Al Qa'ida	Battle during Operation Enduring Freedom in Afghanistan (Paktia Province)
Cast Lead (First Gaza War) (Battle of al-Furqan)	27 December 2008–18 January 2009	Israel	Hamas/ Palestinians	Three weeks war in Gaza strip
Change of Direction, also Second Lebanon War	2006, 12 July–14 August	Israel	Hezbollah, Lebanon	Israeli military intervention after attacks and kidnapping of soldiers
Desert Shield	1990–1991	USA	Iraq	Defensive deployment to prevent Iraq from invading Saudi Arabia
Deliberate Force	1995, 30 August–14 September	NATO	Bosnian Serb Army	Air operations in support of UNPROFOR in former Yugoslavia after Bosnian Serbs threatened and attacked UN Safe Areas
Deny Flight	12 April 1993–20 December 1995	NATO	various	Enforcement of (a UN) no-fly zone in Bosnia and Herzegovina

P.A.L. Ducheine et al. (eds.), *Targeting: The Challenges of Modern Warfare*,
DOI 10.1007/978-94-6265-072-5

Operation (& Alias)	Period	Actor	Addressee/ target state	Description
Desert Shield	2 August 1990–17 January 1991	USA and Coalition	Saudi Arabia	Operations after the Iraqi invasion of Kuwait, leading to the buildup of troops for Desert Storm and defence of Saudi Arabia
Desert Storm/Granby (UK) Also: Gulf War, Second	1991	Coalition (US, UK led)	Iraq	Military intervention in self-defence of Kuwait and with UN Security Council authorization to end the Iraqi occupation of Kuwait
El Dorado Canyon	14 April 1986	USA	Libya	Military action after i.a. bomb explosions in Berlin (discotheque La Belle)
Enduring Freedom/ Operation Veritas (UK)	2001–2014	US & UK led coalition	Afghanistan & Al Qa'ida	Self-defence against Afghanistan and Al Qa'ida, triggered by 9/11 attacks
Gulf War, First,	1991			see Desert Storm/Granby
Gulf War, Second	2003–2004			see Iraqi Freedom/Telic
Granby				see Desert Storm
Intifada, Second	2000–2005			Second Palestinian uprising against Israeli occupation
Iraqi Freedom/ Operation Telic (UK)	2003–2010	US & UK-led coalition	Iraq	Invasion of Iraq, preventive war based on Weapons of Mass Destruction issues
ISAF	2001–present	(NATO-led) coalition	Afghanistan	UN Security Council authorised peace enforcement operation in Afghanistan
Kosovo War	1999			See: Allied Force.
Linebacker (I)	1972, 9 May–23 October	USA	North Vietnam	Bombing campaign during Vietnam War
Linebacker II	1972, 18–29 December	USA	North Vietnam	Strategic bombing campaign during Vietnam War
New Dawn	2010–2011	USA	Iraq	US operation after Iraqi Freedom, prior to the withdrawl from Iraq

Operation (& Alias)	Period	Actor	Addressee/ target state	Description
Odyssee Dawn	2011, 19–31 March	Coaliton (USA, UK, France, etc.)	Libya	Military intervention Libya to enforce UN Security Council Resolution 1973. Followed by NATO-led operation Unified Protector
Overlord (Operation Neptune)	6-6-1944	Allied Forces	Nazi Germany	Battle of Normandy, initiated by Operation Neptune (invasion)
Rolling Thunder I & II	2 March 1965–2 November 1968	USA	North Vietnam	Aerial bombardment campaign against the Democratic Republic of Vietnam (North Vietnam) during the Vietnam War
Six Day War	5–10 June 1967	Israel	Egypt, Jordan, Syria	Israeli pre-emptive war after mobilisation in Arab neighbouring states
Telic				see Iraqi Freedom
Unified Protector	2011, 23 March–31 October	NATO & Coalition	Libya	NATO-led operation enforcing UN SC resolutions 1970 and 1973 concerning the Libyan Civil War
UNPROFOR	1992–1995	UN		UN-operation in former Yugoslavia
Veritas				See Enduring Freedom

Index

P.A.L. Ducheine et al. (eds.), *Targeting: The Challenges of Modern Warfare*,
DOI 10.1007/978-94-6265-072-5

D

E

CPSIA information can be obtained
at www.ICGtesting.com
Printed in the USA
LVOW02*2114070417
530037LV00001B/33/P